Phantom Dream™

VOLUME 4

NATSUKI TAKAYA

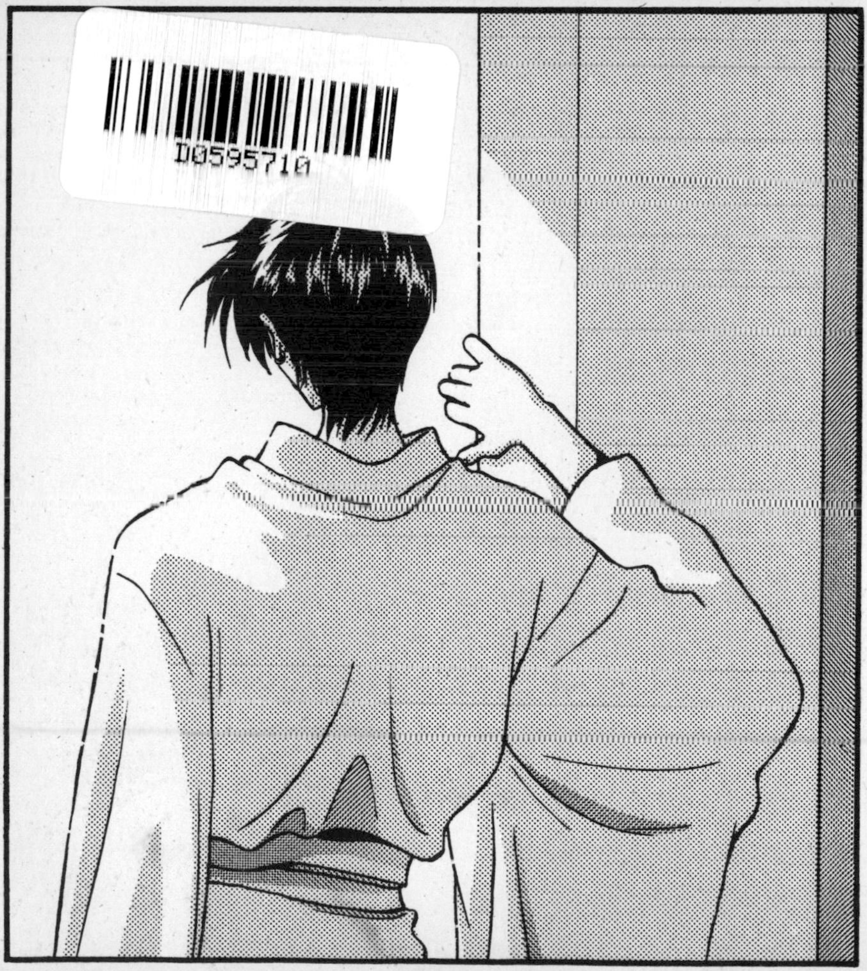

Phantom Dream Volume 4
Written by Natsuki Takaya

Translation - Beni Axia Conrad
English Adaptation - Ysabet Reinhardt MacFarlane
Retouch and Lettering - Star Print Brokers
Production Artist - Michael Paolilli
Graphic Designer - Al-Insan Lashley

Editor - Lillian Diaz-Przybyl
Print Production Manager - Lucas Rivera
Managing Editor - Vy Nguyen
Senior Designer - Louis Csontos
Director of Sales and Manufacturing - Allyson De Simone
Associate Publisher - Marco F. Pavia
President and C.O.O. - John Parker
C.E.O. and Chief Creative Officer - Stu Levy

A **TOKYOPOP** Manga

TOKYOPOP and 🐢 are trademarks or registered trademarks of TOKYOPOP Inc.

TOKYOPOP Inc.
5900 Wilshire Blvd. Suite 2000
Los Angeles, CA 90036

E-mail: info@TOKYOPOP.com
Come visit us online at www.TOKYOPOP.com

ISBN: 978-1-4278-1092-2

First TOKYOPOP printing: November 2009
10 9 8 7 6 5 4 3 2 1
Printed in the USA

Phantom Dream

Volume 4

By Natsuki Takaya

HAMBURG // LONDON // LOS ANGELES // TOKYO

STORY SO FAR:

OUR STORY BEGINS NEARLY A THOUSAND YEARS AGO, WHEN A YOUNG GIRL, SUIGEKKA, WHO WAS BELIEVED TO BE ALL-POWERFUL, WAS SECRETLY REVERED AS THE GUARDIAN OF JAPAN. HER CONSTANT COMPANIONS WERE TWO MAGICIANS, HIRA AND SAGA. HIRA WAS DEEPLY IN LOVE WITH SUIGEKKA, BUT AFTER HER DEATH, HE CHANGED.

CALLING HIMSELF THE KING OF THE GEKKA FAMILY, HIRA TOOK IT UPON HIMSELF TO REINVENT THE WORLD. HIS SPELLS GAVE HIM POWER OVER JASHIN, THE DARKNESS WITHIN HUMAN HEARTS, AND THROUGH HIS INFLUENCE, THE PEOPLE THREW OFF THEIR WEAK EMOTIONS TO BECOME STRONG JAKI.

THE GEKKA FAMILY DREAMS OF A WORLD WHERE ONLY SUCH PEOPLE EXIST.

HOWEVER, SAGA OPPOSED HIM. USING SPELLS OF PROTECTION, HE EXORCISED THE JAKI AND BECAME THE FIRST SHUGOSHI OF THE OTOYA FAMILY. NOW, TAMAKI OTOYA, THE SHUGOSHI WHO INHERITED THE LONG-DEAD SAGA'S BLOOD, AND EIJI, A JAHOUTSUKAI WHO INHERITED THE BLOOD OF KING HIRA, HAVE INHERITED THEIR ANCIENT CONFLICT AS WELL.

JASHIN: POWERFUL NEGATIVE EMOTIONS, WHICH, IF LEFT UNCHECKED, TRANSFORM PEOPLE INTO JAKI.

JAKI: A TYPE OF DEMON OR MALEVOLENT BEING CREATED WHEN A HUMAN LOSES CONTROL OF EXTREME ANGER, HATE AND FEAR.

JARYOKU: BLACK MAGIC. A POWER THAT STEMS FROM JASHIN.

JAHOUTSUKAI: A BLACK MAGICIAN. ONE WHO SPECIALIZES IN USING JARYOKU.

SHUGOSHI: A TYPE OF PRIEST WHO HAS THE POWER TO EXORCISE JASHIN. LITERALLY, A PROTECTOR.

HIGOSHI: ONE TASKED WITH DEFENDING THE SHUGOSHI. A HEREDITARY POSITION OCCUPIED BY MEMBERS OF THE OTOYA BRANCH FAMILIES.

JUZU: PRAYER BEADS.

GOHOU: A PROTECTIVE AVATAR UNIQUE TO EACH SHUGOSHI. THEY TAKE ON DIFFERENT FORMS: TAMAKI'S IS A BIRD, WHILE HIS GRANDFATHER'S WAS A DRAGON.

SHICHIBOUJIN: A SHIELD OF PROTECTION. LITERALLY, A SEPTAGRAM--A SEVEN-POINTED STAR WITHIN A CIRCLE.

SHIEKI: A MAGICAL SERVANT THAT DOES THE SHUGOSHI'S BIDDING. TAMAKI'S SHIEKI WAS A HUMAN BOY, SOUICHI, WHO TAMAKI EXORCISED. HE MANIFESTS AS A BUTTERFLY.

TAMAKI OTOYA: BORN TO SOUETSU, THE PREVIOUS HEAD OF THE OTOYA FAMILY, AND KANAME, A WOMAN TRAINED AS A JAHOUTSUKAI OF THE GEKKA FAMILY, TAMAKI IS YOUNG, BUT POWERFUL. RESENTED BY THE SPRAWLING OTOYA CLAN FOR HIS SUPPOSEDLY "TAINTED" BLOODLINE, HE IS TORN BETWEEN HIS DUTY TO PROTECT PEOPLE FROM BECOMING JAKI, AND HIS FRUSTRATION AT NEVER BEING ABLE TO STOP TERRIBLE THINGS BEFORE THEY HAPPEN--ONLY CLEAN UP THE DAMAGE.

ASAHI: TAMAKI'S FRIEND AND LOVER, ASAHI IS SWEET AND CHEERFUL IN SPITE OF A TROUBLED CHILDHOOD. TRAGICALLY, SHE IS ALSO THE REINCARNATION OF SUIGEKKA, AND HAS RECENTLY CHOSEN TO RETURN TO KING HIRA'S SIDE, FIGHTING AGAINST TAMAKI.

EIJI: A YOUNG JAHOUTSUKAI, WORKING FOR HIRA'S RESURRECTION AND THE CREATION OF HIS IDEAL WORLD. TORMENTED, AND POSSIBLY SLOWLY DYING, EIJI HAS A TWISTED MIX OF LOVE AND RESPECT FOR TAMAKI, IN SPITE OF THEIR OPPOSING GOALS. KAGEHA, A CAT DEMON, IS EIJI'S PROTECTOR AND SOLE FRIEND.

HIDERI: A BRASH YOUNG MAN FROM THE EASTERN OTOYA BRANCH FAMILY. ONE OF TAMAKI'S DESIGNATED PROTECTORS ("HIGOSHI"), HE OFTEN ACTS MORE LIKE AN OLDER BROTHER THAN A GUARDIAN. HE HAD A CRUSH ON TAMAKI'S MOTHER.

MIGIRI: THE SECOND OF THE OTOYA HIGOSHI, SHE IS GENERALLY QUIET, BUT HAS QUITE A TEMPER WHEN PROVOKED. HIDERI IS HER BIG BROTHER, AND SHE ADDRESSES HIM AS "ANIUE."

TOKIWA: TWO YEARS YOUNGER THAN TAMAKI, TOKIWA IS THE THIRD OTOYA HIGOSHI. HE SEES TAMAKI AS AN OLDER BROTHER FIGURE, AND ADDRESSES HIM AS SUCH, CALLING HIM "NII-SAN."

Contents

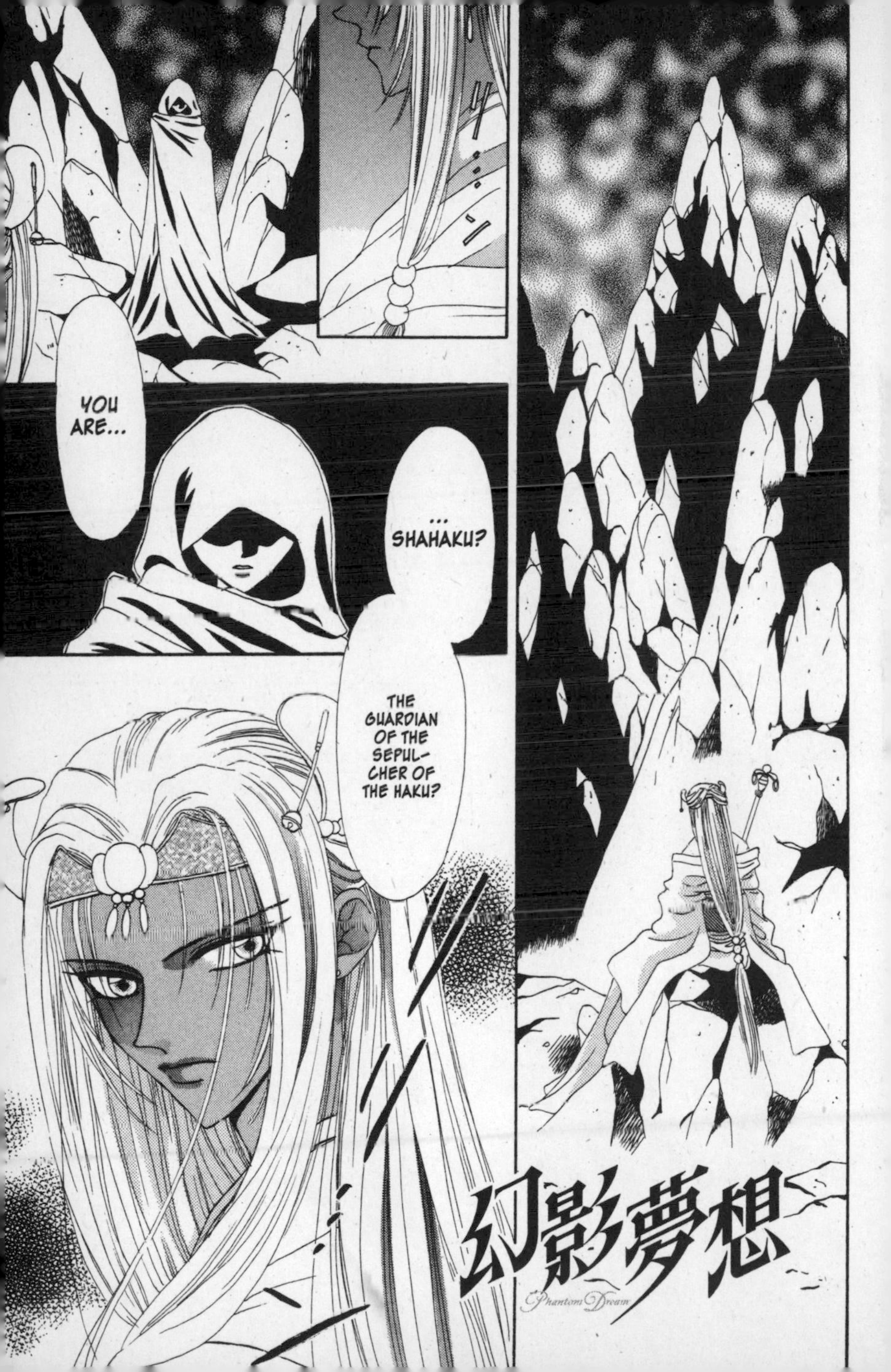
幻影夢想
Phantom Dream
YOU ARE...
...SHAHAKU?
THE GUARDIAN OF THE SEPULCHER OF THE HAKU?

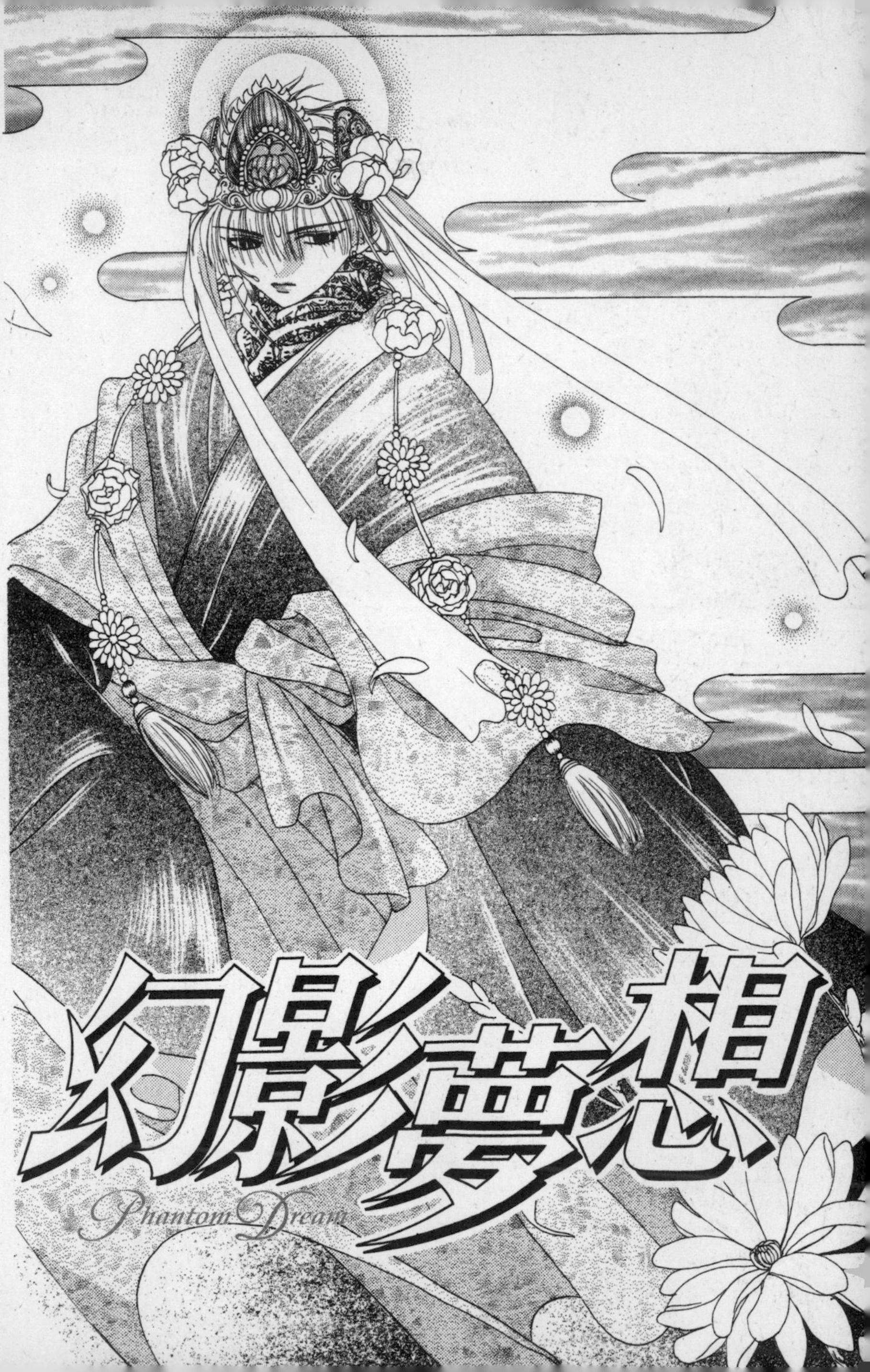
幻影夢想
Phantom Dream

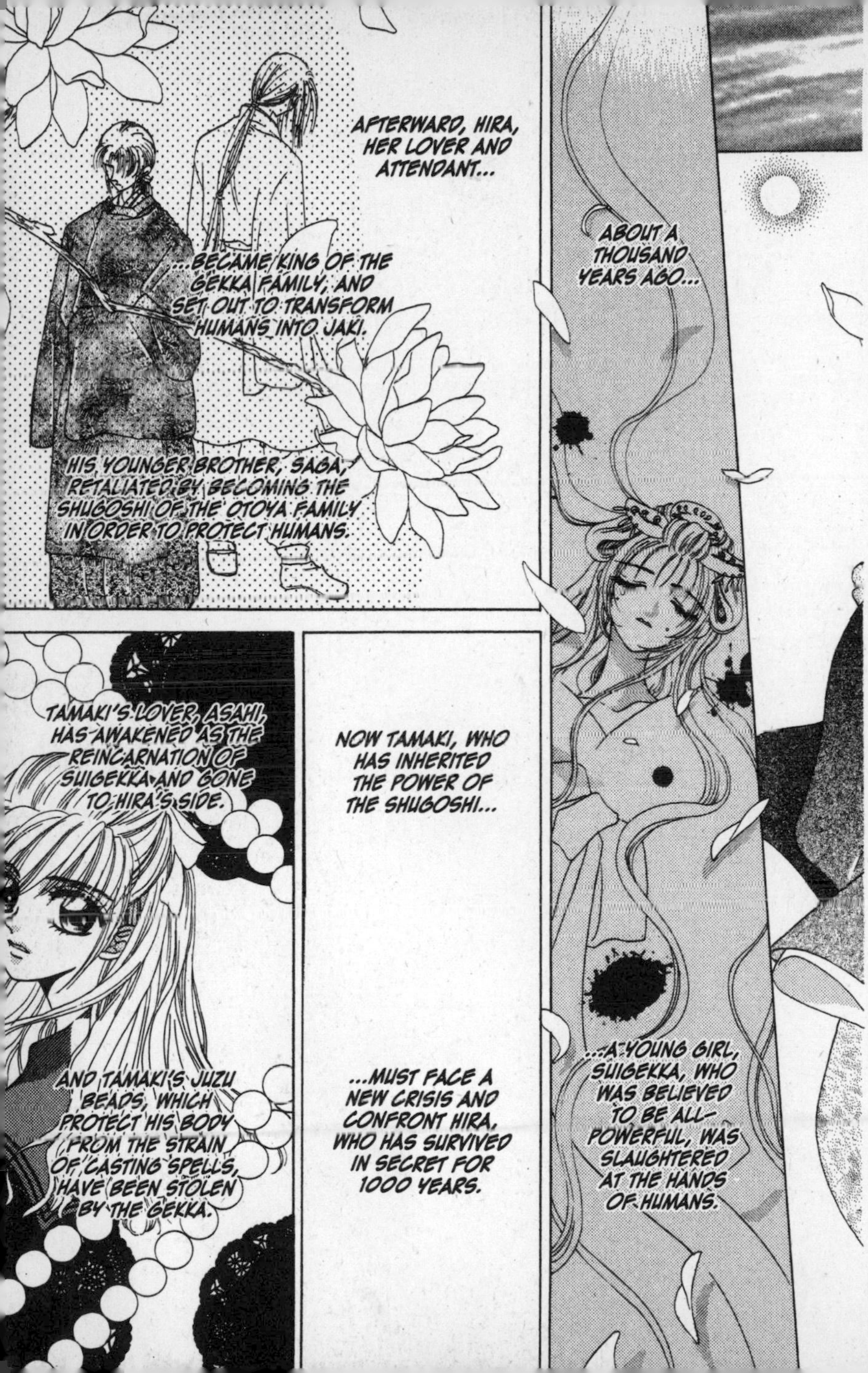
ABOUT A THOUSAND YEARS AGO...
...A YOUNG GIRL, SUIGEKKA, WHO WAS BELIEVED TO BE ALL-POWERFUL, WAS SLAUGHTERED AT THE HANDS OF HUMANS.
AFTERWARD, HIRA, HER LOVER AND ATTENDANT...
...BECAME KING OF THE GEKKA FAMILY, AND SET OUT TO TRANSFORM HUMANS INTO JAKI.
HIS YOUNGER BROTHER, SAGA, RETALIATED BY BECOMING THE SHUGOSHI OF THE OTOYA FAMILY IN ORDER TO PROTECT HUMANS.
NOW TAMAKI, WHO HAS INHERITED THE POWER OF THE SHUGOSHI...
...MUST FACE A NEW CRISIS AND CONFRONT HIRA, WHO HAS SURVIVED IN SECRET FOR 1000 YEARS.
TAMAKI'S LOVER, ASAHI, HAS AWAKENED AS THE REINCARNATION OF SUIGEKKA AND GONE TO HIRA'S SIDE.
AND TAMAKI'S JUZU BEADS, WHICH PROTECT HIS BODY FROM THE STRAIN OF CASTING SPELLS, HAVE BEEN STOLEN BY THE GEKKA.

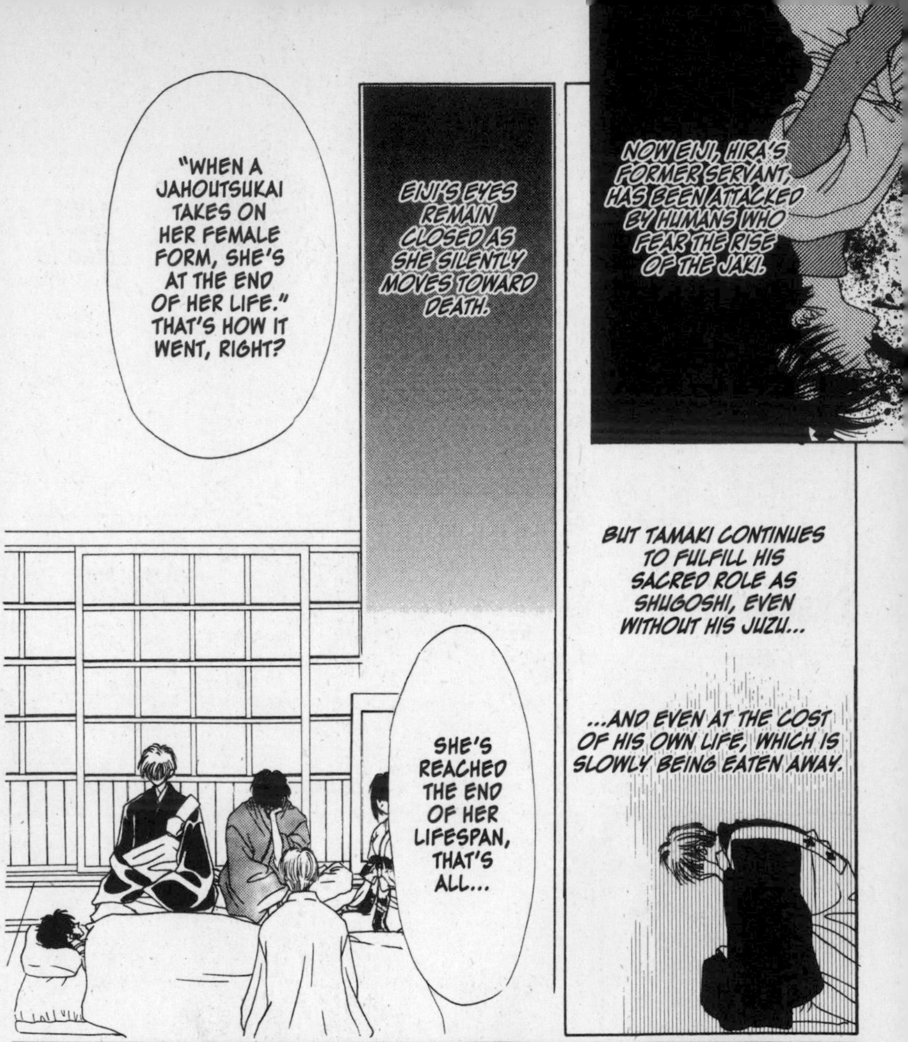
NOW EIJI, HIRA'S FORMER SERVANT, HAS BEEN ATTACKED BY HUMANS WHO FEAR THE RISE OF THE JAKI.
BUT TAMAKI CONTINUES TO FULFILL HIS SACRED ROLE AS SHUGOSHI, EVEN WITHOUT HIS JUZU...
...AND EVEN AT THE COST OF HIS OWN LIFE, WHICH IS SLOWLY BEING EATEN AWAY.
EIJI'S EYES REMAIN CLOSED AS SHE SILENTLY MOVES TOWARD DEATH.
"WHEN A JAHOUTSUKAI TAKES ON HER FEMALE FORM, SHE'S AT THE END OF HER LIFE." THAT'S HOW IT WENT, RIGHT?
SHE'S REACHED THE END OF HER LIFESPAN, THAT'S ALL...

ULTRA SPECIAL *THINGS THAT DON'T MATTER I*

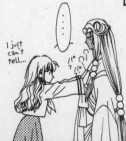

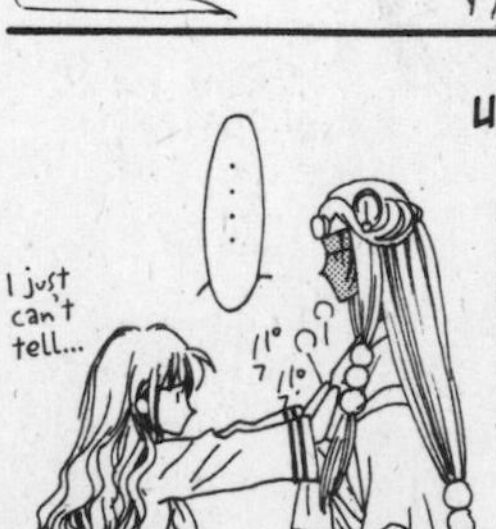
......
I just can't tell...

Shahaku is a man...probably. (laughs) I hadn't really thought about it while drawing. I like ambivalence, like androgyny, so...if a character appears and you think, "I just can't tell if it's a man or a woman...!" please just think of them as androgynous. (laughs)

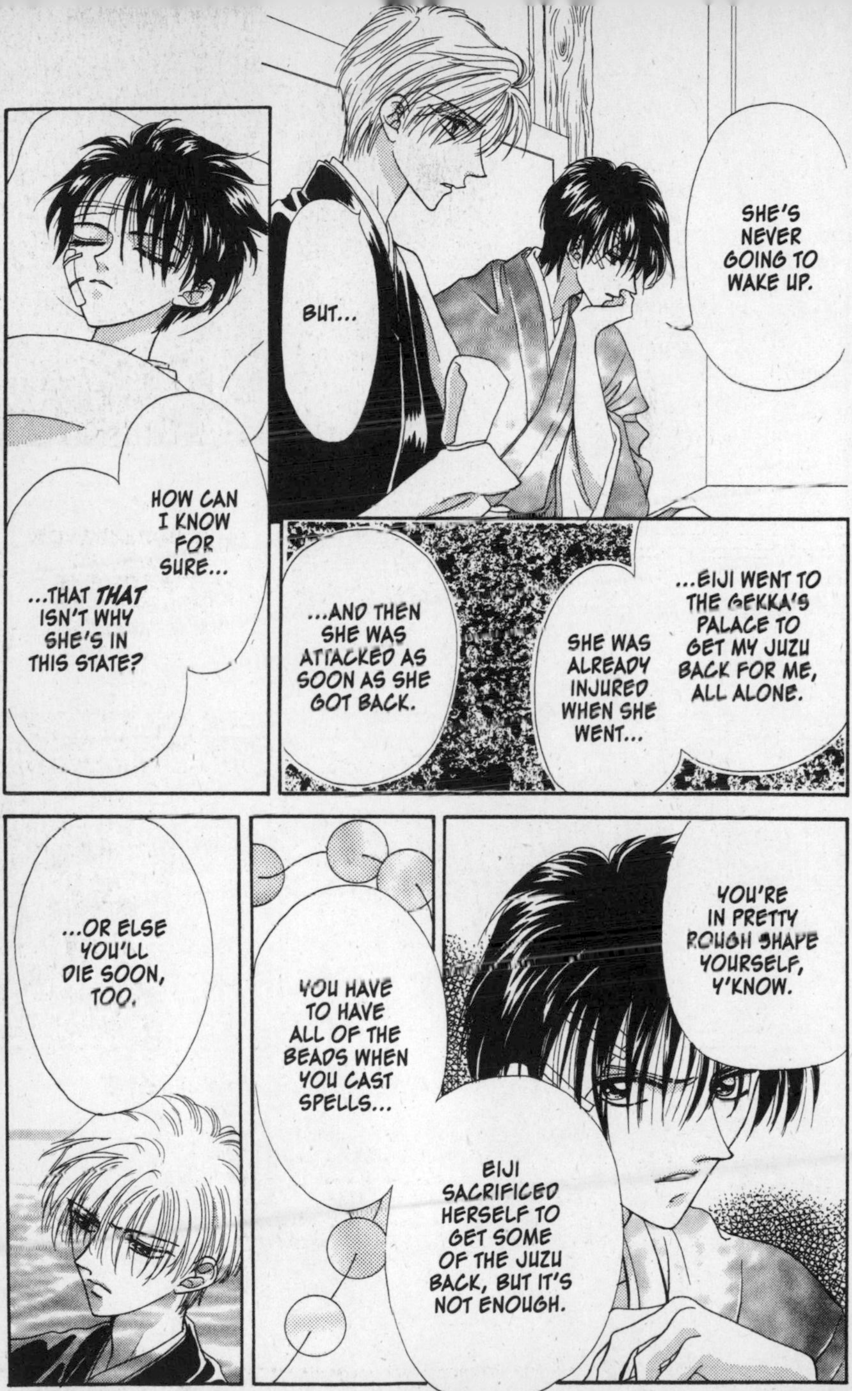
SHE'S NEVER GOING TO WAKE UP.
BUT...
...EIJI WENT TO THE GEKKA'S PALACE TO GET MY JUZU BACK FOR ME, ALL ALONE.
SHE WAS ALREADY INJURED WHEN SHE WENT...
...AND THEN SHE WAS ATTACKED AS SOON AS SHE GOT BACK.
HOW CAN I KNOW FOR SURE...
...THAT *THAT* ISN'T WHY SHE'S IN THIS STATE?
YOU'RE IN PRETTY ROUGH SHAPE YOURSELF, Y'KNOW.
EIJI SACRIFICED HERSELF TO GET SOME OF THE JUZU BACK, BUT IT'S NOT ENOUGH.
YOU HAVE TO HAVE ALL OF THE BEADS WHEN YOU CAST SPELLS...
...OR ELSE YOU'LL DIE SOON, TOO.

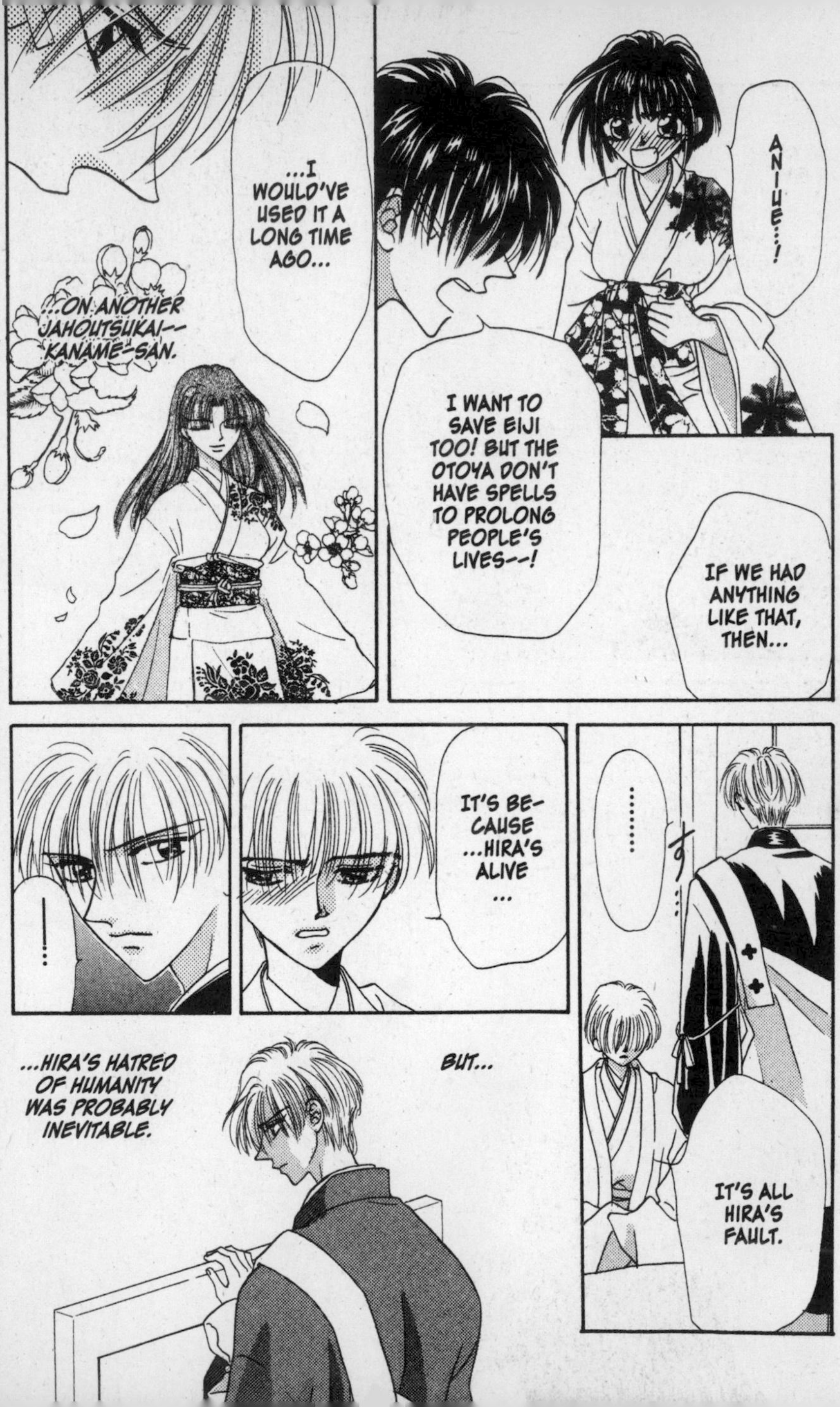
ANIUE...!
I WANT TO SAVE EIJI TOO! BUT THE OTOYA DON'T HAVE SPELLS TO PROLONG PEOPLE'S LIVES--!
IF WE HAD ANYTHING LIKE THAT, THEN...
...I WOULD'VE USED IT A LONG TIME AGO...
...ON ANOTHER JAHOUTSUKAI--KANAME-SAN.
......
す...
IT'S ALL HIRA'S FAULT.
IT'S BE-CAUSE ...HIRA'S ALIVE ...
...!
BUT...
...HIRA'S HATRED OF HUMANITY WAS PROBABLY INEVITABLE.

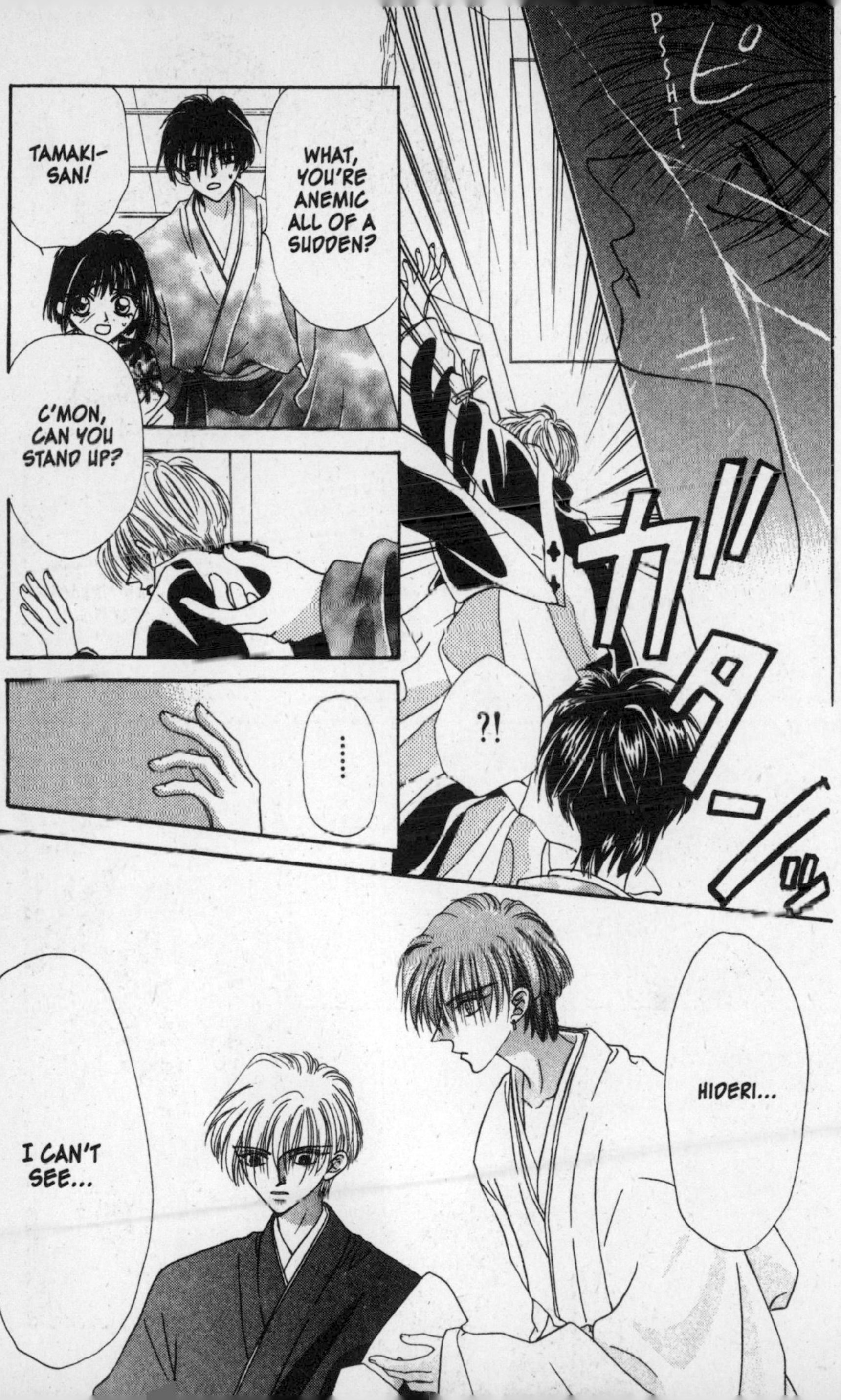
PSSHT!
?!
WHAT, YOU'RE ANEMIC ALL OF A SUDDEN?
TAMAKI-SAN!
C'MON, CAN YOU STAND UP?
......
HIDERI...
I CAN'T SEE...

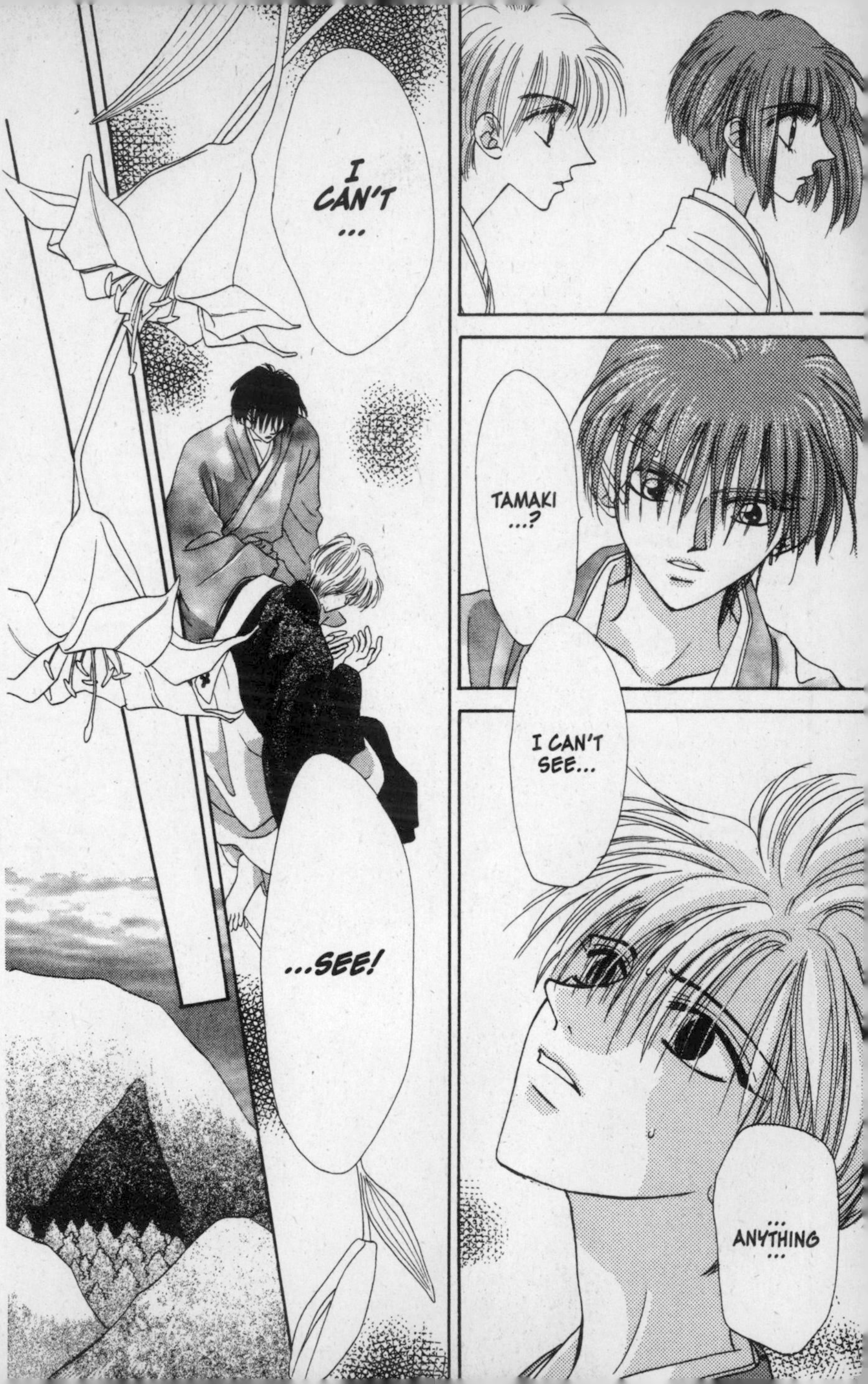
TAMAKI ...?
I CAN'T SEE...
... ANYTHING ...
I CAN'T ...
...SEE!

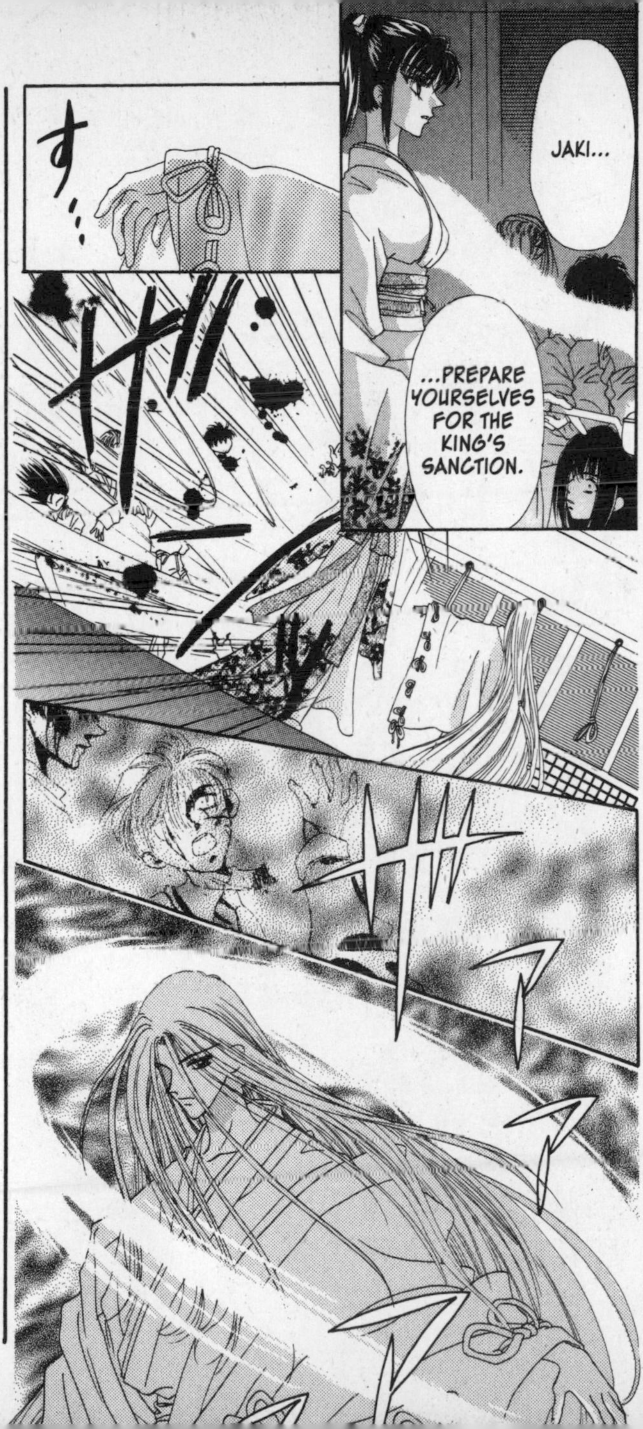
JAKI...
...PREPARE YOURSELVES FOR THE KING'S SANCTION.
す...

Phantom Dream

Scroll One

Nice to meet you! Hello! This is Takaya. ♥ It's been a while since the last volume of Phantom Dream. Maybe... about a year? Since then, Tsubasa: Those With Wings and other stuff came out, so I can't be sure. I've heard from people who only read Dream in the serialized chapters, asking "Not yet?" but...if nothing else, it's supposed to be six volumes, so it's amaaaazing! I'm sooo happy! It's like that. (...like Shinohara, you know?) Thank you!

Well, that's how it goes, and now Hideri's gracing the cover of volume 4. There were plenty of people who thought, "It'll be Kaname, right?" but it was him. (laughs) Now the only one left is "him." Who could it be...? It's soooo obvious. It's not like I'm trying to keep it a secret, either. (laughs)

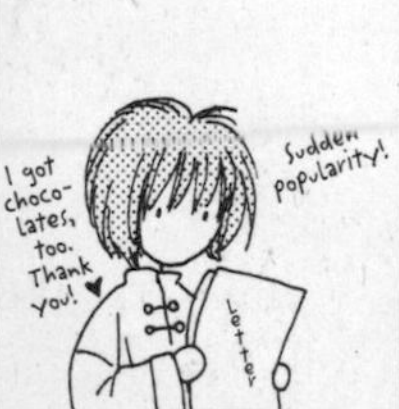
I got chocolates, too. Thank you! ♥
Sudden popularity!
Letter

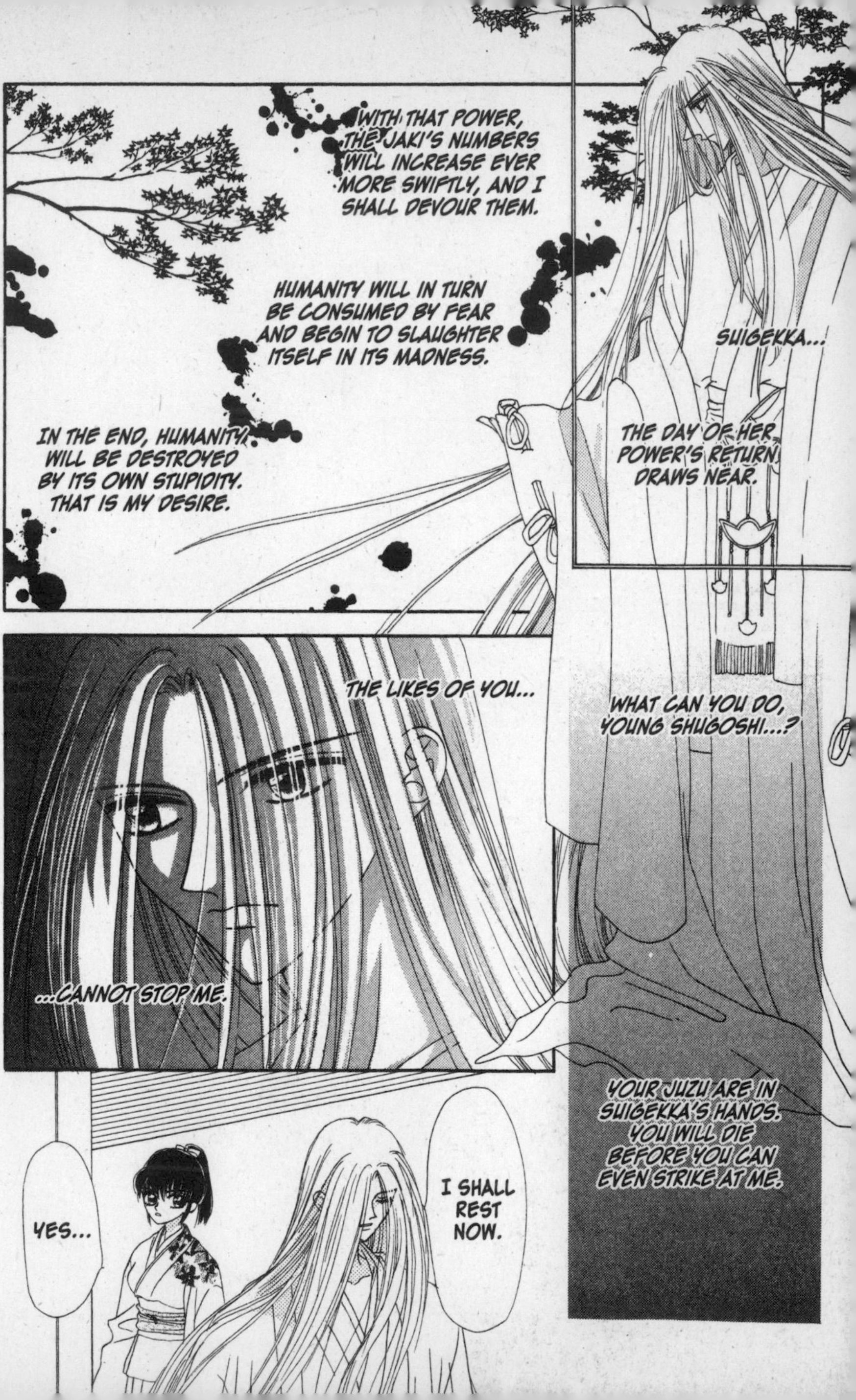
SUIGEKKA...
THE DAY OF HER POWER'S RETURN DRAWS NEAR.
WITH THAT POWER, THE JAKI'S NUMBERS WILL INCREASE EVER MORE SWIFTLY, AND I SHALL DEVOUR THEM.
HUMANITY WILL IN TURN BE CONSUMED BY FEAR AND BEGIN TO SLAUGHTER ITSELF IN ITS MADNESS.
IN THE END, HUMANITY WILL BE DESTROYED BY ITS OWN STUPIDITY. THAT IS MY DESIRE.
WHAT CAN YOU DO, YOUNG SHUGOSHI...?
YOUR JUZU ARE IN SUIGEKKA'S HANDS. YOU WILL DIE BEFORE YOU CAN EVEN STRIKE AT ME.
THE LIKES OF YOU...
...CANNOT STOP ME.
I SHALL REST NOW.
YES...

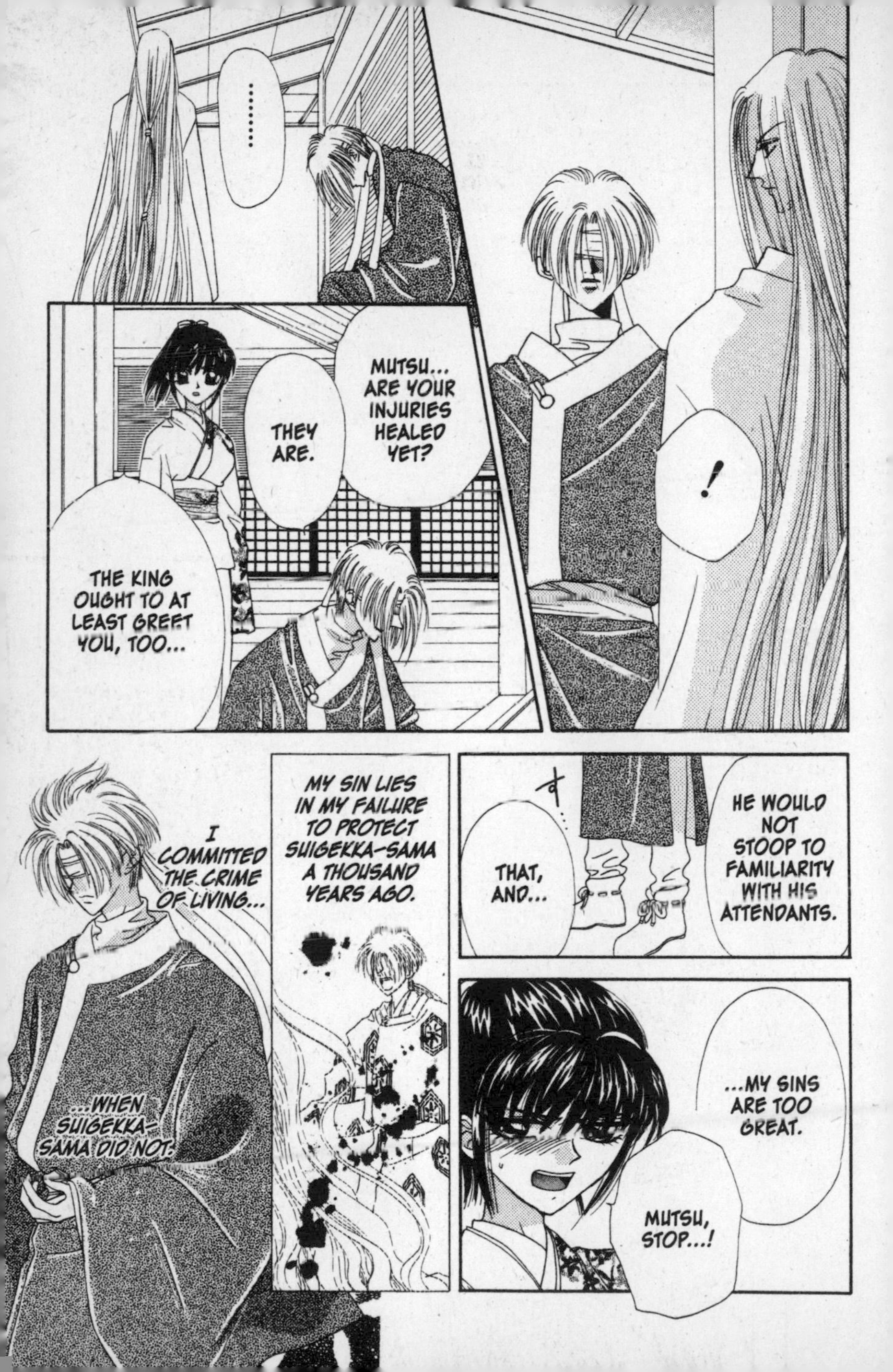
!
……
MUTSU... ARE YOUR INJURIES HEALED YET?
THEY ARE.
THE KING OUGHT TO AT LEAST GREET YOU, TOO...
HE WOULD NOT STOOP TO FAMILIARITY WITH HIS ATTENDANTS.
す
THAT, AND...
...MY SINS ARE TOO GREAT.
MUTSU, STOP...!
MY SIN LIES IN MY FAILURE TO PROTECT SUIGEKKA-SAMA A THOUSAND YEARS AGO.
I COMMITTED THE CRIME OF LIVING...
...WHEN SUIGEKKA-SAMA DID NOT.

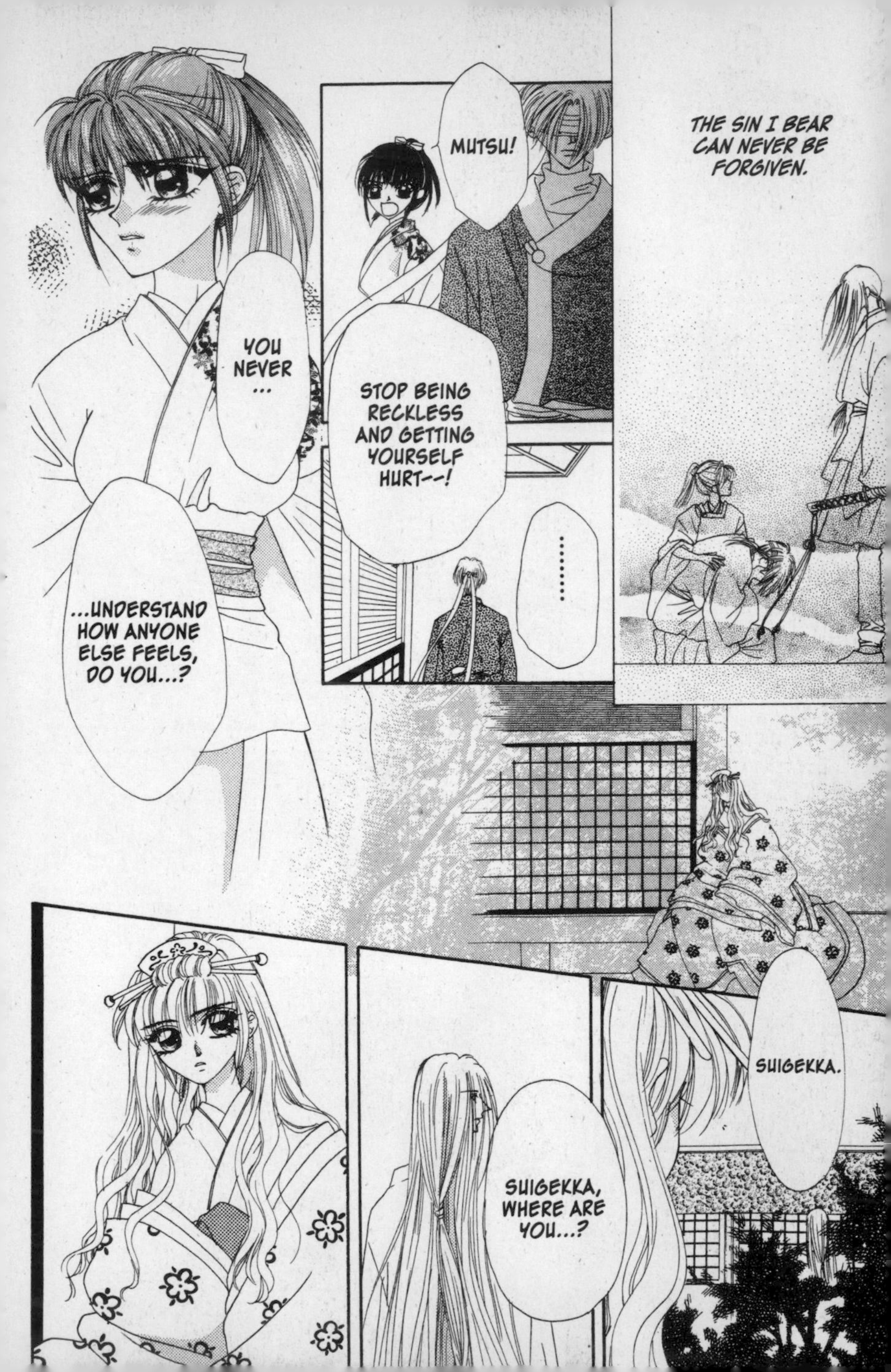

THE SIN I BEAR CAN NEVER BE FORGIVEN.
MUTSU!
STOP BEING RECKLESS AND GETTING YOURSELF HURT--!
......
YOU NEVER ...
...UNDERSTAND HOW ANYONE ELSE FEELS, DO YOU...?
SUIGEKKA.
SUIGEKKA, WHERE ARE YOU...?

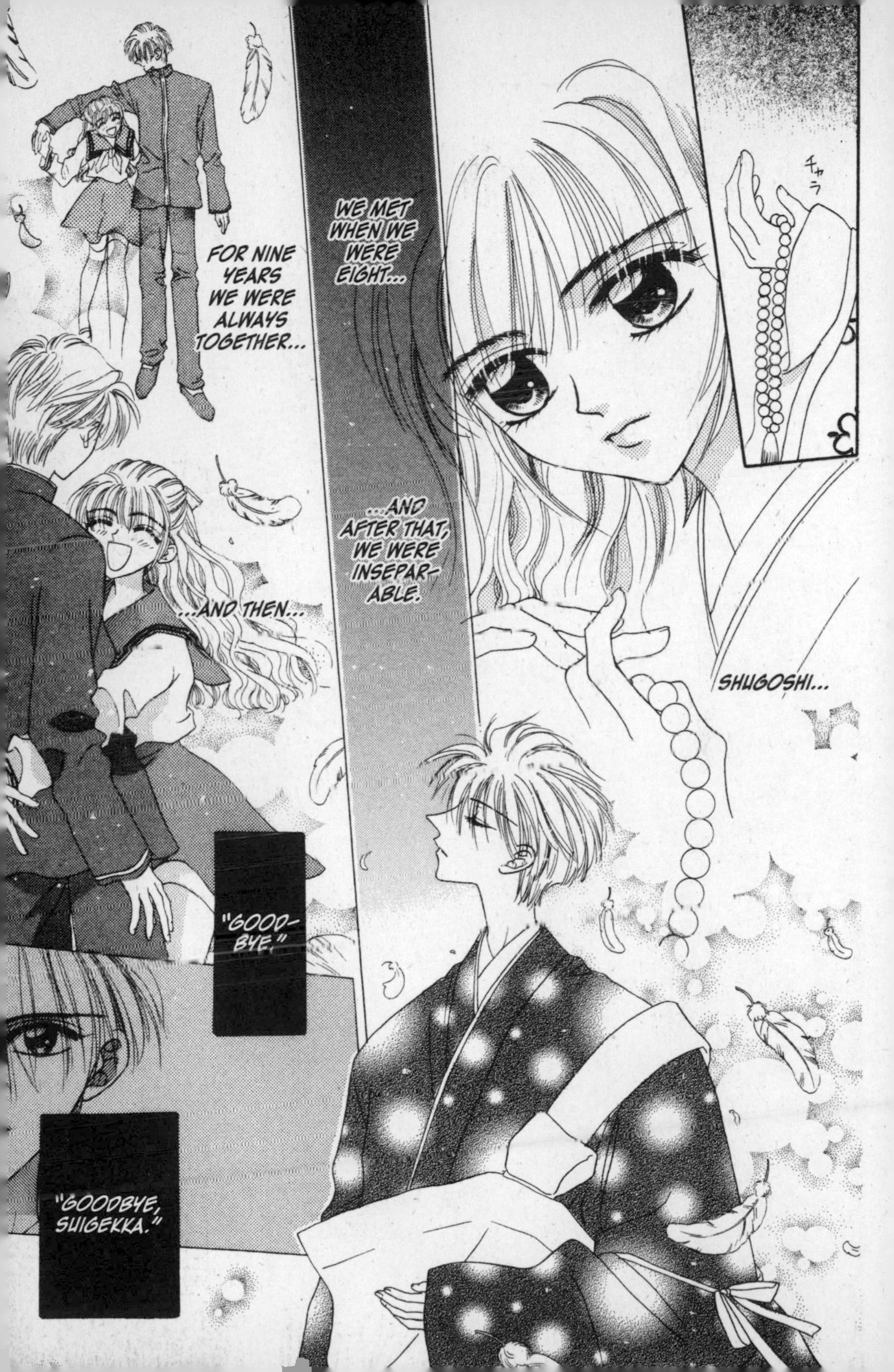
チャラ
SHUGOSHI...
WE MET WHEN WE WERE EIGHT...
...AND AFTER THAT, WE WERE INSEPARABLE.
FOR NINE YEARS WE WERE ALWAYS TOGETHER...
...AND THEN...
"GOOD-BYE."
"GOODBYE, SUIGEKKA."

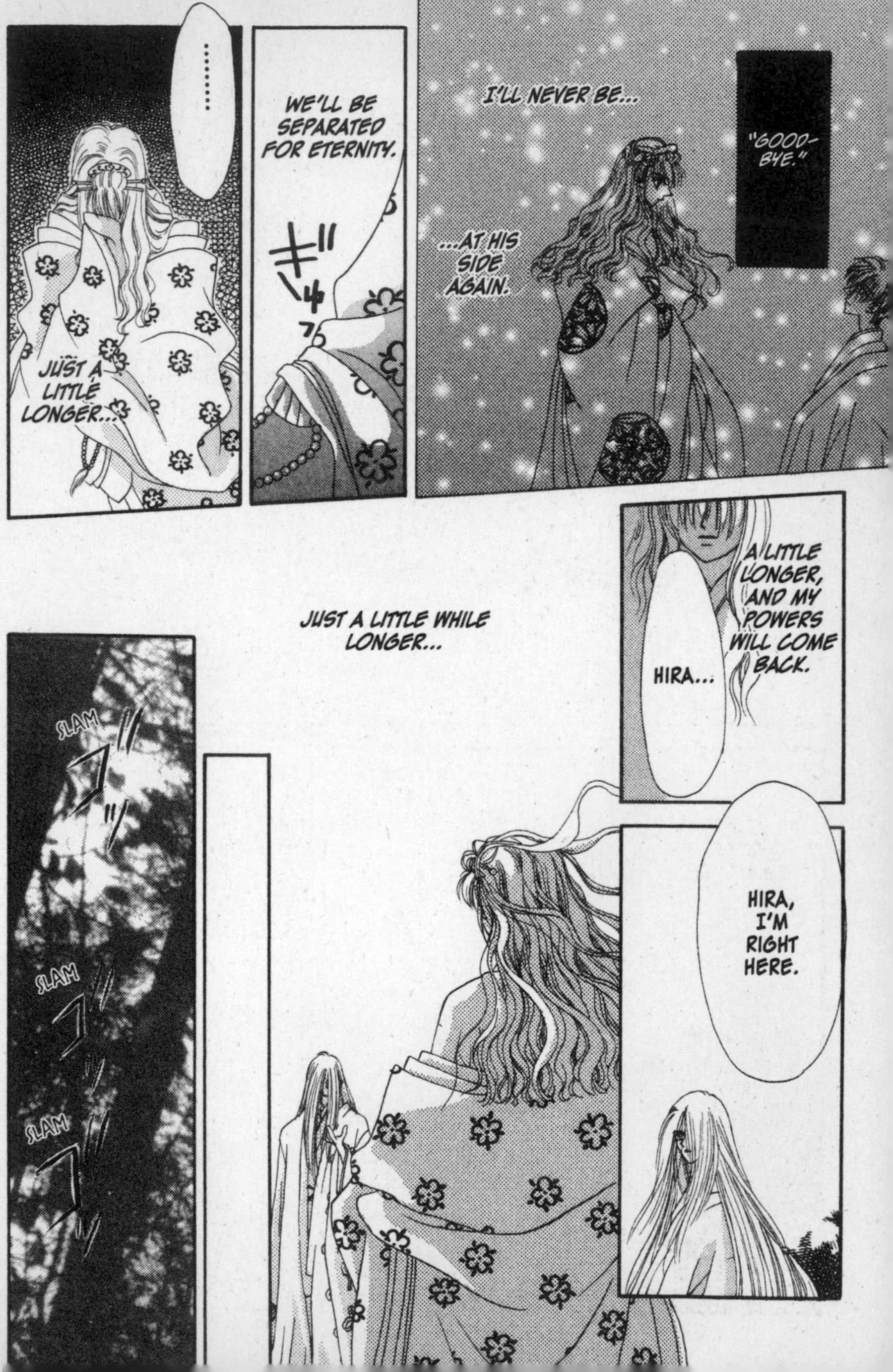
"GOOD-BYE."
I'LL NEVER BE...
...AT HIS SIDE AGAIN.
WE'LL BE SEPARATED FOR ETERNITY.
......
JUST A LITTLE LONGER...
A LITTLE LONGER, AND MY POWERS WILL COME BACK.
HIRA...
JUST A LITTLE WHILE LONGER...
HIRA, I'M RIGHT HERE.
SLAM
SLAM
SLAM

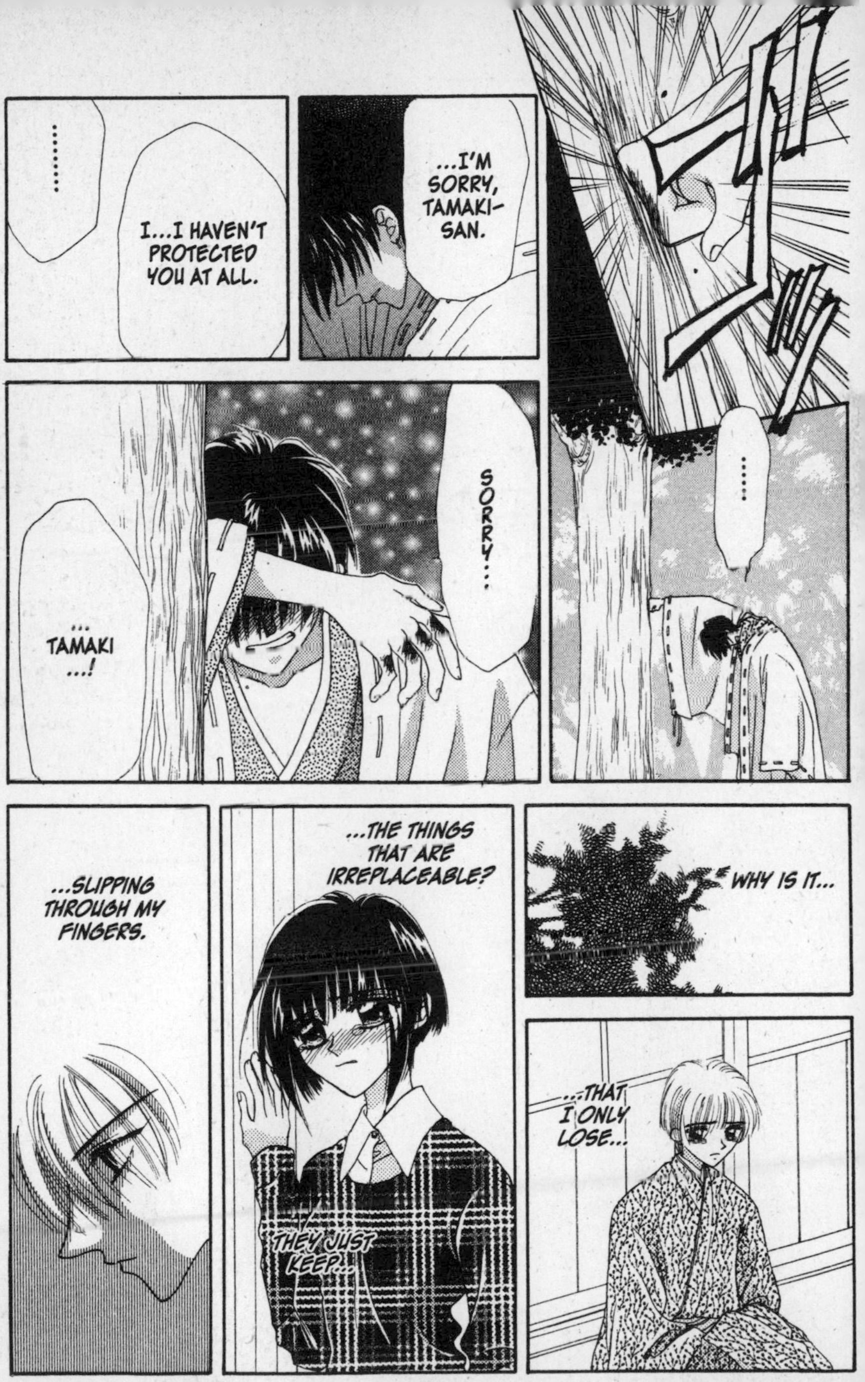
...I'M SORRY, TAMAKI-SAN.
......
I...I HAVEN'T PROTECTED YOU AT ALL.
......
SORRY...
...TAMAKI...!
WHY IS IT...
...THAT I ONLY LOSE...
...THE THINGS THAT ARE IRREPLACEABLE?
THEY JUST KEEP...
...SLIPPING THROUGH MY FINGERS.

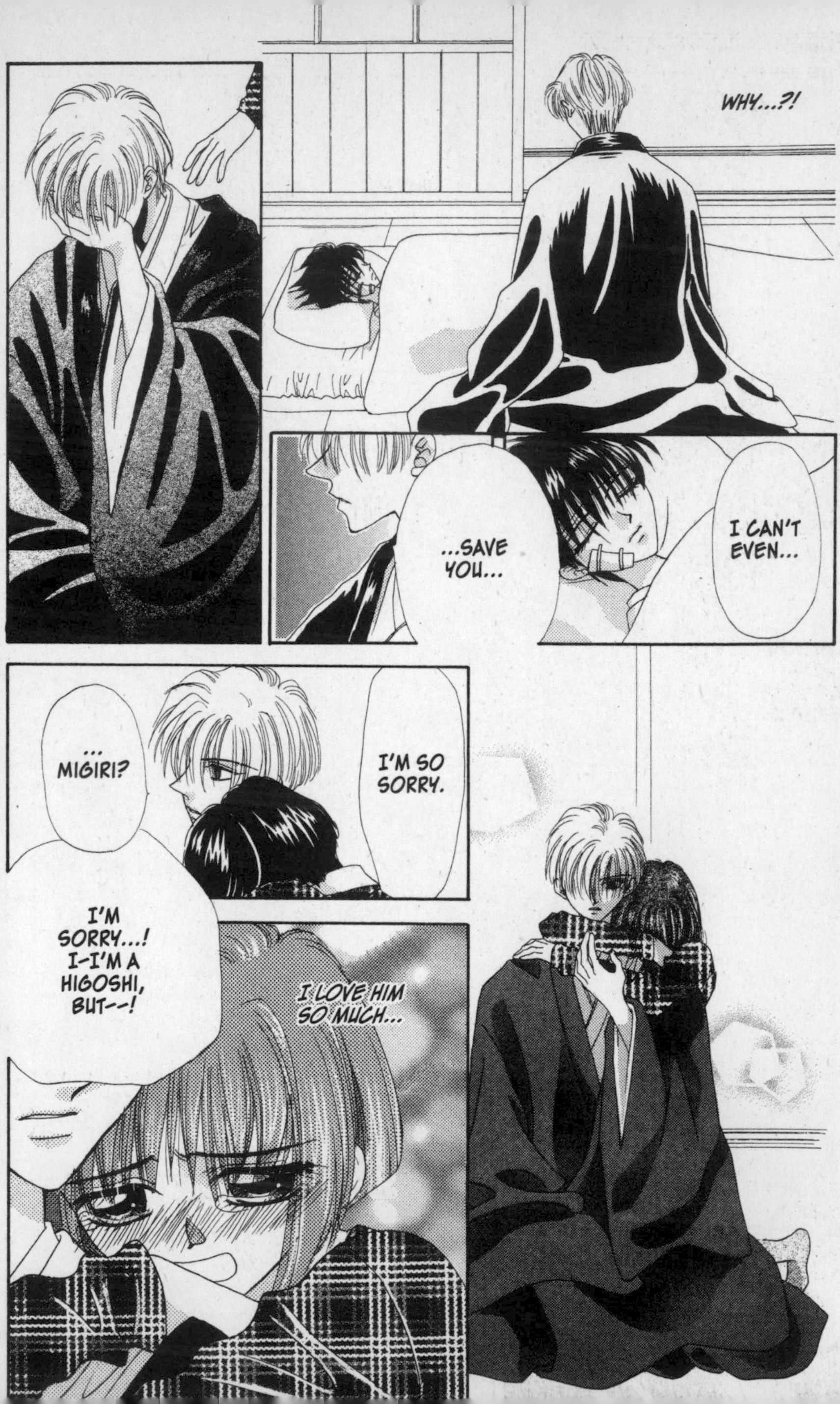
WHY...?!
I CAN'T EVEN...
...SAVE YOU...
I'M SO SORRY.
...MIGIRI?
I'M SORRY...! I-I'M A HIGOSHI, BUT--!
I LOVE HIM SO MUCH...

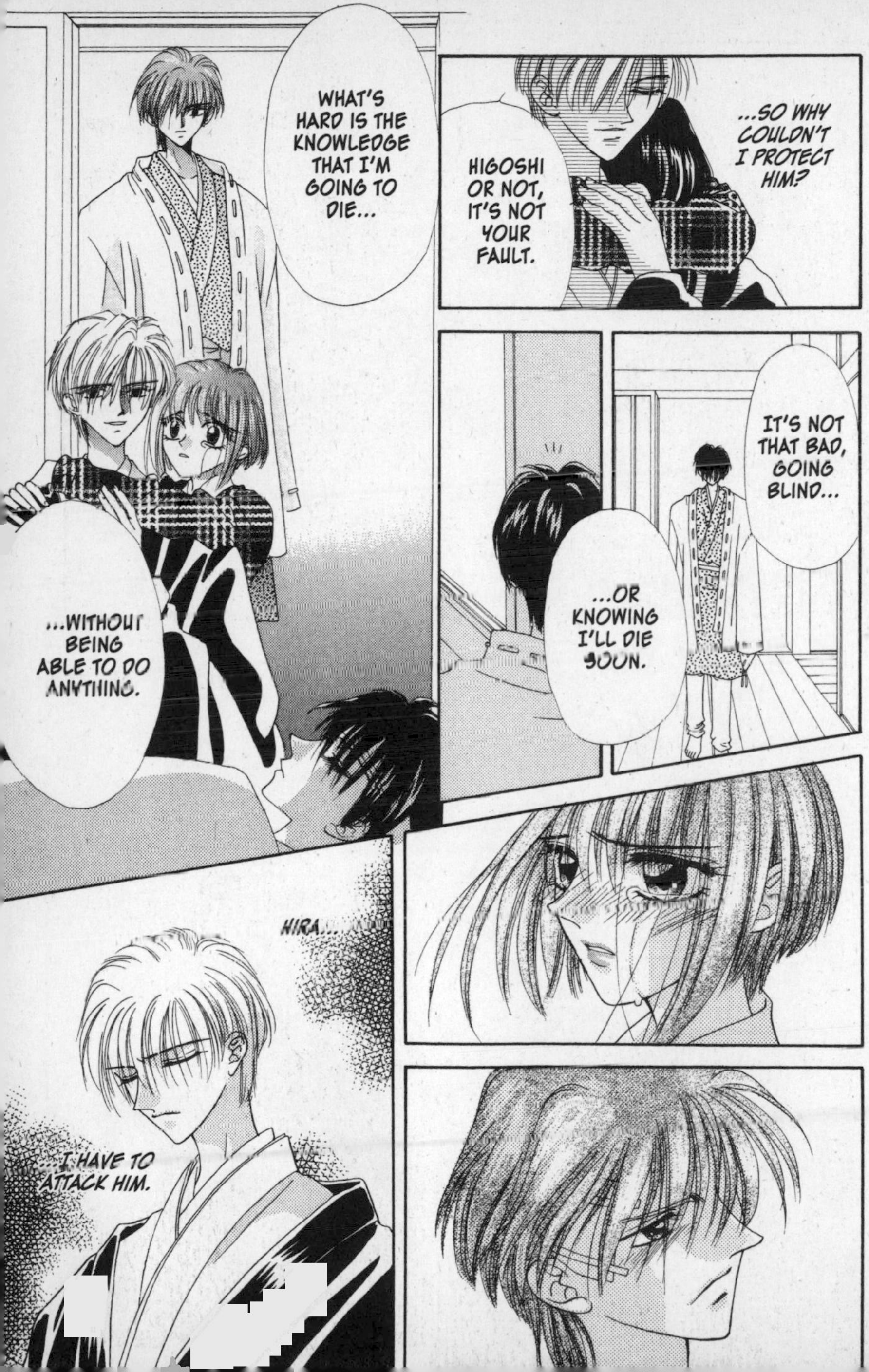
...SO WHY COULDN'T I PROTECT HIM?
HIGOSHI OR NOT, IT'S NOT YOUR FAULT.
IT'S NOT THAT BAD, GOING BLIND...
...OR KNOWING I'LL DIE SOON.
WHAT'S HARD IS THE KNOWLEDGE THAT I'M GOING TO DIE...
...WITHOUT BEING ABLE TO DO ANYTHING.
HIRA...
...I HAVE TO ATTACK HIM.

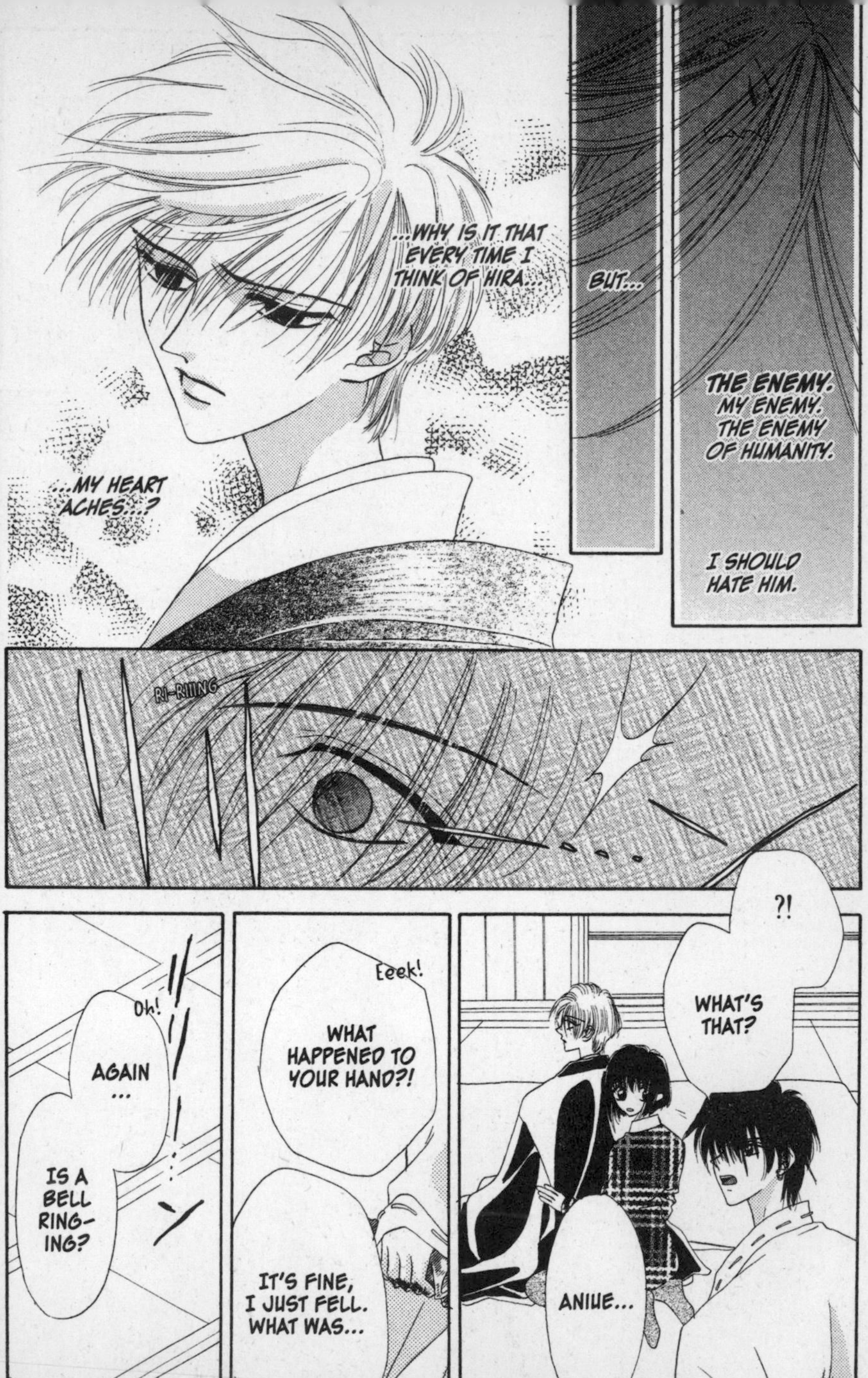
THE ENEMY. MY ENEMY. THE ENEMY OF HUMANITY.
I SHOULD HATE HIM.
BUT...
...WHY IS IT THAT EVERY TIME I THINK OF HIRA...
...MY HEART ACHES...?
RI-RIIING
?!
WHAT'S THAT?
ANIUE...
Eeek!
WHAT HAPPENED TO YOUR HAND?!
IT'S FINE, I JUST FELL. WHAT WAS...
Oh!
AGAIN ...
IS A BELL RING-ING?

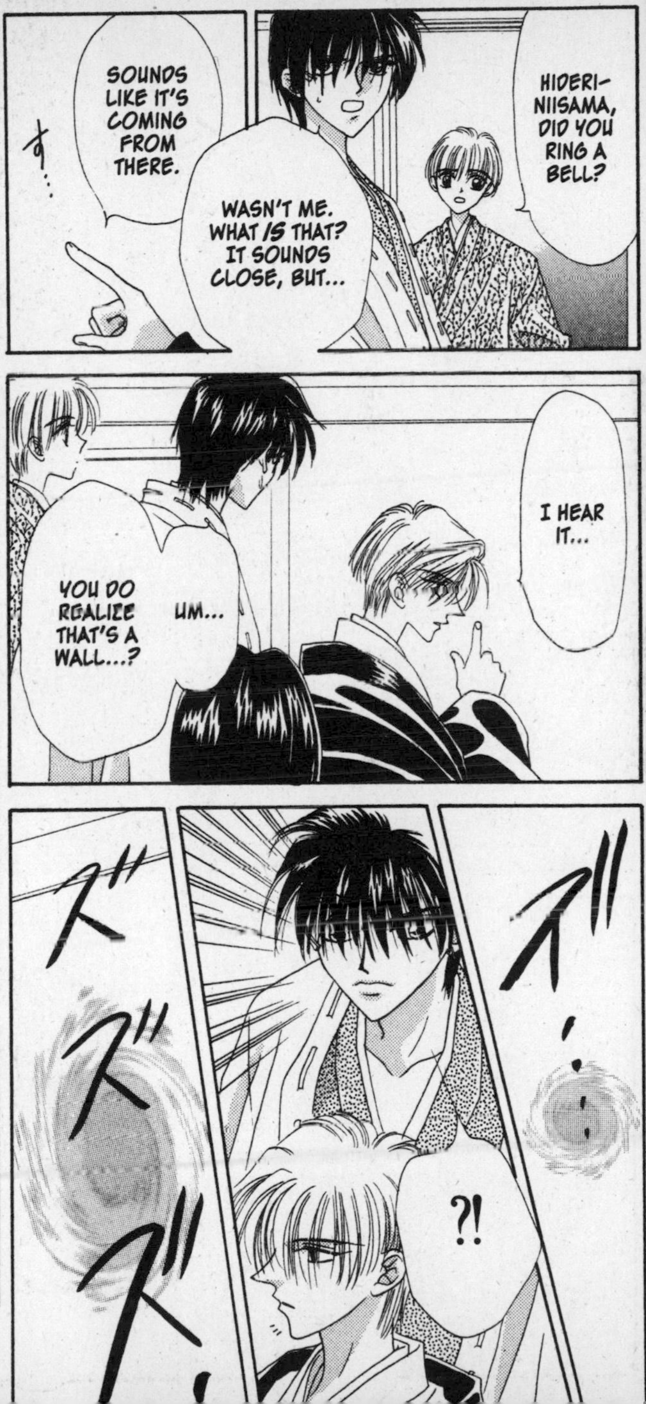
HIDERI-NIISAMA, DID YOU RING A BELL?
WASN'T ME. WHAT *IS* THAT? IT SOUNDS CLOSE, BUT...
SOUNDS LIKE IT'S COMING FROM THERE.
す…
I HEAR IT...
UM...
YOU DO REALIZE THAT'S A WALL...?
ズ
?!
ズ
ズ
ズ

Scroll Two

I had a bit of a fever and had to stay in bed. Of course, it happened just as I had a deadline looming. I guess the root of the problem is that I'm sickly or have a weak body or something. I get a lot of fevers, and I tend to be anemic. Before I started high school I used to throw up a lot. I think that was because of stress, but...that doesn't change the fact that I'm kind of ditzy. But there are lots of people who're even less healthy than I am, so I don't think I'm very convincing. Yep. They get so sick that it's not even funny, and every once in a while I get scared. (laughs) Take care of yourself, everybody! (laughs) ♥

Take the case of a certain manga creator:

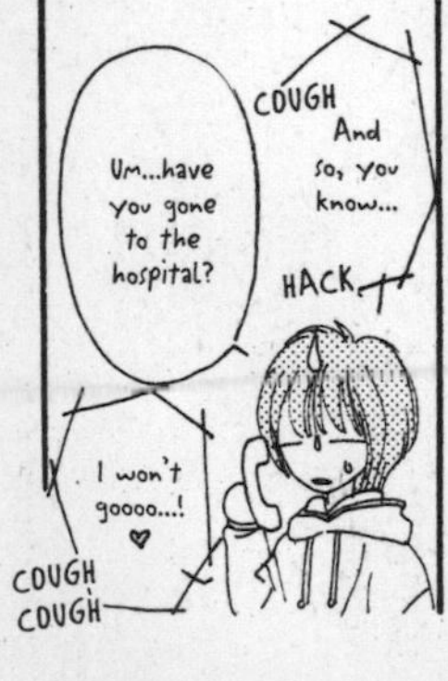
COUGH
And so, you know...
Um...have you gone to the hospital?
HACK
I won't goooo...! ♥
COUGH COUGH

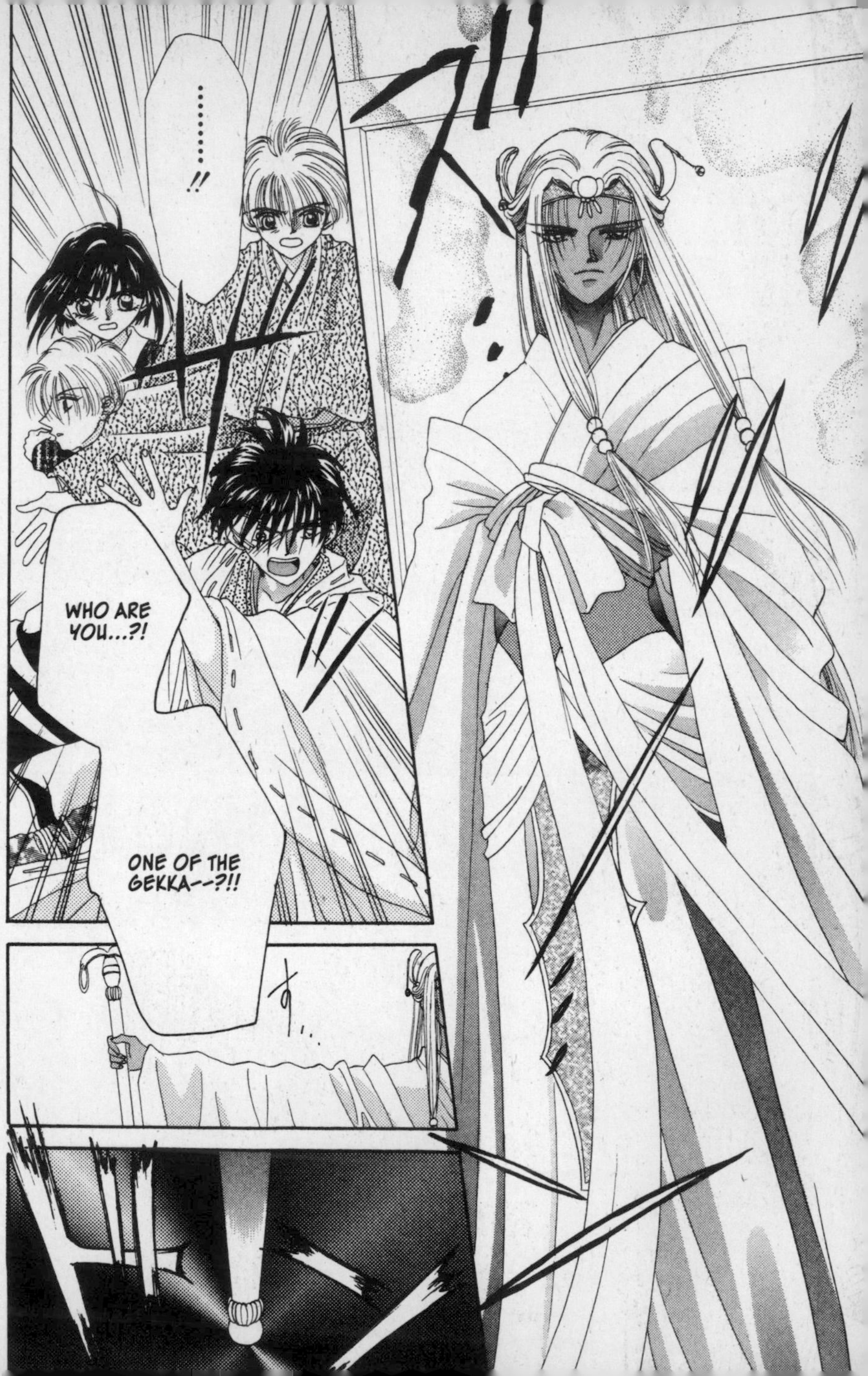
......
!!
WHO ARE YOU...?!
ONE OF THE GEKKA--?!!

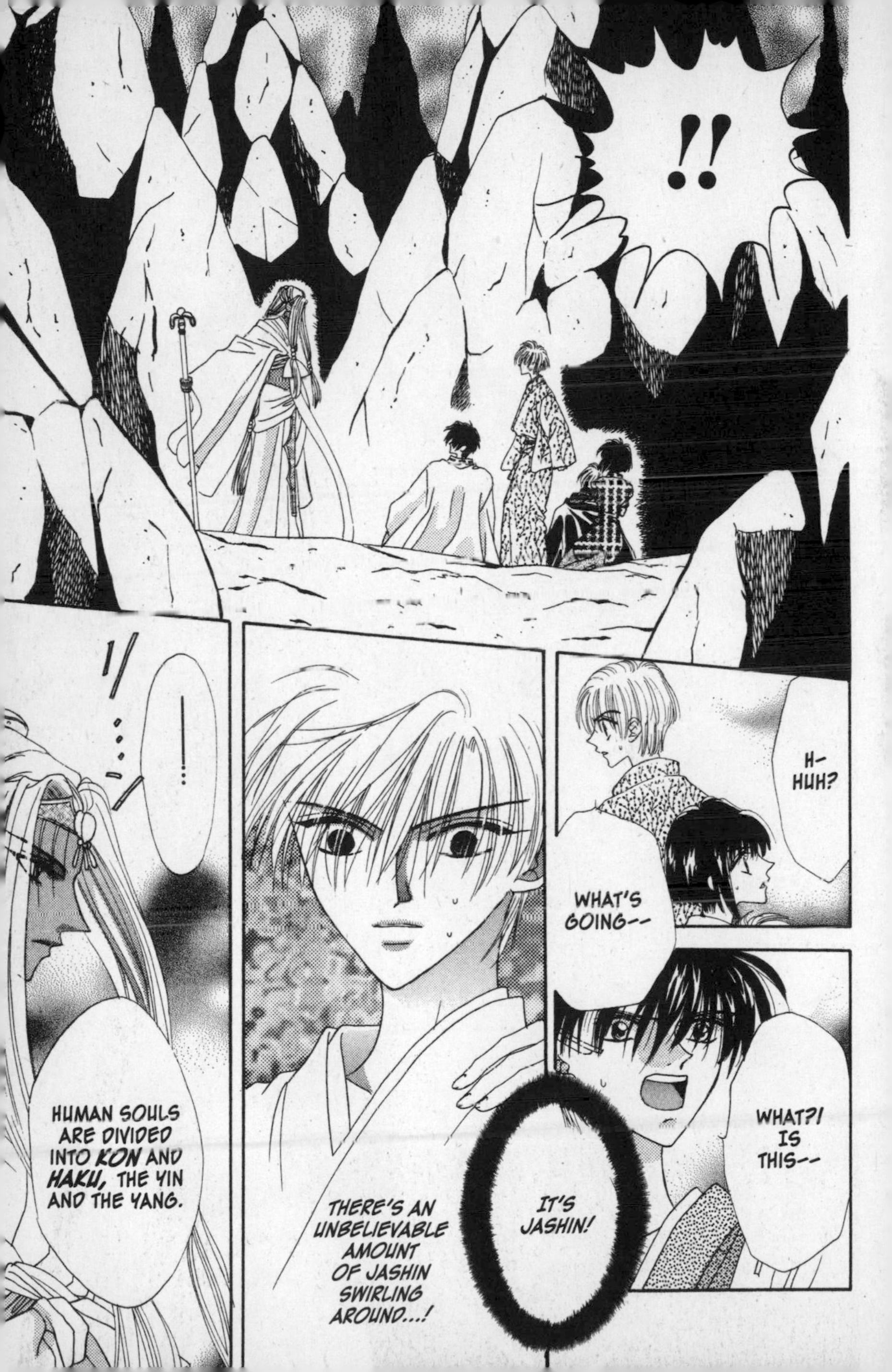
!!
H-HUH?
WHAT'S GOING--
WHAT?! IS THIS--
IT'S JASHIN!
THERE'S AN UNBELIEVABLE AMOUNT OF JASHIN SWIRLING AROUND...!
...!
HUMAN SOULS ARE DIVIDED INTO KON AND HAKU, THE YIN AND THE YANG.

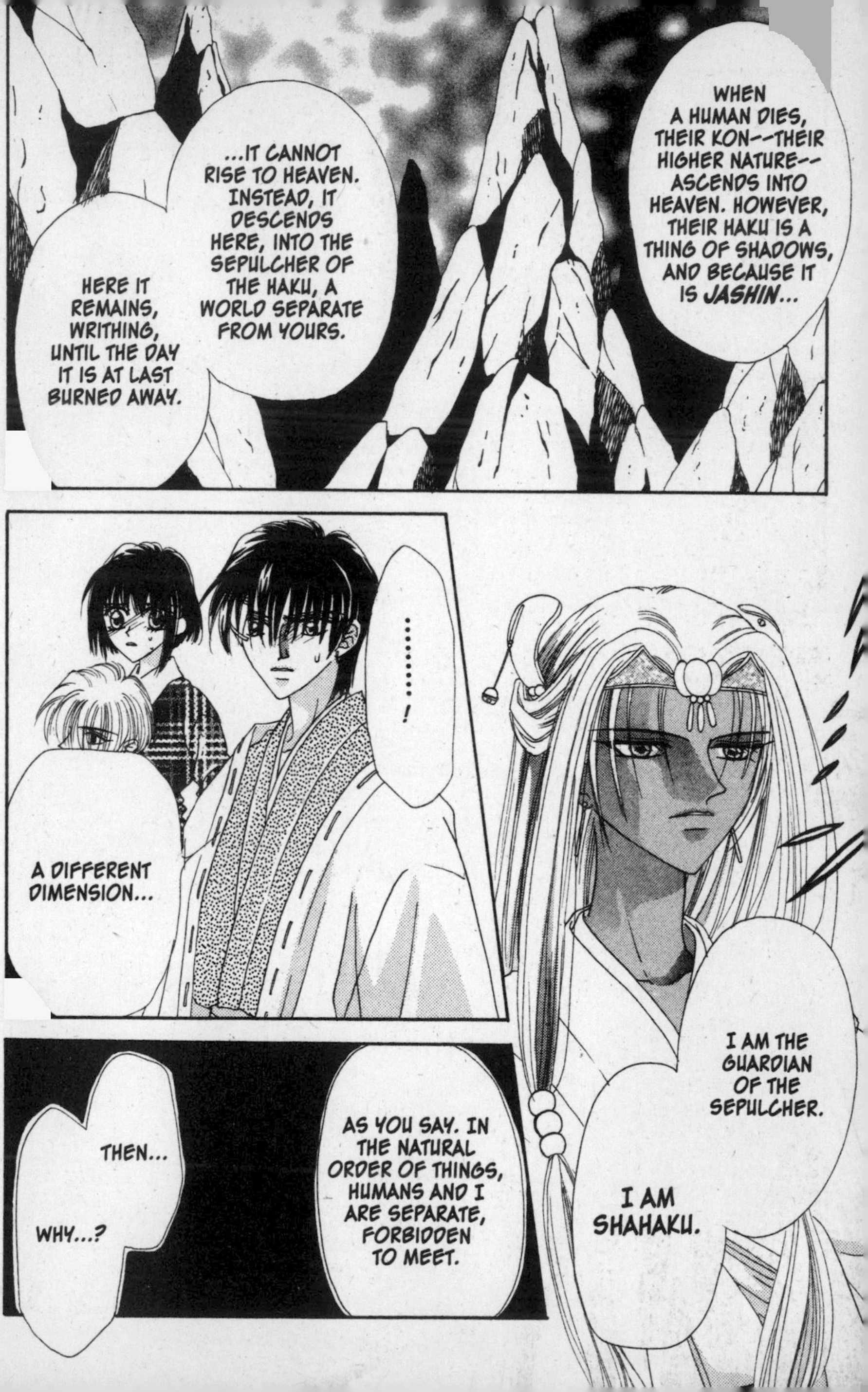
WHEN A HUMAN DIES, THEIR KON--THEIR HIGHER NATURE--ASCENDS INTO HEAVEN. HOWEVER, THEIR HAKU IS A THING OF SHADOWS, AND BECAUSE IT IS *JASHIN*...
...IT CANNOT RISE TO HEAVEN. INSTEAD, IT DESCENDS HERE, INTO THE SEPULCHER OF THE HAKU, A WORLD SEPARATE FROM YOURS.
HERE IT REMAINS, WRITHING, UNTIL THE DAY IT IS AT LAST BURNED AWAY.
I AM THE GUARDIAN OF THE SEPULCHER.
I AM SHAHAKU.
......!
A DIFFERENT DIMENSION...
AS YOU SAY. IN THE NATURAL ORDER OF THINGS, HUMANS AND I ARE SEPARATE, FORBIDDEN TO MEET.
THEN...
WHY...?

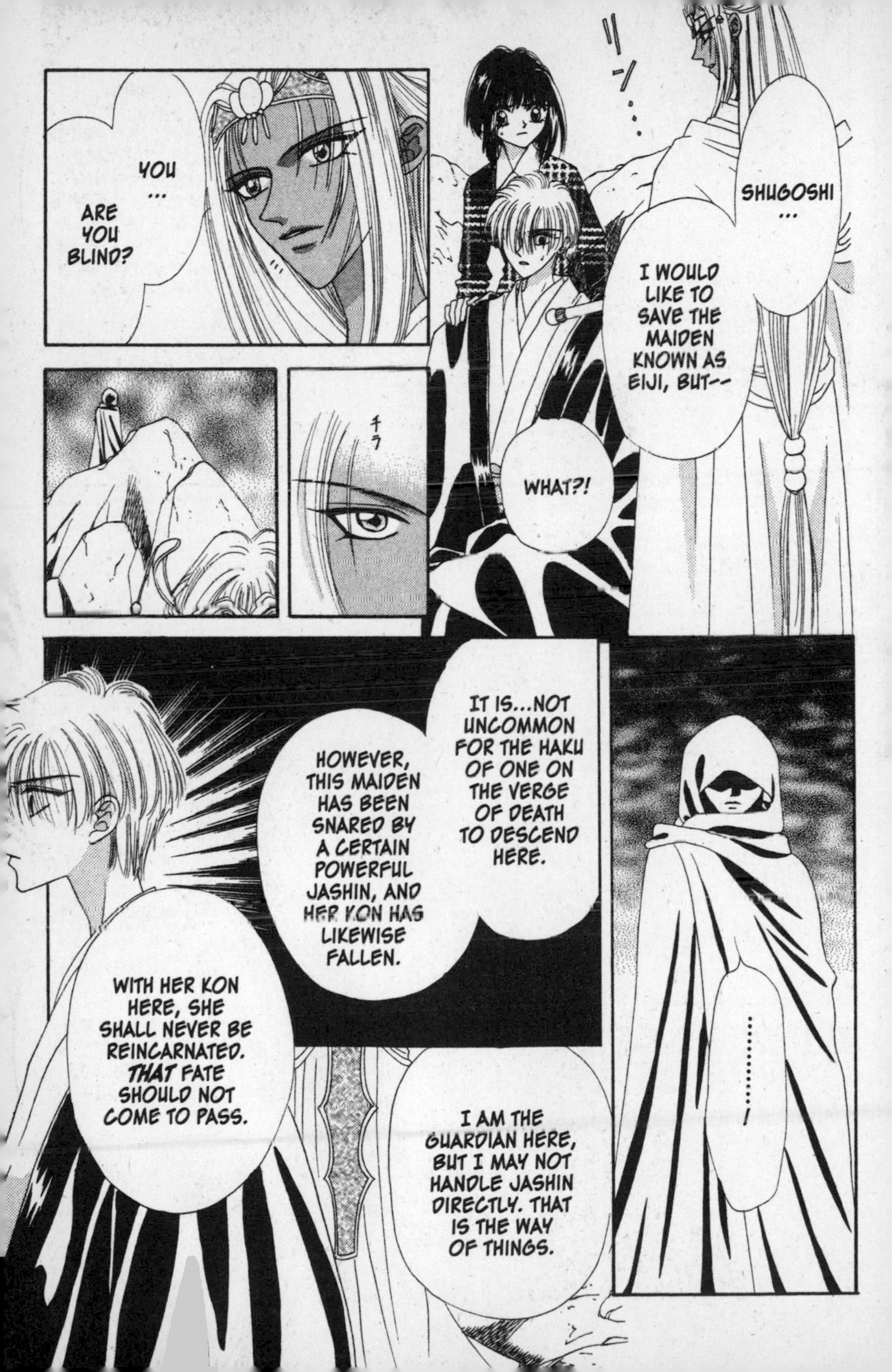
SHUGOSHI ...
I WOULD LIKE TO SAVE THE MAIDEN KNOWN AS EIJI, BUT--
WHAT?!
YOU ... ARE YOU BLIND?
チラ
......!
IT IS...NOT UNCOMMON FOR THE HAKU OF ONE ON THE VERGE OF DEATH TO DESCEND HERE.
HOWEVER, THIS MAIDEN HAS BEEN SNARED BY A CERTAIN POWERFUL JASHIN, AND HER KON HAS LIKEWISE FALLEN.
WITH HER KON HERE, SHE SHALL NEVER BE REINCARNATED. *THAT* FATE SHOULD NOT COME TO PASS.
I AM THE GUARDIAN HERE, BUT I MAY NOT HANDLE JASHIN DIRECTLY. THAT IS THE WAY OF THINGS.

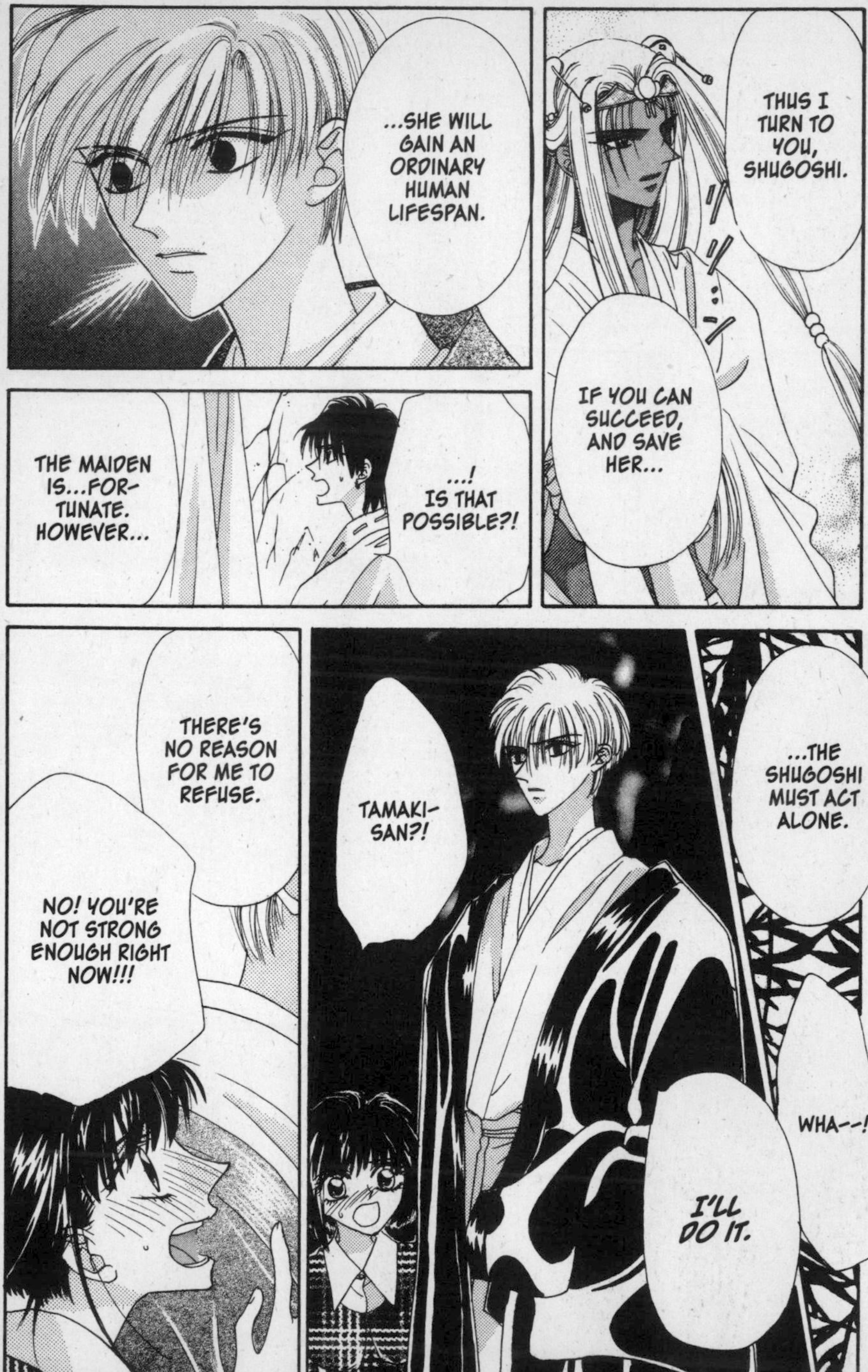
THUS I TURN TO YOU, SHUGOSHI.
IF YOU CAN SUCCEED, AND SAVE HER...
...SHE WILL GAIN AN ORDINARY HUMAN LIFESPAN.
...! IS THAT POSSIBLE?!
THE MAIDEN IS...FOR-TUNATE. HOWEVER...
...THE SHUGOSHI MUST ACT ALONE.
WHA--!
I'LL DO IT.
TAMAKI-SAN?!
THERE'S NO REASON FOR ME TO REFUSE.
NO! YOU'RE NOT STRONG ENOUGH RIGHT NOW!!!

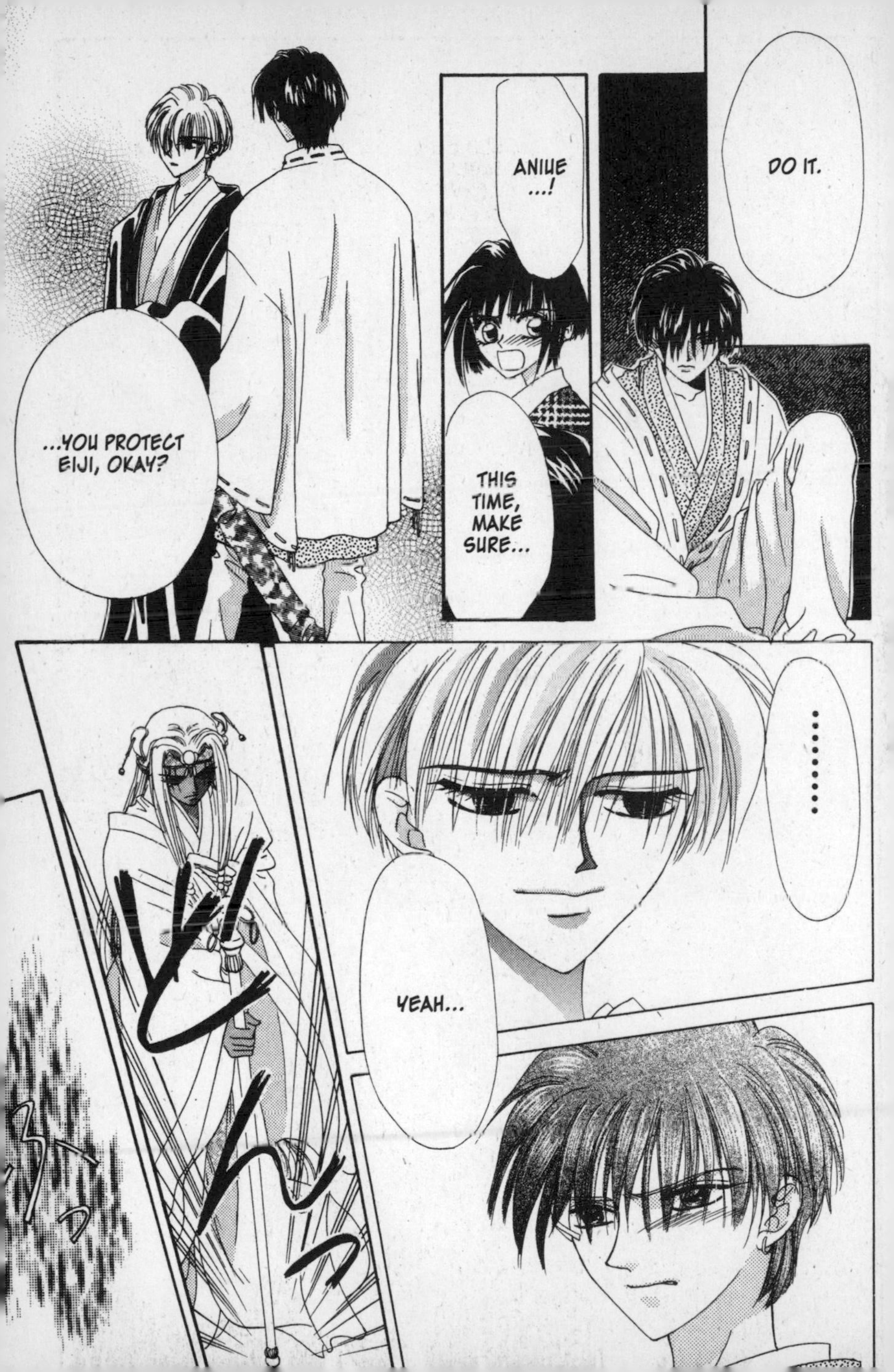
DO IT.
ANIUE ...!
THIS TIME, MAKE SURE...
...YOU PROTECT EIJI, OKAY?
......
YEAH...

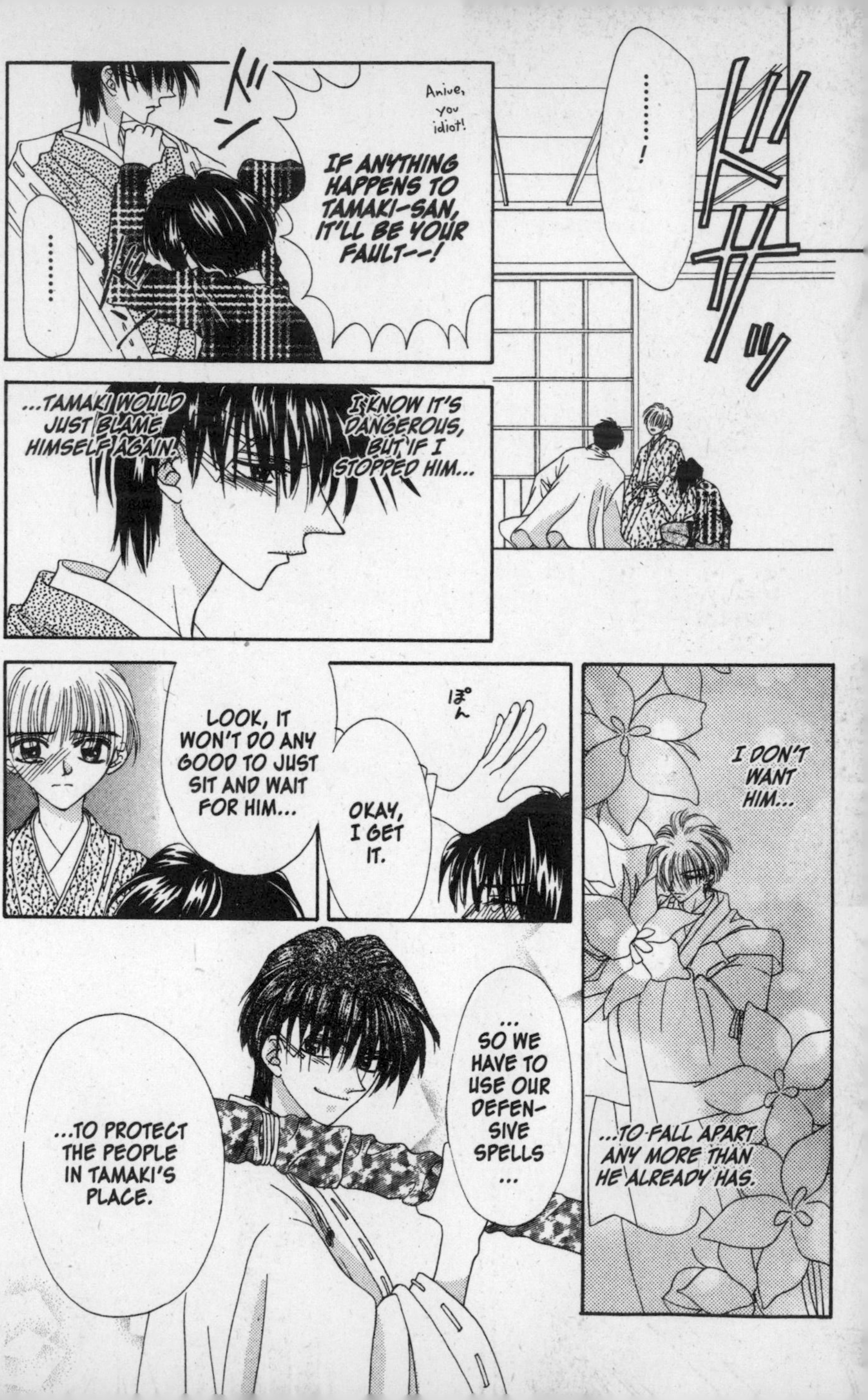
……!
ドドサッ
Aniue, you idiot!
IF ANYTHING HAPPENS TO TAMAKI-SAN, IT'LL BE YOUR FAULT--!
……
I KNOW IT'S DANGEROUS, BUT IF I STOPPED HIM...
...TAMAKI WOULD JUST BLAME HIMSELF AGAIN.
I DON'T WANT HIM...
...TO FALL APART ANY MORE THAN HE ALREADY HAS.
ぽん
OKAY, I GET IT.
LOOK, IT WON'T DO ANY GOOD TO JUST SIT AND WAIT FOR HIM...
... SO WE HAVE TO USE OUR DEFEN-SIVE SPELLS ...
...TO PROTECT THE PEOPLE IN TAMAKI'S PLACE.

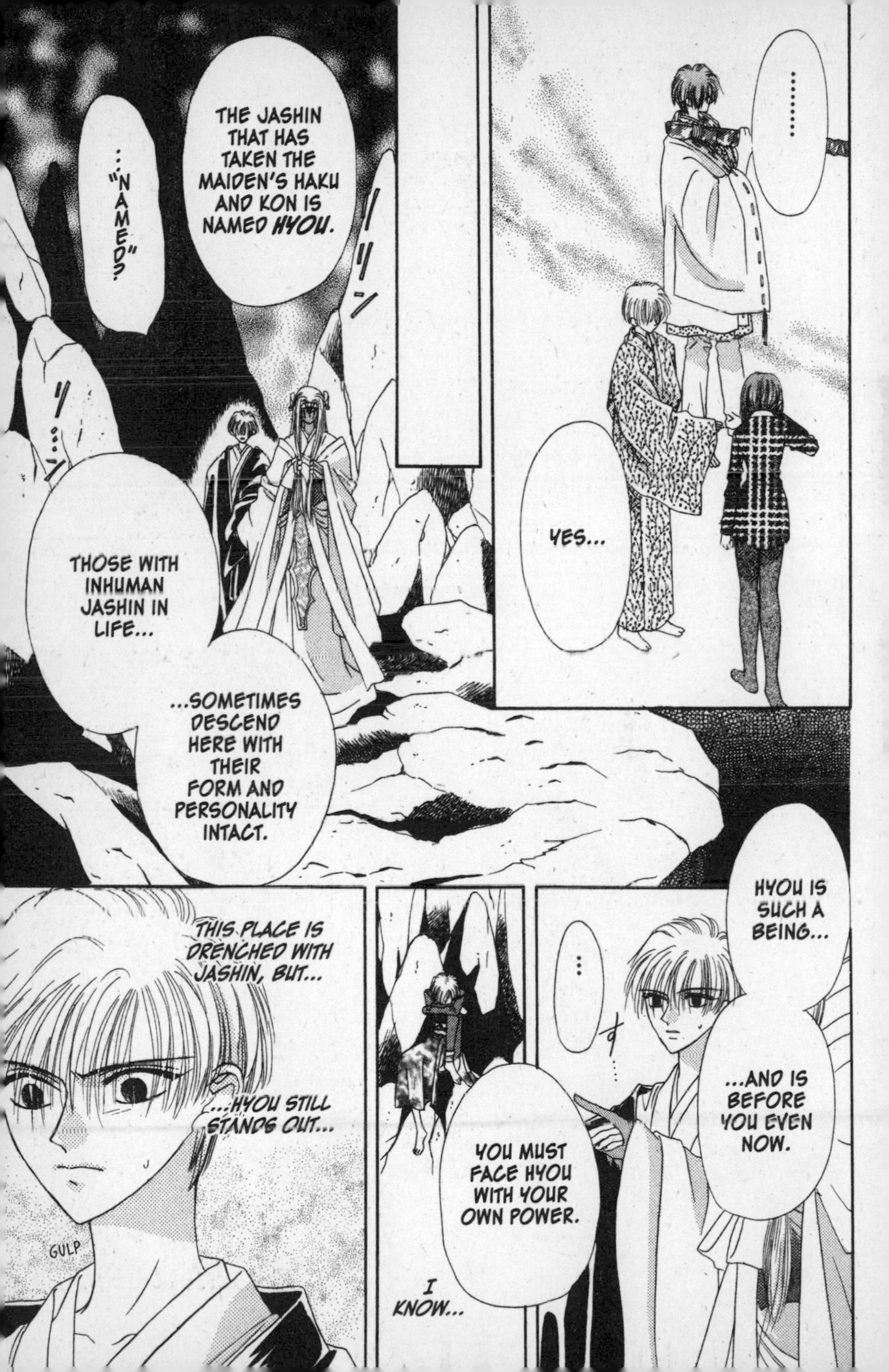
....
YES...
THE JASHIN THAT HAS TAKEN THE MAIDEN'S HAKU AND KON IS NAMED HYOU.
..."NAMED"?
THOSE WITH INHUMAN JASHIN IN LIFE...
...SOMETIMES DESCEND HERE WITH THEIR FORM AND PERSONALITY INTACT.
HYOU IS SUCH A BEING...
...
...AND IS BEFORE YOU EVEN NOW.
YOU MUST FACE HYOU WITH YOUR OWN POWER.
I KNOW...
THIS PLACE IS DRENCHED WITH JASHIN, BUT...
...HYOU STILL STANDS OUT...
GULP

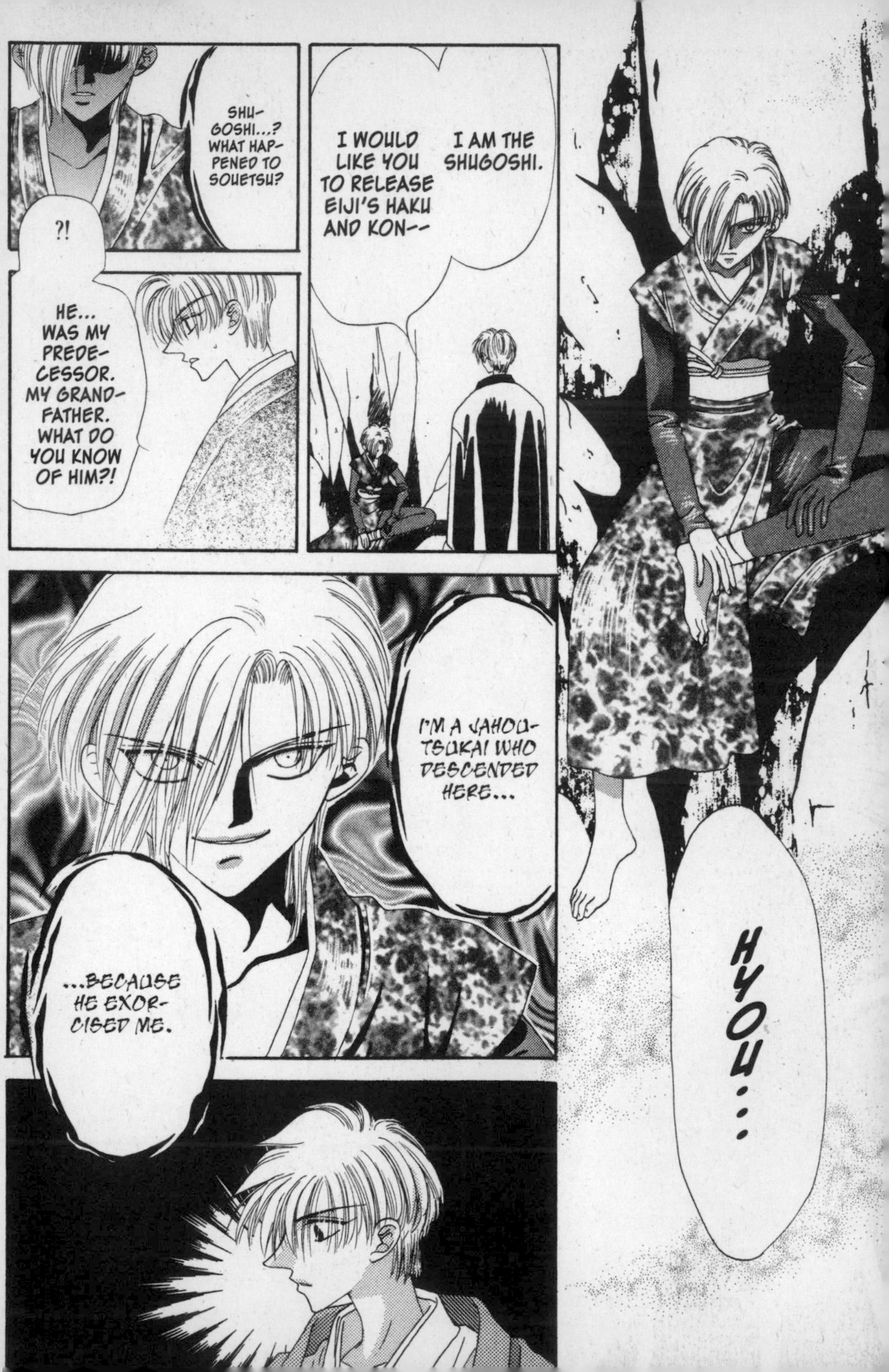
HYOU...
I AM THE SHUGOSHI.
I WOULD LIKE YOU TO RELEASE EIJI'S HAKU AND KON--
SHUGOSHI...? WHAT HAPPENED TO SOUETSU?
?!
HE... WAS MY PREDECESSOR. MY GRANDFATHER. WHAT DO YOU KNOW OF HIM?!
I'M A JAHOU-TSUKAI WHO DESCENDED HERE...
...BECAUSE HE EXORCISED ME.

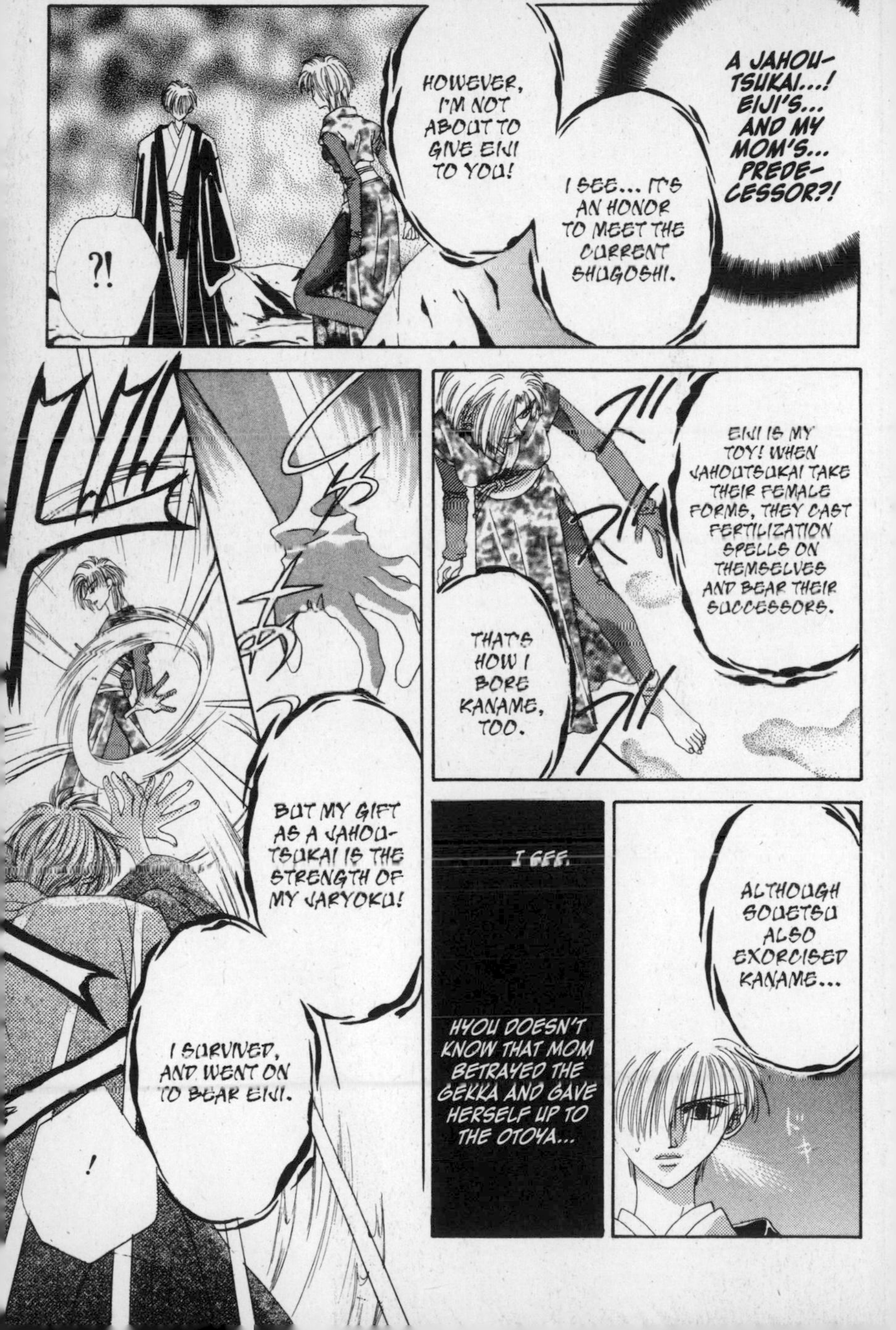

A JAHOU-TSUKAI...! EIJI'S... AND MY MOM'S... PREDECESSOR?!
I SEE... IT'S AN HONOR TO MEET THE CURRENT SHUGOSHI.
HOWEVER, I'M NOT ABOUT TO GIVE EIJI TO YOU!
?!
EIJI IS MY TOY! WHEN JAHOUTSUKAI TAKE THEIR FEMALE FORMS, THEY CAST FERTILIZATION SPELLS ON THEMSELVES AND BEAR THEIR SUCCESSORS.
THAT'S HOW I BORE KANAME, TOO.
ALTHOUGH SOUETSU ALSO EXORCISED KANAME...
I SEE.
HYOU DOESN'T KNOW THAT MOM BETRAYED THE GEKKA AND GAVE HERSELF UP TO THE OTOYA...
BUT MY GIFT AS A JAHOU-TSUKAI IS THE STRENGTH OF MY JARYOKU!
I SURVIVED, AND WENT ON TO BEAR EIJI.
!

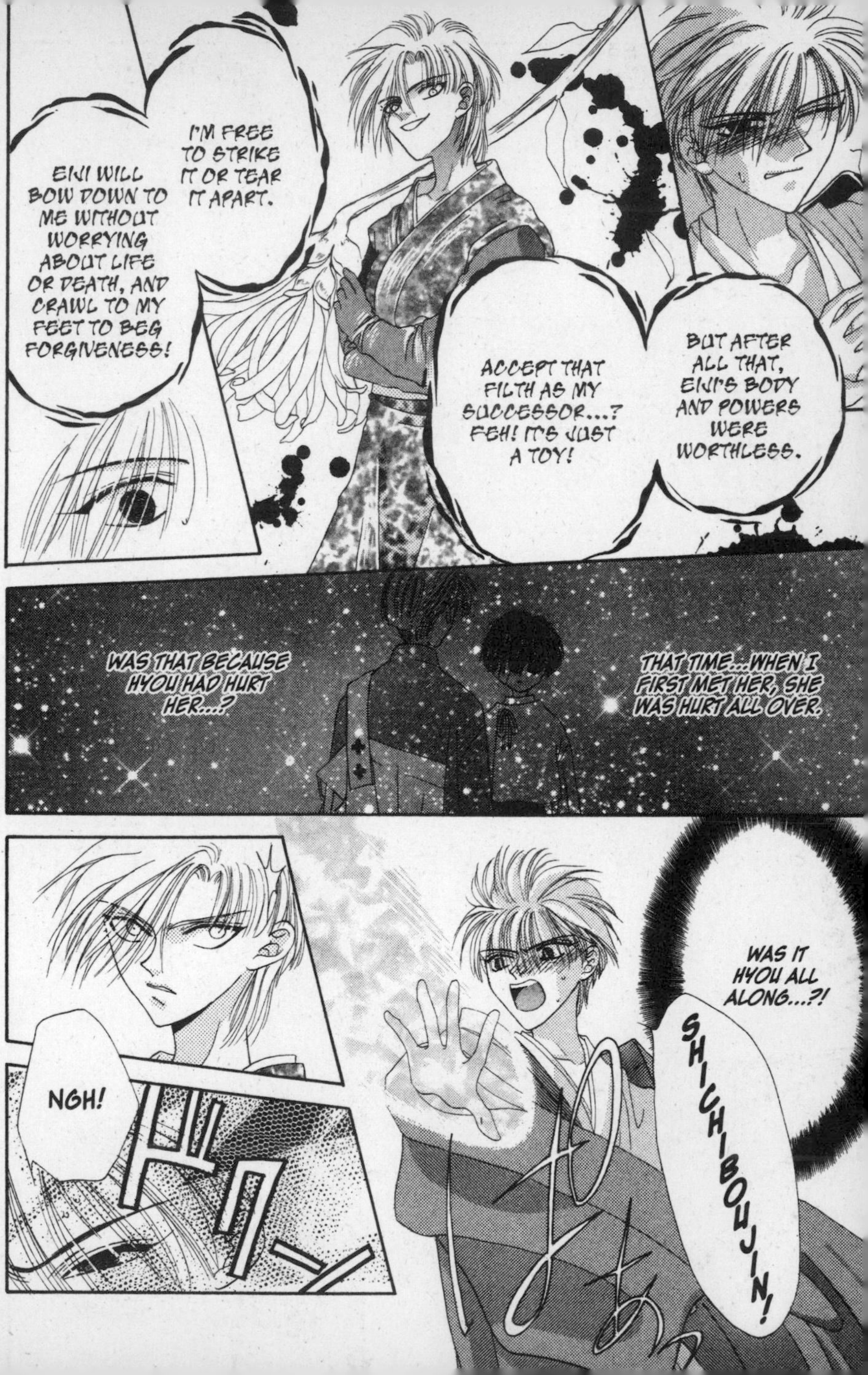
BUT AFTER ALL THAT, EIJI'S BODY AND POWERS WERE WORTHLESS.
ACCEPT THAT FILTH AS MY SUCCESSOR...? FEH! IT'S JUST A TOY!
I'M FREE TO STRIKE IT OR TEAR IT APART.
EIJI WILL BOW DOWN TO ME WITHOUT WORRYING ABOUT LIFE OR DEATH, AND CRAWL TO MY FEET TO BEG FORGIVENESS!
THAT TIME...WHEN I FIRST MET HER, SHE WAS HURT ALL OVER.
WAS THAT BECAUSE HYOU HAD HURT HER...?
WAS IT HYOU ALL ALONG...?!
SHICHIBOUJIN!
NGH!

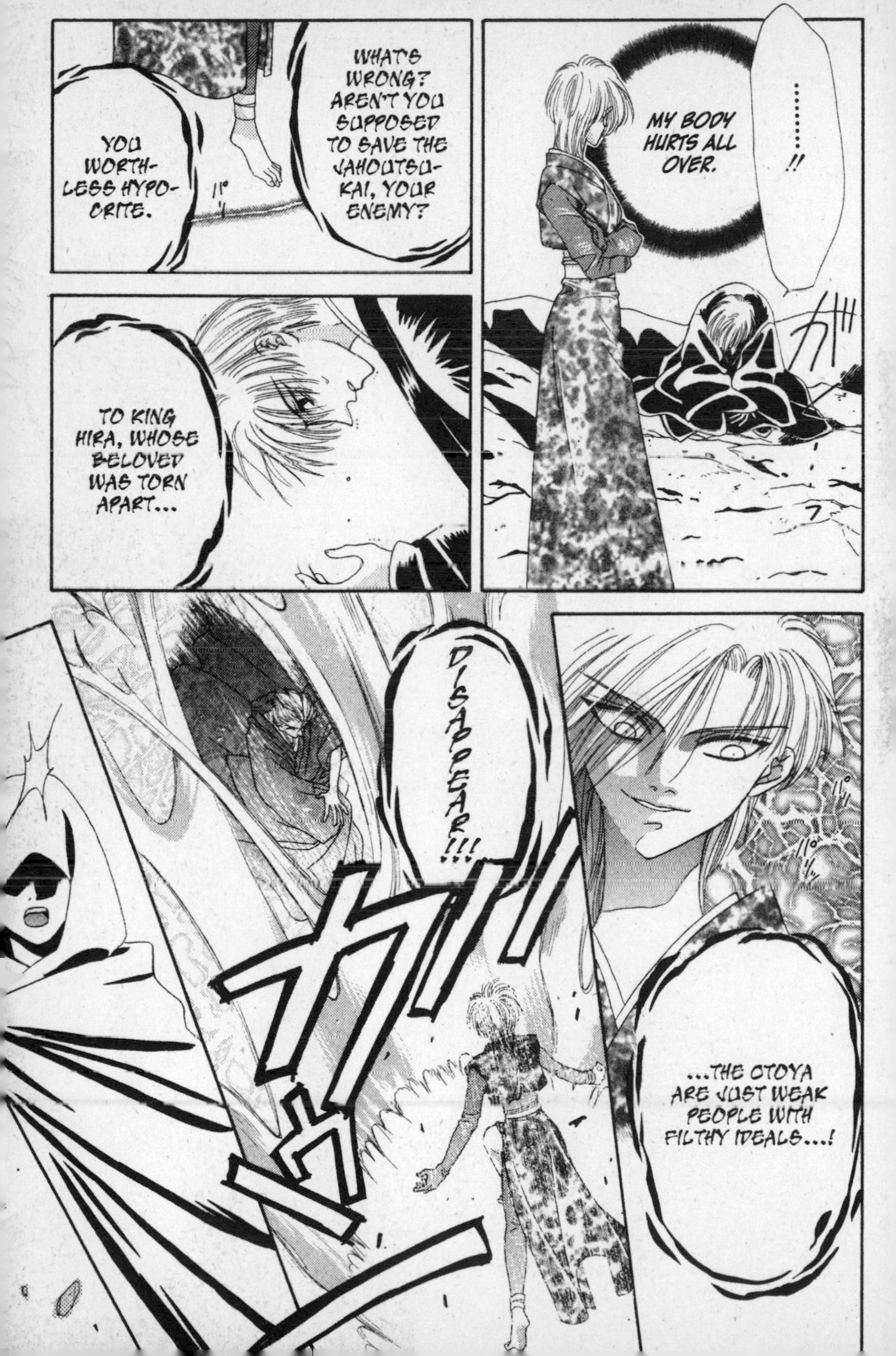
......!!
MY BODY HURTS ALL OVER.
WHAT'S WRONG? AREN'T YOU SUPPOSED TO SAVE THE JAHOUTSU-KAI, YOUR ENEMY?
YOU WORTH-LESS HYPO-CRITE.
TO KING HIRA, WHOSE BELOVED WAS TORN APART...
...THE OTOYA ARE JUST WEAK PEOPLE WITH FILTHY IDEALS...!
DISAPPEAR!!!

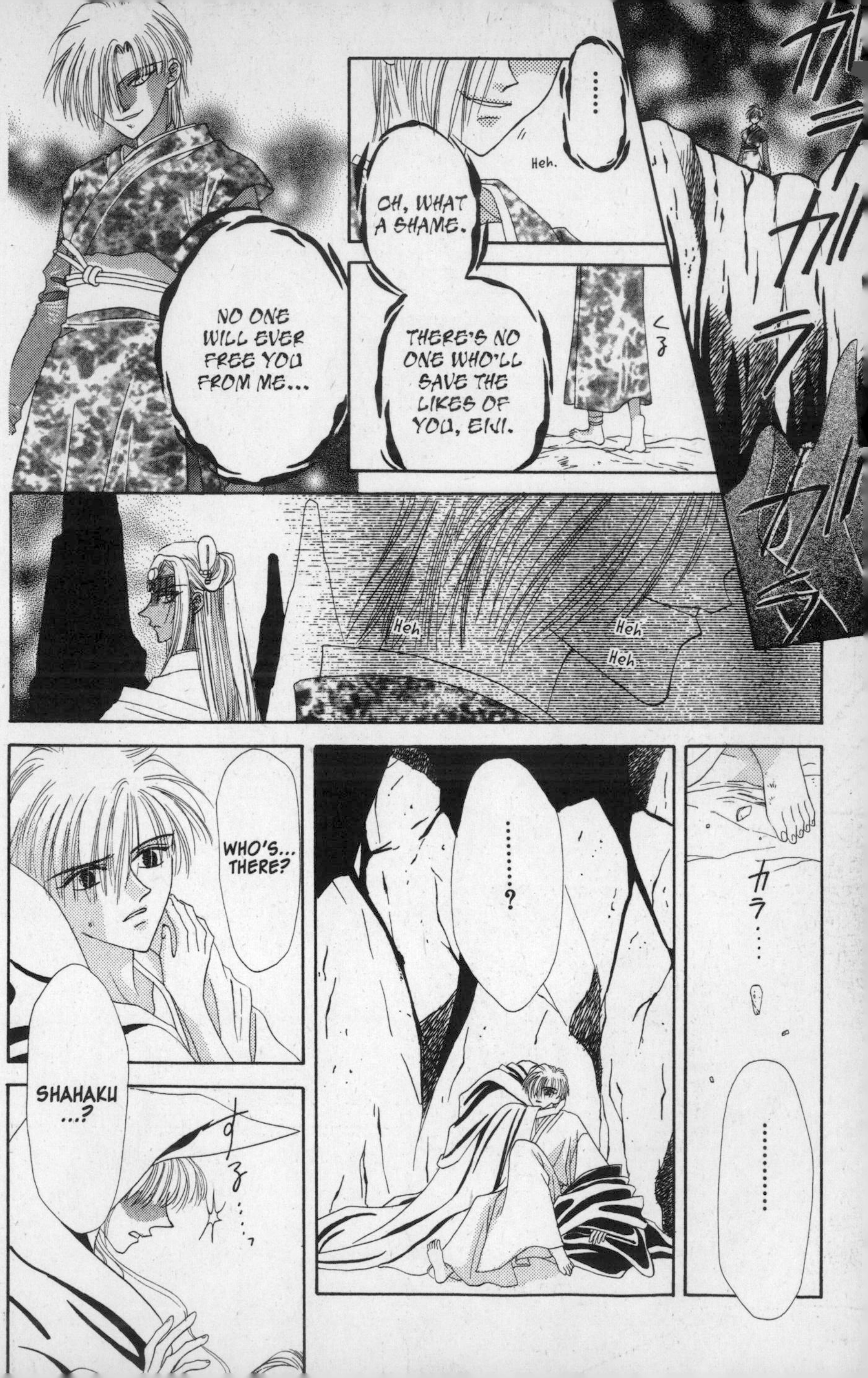
......
Heh.
OH, WHAT A SHAME.
THERE'S NO ONE WHO'LL SAVE THE LIKES OF YOU, EIJI.
NO ONE WILL EVER FREE YOU FROM ME...
Heh
Heh
Heh
カラ……
......
......?
WHO'S... THERE?
SHAHAKU ...?

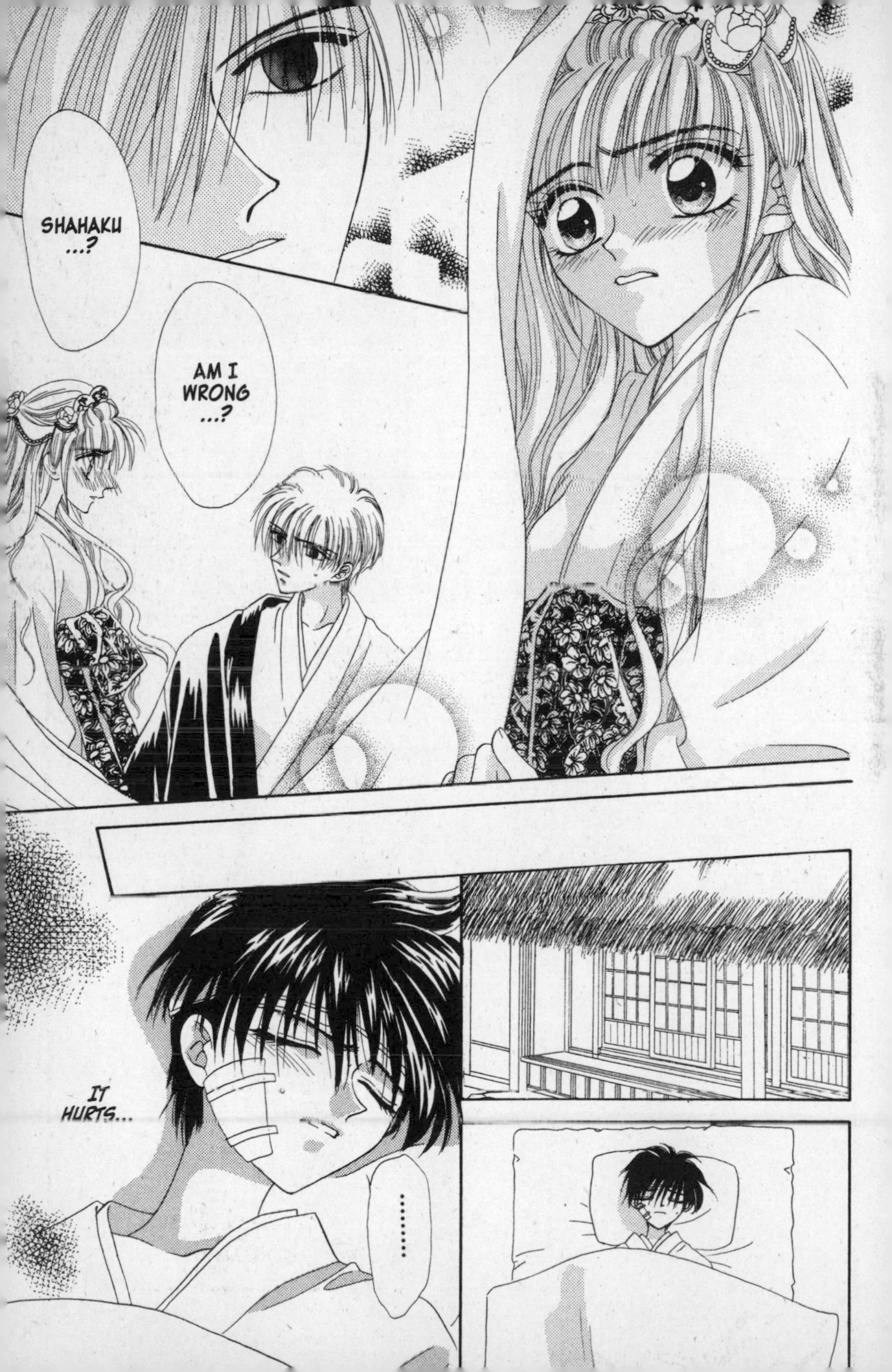
SHAHAKU ...?
AM I WRONG ...?
......
IT HURTS...

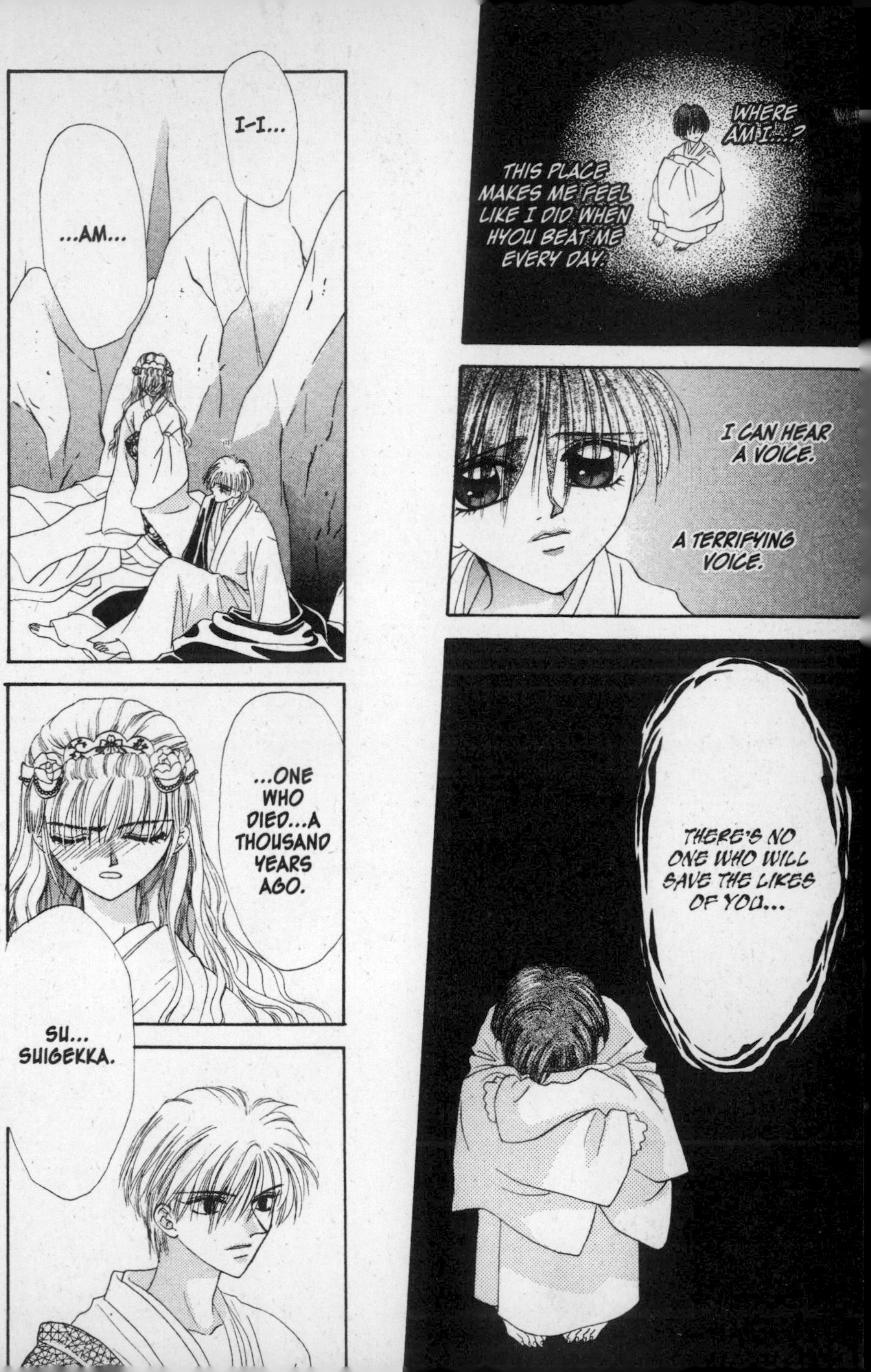
WHERE AM I...?
THIS PLACE MAKES ME FEEL LIKE I DID WHEN HYOU BEAT ME EVERY DAY.
I CAN HEAR A VOICE.
A TERRIFYING VOICE.
THERE'S NO ONE WHO WILL SAVE THE LIKES OF YOU...
I-I...
...AM...
...ONE WHO DIED...A THOUSAND YEARS AGO.
SU... SUIGEKKA.

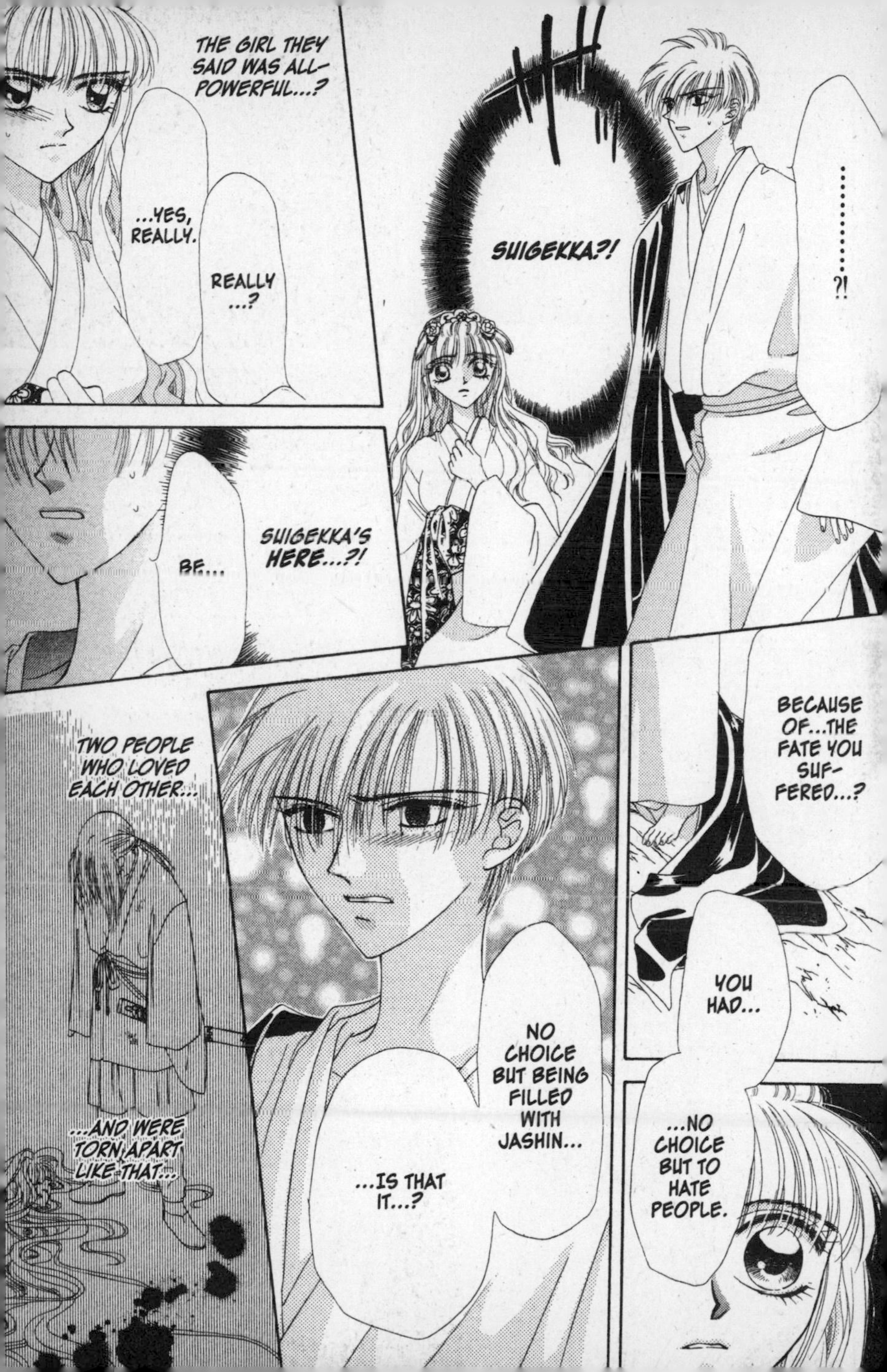
......?!
SUIGEKKA?!
THE GIRL THEY SAID WAS ALL-POWERFUL...?
...YES, REALLY.
REALLY...?
SUIGEKKA'S HERE...?!
BE...
BECAUSE OF...THE FATE YOU SUFFERED...?
YOU HAD...
...NO CHOICE BUT TO HATE PEOPLE.
NO CHOICE BUT BEING FILLED WITH JASHIN...
...IS THAT IT...?
TWO PEOPLE WHO LOVED EACH OTHER...
...AND WERE TORN APART LIKE THAT...

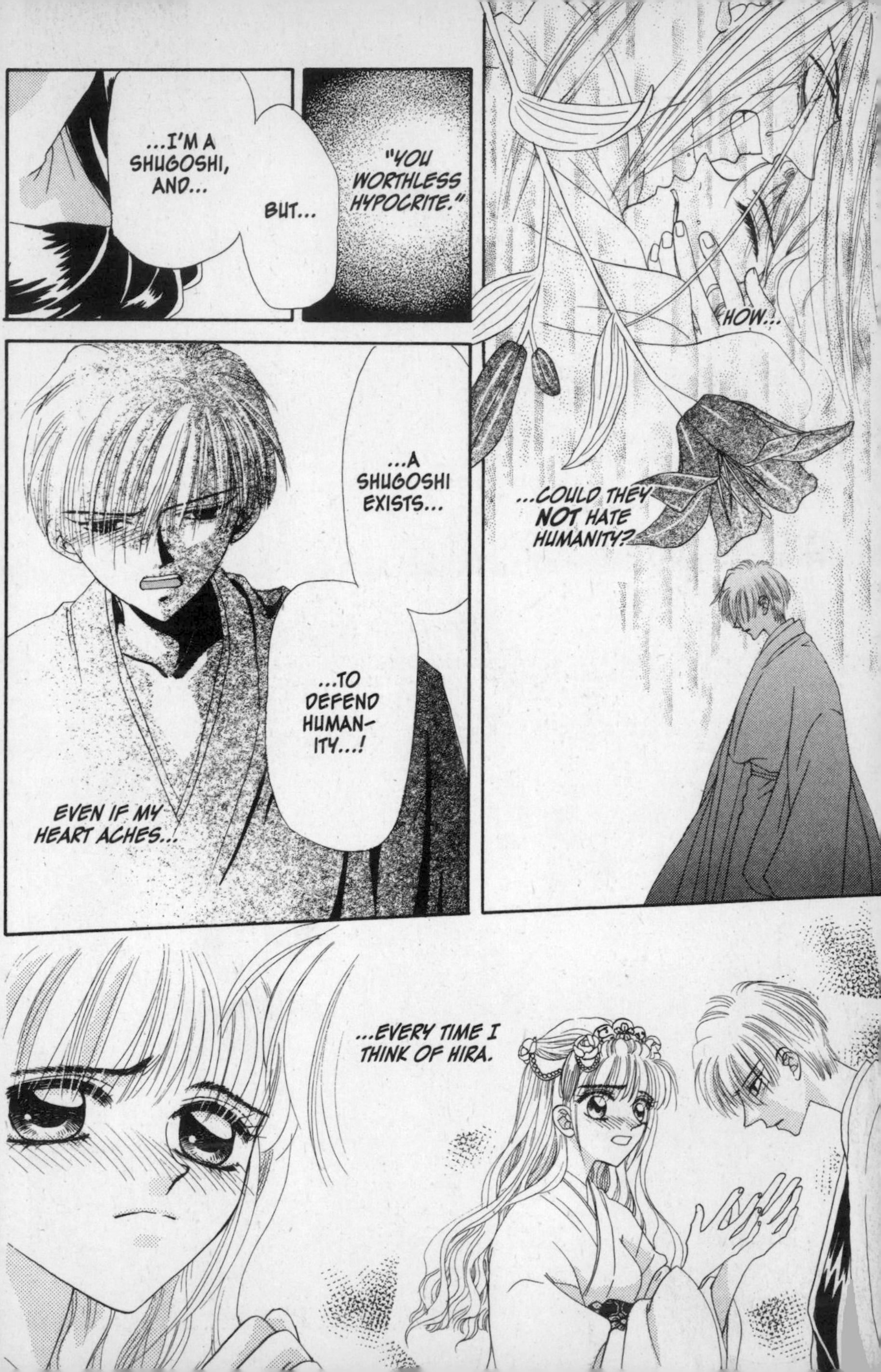
HOW...
...COULD THEY NOT HATE HUMANITY?
"YOU WORTHLESS HYPOCRITE."
BUT...
...I'M A SHUGOSHI, AND...
...A SHUGOSHI EXISTS...
...TO DEFEND HUMAN-ITY...!
EVEN IF MY HEART ACHES...
...EVERY TIME I THINK OF HIRA.

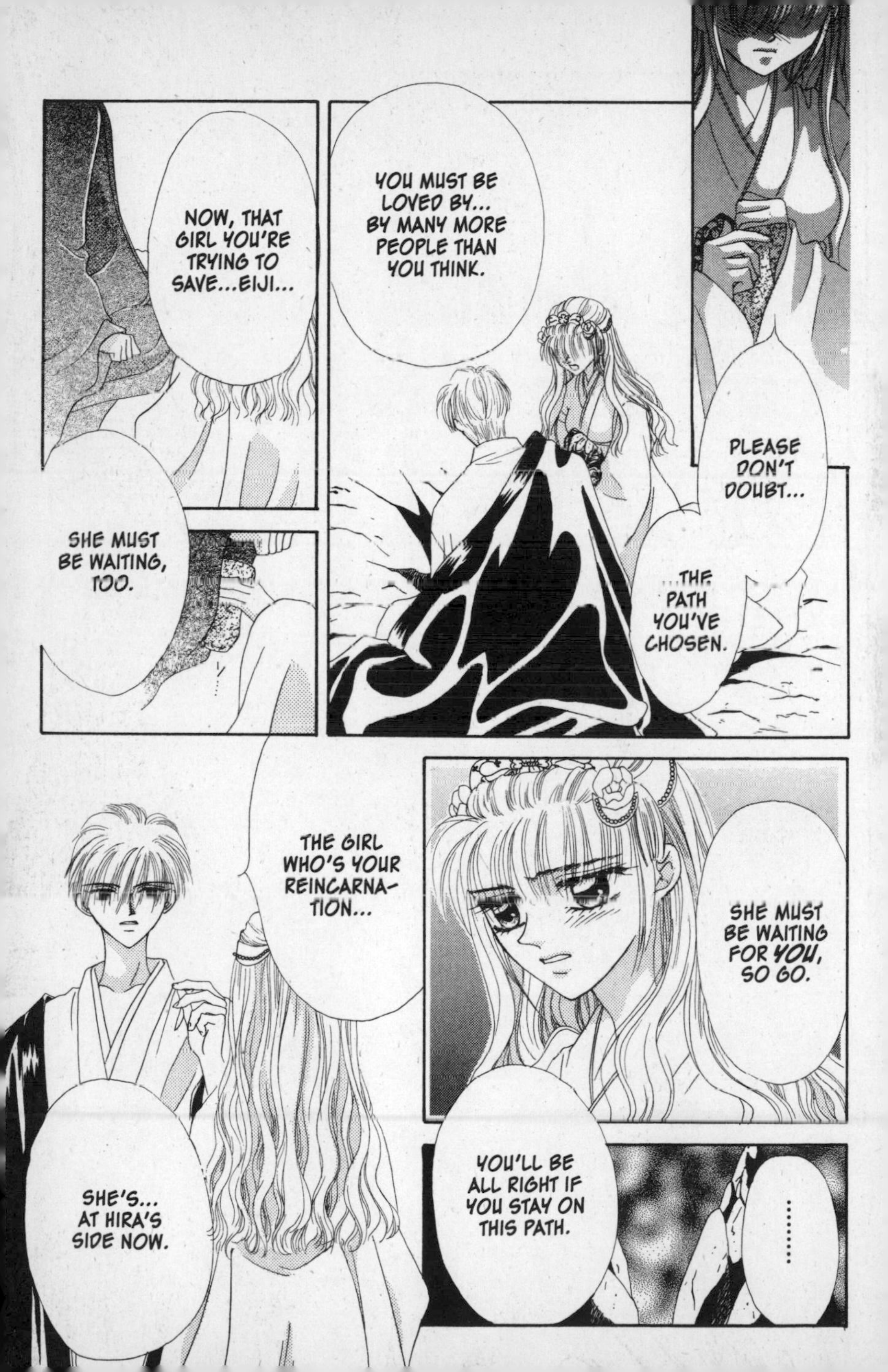
YOU MUST BE LOVED BY... BY MANY MORE PEOPLE THAN YOU THINK.
PLEASE DON'T DOUBT...
...THE PATH YOU'VE CHOSEN.
NOW, THAT GIRL YOU'RE TRYING TO SAVE...EIJI...
SHE MUST BE WAITING, TOO.
THE GIRL WHO'S YOUR REINCARNATION...
SHE'S... AT HIRA'S SIDE NOW.
SHE MUST BE WAITING FOR *YOU*, SO GO.
YOU'LL BE ALL RIGHT IF YOU STAY ON THIS PATH.
......

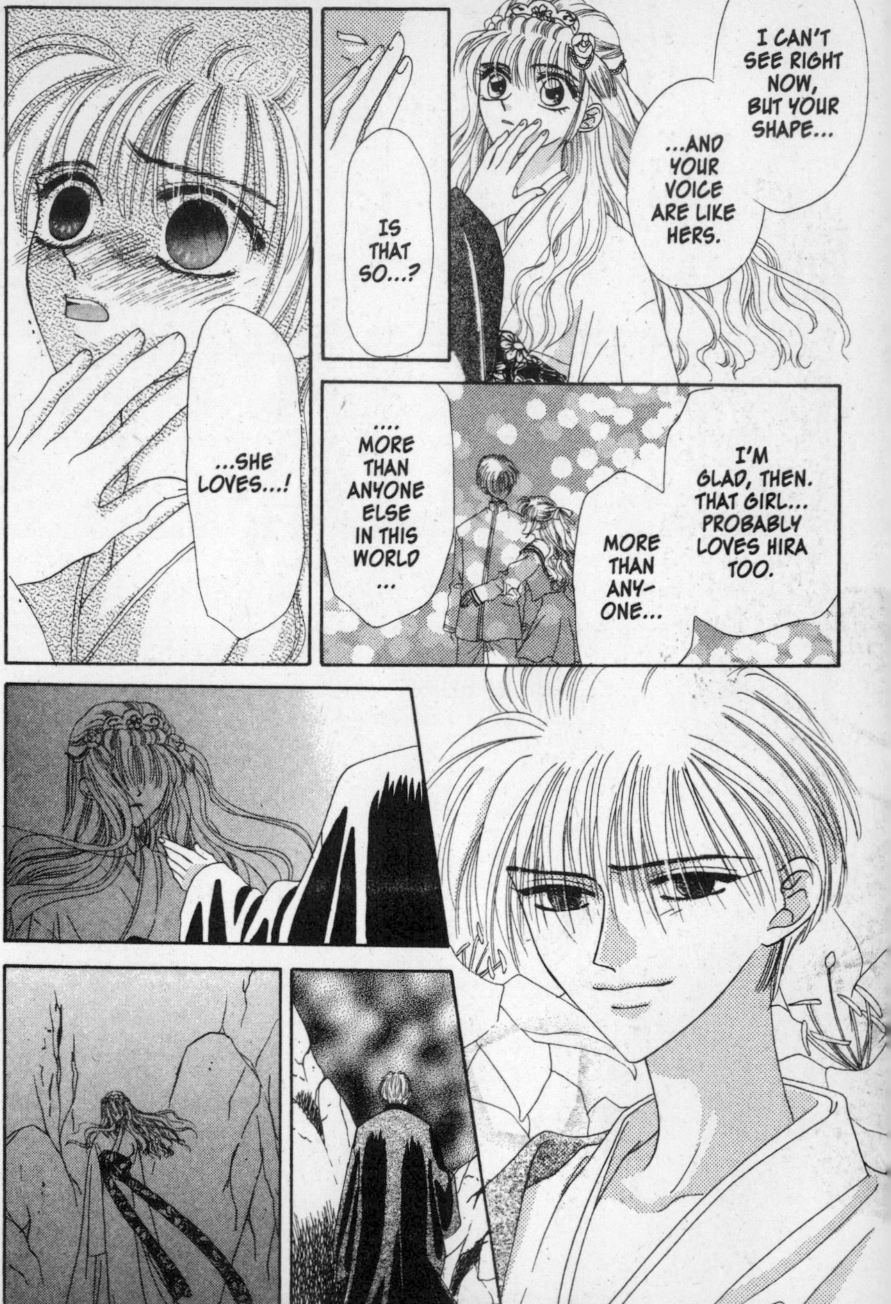
I CAN'T SEE RIGHT NOW, BUT YOUR SHAPE...
...AND YOUR VOICE ARE LIKE HERS.
IS THAT SO...?
I'M GLAD, THEN. THAT GIRL... PROBABLY LOVES HIRA TOO.
MORE THAN ANY-ONE...
.... MORE THAN ANYONE ELSE IN THIS WORLD ...
...SHE LOVES...!

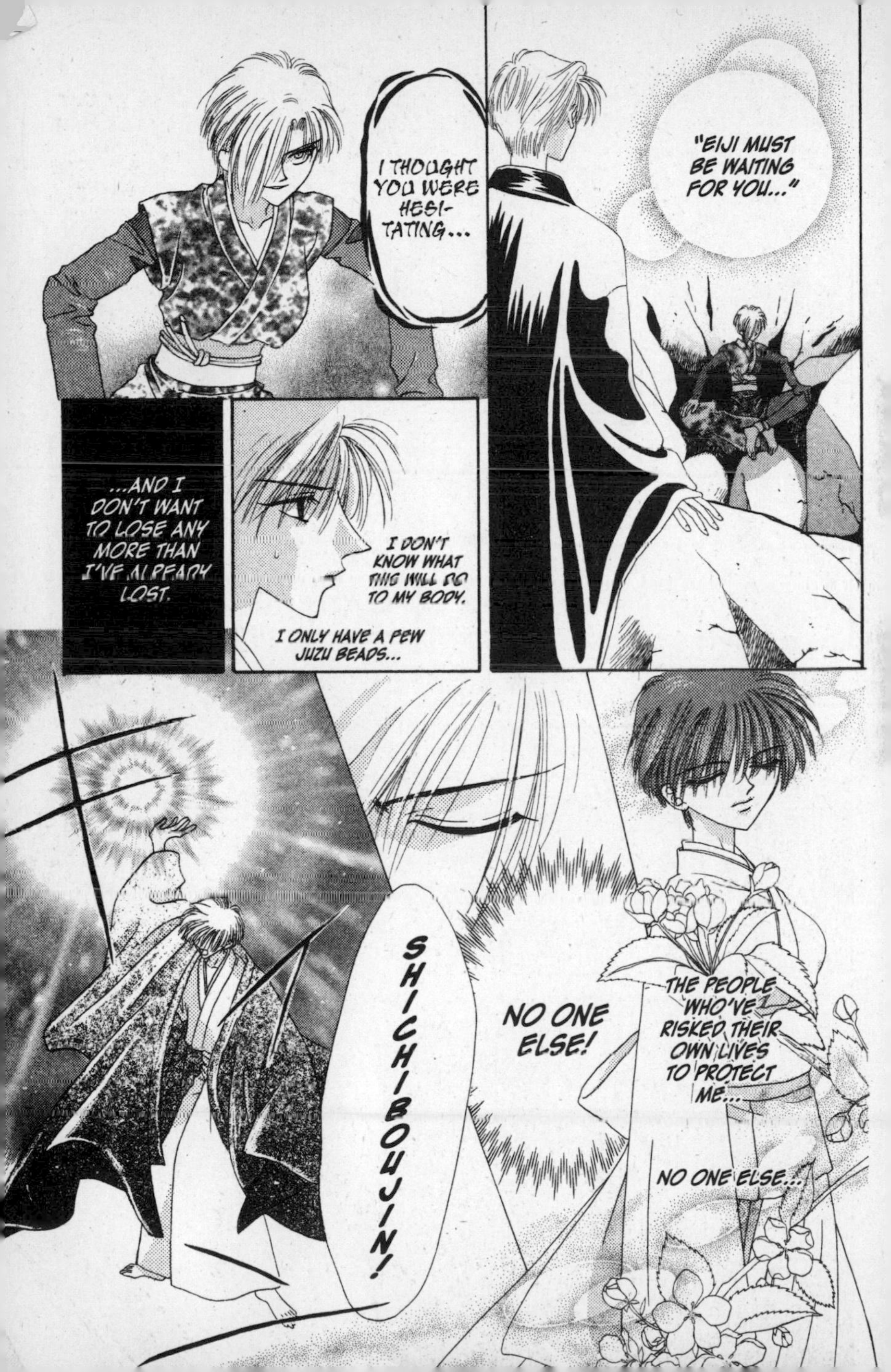
"EIJI MUST BE WAITING FOR YOU..."
I THOUGHT YOU WERE HESI-TATING...
I DON'T KNOW WHAT THIS WILL DO TO MY BODY.
I ONLY HAVE A FEW JUZU BEADS...
...AND I DON'T WANT TO LOSE ANY MORE THAN I'VE ALREADY LOST.
THE PEOPLE WHO'VE RISKED THEIR OWN LIVES TO PROTECT ME...
NO ONE ELSE...
NO ONE ELSE!
SHICHIBOUJIN!

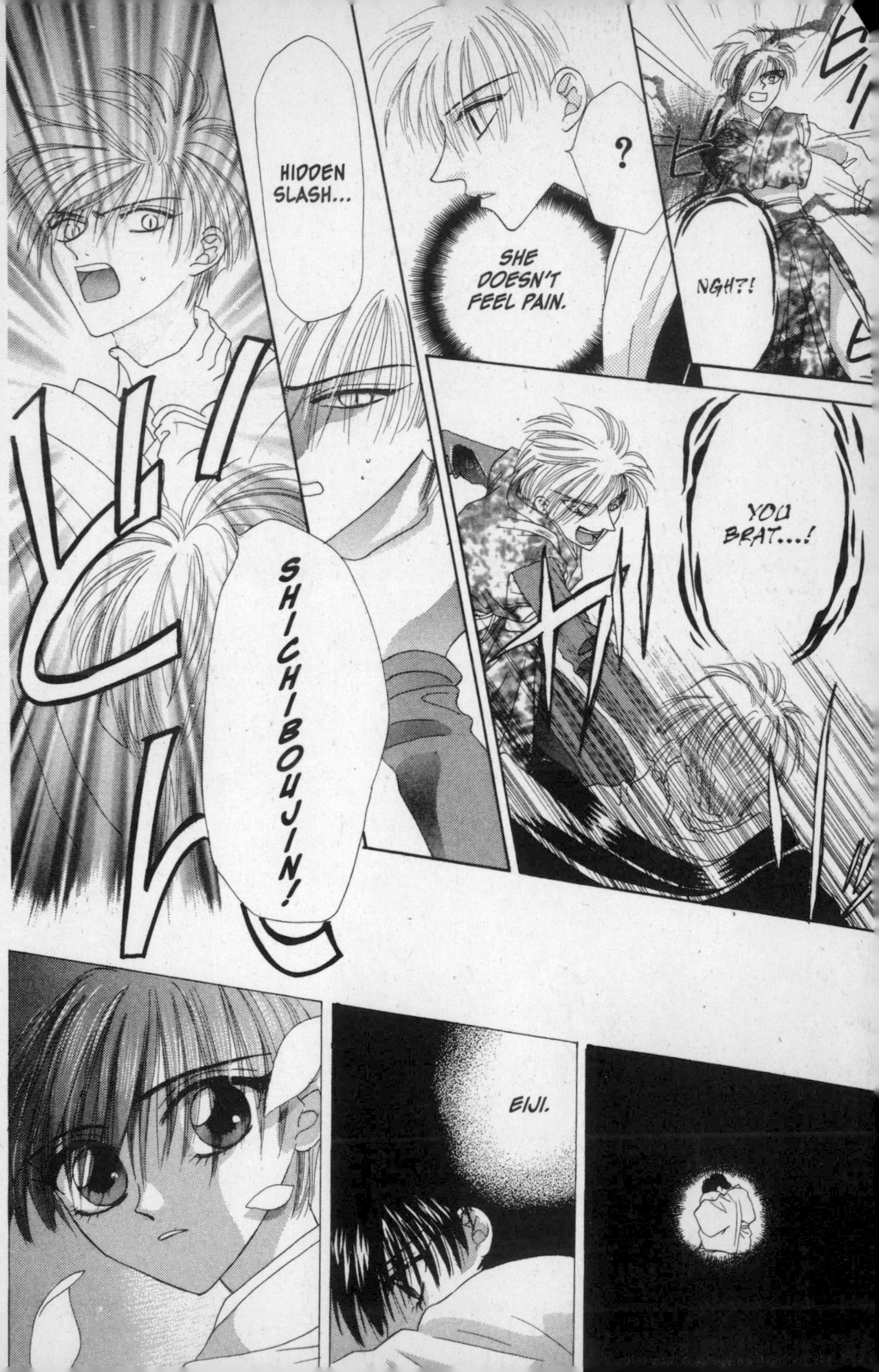
NGH?!
?
SHE DOESN'T FEEL PAIN.
YOU BRAT...!
HIDDEN SLASH...
SHICHIBOUJIN!
EIJI.

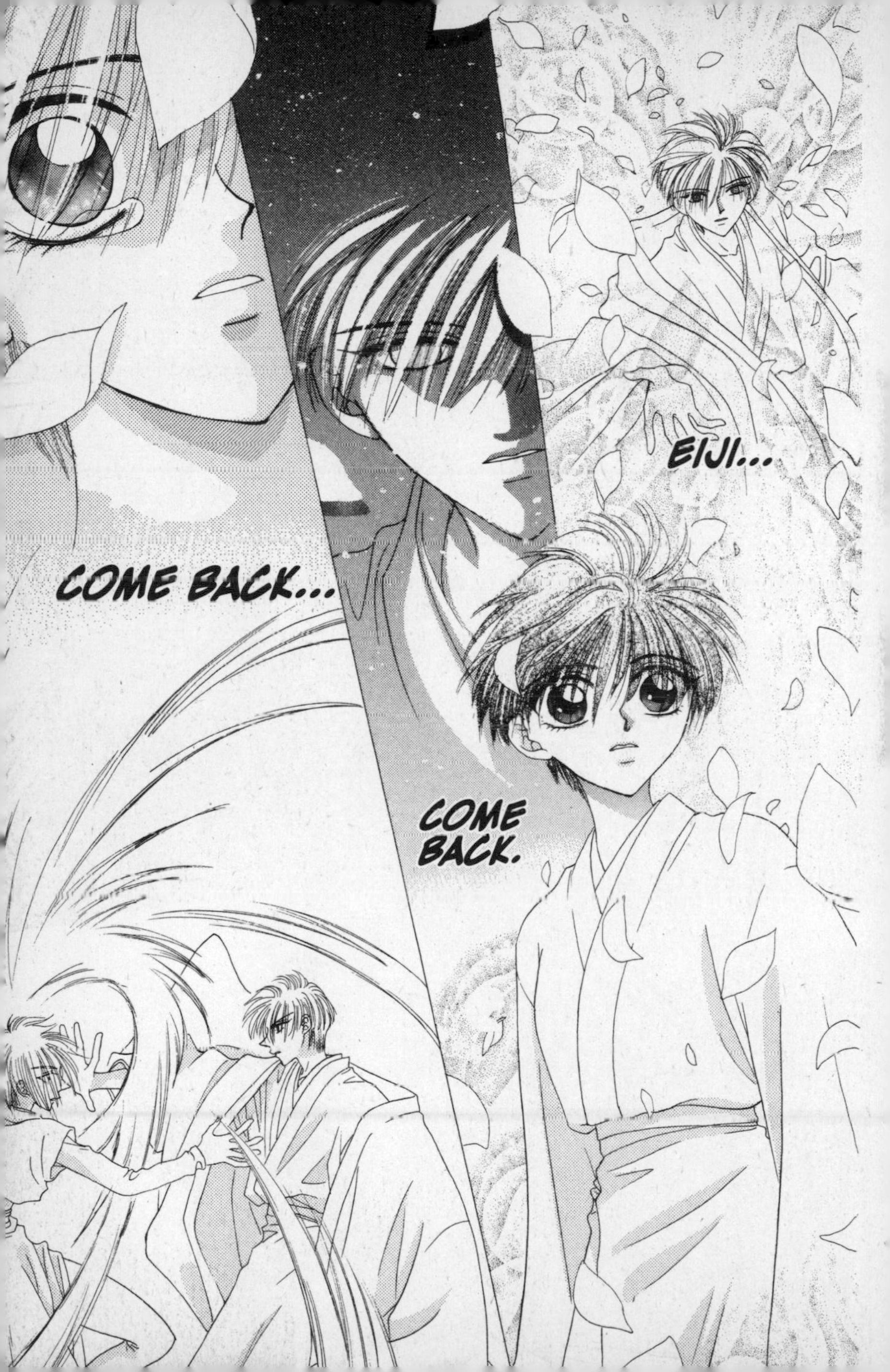
EIJI...
COME BACK.
COME BACK...

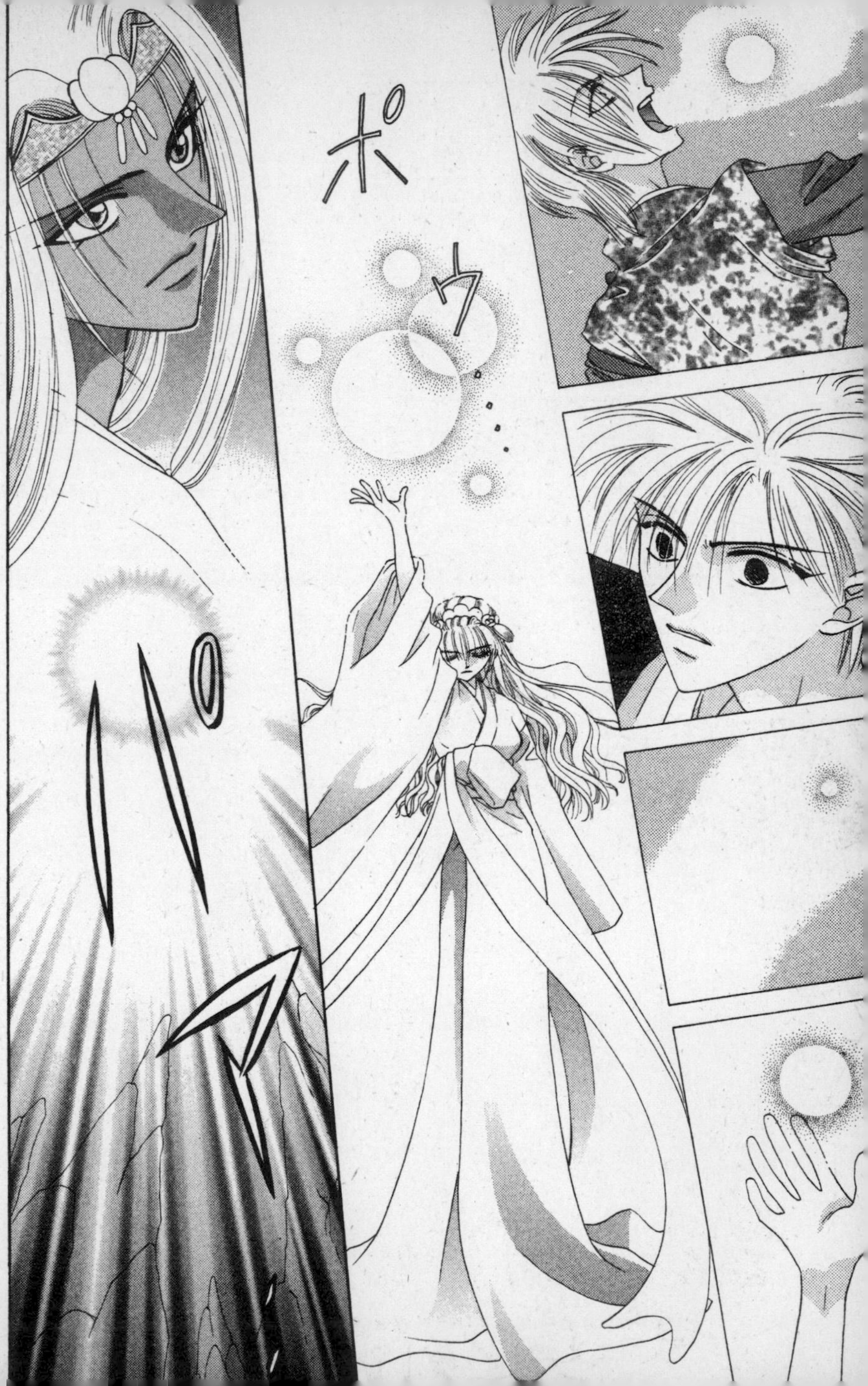
ポウ
パァ

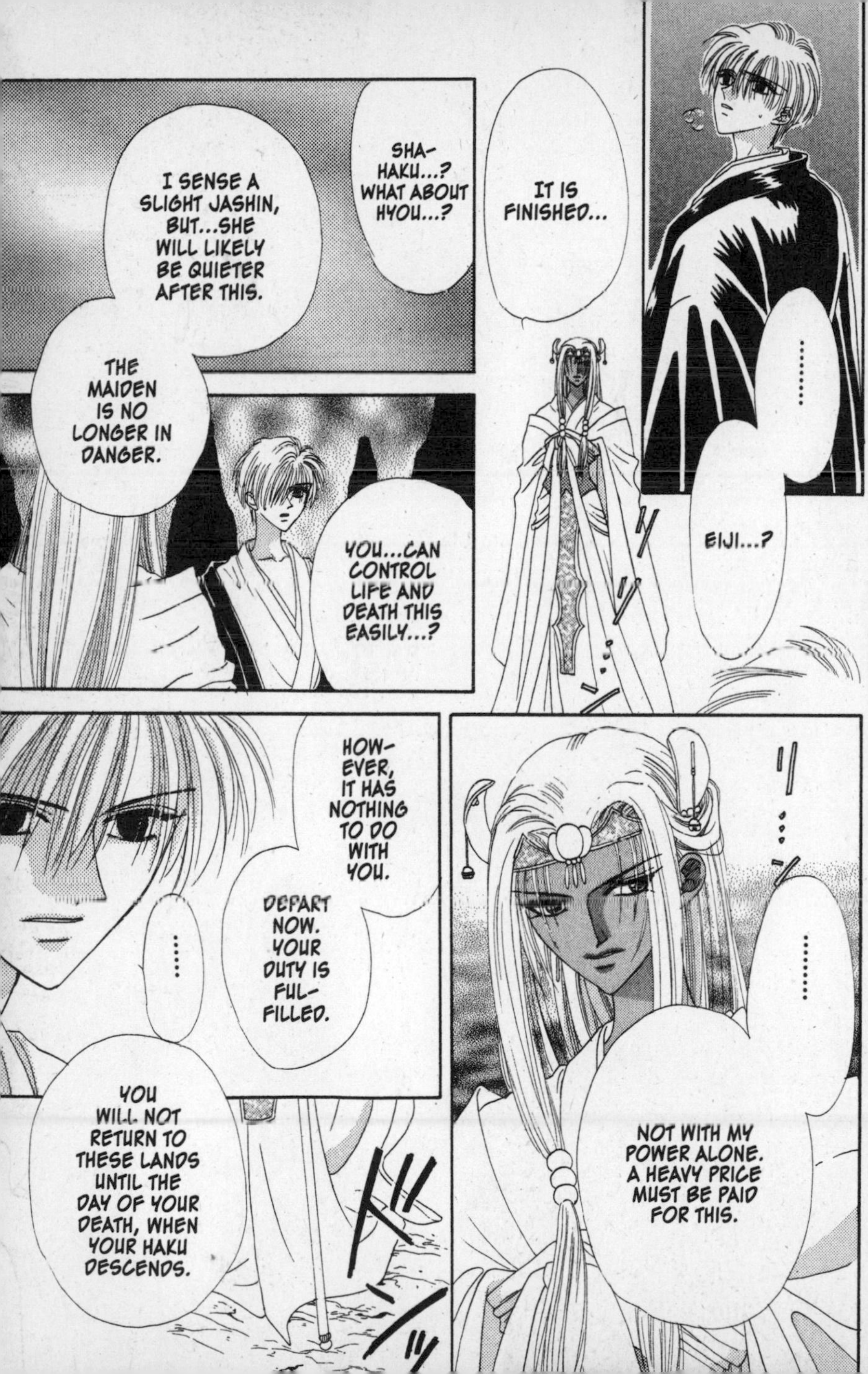
IT IS FINISHED...
......
EIJI...?
SHA-HAKU...? WHAT ABOUT HYOU...?
I SENSE A SLIGHT JASHIN, BUT...SHE WILL LIKELY BE QUIETER AFTER THIS.
THE MAIDEN IS NO LONGER IN DANGER.
YOU...CAN CONTROL LIFE AND DEATH THIS EASILY...?
......
NOT WITH MY POWER ALONE. A HEAVY PRICE MUST BE PAID FOR THIS.
HOW-EVER, IT HAS NOTHING TO DO WITH YOU.
DEPART NOW. YOUR DUTY IS FUL-FILLED.
......
YOU WILL NOT RETURN TO THESE LANDS UNTIL THE DAY OF YOUR DEATH, WHEN YOUR HAKU DESCENDS.

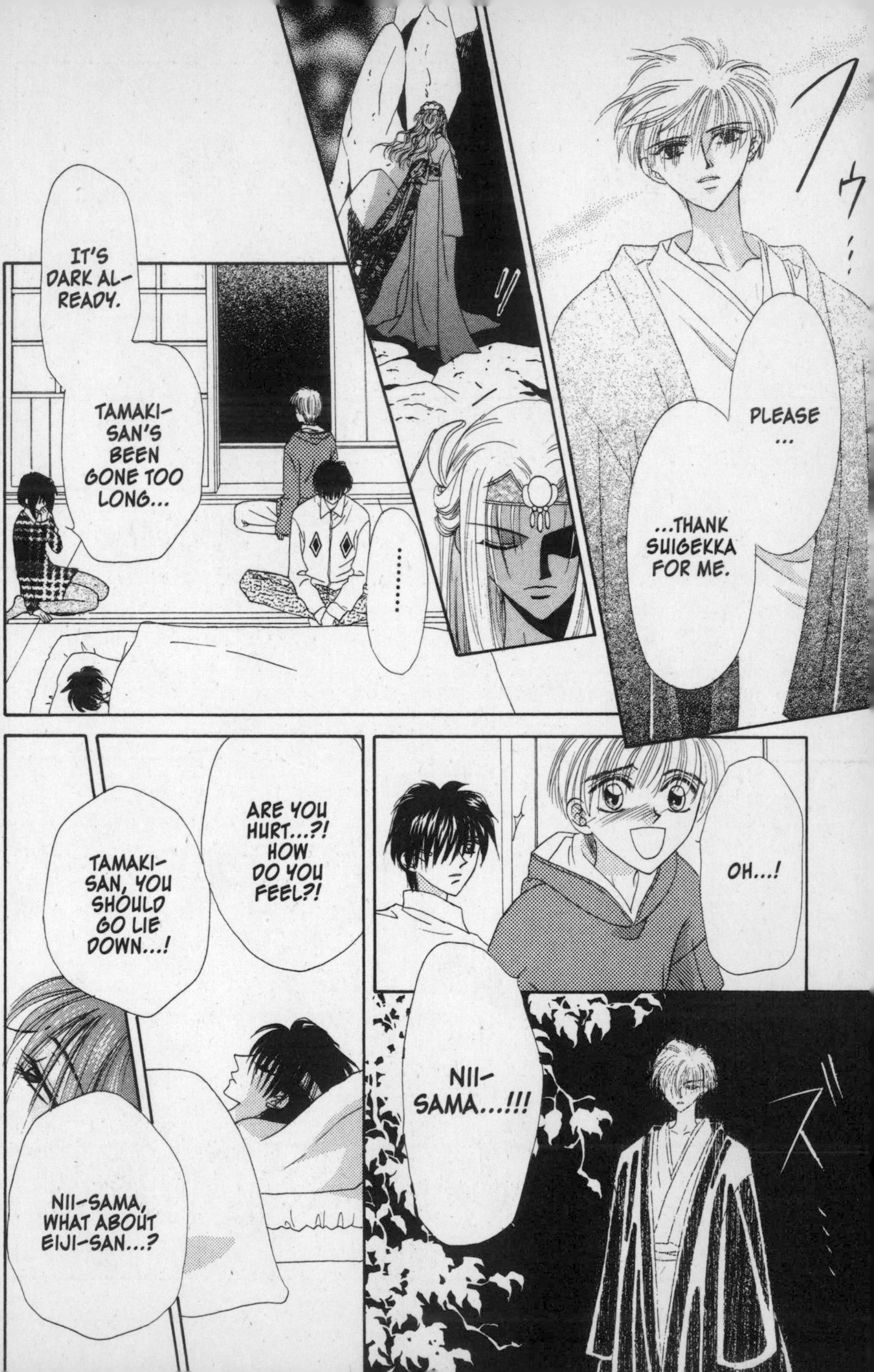
PLEASE ...
...THANK SUIGEKKA FOR ME.
IT'S DARK AL-READY.
TAMAKI-SAN'S BEEN GONE TOO LONG...
......
OH...!
NII-SAMA...!!!
ARE YOU HURT...?! HOW DO YOU FEEL?!
TAMAKI-SAN, YOU SHOULD GO LIE DOWN...!
NII-SAMA, WHAT ABOUT EIJI-SAN...?

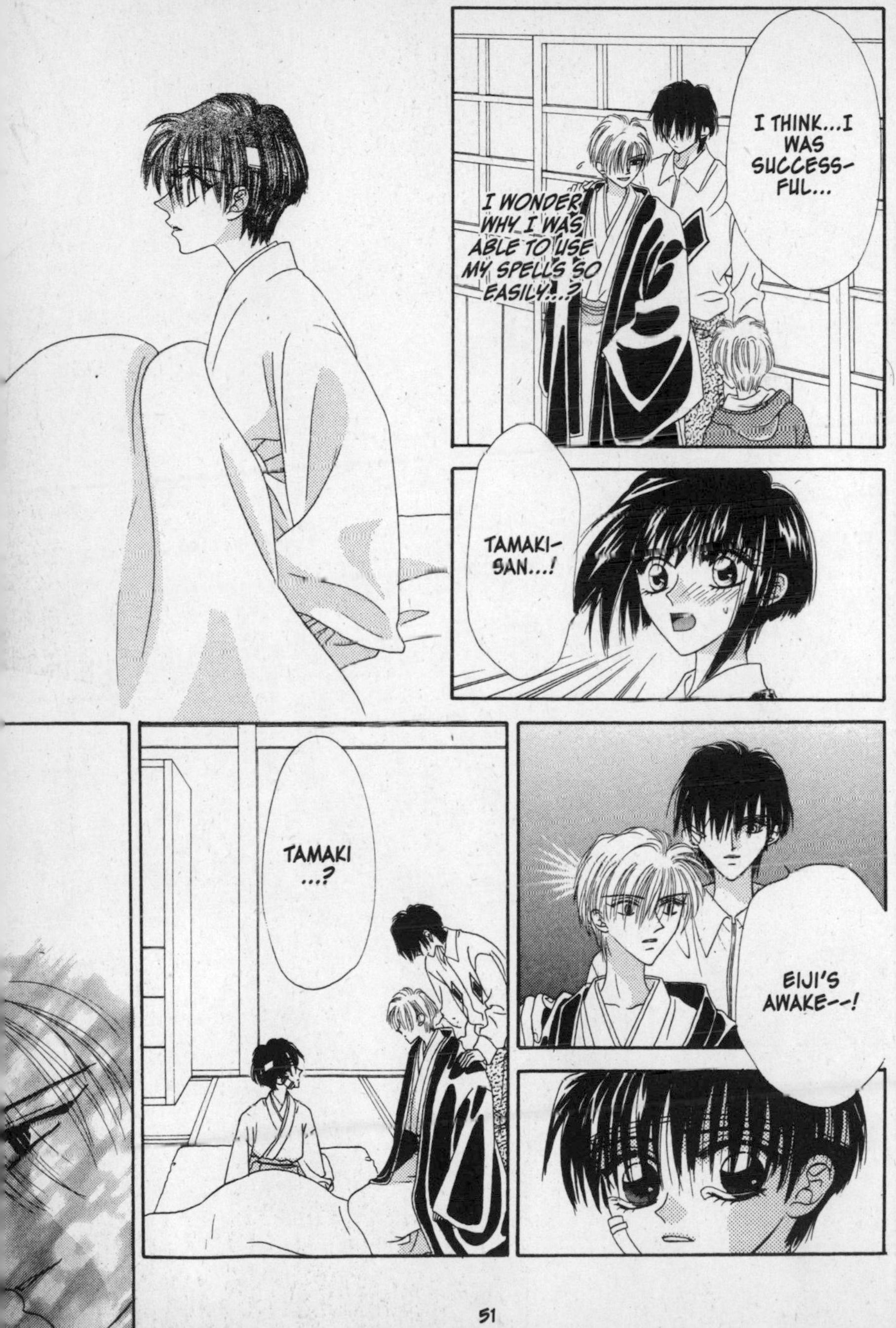
I THINK...I WAS SUCCESSFUL...
I WONDER WHY I WAS ABLE TO USE MY SPELLS SO EASILY...?
TAMAKI-SAN...!
EIJI'S AWAKE--!
TAMAKI ...?

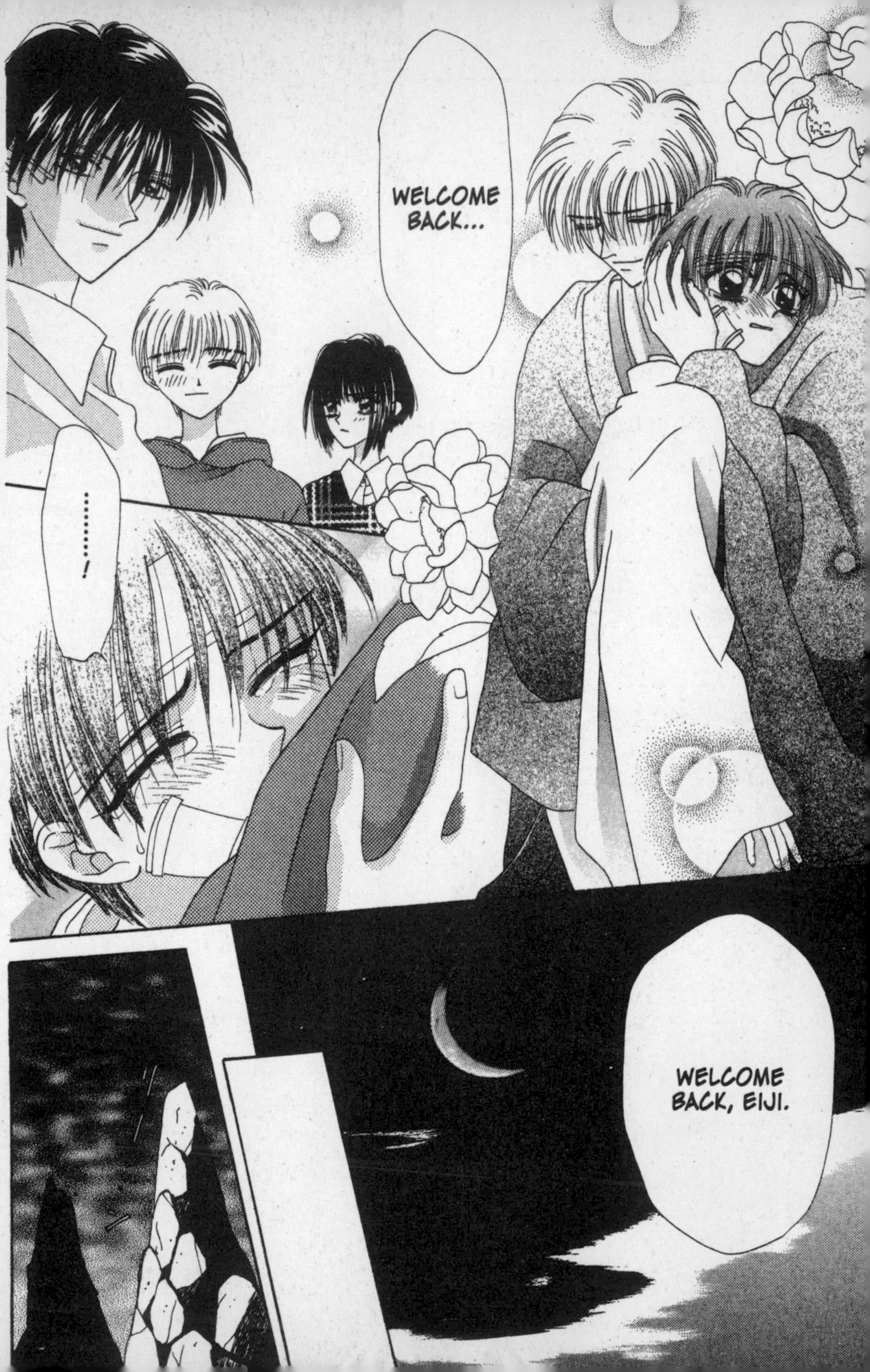
WELCOME BACK...
......!
WELCOME BACK, EIJI.

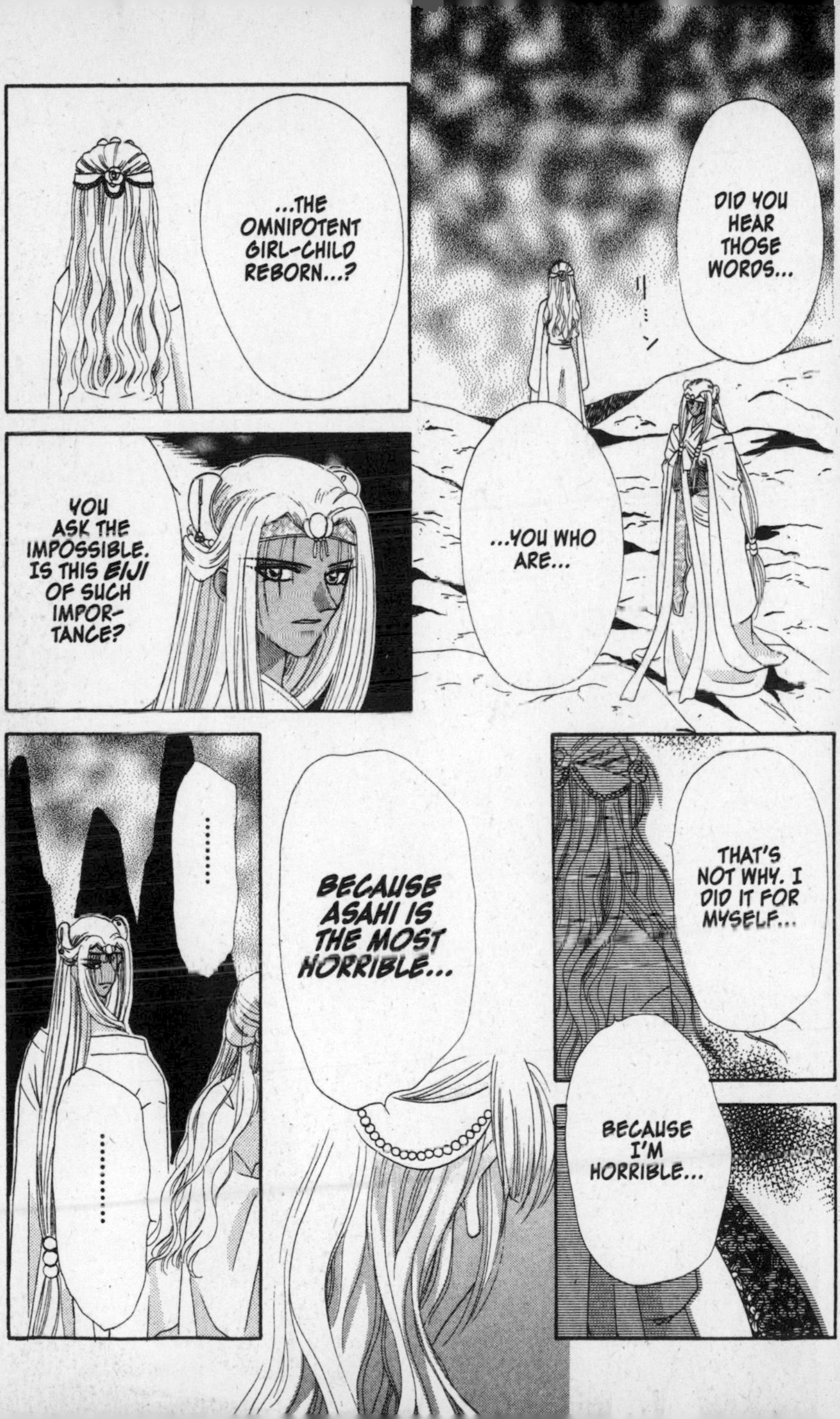
DID YOU HEAR THOSE WORDS...
...YOU WHO ARE...
...THE OMNIPOTENT GIRL-CHILD REBORN...?
YOU ASK THE IMPOSSIBLE. IS THIS *EIJI* OF SUCH IMPORTANCE?
THAT'S NOT WHY. I DID IT FOR MYSELF...
BECAUSE I'M HORRIBLE...
BECAUSE ASAHI IS THE MOST HORRIBLE...
......
......

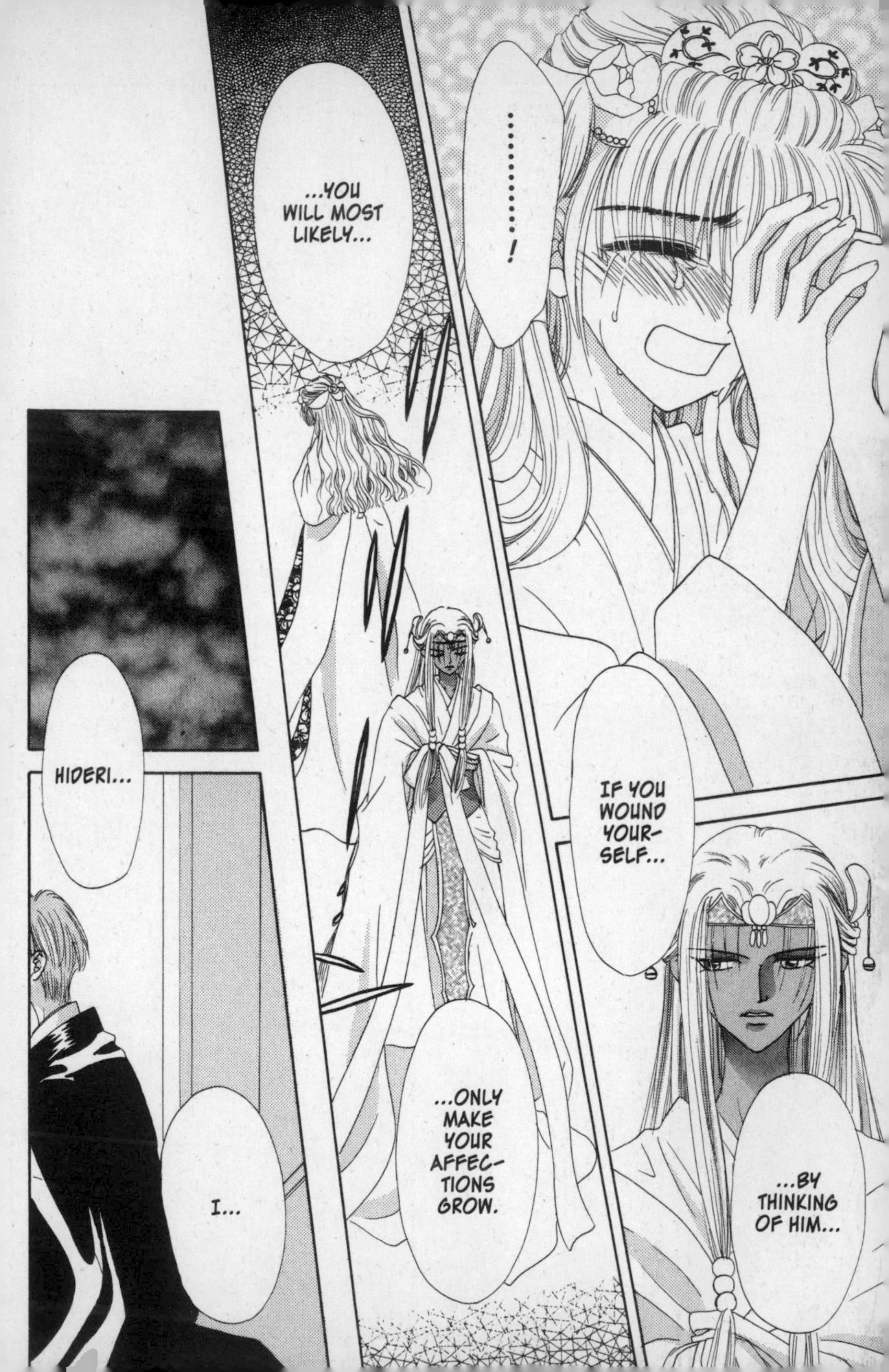
......!
IF YOU WOUND YOUR-SELF...
...BY THINKING OF HIM...
...YOU WILL MOST LIKELY...
...ONLY MAKE YOUR AFFEC-TIONS GROW.
HIDERI...
I...

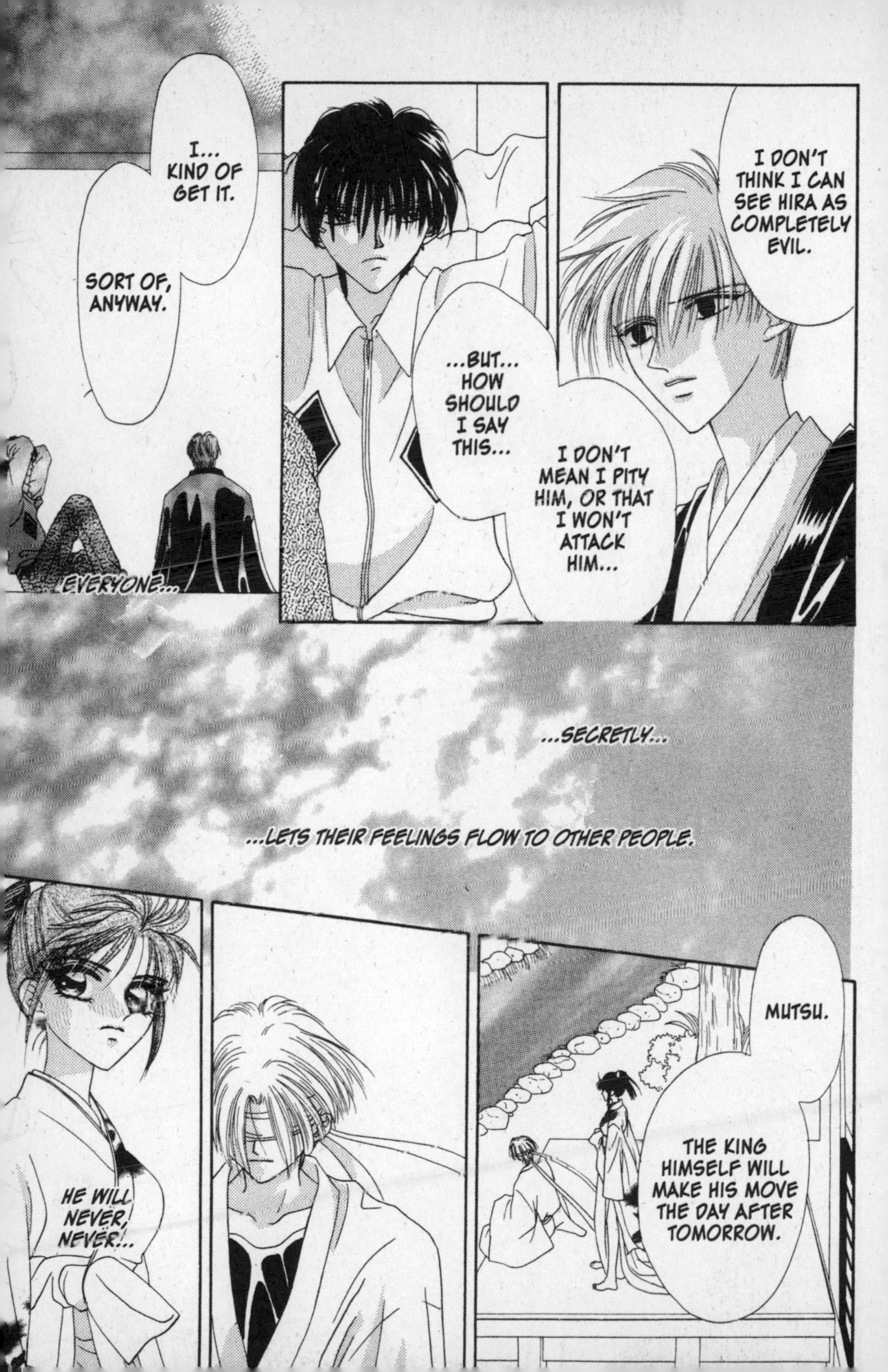
I DON'T THINK I CAN SEE HIRA AS COMPLETELY EVIL.
I DON'T MEAN I PITY HIM, OR THAT I WON'T ATTACK HIM...
...BUT... HOW SHOULD I SAY THIS...
I... KIND OF GET IT.
SORT OF, ANYWAY.
EVERYONE...
...SECRETLY...
...LETS THEIR FEELINGS FLOW TO OTHER PEOPLE.
MUTSU.
THE KING HIMSELF WILL MAKE HIS MOVE THE DAY AFTER TOMORROW.
HE WILL NEVER, NEVËR...

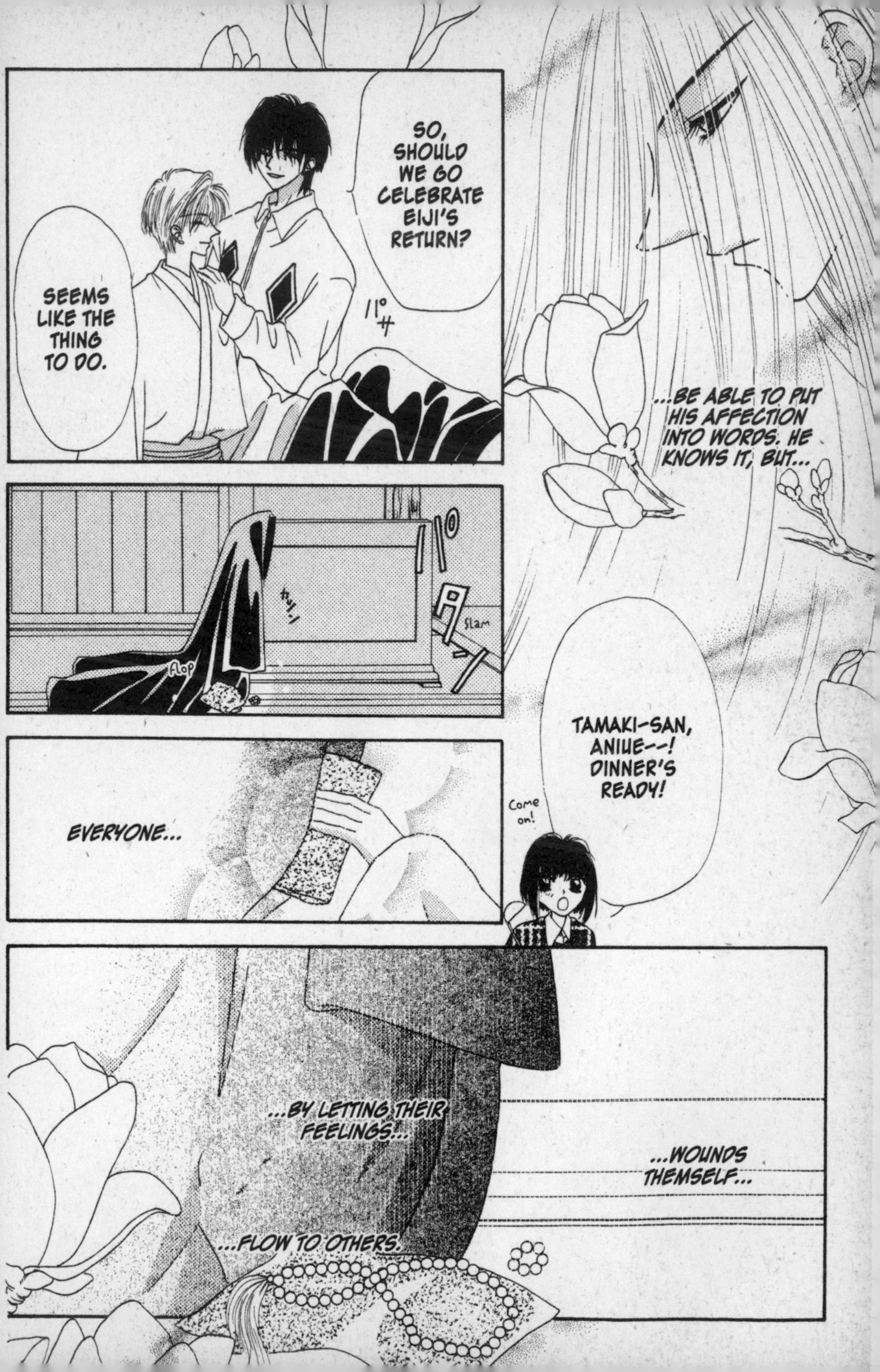
...BE ABLE TO PUT HIS AFFECTION INTO WORDS. HE KNOWS IT, BUT...
TAMAKI-SAN, ANIUE--! DINNER'S READY!
Come on!
SO, SHOULD WE GO CELEBRATE EIJI'S RETURN?
SEEMS LIKE THE THING TO DO.
Slam
Flop
EVERYONE...
...WOUNDS THEMSELF...
...BY LETTING THEIR FEELINGS...
...FLOW TO OTHERS.

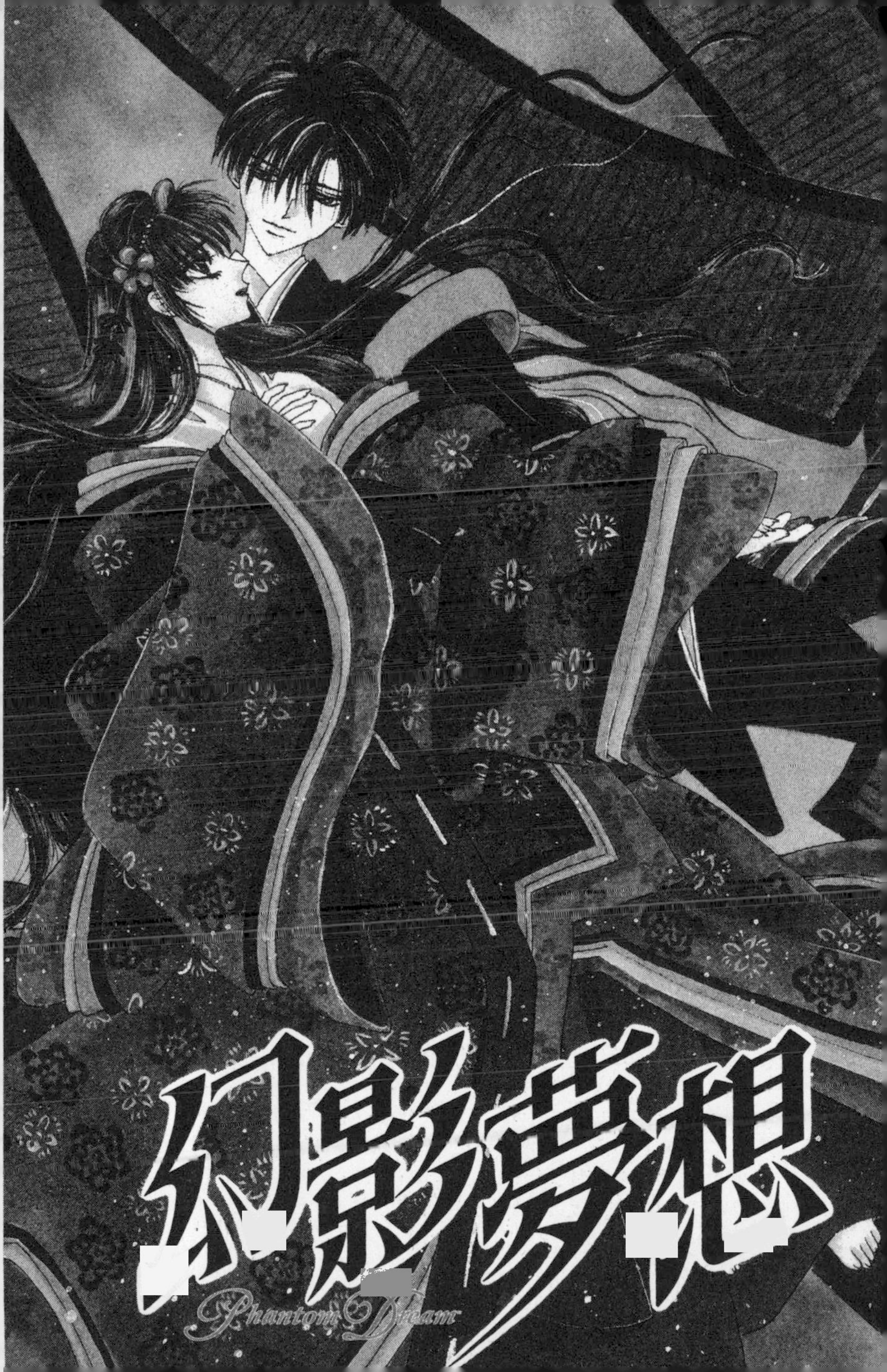
幻影夢想
Phantom Dream

*Note: in Buddhism, there are ten sins (the toaku) which are rooted in three different types of human action (the sangou): physical, verbal and mental.

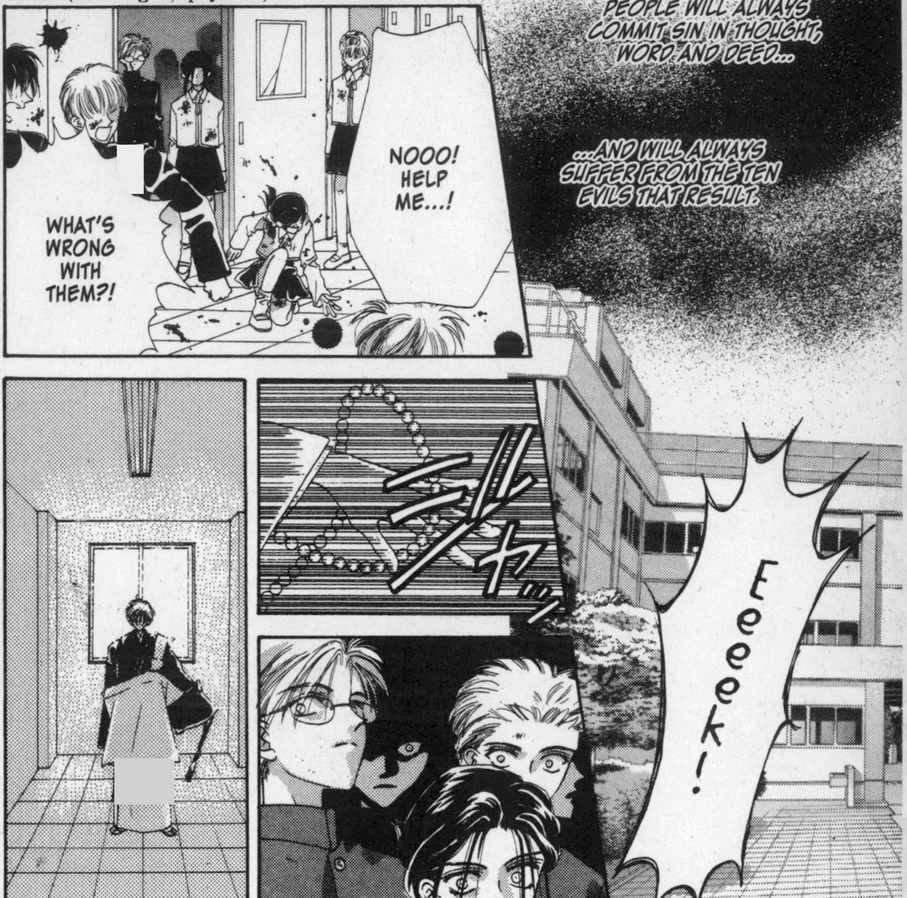
PEOPLE WILL ALWAYS COMMIT SIN IN THOUGHT, WORD AND DEED...
...AND WILL ALWAYS SUFFER FROM THE TEN EVILS THAT RESULT.
NOOO! HELP ME...!
WHAT'S WRONG WITH THEM?!
Eeeek!

ULTRA SPECIAL *THINGS THAT DON'T MATTER II*

Starting with this chapter, I've had an assistant coming in to help me. Until now I've done Dream entirely by myself, so I was happy! But it's hard to say, "please do it like this." I worry about it a little. So far, the absolute worst instruction I've given is, "Do it with sensitivity." That one little phrase will make a person's will to do something evaporate. I don't say that anymore, though...!

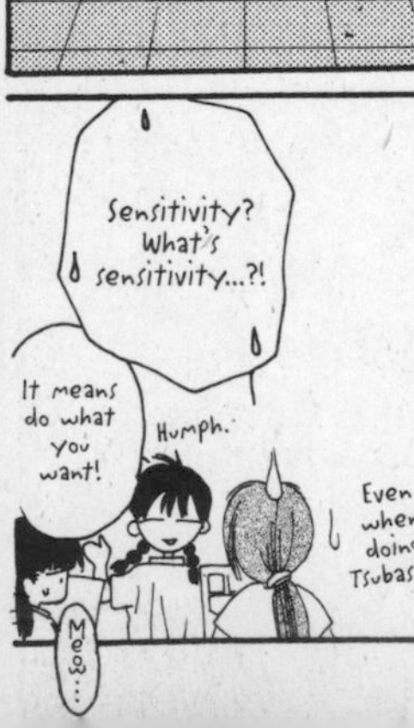
Sensitivity? What's sensitivity...?!
Even when doing Tsubasa...
Humph.
It means do what you want!
Meow...

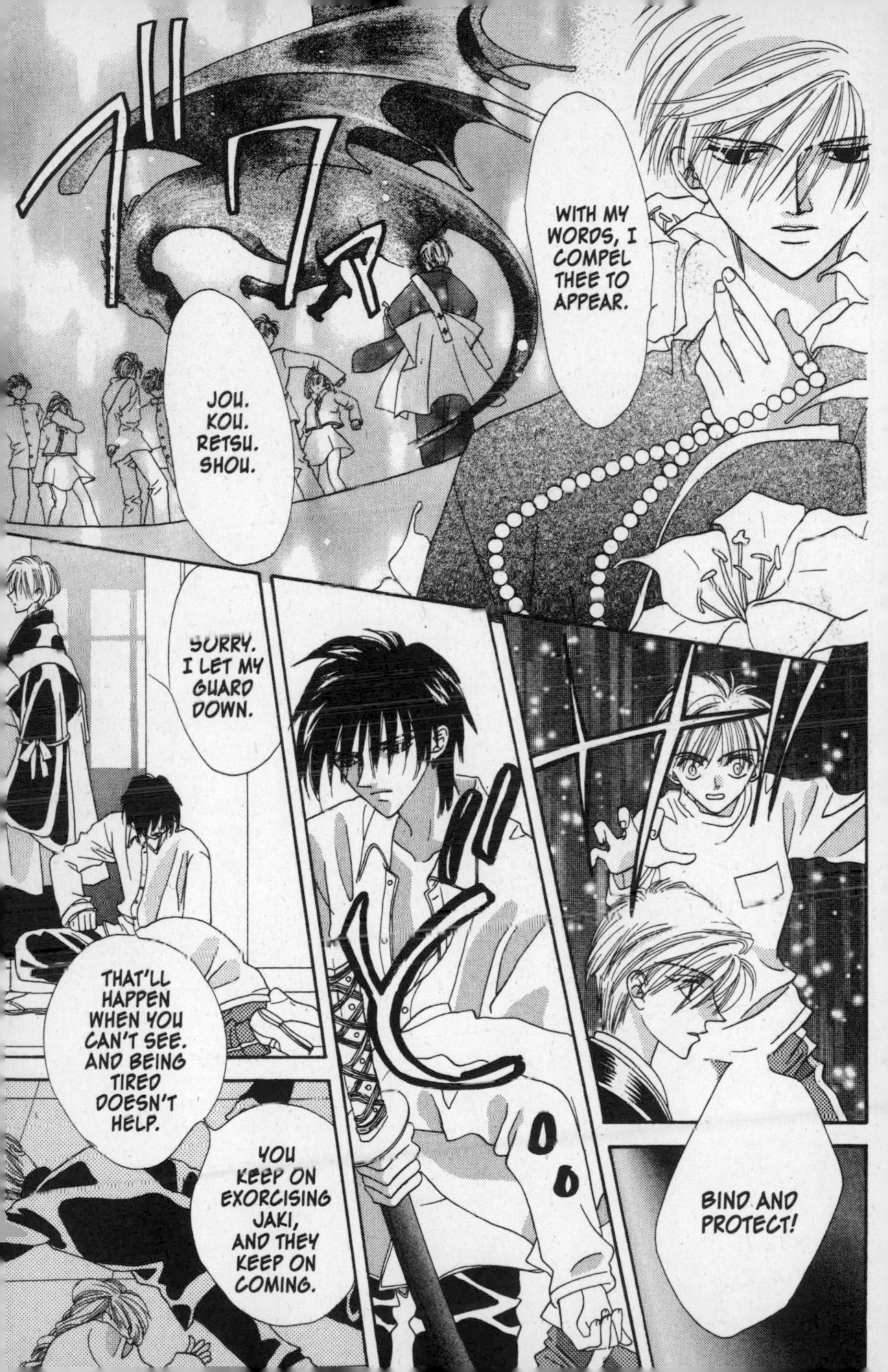
WITH MY WORDS, I COMPEL THEE TO APPEAR.
JOU. KOU. RETSU. SHOU.
BIND AND PROTECT!
SORRY. I LET MY GUARD DOWN.
THAT'LL HAPPEN WHEN YOU CAN'T SEE. AND BEING TIRED DOESN'T HELP.
YOU KEEP ON EXORCISING JAKI, AND THEY KEEP ON COMING.

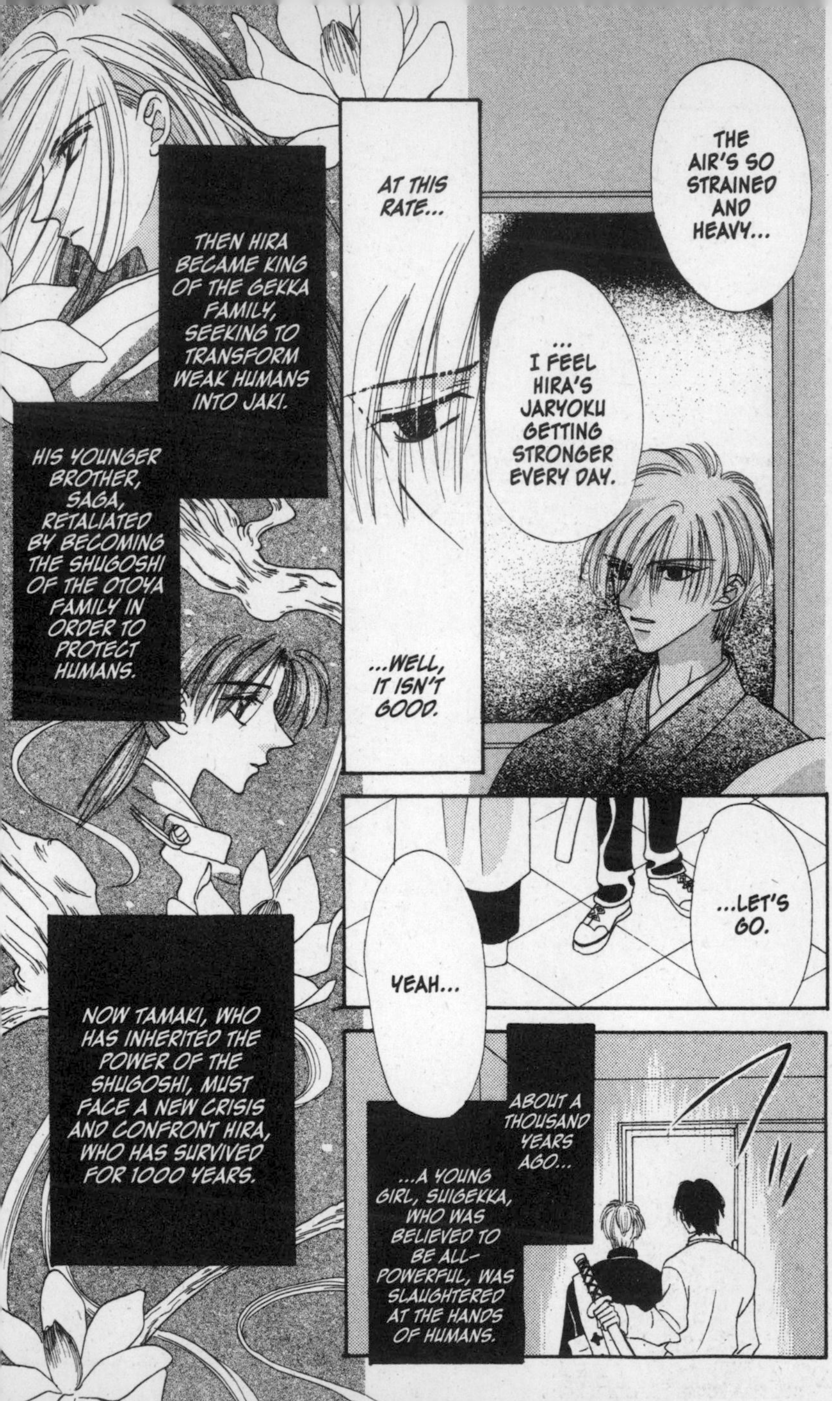
THE AIR'S SO STRAINED AND HEAVY...
... I FEEL HIRA'S JARYOKU GETTING STRONGER EVERY DAY.
AT THIS RATE...
...WELL, IT ISN'T GOOD.
...LET'S GO.
YEAH...
ABOUT A THOUSAND YEARS AGO...
...A YOUNG GIRL, SUIGEKKA, WHO WAS BELIEVED TO BE ALL-POWERFUL, WAS SLAUGHTERED AT THE HANDS OF HUMANS.
THEN HIRA BECAME KING OF THE GEKKA FAMILY, SEEKING TO TRANSFORM WEAK HUMANS INTO JAKI.
HIS YOUNGER BROTHER, SAGA, RETALIATED BY BECOMING THE SHUGOSHI OF THE OTOYA FAMILY IN ORDER TO PROTECT HUMANS.
NOW TAMAKI, WHO HAS INHERITED THE POWER OF THE SHUGOSHI, MUST FACE A NEW CRISIS AND CONFRONT HIRA, WHO HAS SURVIVED FOR 1000 YEARS.

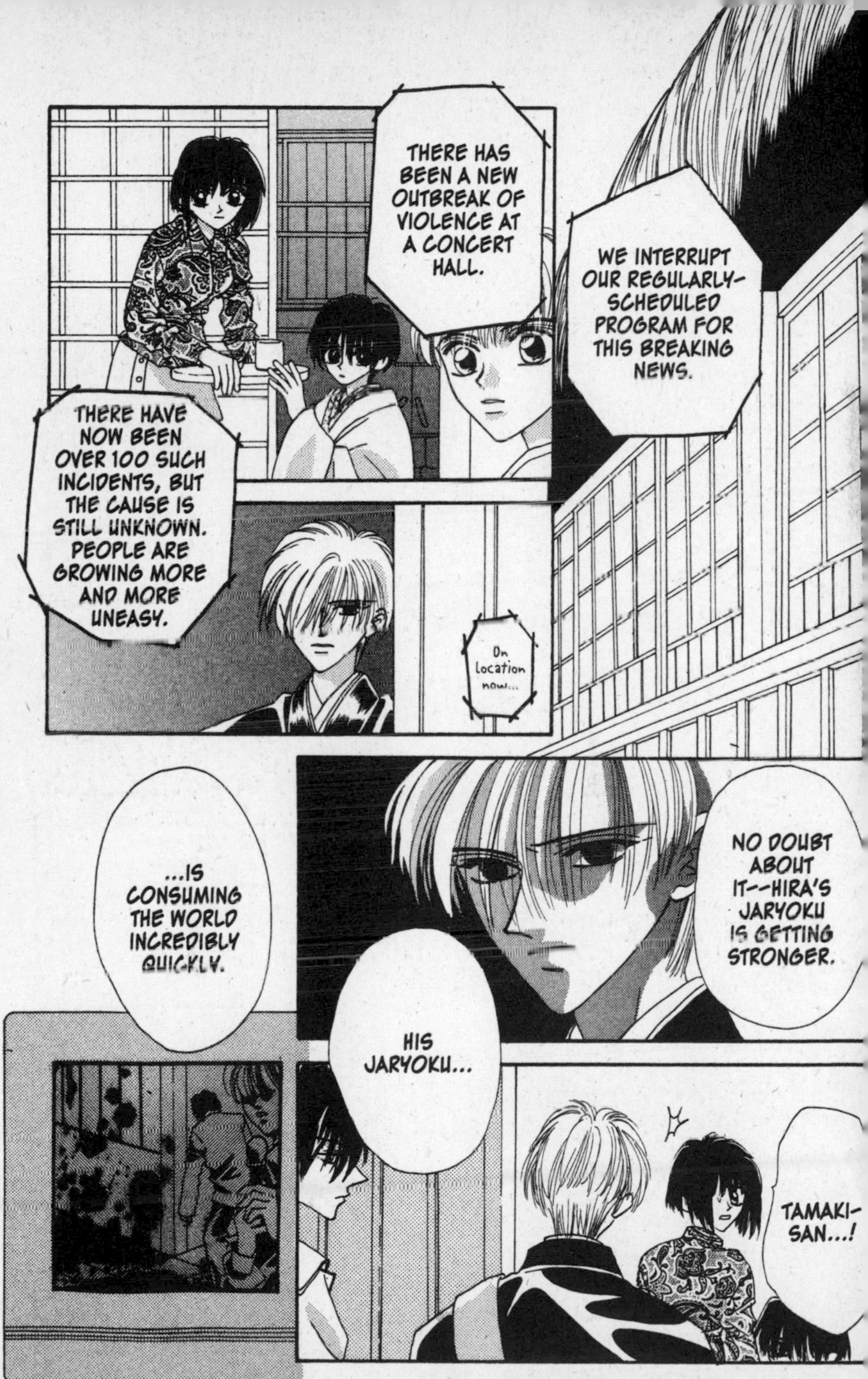
WE INTERRUPT OUR REGULARLY-SCHEDULED PROGRAM FOR THIS BREAKING NEWS.
THERE HAS BEEN A NEW OUTBREAK OF VIOLENCE AT A CONCERT HALL.
THERE HAVE NOW BEEN OVER 100 SUCH INCIDENTS, BUT THE CAUSE IS STILL UNKNOWN. PEOPLE ARE GROWING MORE AND MORE UNEASY.
On location now...
NO DOUBT ABOUT IT--HIRA'S JARYOKU IS GETTING STRONGER.
HIS JARYOKU...
...IS CONSUMING THE WORLD INCREDIBLY QUICKLY.
TAMAKI-SAN...!

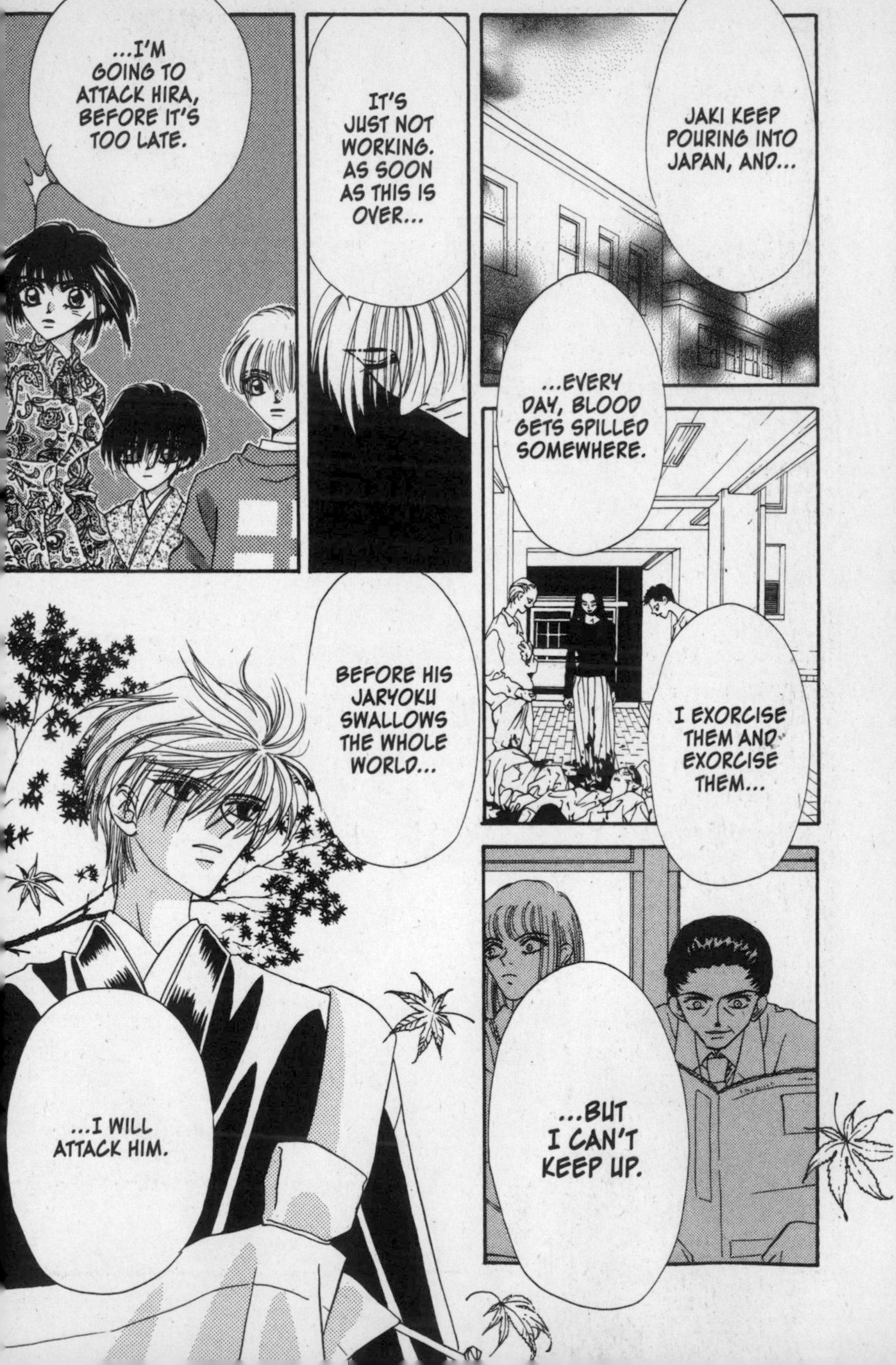
JAKI KEEP POURING INTO JAPAN, AND...
...EVERY DAY, BLOOD GETS SPILLED SOMEWHERE.
I EXORCISE THEM AND EXORCISE THEM...
...BUT I CAN'T KEEP UP.
IT'S JUST NOT WORKING. AS SOON AS THIS IS OVER...
...I'M GOING TO ATTACK HIRA, BEFORE IT'S TOO LATE.
BEFORE HIS JARYOKU SWALLOWS THE WHOLE WORLD...
...I WILL ATTACK HIM.

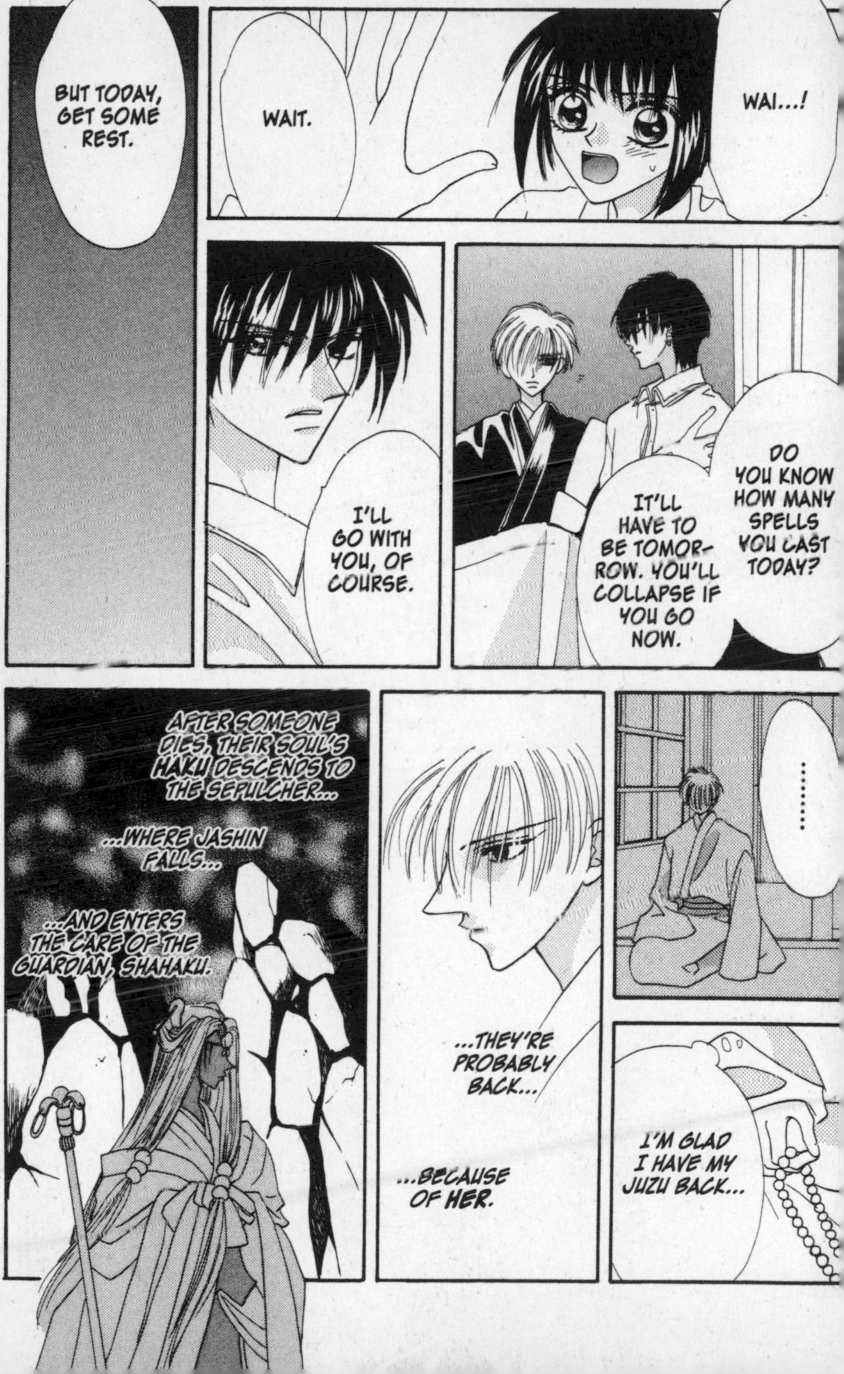
WAI...!
WAIT.
DO YOU KNOW HOW MANY SPELLS YOU CAST TODAY?
IT'LL HAVE TO BE TOMORROW. YOU'LL COLLAPSE IF YOU GO NOW.
I'LL GO WITH YOU, OF COURSE.
BUT TODAY, GET SOME REST.
......
I'M GLAD I HAVE MY JUZU BACK...
...THEY'RE PROBABLY BACK...
...BECAUSE OF HER.
AFTER SOMEONE DIES, THEIR SOUL'S HAKU DESCENDS TO THE SEPULCHER...
...WHERE JASHIN FALLS...
...AND ENTERS THE CARE OF THE GUARDIAN, SHAHAKU.

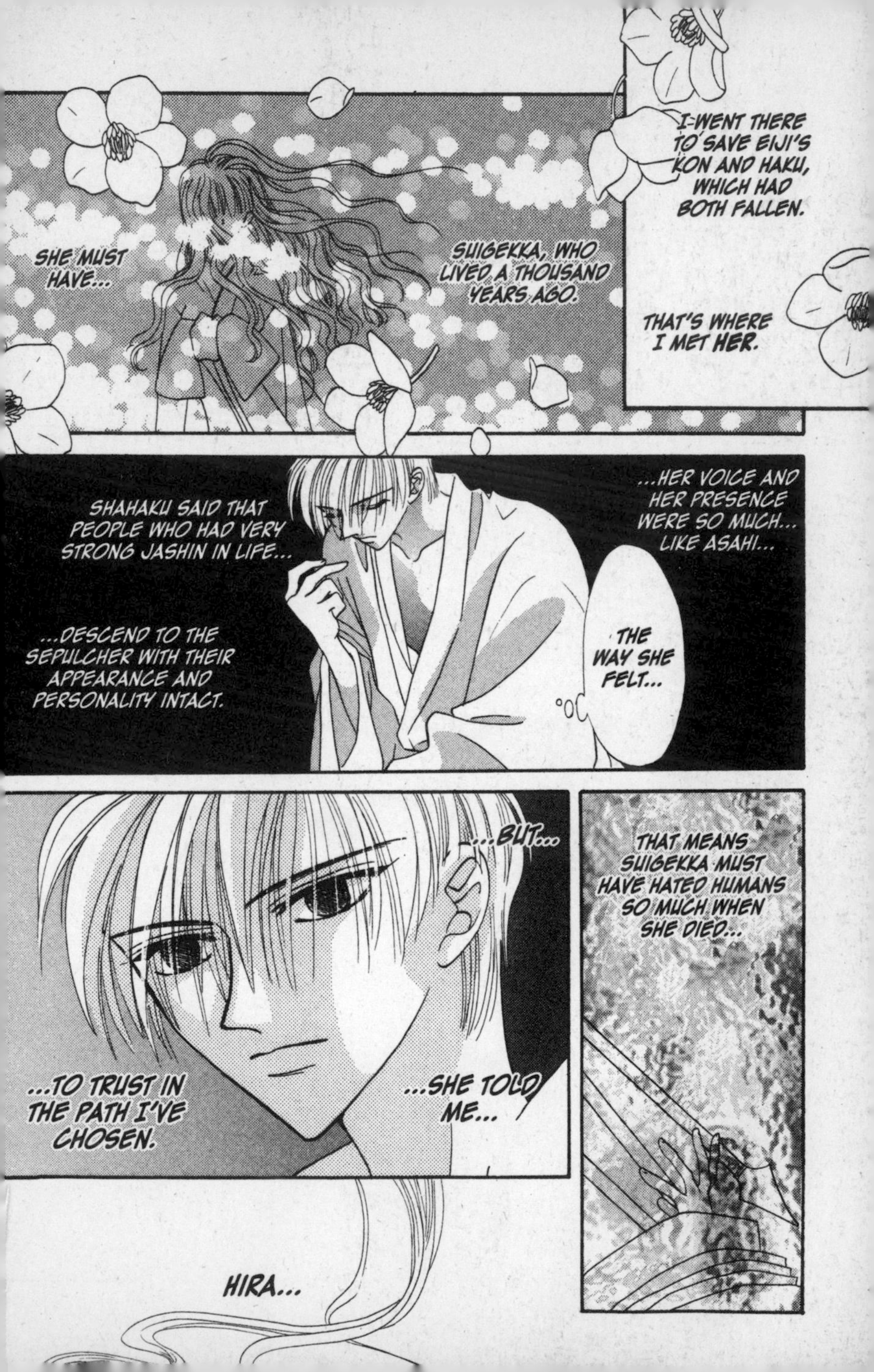
I-WENT THERE TO SAVE EIJI'S KON AND HAKU, WHICH HAD BOTH FALLEN.
THAT'S WHERE I MET **HER**.
SUIGEKKA, WHO LIVED A THOUSAND YEARS AGO.
SHE MUST HAVE...
...HER VOICE AND HER PRESENCE WERE SO MUCH... LIKE ASAHI...
THE WAY SHE FELT...
SHAHAKU SAID THAT PEOPLE WHO HAD VERY STRONG JASHIN IN LIFE...
...DESCEND TO THE SEPULCHER WITH THEIR APPEARANCE AND PERSONALITY INTACT.
THAT MEANS SUIGEKKA MUST HAVE HATED HUMANS SO MUCH WHEN SHE DIED...
...BUT...
...SHE TOLD ME...
...TO TRUST IN THE PATH I'VE CHOSEN.
HIRA...

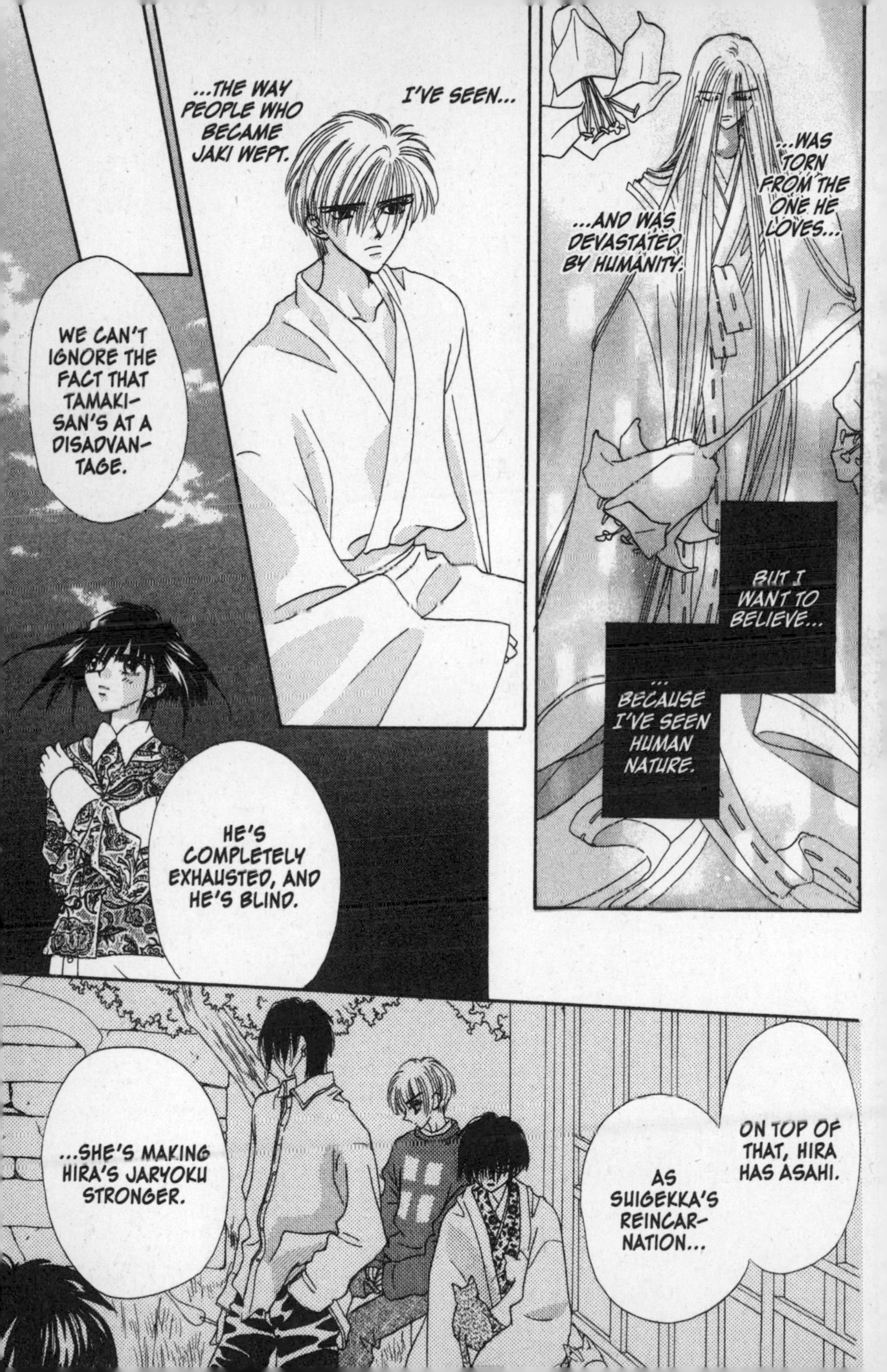
...WAS TORN FROM THE ONE HE LOVES...
...AND WAS DEVASTATED BY HUMANITY.
BUT I WANT TO BELIEVE...
...BECAUSE I'VE SEEN HUMAN NATURE.
I'VE SEEN...
...THE WAY PEOPLE WHO BECAME JAKI WEPT.
WE CAN'T IGNORE THE FACT THAT TAMAKI-SAN'S AT A DISADVANTAGE.
HE'S COMPLETELY EXHAUSTED, AND HE'S BLIND.
ON TOP OF THAT, HIRA HAS ASAHI.
AS SUIGEKKA'S REINCARNATION...
...SHE'S MAKING HIRA'S JARYOKU STRONGER.

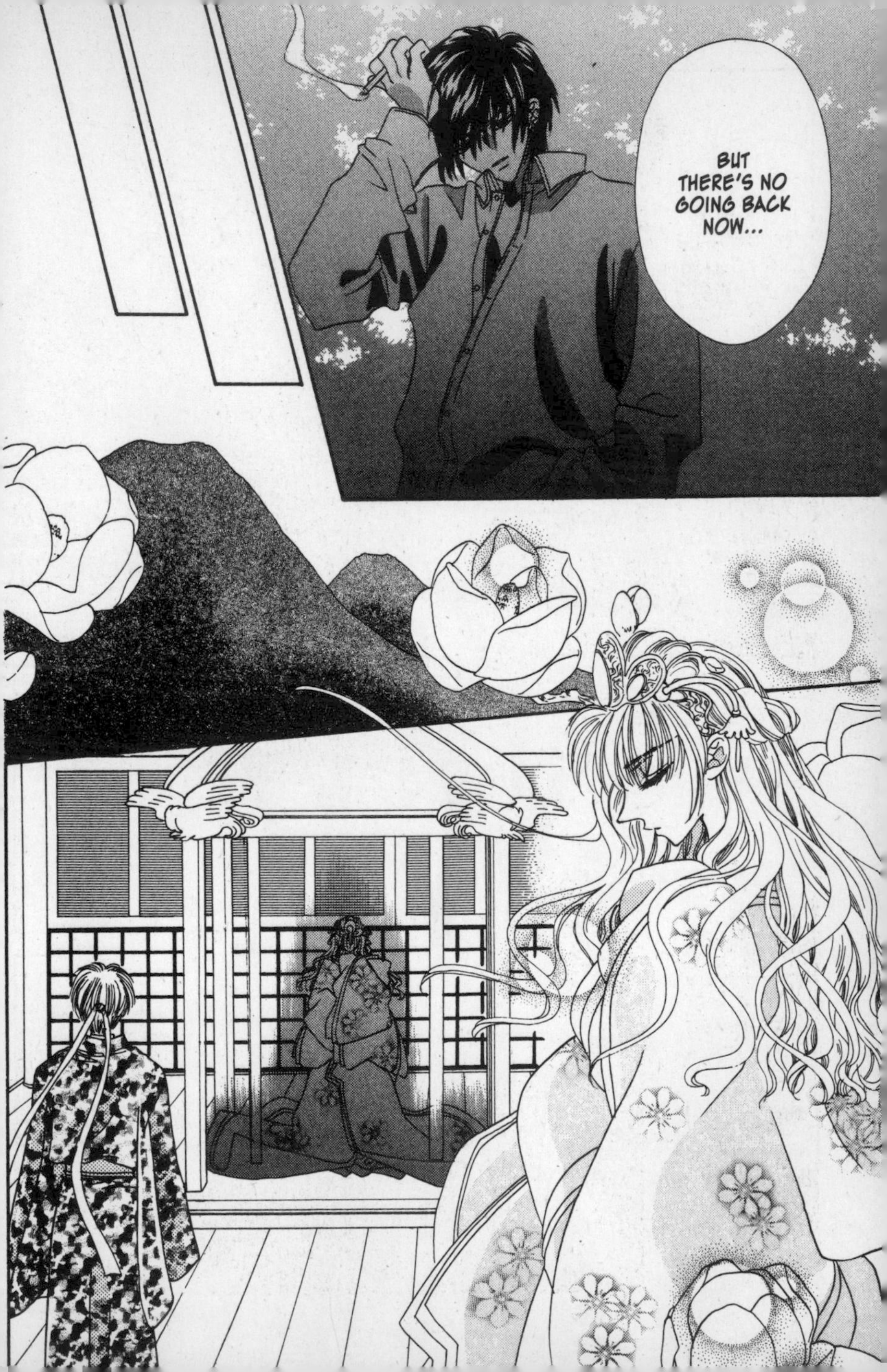
BUT THERE'S NO GOING BACK NOW...

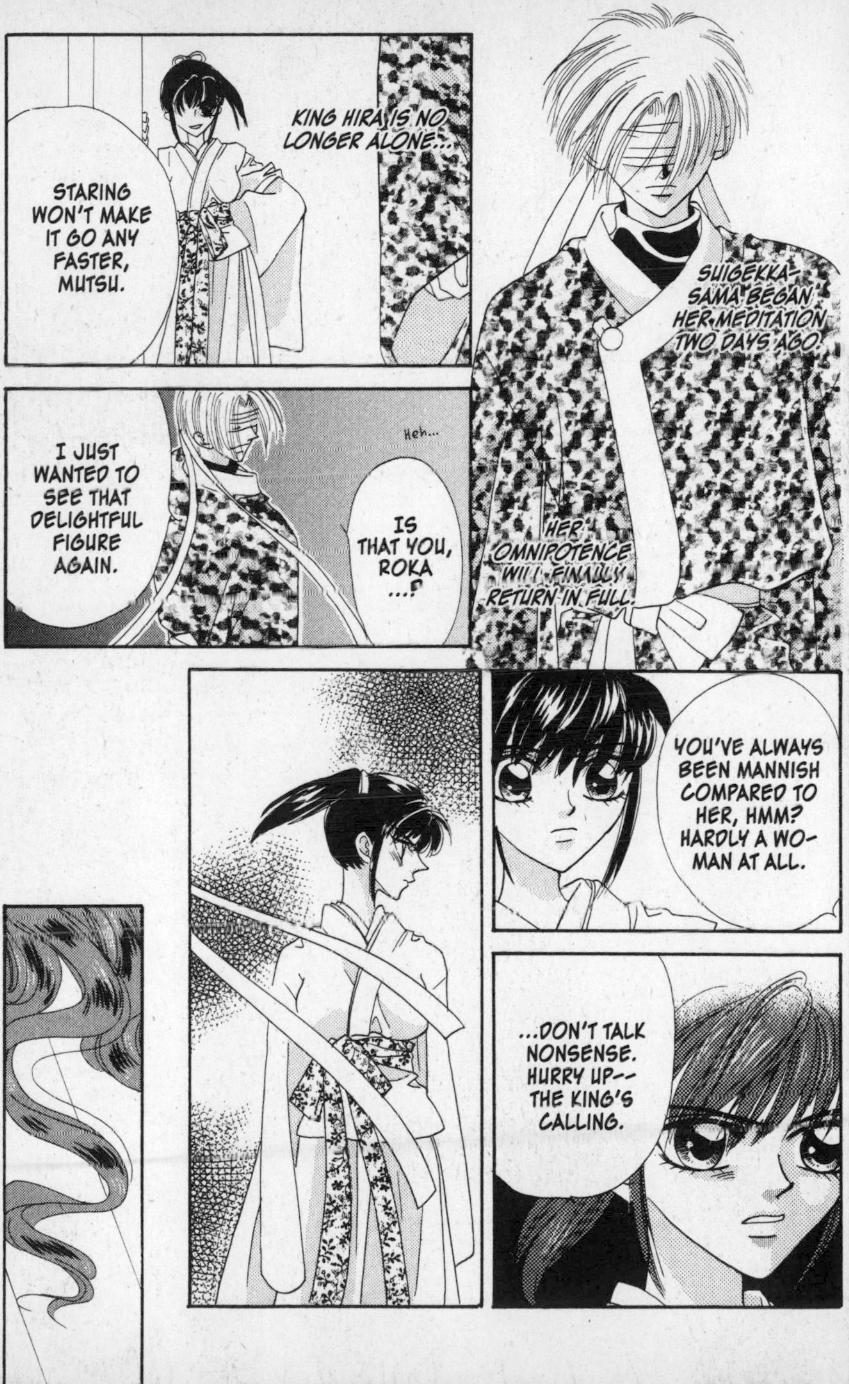
SUIGEKKA-SAMA BEGAN HER MEDITATION TWO DAYS AGO.
HER OMNIPOTENCE WILL FINALLY RETURN IN FULL.
KING HIRA IS NO LONGER ALONE...
STARING WON'T MAKE IT GO ANY FASTER, MUTSU.
Heh...
IS THAT YOU, ROKA...?
I JUST WANTED TO SEE THAT DELIGHTFUL FIGURE AGAIN.
YOU'VE ALWAYS BEEN MANNISH COMPARED TO HER, HMM? HARDLY A WO-MAN AT ALL.
...DON'T TALK NONSENSE. HURRY UP-- THE KING'S CALLING.

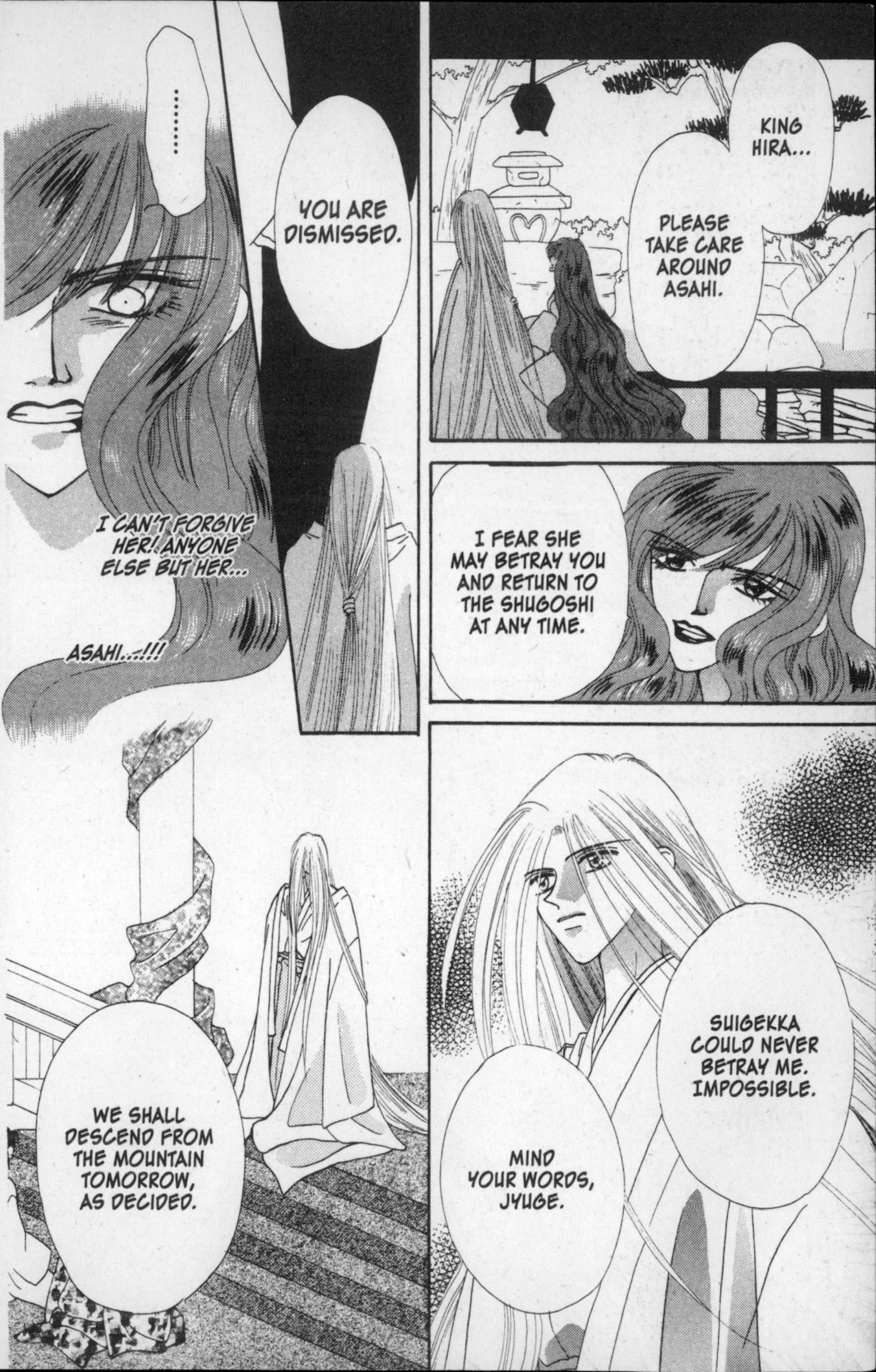

KING HIRA...
PLEASE TAKE CARE AROUND ASAHI.
I FEAR SHE MAY BETRAY YOU AND RETURN TO THE SHUGOSHI AT ANY TIME.
YOU ARE DISMISSED.
......
I CAN'T FORGIVE HER! ANYONE ELSE BUT HER...
ASAHI...!!!
SUIGEKKA COULD NEVER BETRAY ME. IMPOSSIBLE.
MIND YOUR WORDS, JYUGE.
WE SHALL DESCEND FROM THE MOUNTAIN TOMORROW, AS DECIDED.

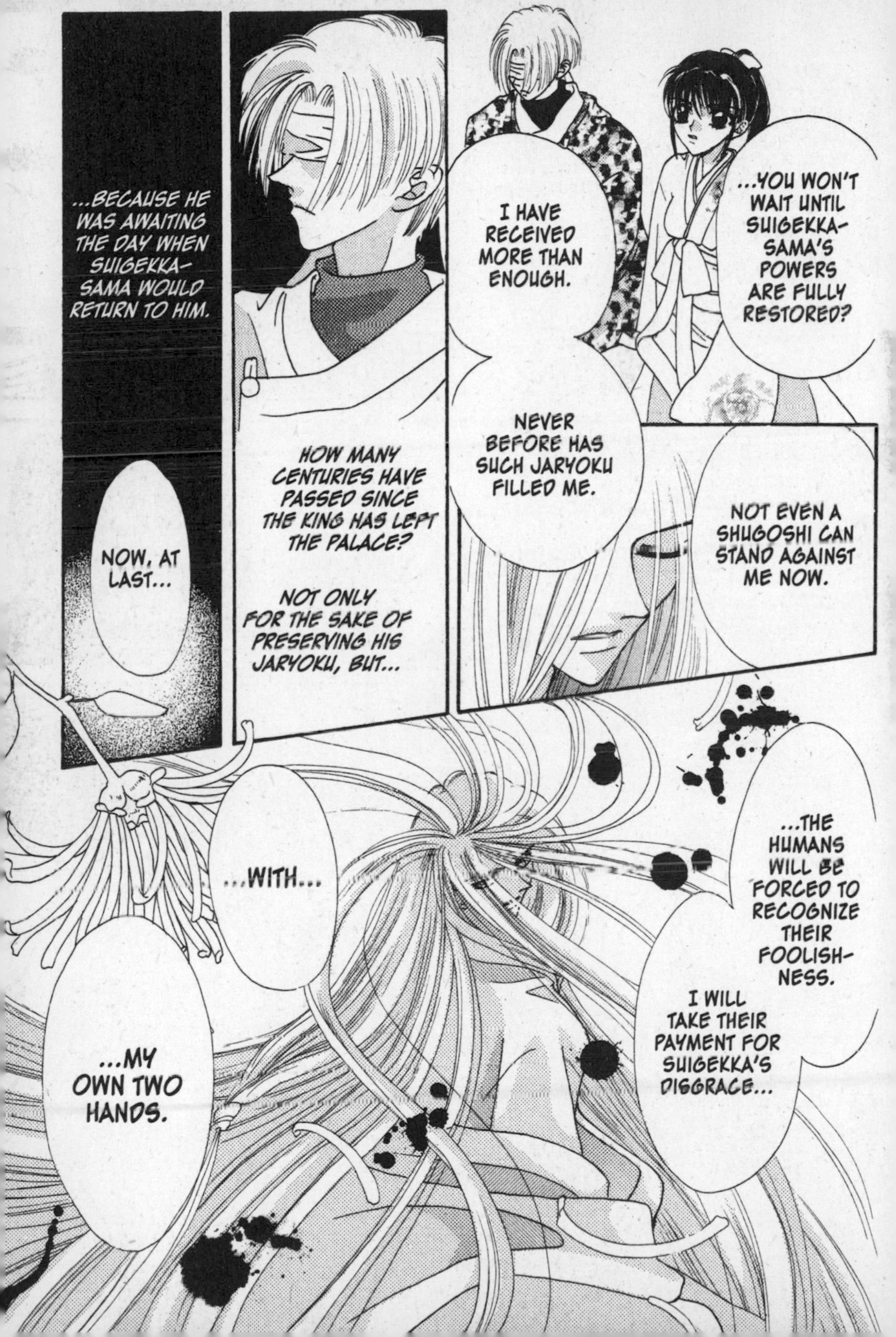
...YOU WON'T WAIT UNTIL SUIGEKKA-SAMA'S POWERS ARE FULLY RESTORED?
I HAVE RECEIVED MORE THAN ENOUGH.
NEVER BEFORE HAS SUCH JARYOKU FILLED ME.
NOT EVEN A SHUGOSHI CAN STAND AGAINST ME NOW.
HOW MANY CENTURIES HAVE PASSED SINCE THE KING HAS LEFT THE PALACE?
NOT ONLY FOR THE SAKE OF PRESERVING HIS JARYOKU, BUT...
...BECAUSE HE WAS AWAITING THE DAY WHEN SUIGEKKA-SAMA WOULD RETURN TO HIM.
NOW, AT LAST...
...THE HUMANS WILL BE FORCED TO RECOGNIZE THEIR FOOLISHNESS.
I WILL TAKE THEIR PAYMENT FOR SUIGEKKA'S DISGRACE...
...WITH...
...MY OWN TWO HANDS.

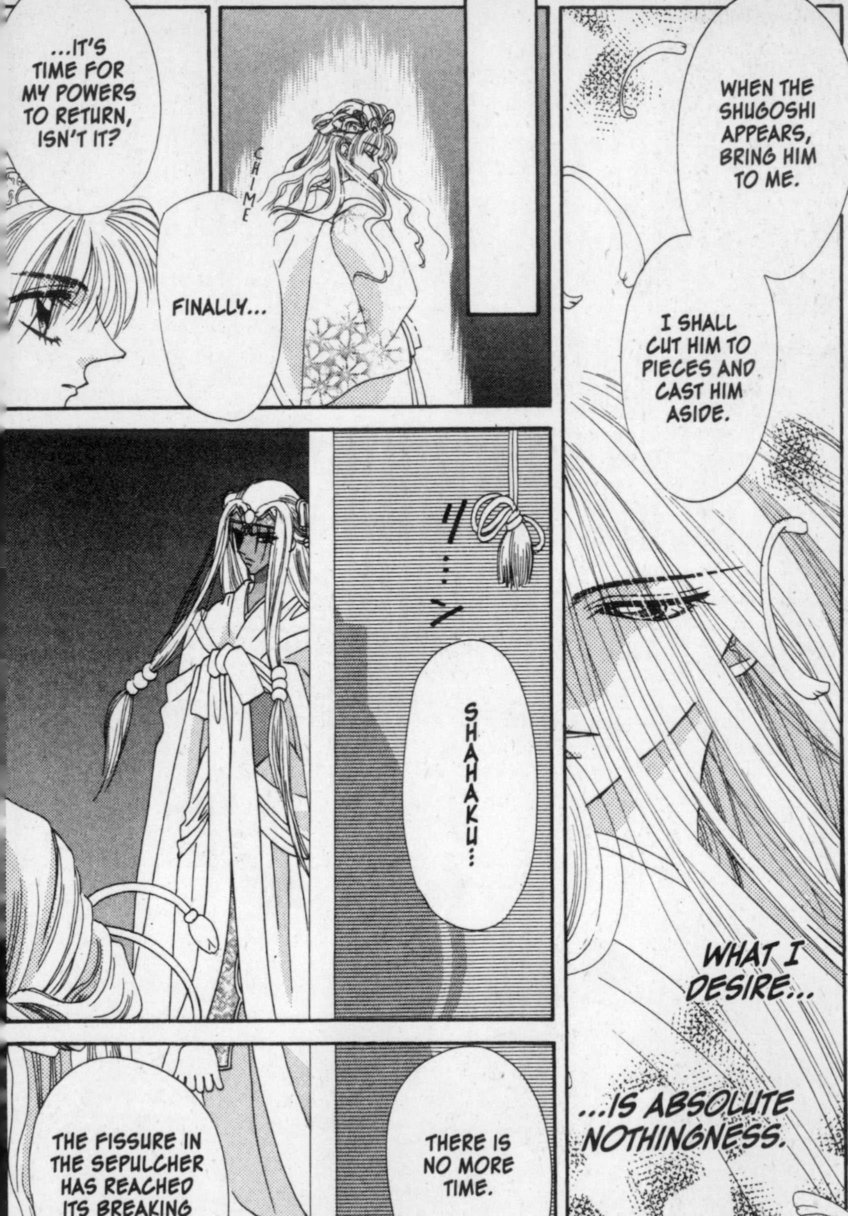
WHEN THE SHUGOSHI APPEARS, BRING HIM TO ME.
I SHALL CUT HIM TO PIECES AND CAST HIM ASIDE.
WHAT I DESIRE...
...IS ABSOLUTE NOTHINGNESS.
CHIME
...IT'S TIME FOR MY POWERS TO RETURN, ISN'T IT?
FINALLY...
リ…ン
SHAHAKU...
THERE IS NO MORE TIME.
THE FISSURE IN THE SEPULCHER HAS REACHED ITS BREAKING POINT.

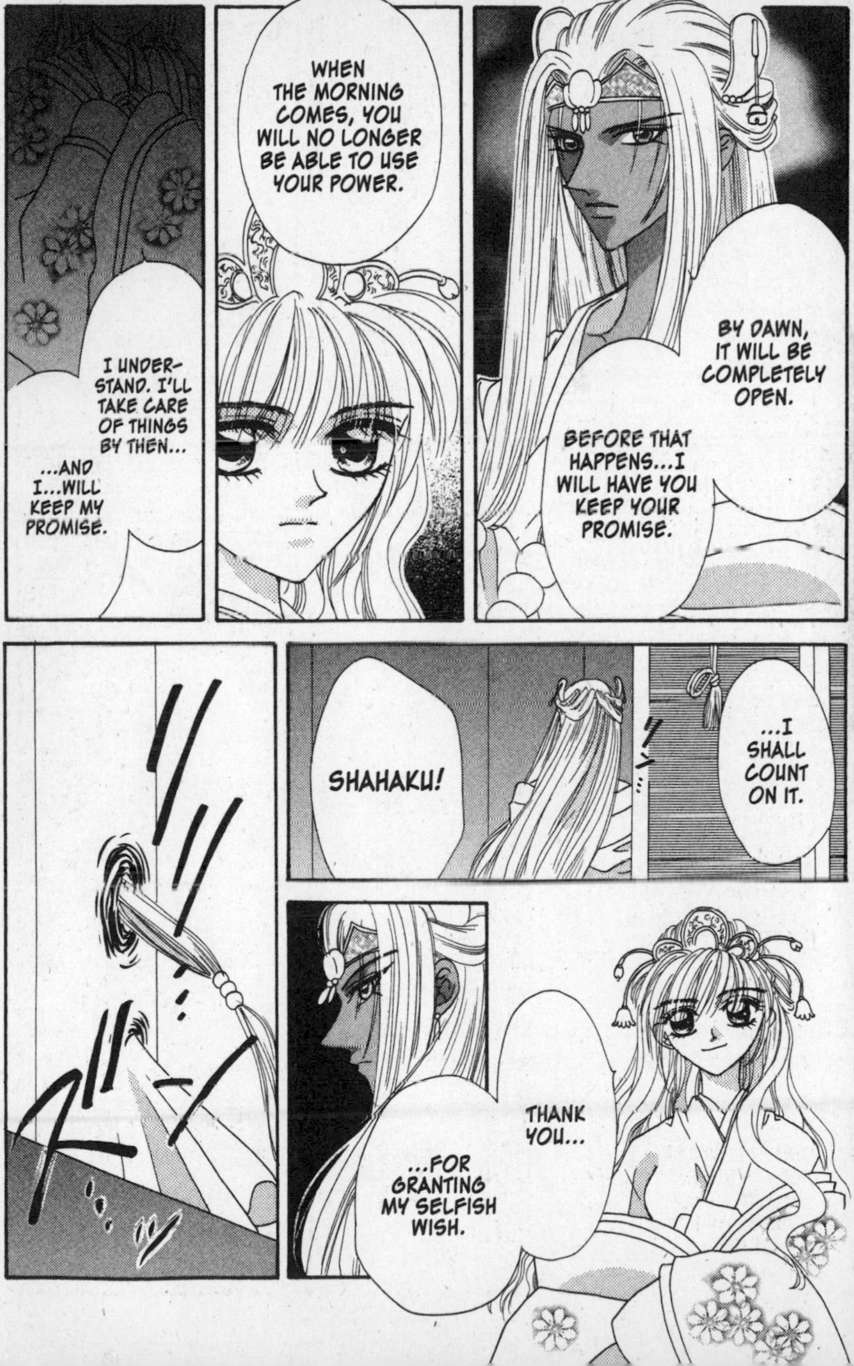
BY DAWN, IT WILL BE COMPLETELY OPEN.
BEFORE THAT HAPPENS...I WILL HAVE YOU KEEP YOUR PROMISE.
WHEN THE MORNING COMES, YOU WILL NO LONGER BE ABLE TO USE YOUR POWER.
I UNDER-STAND. I'LL TAKE CARE OF THINGS BY THEN...
...AND I...WILL KEEP MY PROMISE.
...I SHALL COUNT ON IT.
SHAHAKU!
THANK YOU...
...FOR GRANTING MY SELFISH WISH.

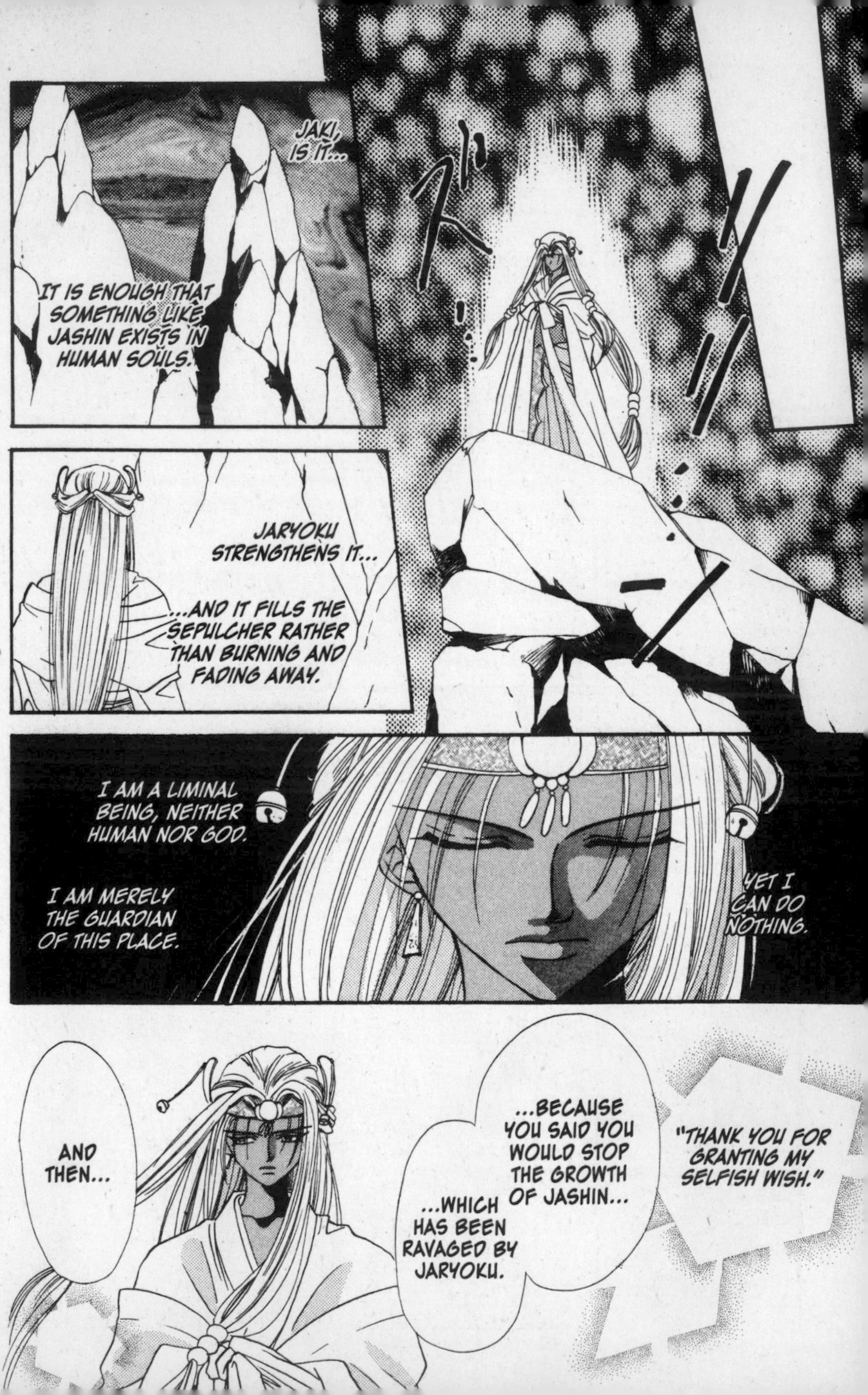
JAKI, IS IT...
IT IS ENOUGH THAT SOMETHING LIKE JASHIN EXISTS IN HUMAN SOULS.
JARYOKU STRENGTHENS IT...
...AND IT FILLS THE SEPULCHER RATHER THAN BURNING AND FADING AWAY.
I AM A LIMINAL BEING, NEITHER HUMAN NOR GOD.
I AM MERELY THE GUARDIAN OF THIS PLACE.
YET I CAN DO NOTHING.
"THANK YOU FOR GRANTING MY SELFISH WISH."
...BECAUSE YOU SAID YOU WOULD STOP THE GROWTH OF JASHIN...
...WHICH HAS BEEN RAVAGED BY JARYOKU.
AND THEN...

Scroll Three

There are lots of things I like, and one of them is dollhouses. Dollhouses! Miniature ones. I really like them, you know--I love them! Totally crazy about them. See, miniatures are neat. They touch people's hearts...but that's enough about that. (laughs) The _ppen House they have in a certain place is a holy spot for me. If you go even once, see, it'll mean you've been swallowed up by dollhouses' allure too. People say I don't cry much, but even I get all teary-eyed when I see miniatures. It's just like when I see Ka_ru-kun and _raudo-kun, you know? (Um, even if you blank out some letters, it's still obvious, Takaya-san.) I like the standard-sized dollhouses with two or more stories, an attic, stairs that really connect things (a lot of them don't have openings at the top!), hallways, windows that really open, and...and...

To be continued...

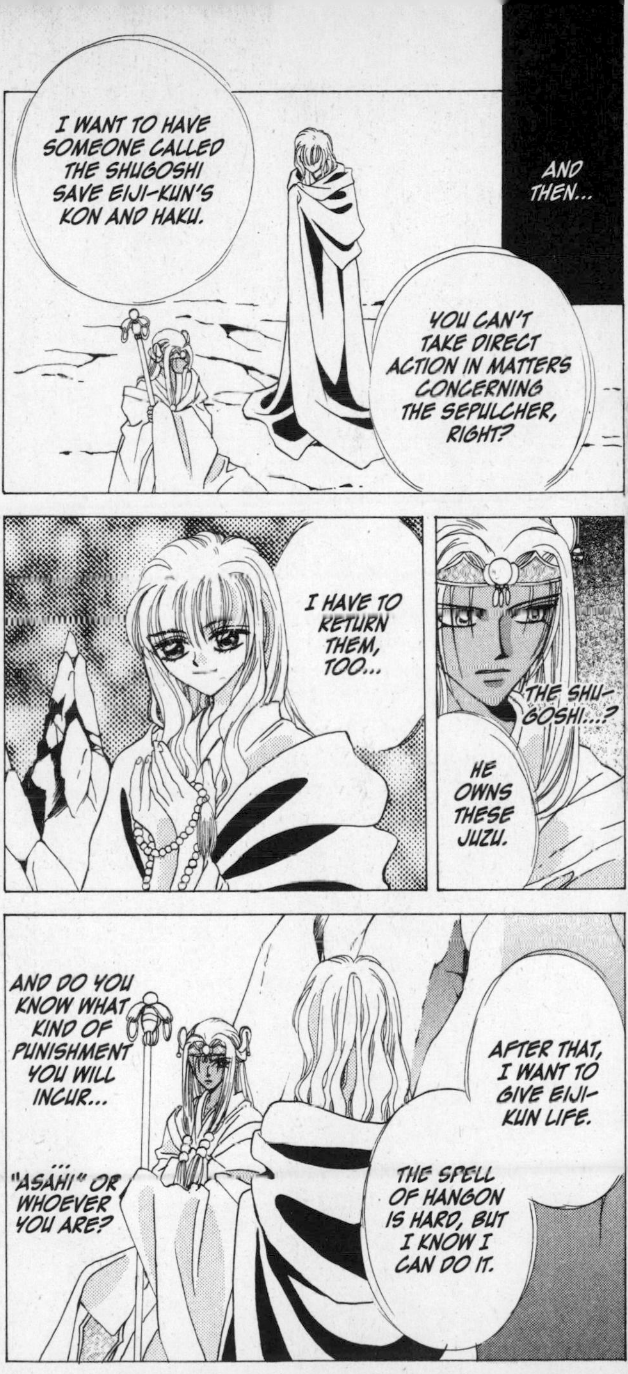
AND THEN...
YOU CAN'T TAKE DIRECT ACTION IN MATTERS CONCERNING THE SEPULCHER, RIGHT?
I WANT TO HAVE SOMEONE CALLED THE SHUGOSHI SAVE EIJI-KUN'S KON AND HAKU.
THE SHU-GOSHI...?
HE OWNS THESE JUZU.
I HAVE TO RETURN THEM, TOO...
AFTER THAT, I WANT TO GIVE EIJI-KUN LIFE.
THE SPELL OF HANGON IS HARD, BUT I KNOW I CAN DO IT.
AND DO YOU KNOW WHAT KIND OF PUNISHMENT YOU WILL INCUR...
..."ASAHI" OR WHOEVER YOU ARE?

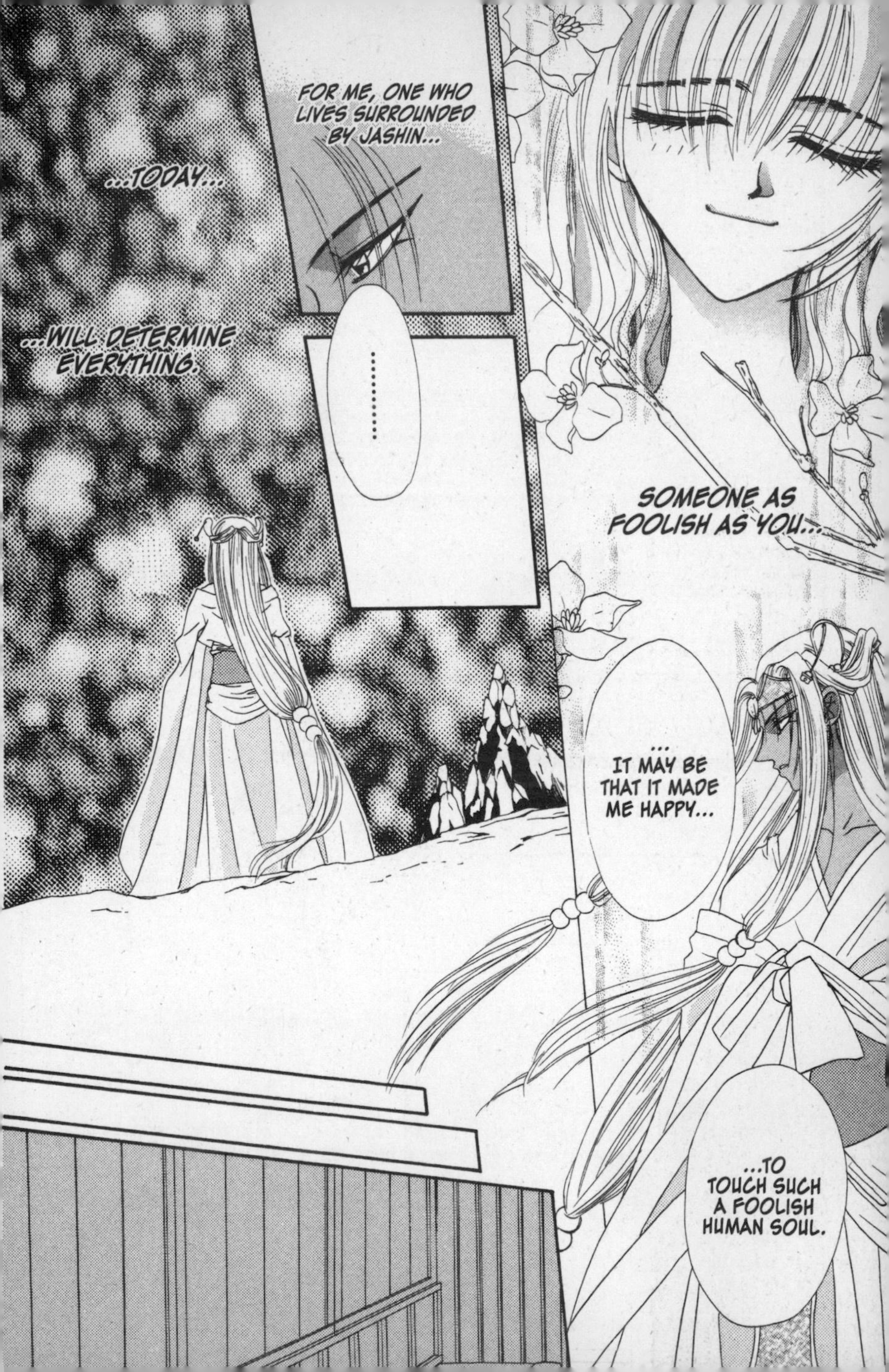
SOMEONE AS FOOLISH AS YOU...
FOR ME, ONE WHO LIVES SURROUNDED BY JASHIN...
... IT MAY BE THAT IT MADE ME HAPPY...
...TO TOUCH SUCH A FOOLISH HUMAN SOUL.
......
...TODAY...
...WILL DETERMINE EVERYTHING.

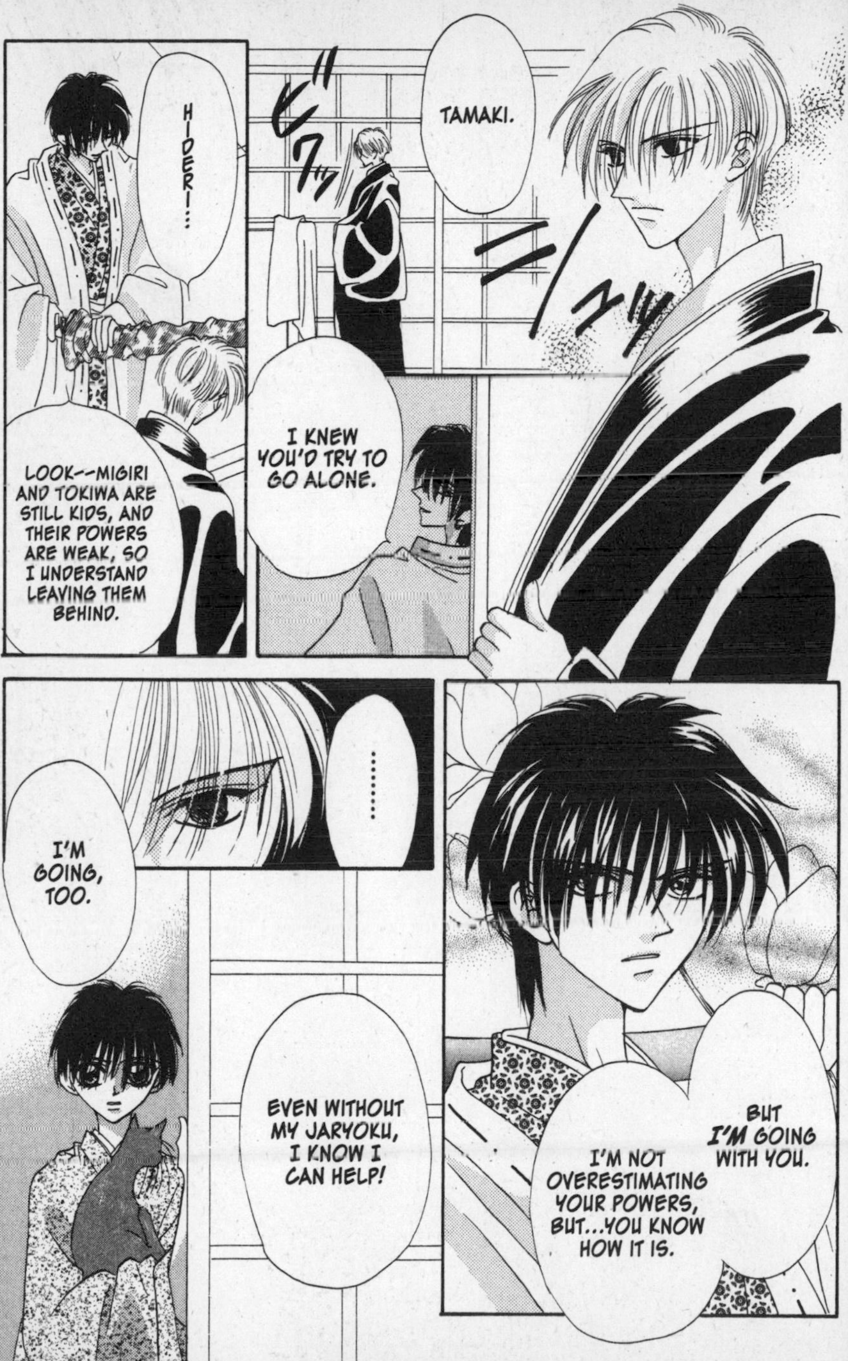
TAMAKI.
I KNEW YOU'D TRY TO GO ALONE.
HIDERI...
LOOK--MIGIRI AND TOKIWA ARE STILL KIDS, AND THEIR POWERS ARE WEAK, SO I UNDERSTAND LEAVING THEM BEHIND.
BUT *I'M* GOING WITH YOU.
I'M NOT OVERESTIMATING YOUR POWERS, BUT...YOU KNOW HOW IT IS.
......
I'M GOING, TOO.
EVEN WITHOUT MY JARYOKU, I KNOW I CAN HELP!

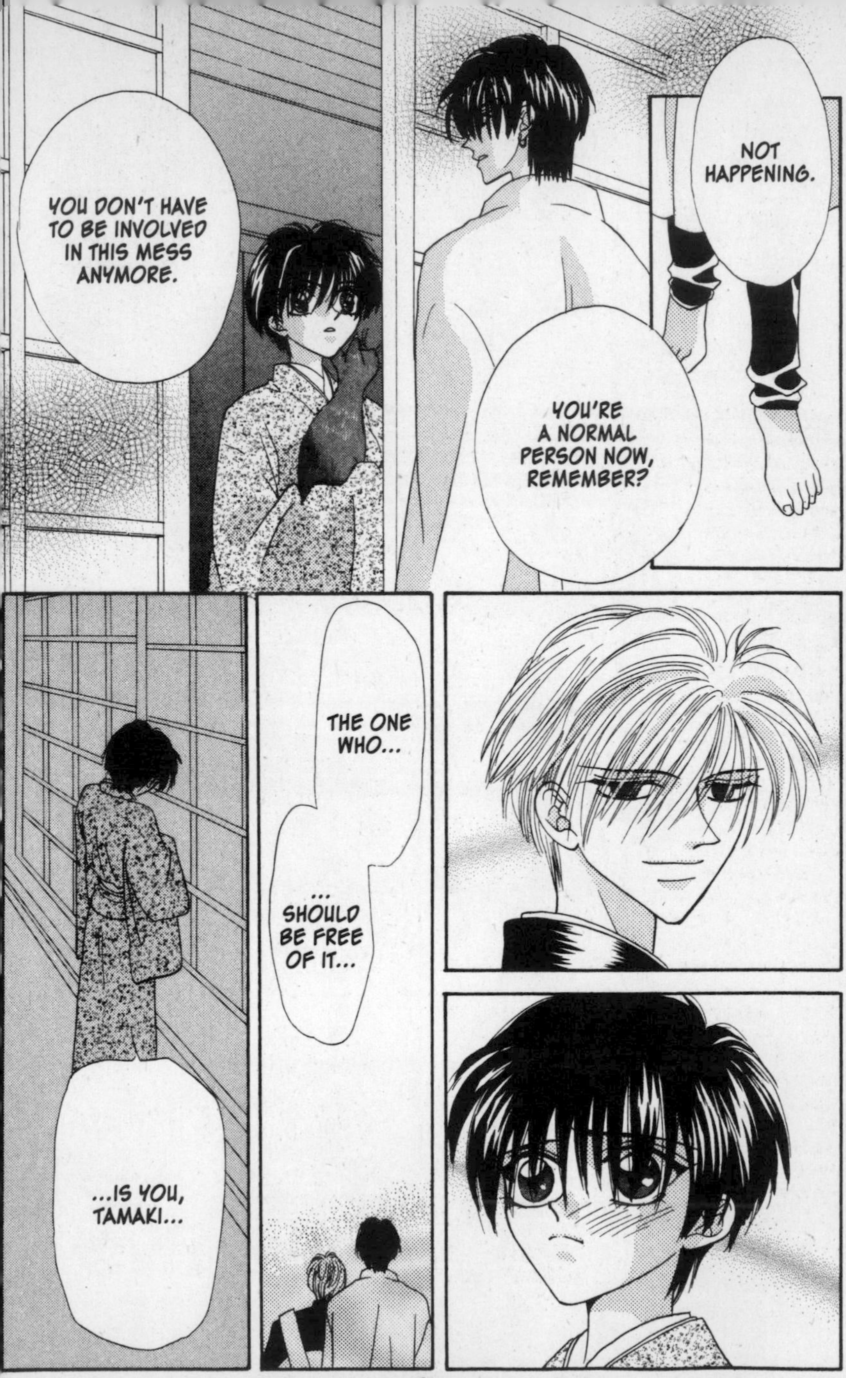
NOT HAPPENING.
YOU'RE A NORMAL PERSON NOW, REMEMBER?
YOU DON'T HAVE TO BE INVOLVED IN THIS MESS ANYMORE.
THE ONE WHO...
...SHOULD BE FREE OF IT...
...IS YOU, TAMAKI...

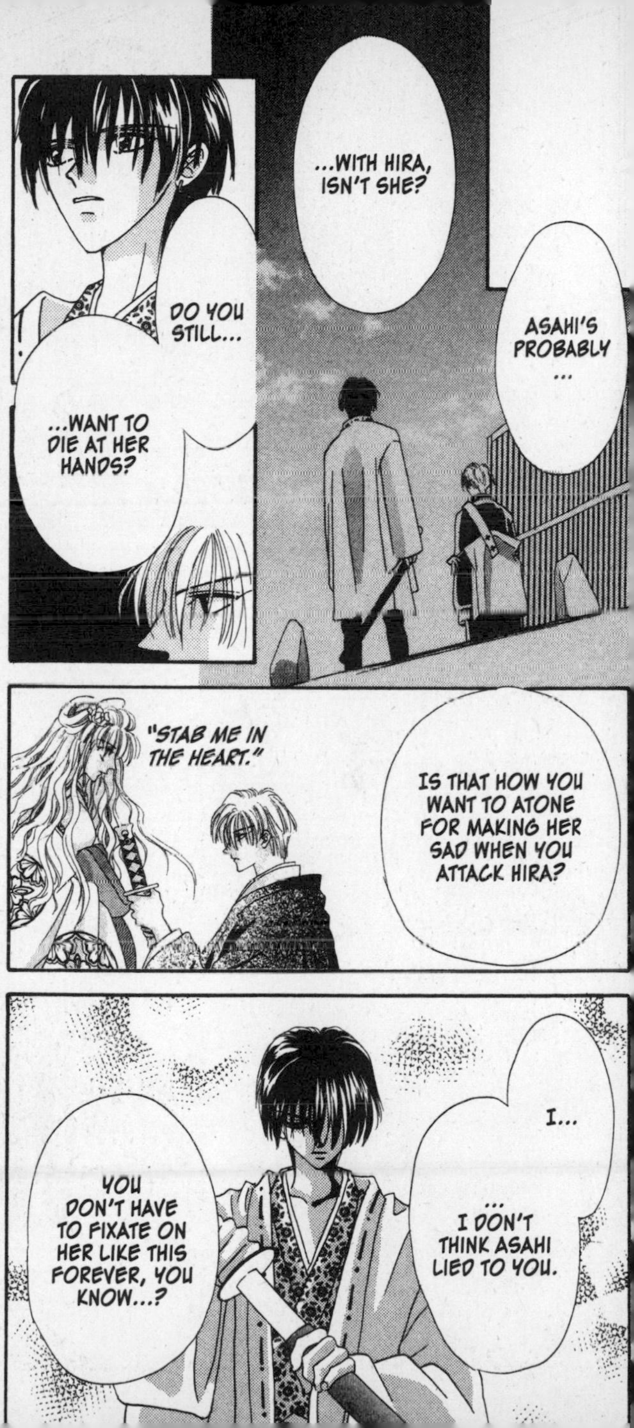
ASAHI'S PROBABLY ...
...WITH HIRA, ISN'T SHE?
DO YOU STILL...
...WANT TO DIE AT HER HANDS?
IS THAT HOW YOU WANT TO ATONE FOR MAKING HER SAD WHEN YOU ATTACK HIRA?
"STAB ME IN THE HEART."
I...
... I DON'T THINK ASAHI LIED TO YOU.
YOU DON'T HAVE TO FIXATE ON HER LIKE THIS FOREVER, YOU KNOW...?

Scroll Four

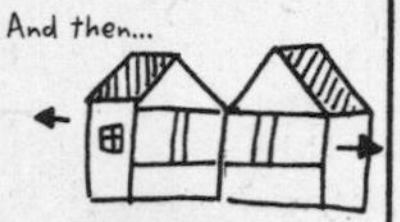
And then...

The kind that open up like this are nice, aren't they? The kind where the lamps really light up, and of course the furniture works and you can move it around! It's so boring if they're glued in place. Oooh, I want one, I want one, I want one...!!! But you know, once I found a wonderful dollhouse and then found out that it cost ¥1,000,000! A million! I mean, there are full tableware sets that cost tens of thousands of yen, too. They're expensive, huh? Sigh. I guess it'd be best to make one myself, but that's kind of... well. Plus when I've had free time lately, I've been sleeping or playing games. Ooh, but dollhouses really are nice, aren't they? I don't really want dolls, though. I don't really like them. The magic of miniatures makes me happy...

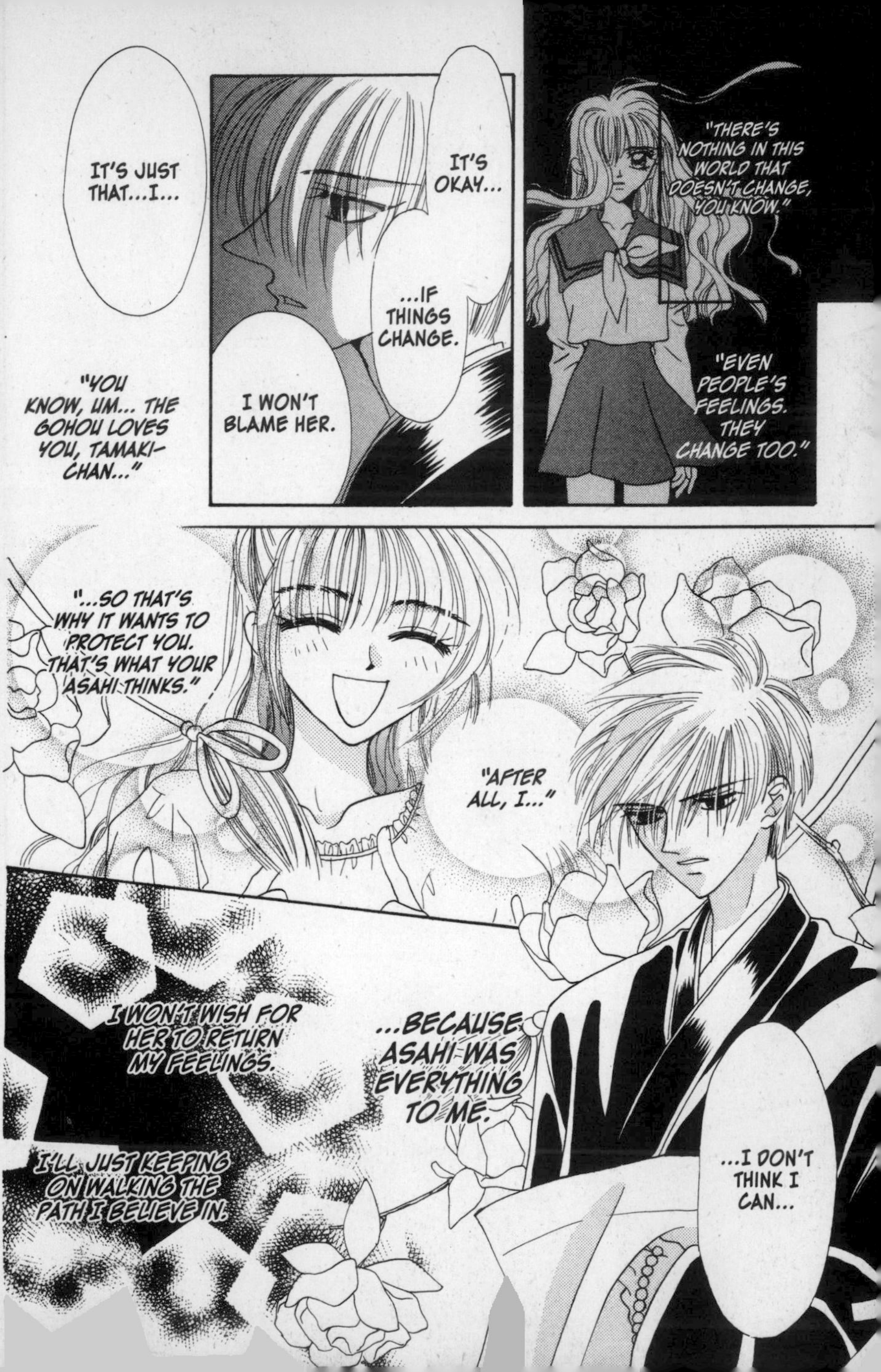
"THERE'S NOTHING IN THIS WORLD THAT DOESN'T CHANGE, YOU KNOW."
"EVEN PEOPLE'S FEELINGS. THEY CHANGE TOO."
IT'S OKAY...
...IF THINGS CHANGE.
I WON'T BLAME HER.
IT'S JUST THAT...I...
"YOU KNOW, UM... THE GOHOU LOVES YOU, TAMAKI-CHAN..."
"...SO THAT'S WHY IT WANTS TO PROTECT YOU. THAT'S WHAT YOUR ASAHI THINKS."
"AFTER ALL, I..."
...I DON'T THINK I CAN...
...BECAUSE ASAHI WAS EVERYTHING TO ME.
I WON'T WISH FOR HER TO RETURN MY FEELINGS.
I'LL JUST KEEPING ON WALKING THE PATH I BELIEVE IN.

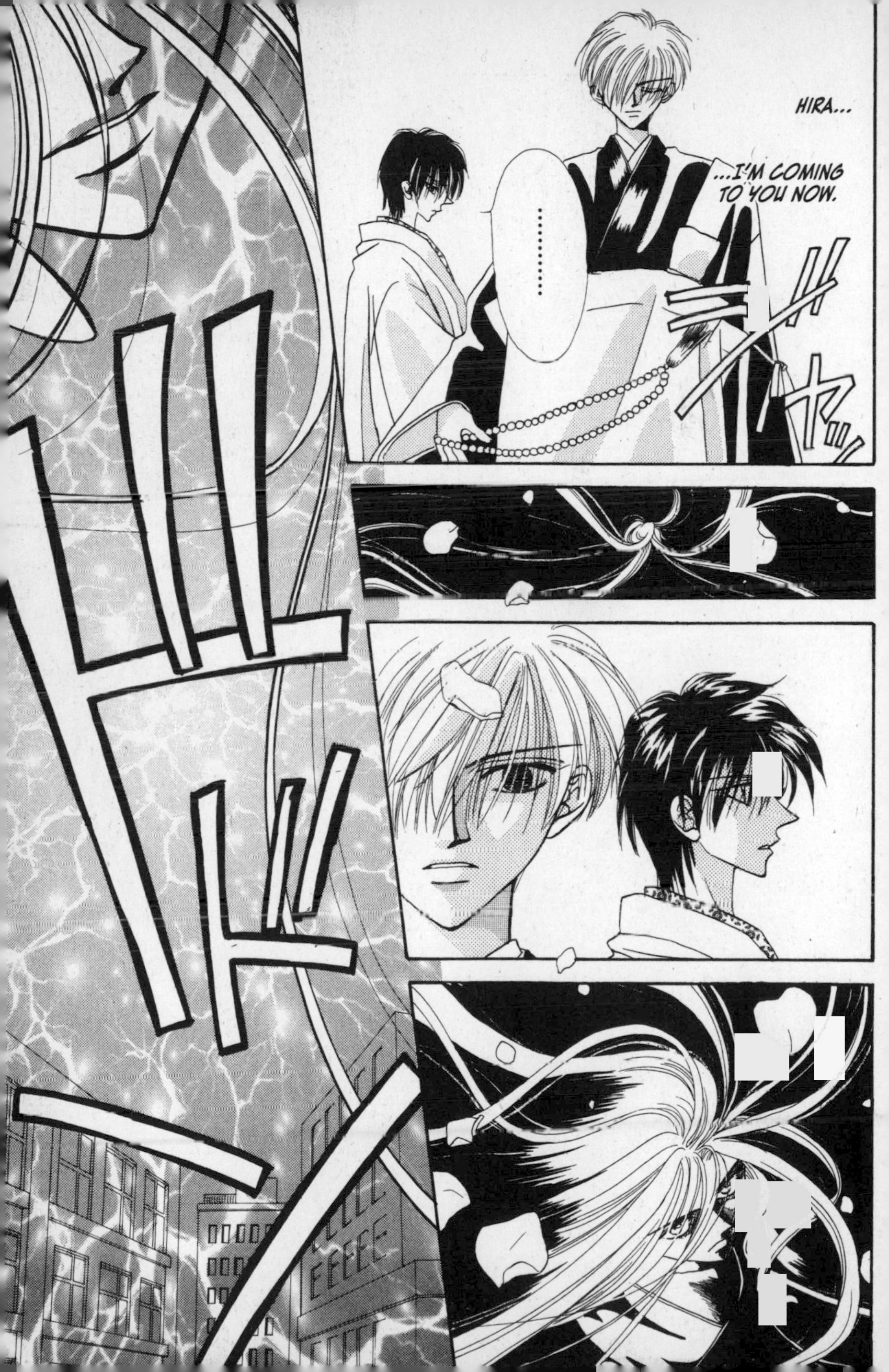
HIRA...
...I'M COMING TO YOU NOW.
......

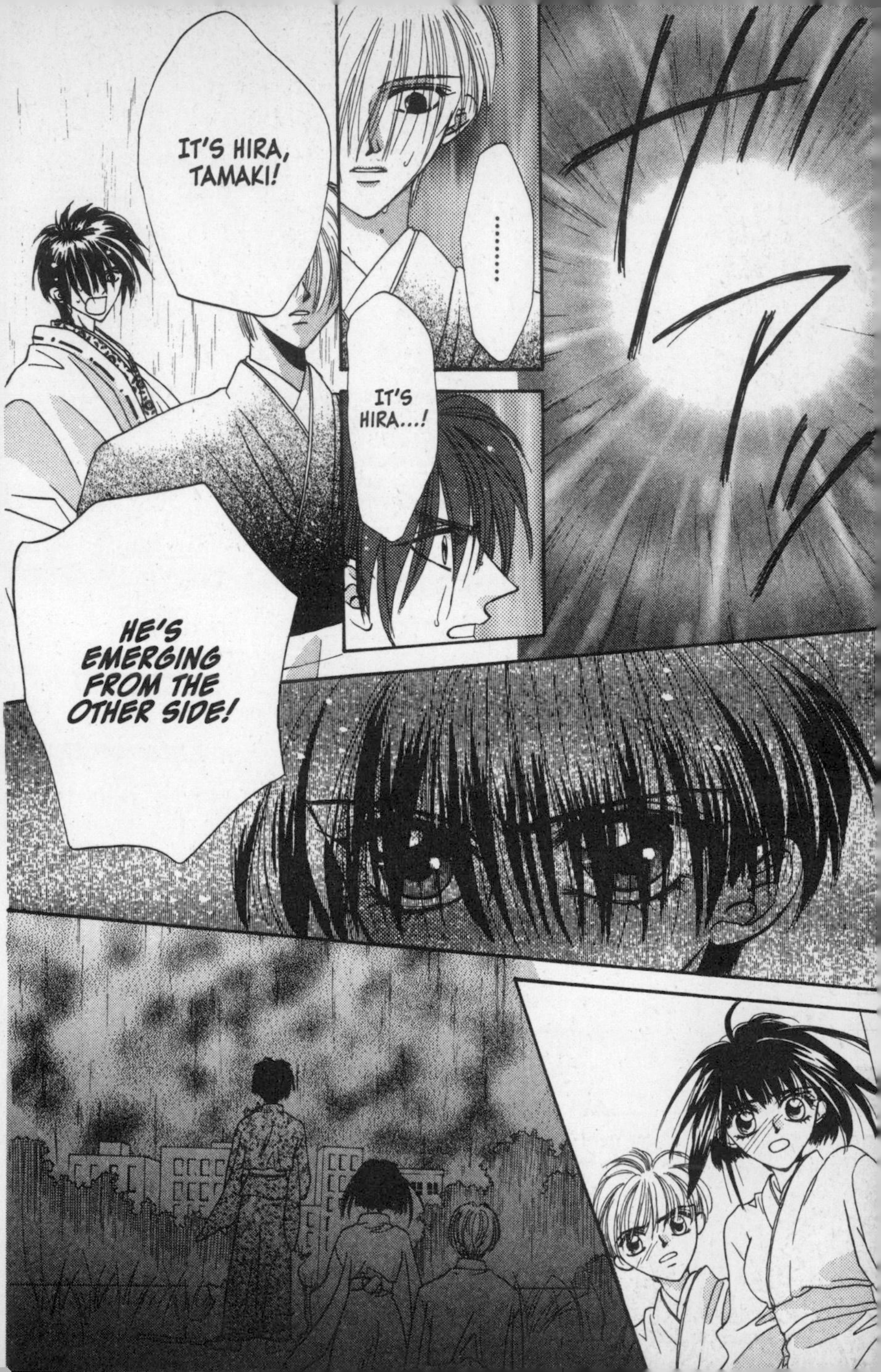
......
IT'S HIRA...!
IT'S HIRA, TAMAKI!
HE'S EMERGING FROM THE OTHER SIDE!

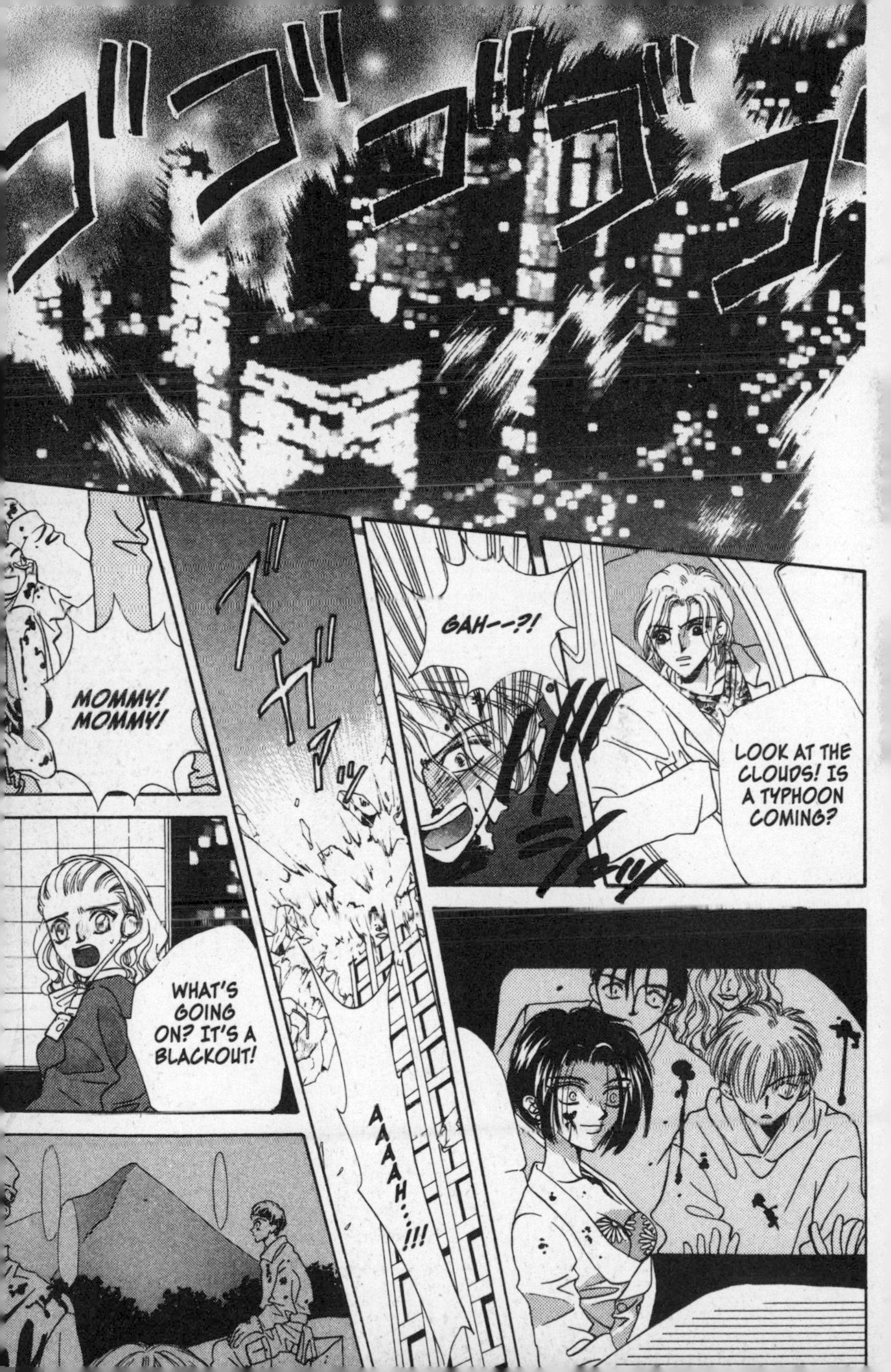
LOOK AT THE CLOUDS! IS A TYPHOON COMING?
GAH--?!
AAAAH...!!!
MOMMY! MOMMY!
WHAT'S GOING ON? IT'S A BLACKOUT!

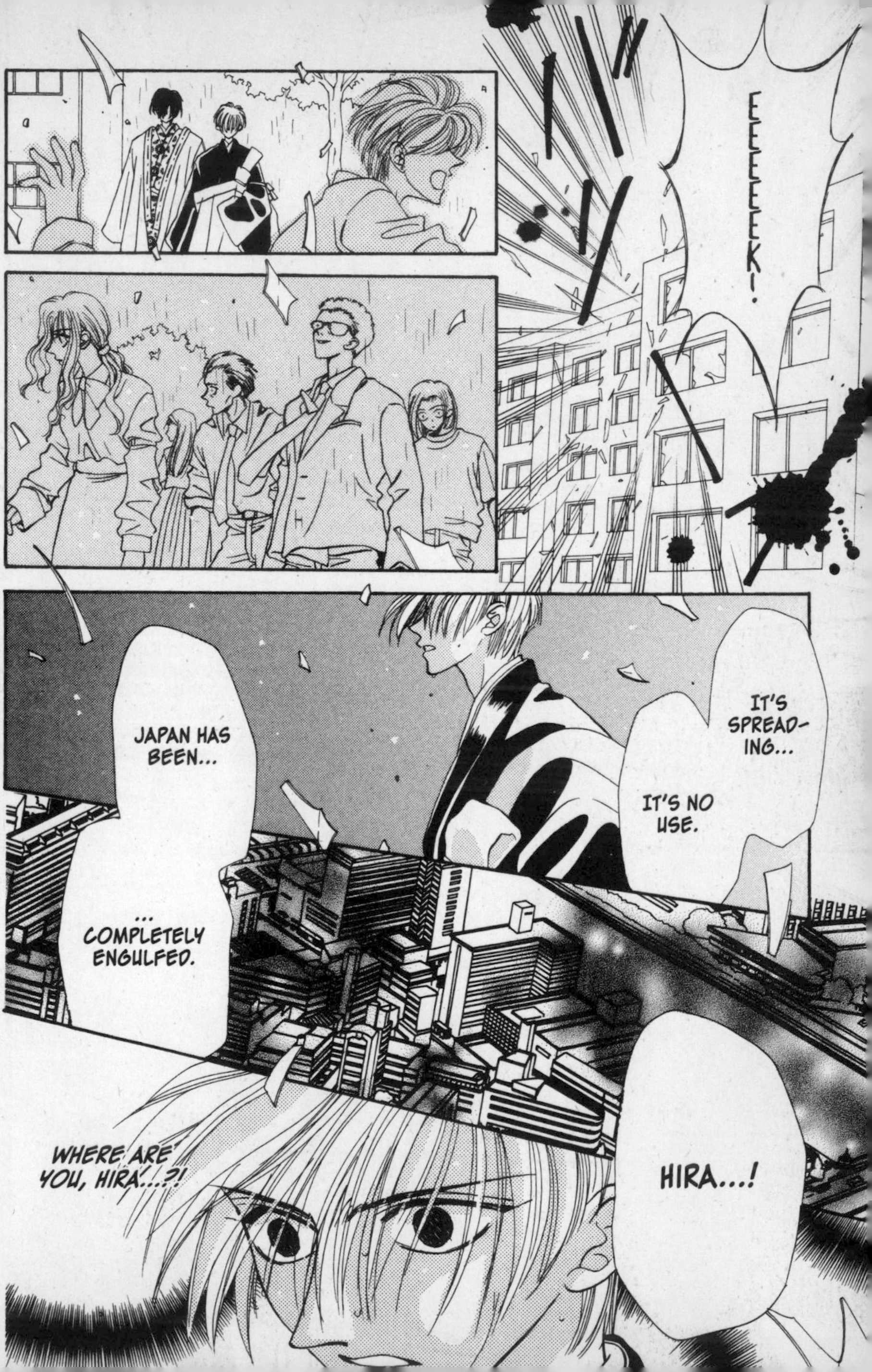
EEEEEEK!
IT'S SPREADING...
IT'S NO USE.
JAPAN HAS BEEN...
...COMPLETELY ENGULFED.
HIRA...!
WHERE ARE YOU, HIRA...?!

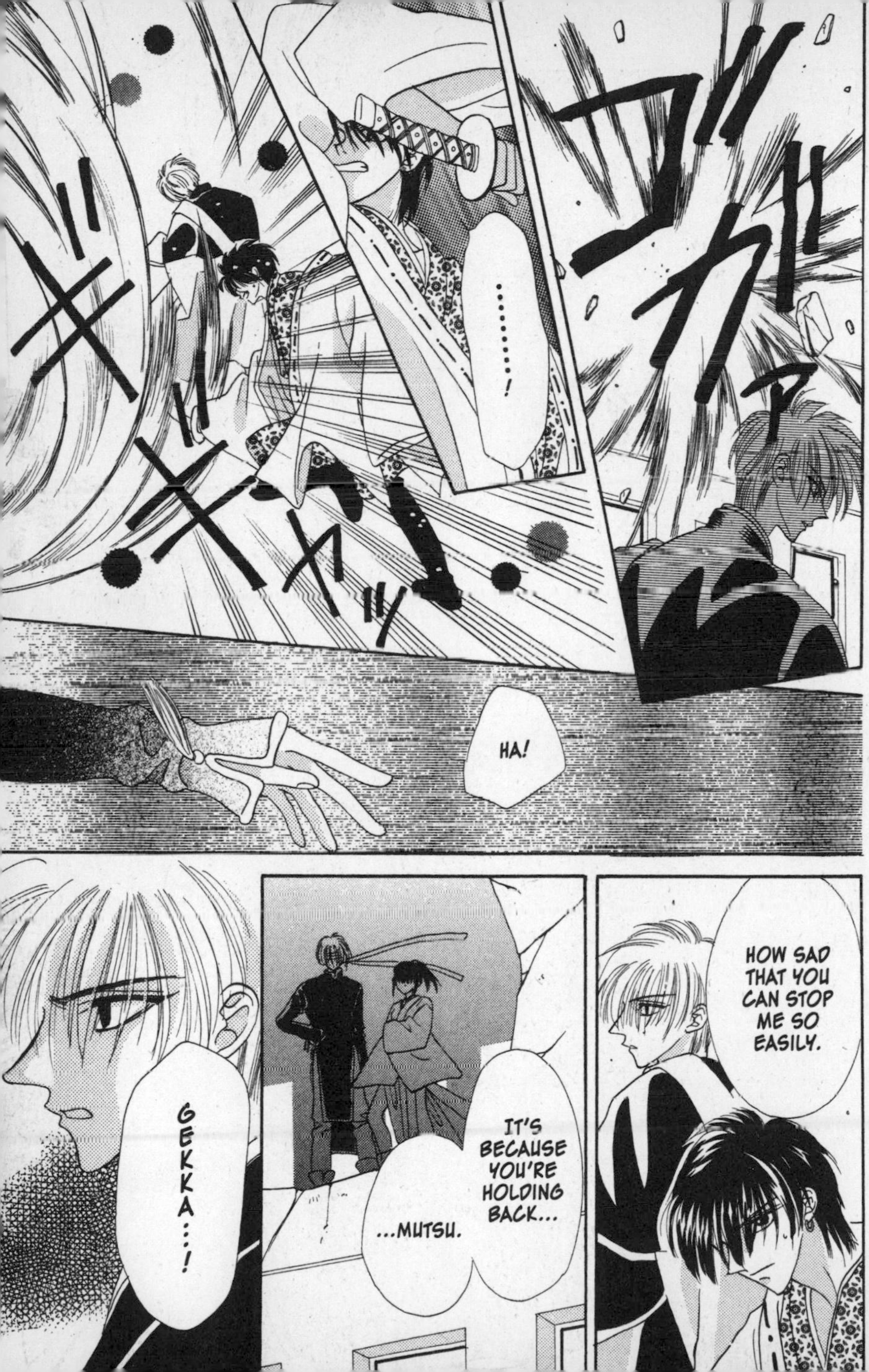
......!
HA!
HOW SAD THAT YOU CAN STOP ME SO EASILY.
IT'S BECAUSE YOU'RE HOLDING BACK...
...MUTSU.
GEKKA...!

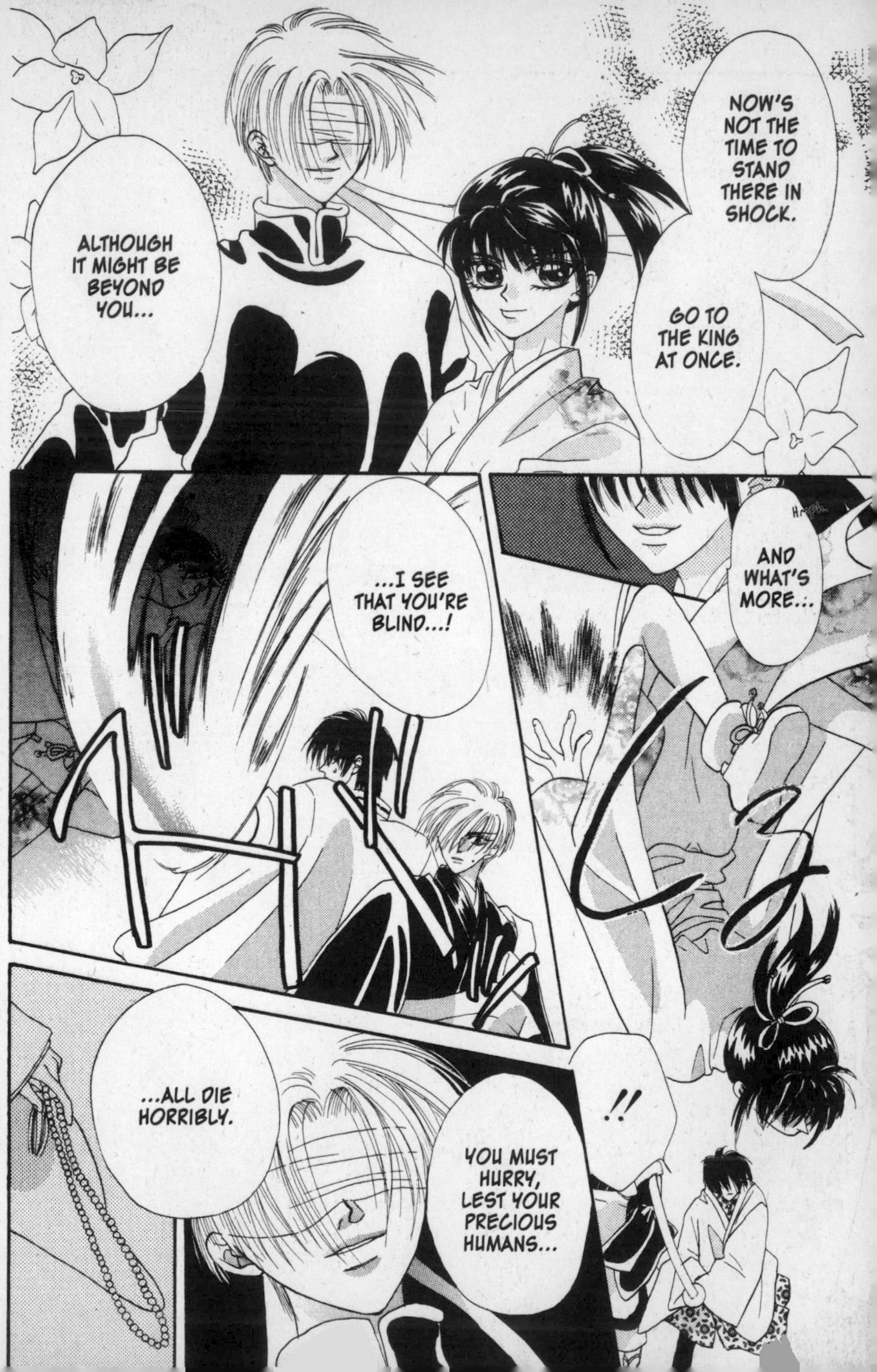
NOW'S NOT THE TIME TO STAND THERE IN SHOCK.
GO TO THE KING AT ONCE.
ALTHOUGH IT MIGHT BE BEYOND YOU...
Hmph.
AND WHAT'S MORE...
...I SEE THAT YOU'RE BLIND...!
!!
YOU MUST HURRY, LEST YOUR PRECIOUS HUMANS...
...ALL DIE HORRIBLY.

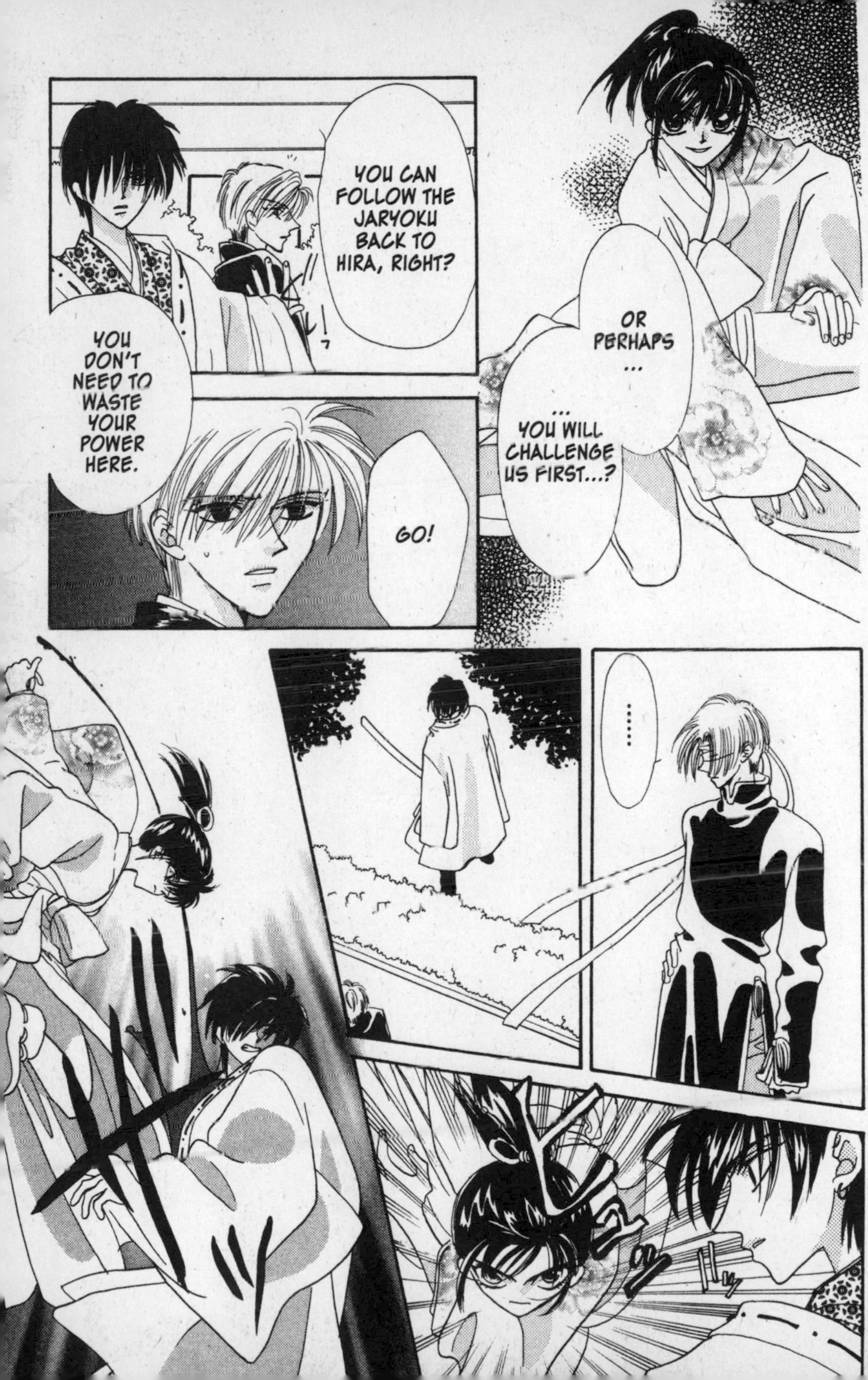
OR PERHAPS...
...YOU WILL CHALLENGE US FIRST...?
YOU CAN FOLLOW THE JARYOKU BACK TO HIRA, RIGHT?
YOU DON'T NEED TO WASTE YOUR POWER HERE.
GO!
......

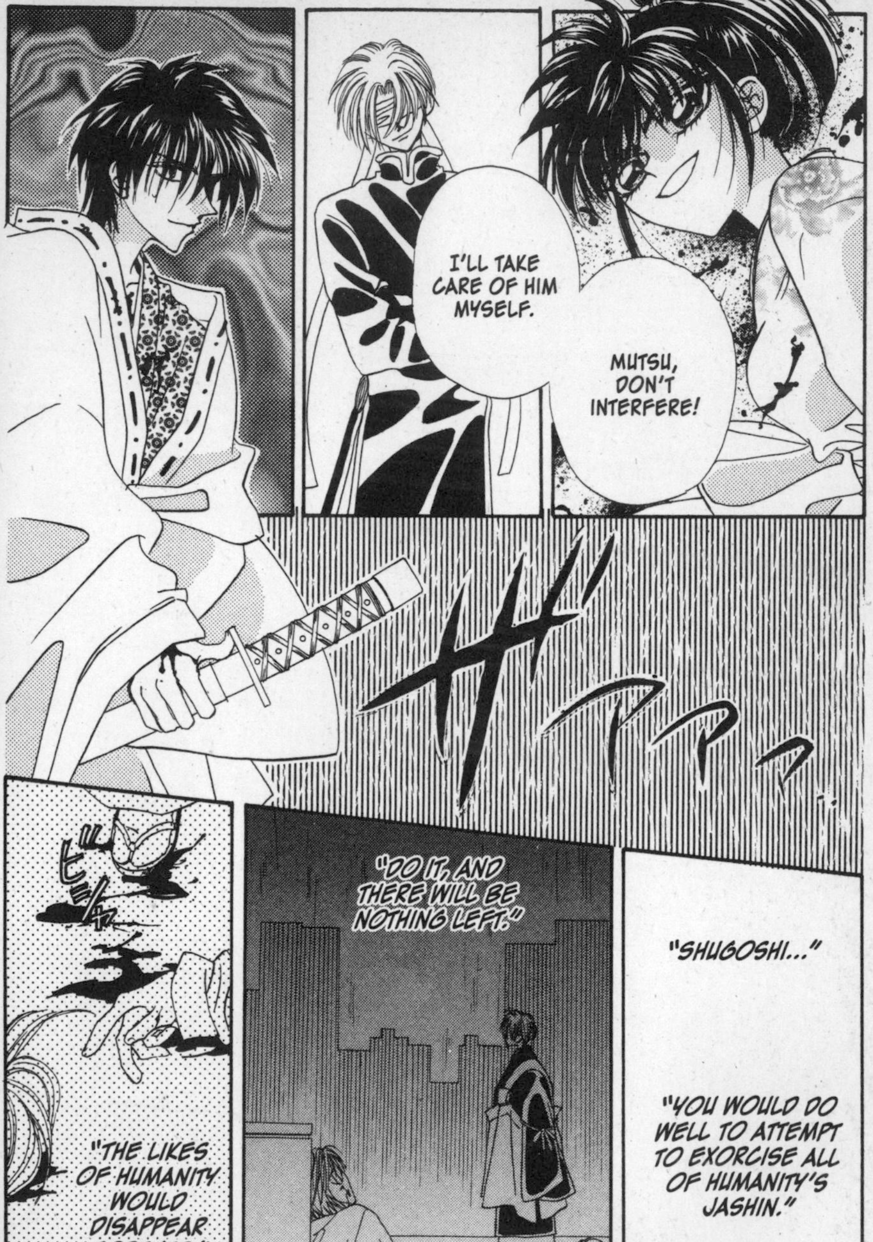
I'LL TAKE CARE OF HIM MYSELF.
MUTSU, DON'T INTERFERE!
"SHUGOSHI..."
"YOU WOULD DO WELL TO ATTEMPT TO EXORCISE ALL OF HUMANITY'S JASHIN."
"DO IT, AND THERE WILL BE NOTHING LEFT."
"THE LIKES OF HUMANITY WOULD DISAPPEAR FOREVER."

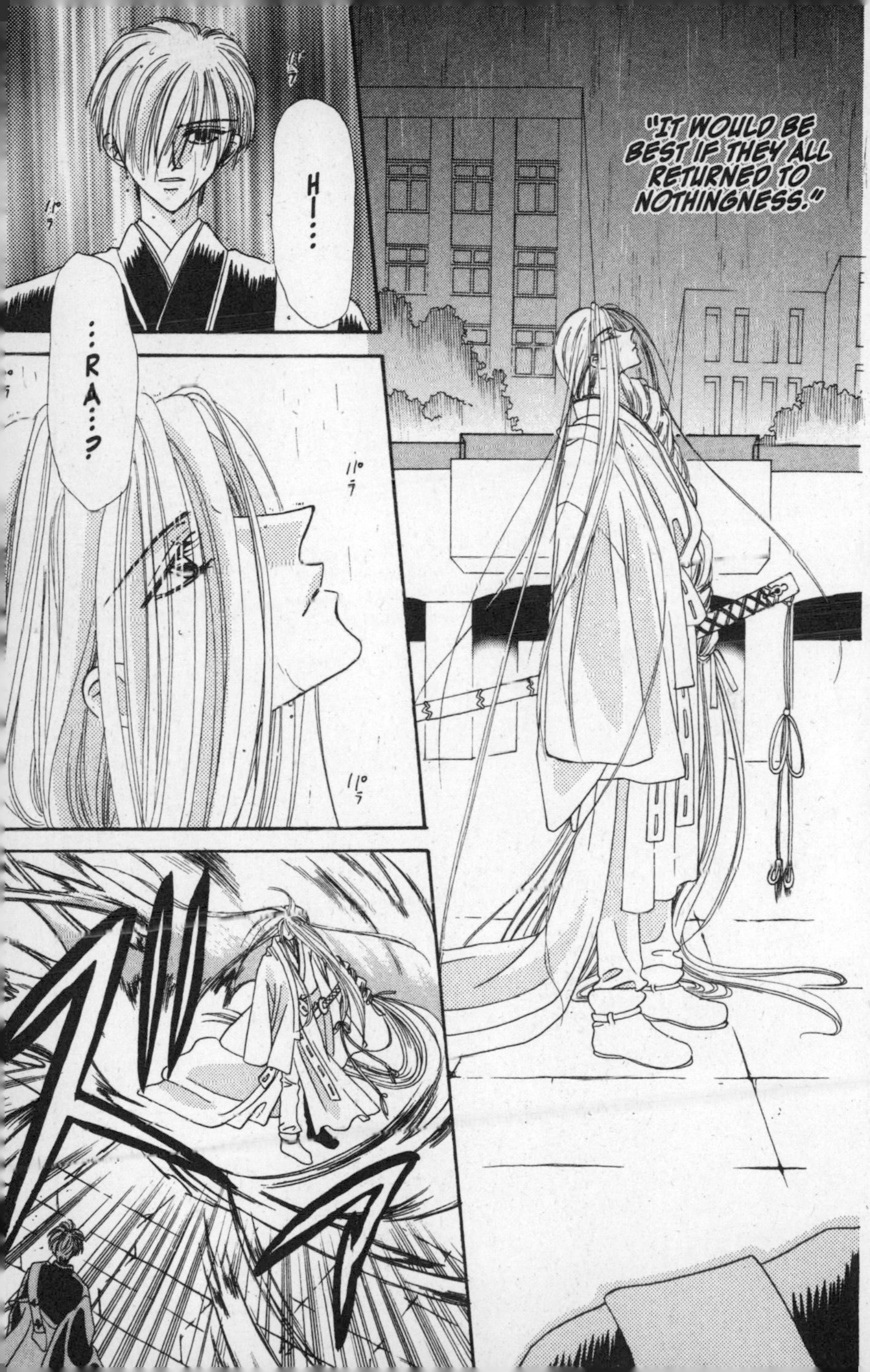
"IT WOULD BE BEST IF THEY ALL RETURNED TO NOTHINGNESS."
HI...
...RA...?

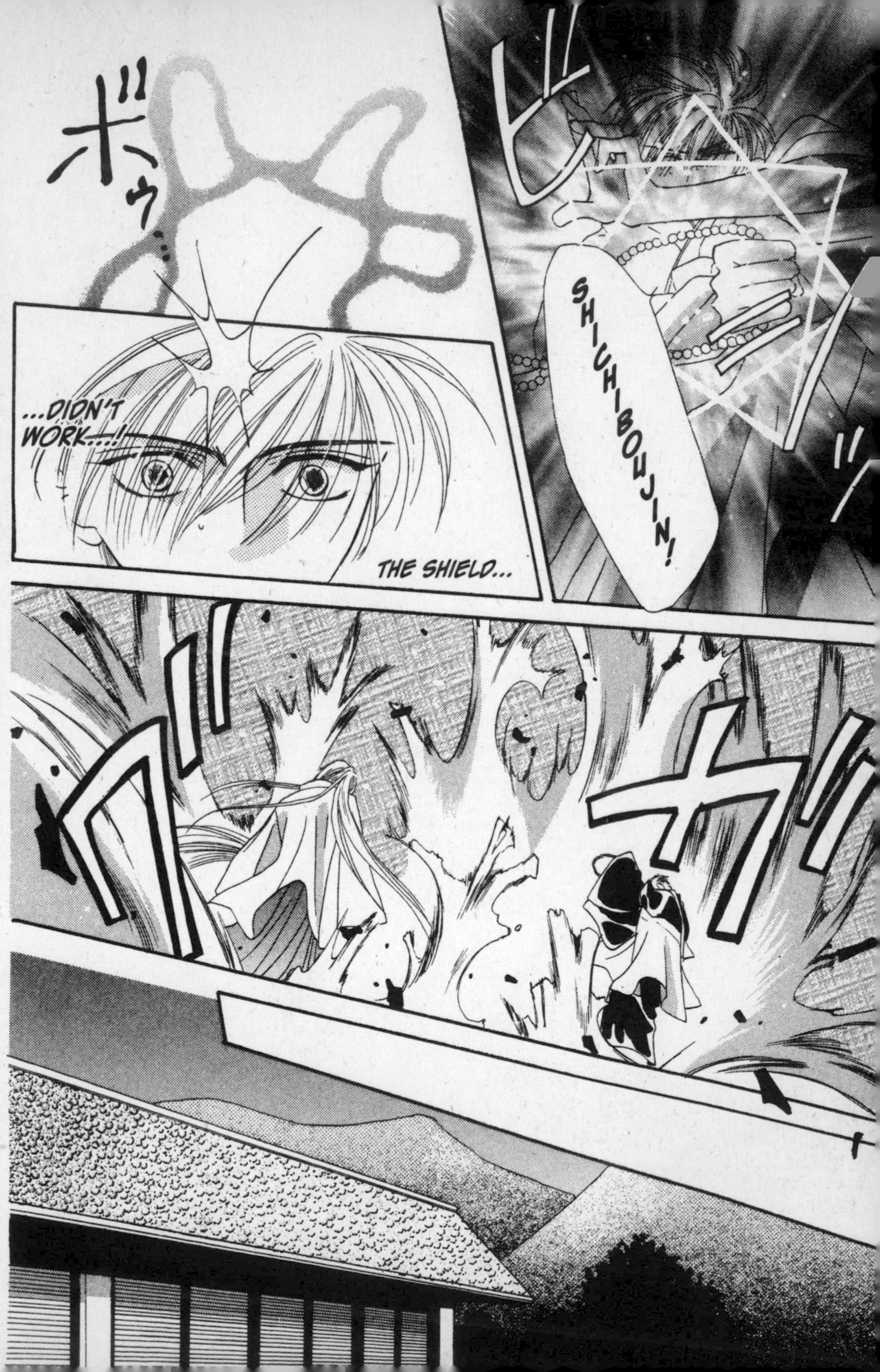
SHICHIBOUJIN!
ボウ
THE SHIELD...
...DIDN'T WORK...!

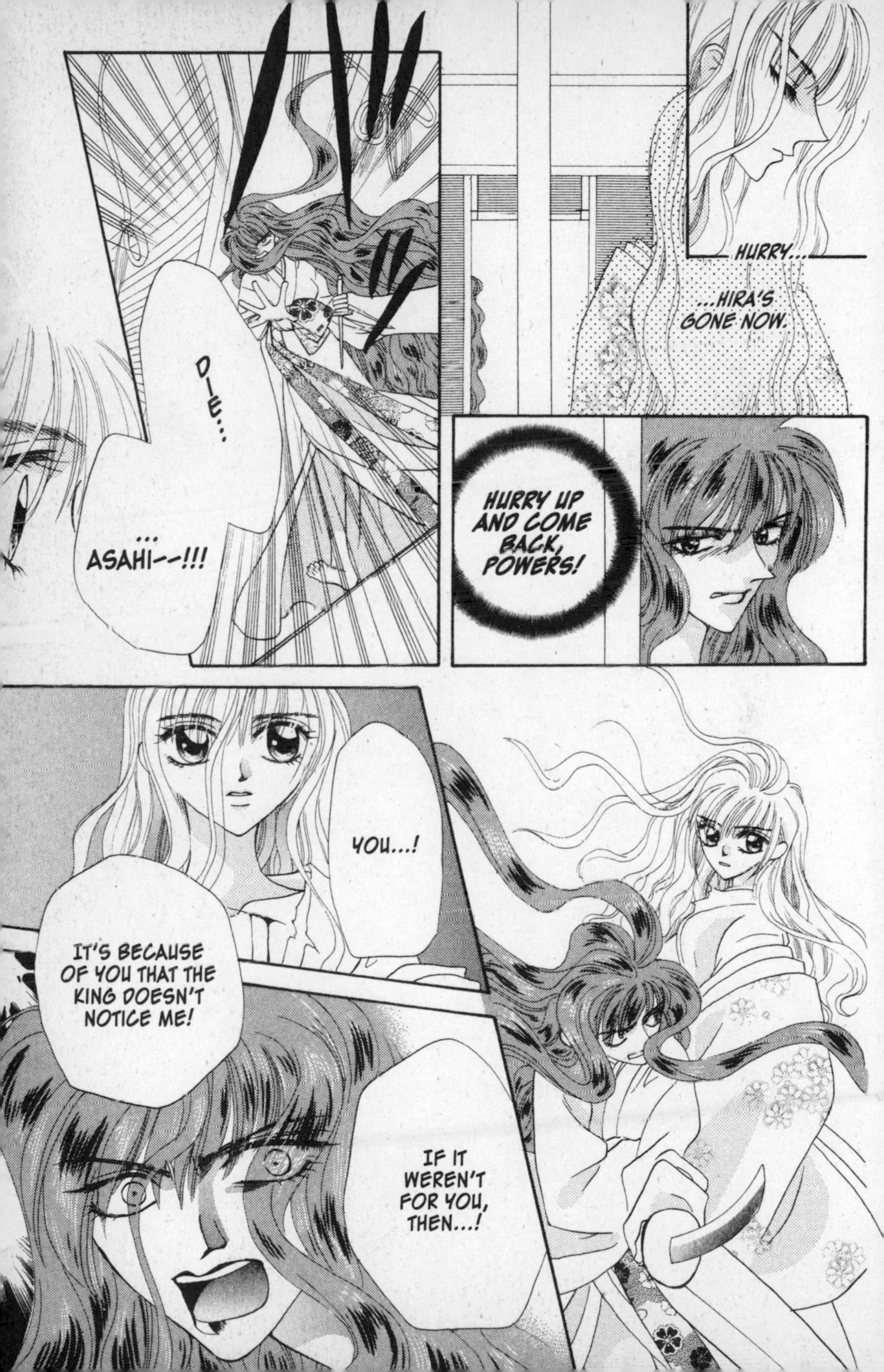
HURRY...
...HIRA'S GONE NOW.
HURRY UP AND COME BACK, POWERS!
DIE...
... ASAHI--!!!
YOU...!
IT'S BECAUSE OF YOU THAT THE KING DOESN'T NOTICE ME!
IF IT WEREN'T FOR YOU, THEN...!

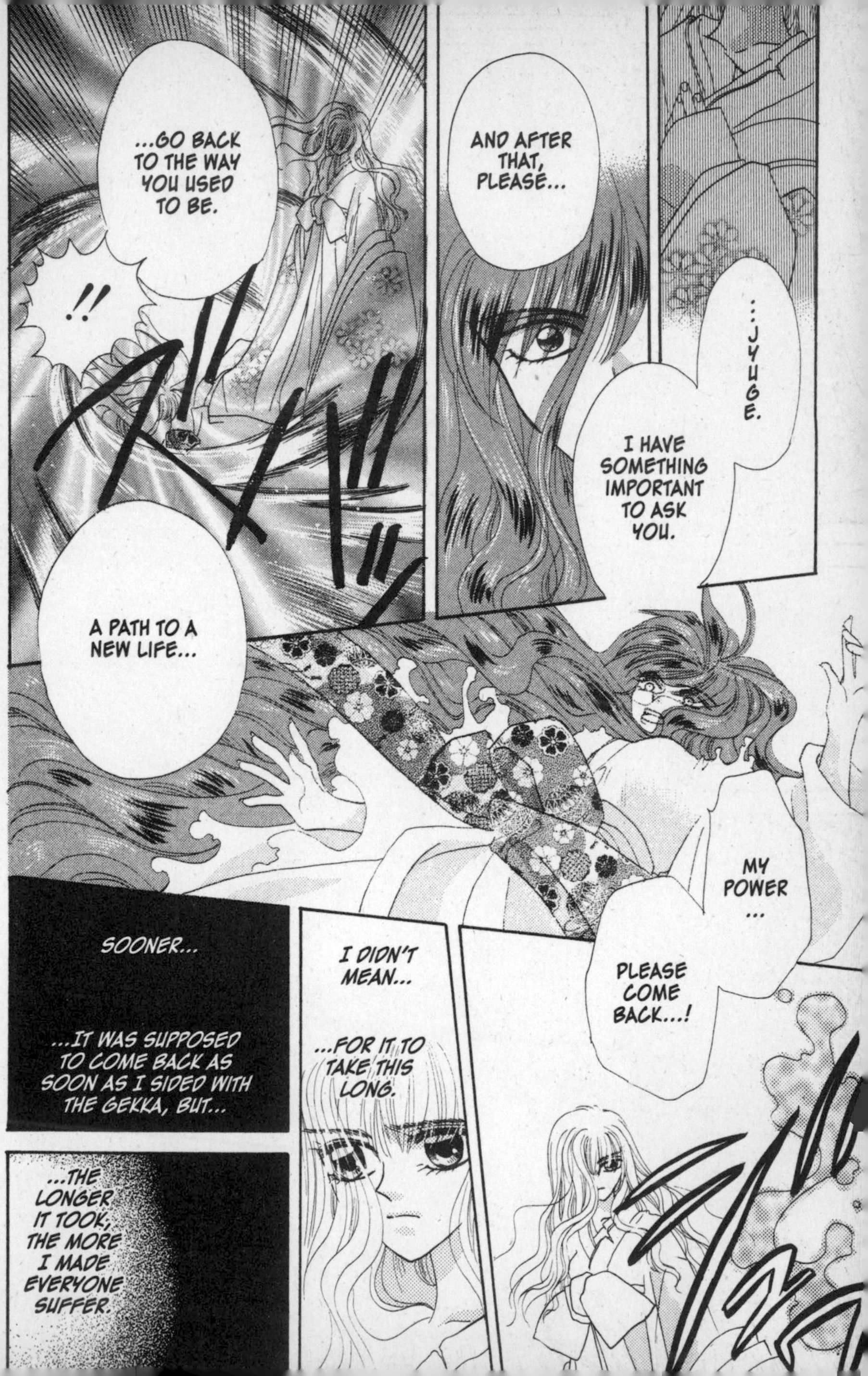

...JYUGE.
I HAVE SOMETHING IMPORTANT TO ASK YOU.
AND AFTER THAT, PLEASE...
...GO BACK TO THE WAY YOU USED TO BE.
!!
A PATH TO A NEW LIFE...
MY POWER...
PLEASE COME BACK...!
I DIDN'T MEAN...
...FOR IT TO TAKE THIS LONG.
SOONER...
...IT WAS SUPPOSED TO COME BACK AS SOON AS I SIDED WITH THE GEKKA, BUT...
...THE LONGER IT TOOK, THE MORE I MADE EVERYONE SUFFER.

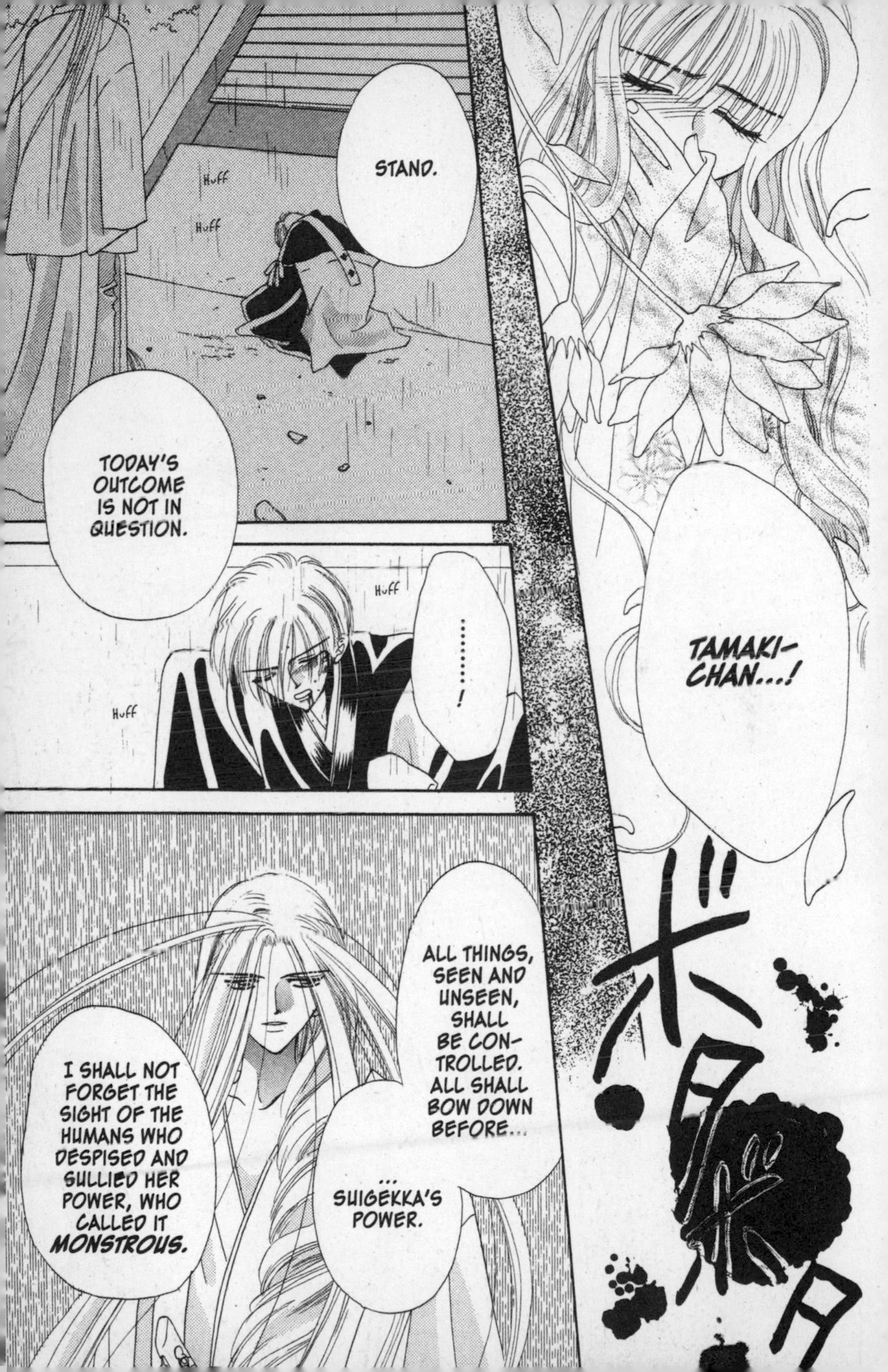
TAMAKI-CHAN...!
STAND.
Huff
Huff
TODAY'S OUTCOME IS NOT IN QUESTION.
Huff
......!
Huff
ALL THINGS, SEEN AND UNSEEN, SHALL BE CONTROLLED. ALL SHALL BOW DOWN BEFORE...
... SUIGEKKA'S POWER.
I SHALL NOT FORGET THE SIGHT OF THE HUMANS WHO DESPISED AND SULLIED HER POWER, WHO CALLED IT *MONSTROUS.*

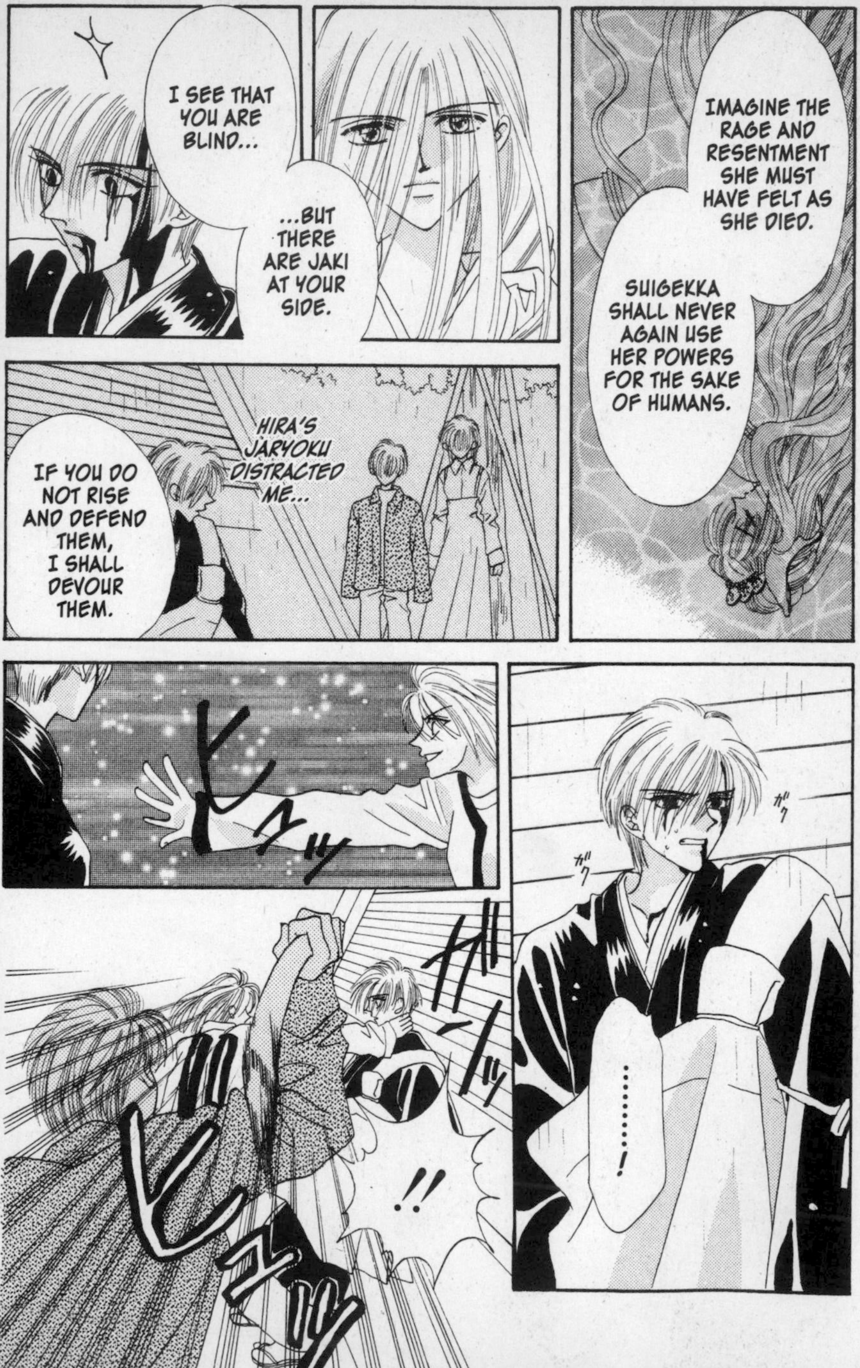
IMAGINE THE RAGE AND RESENTMENT SHE MUST HAVE FELT AS SHE DIED.
SUIGEKKA SHALL NEVER AGAIN USE HER POWERS FOR THE SAKE OF HUMANS.
I SEE THAT YOU ARE BLIND...
...BUT THERE ARE JAKI AT YOUR SIDE.
HIRA'S JARYOKU DISTRACTED ME...
IF YOU DO NOT RISE AND DEFEND THEM, I SHALL DEVOUR THEM.
ガク
ガク
......!
!!

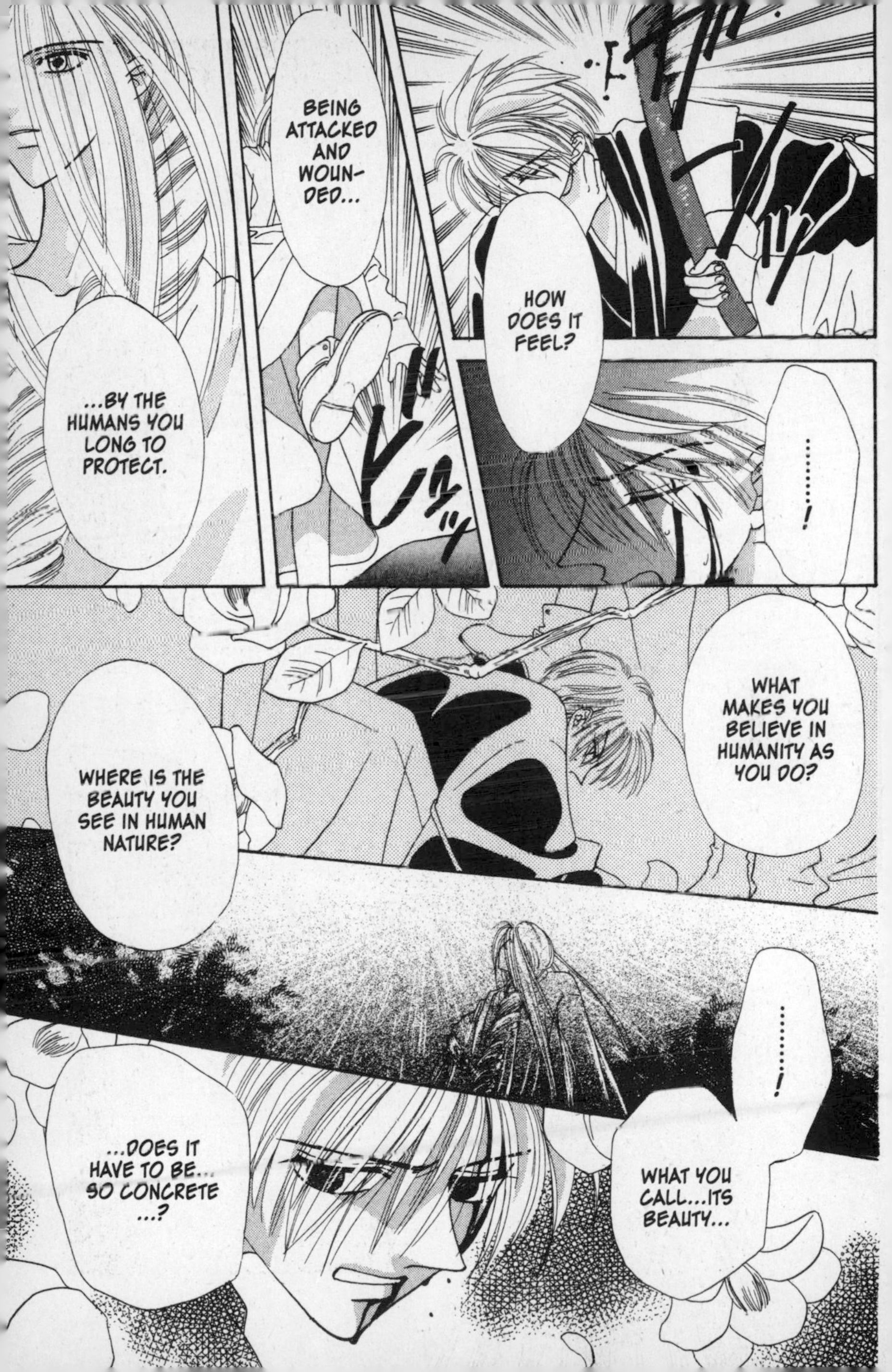
BEING ATTACKED AND WOUN-DED...
...BY THE HUMANS YOU LONG TO PROTECT.
HOW DOES IT FEEL?
......!
WHAT MAKES YOU BELIEVE IN HUMANITY AS YOU DO?
WHERE IS THE BEAUTY YOU SEE IN HUMAN NATURE?
......!
WHAT YOU CALL...ITS BEAUTY...
...DOES IT HAVE TO BE... SO CONCRETE ...?

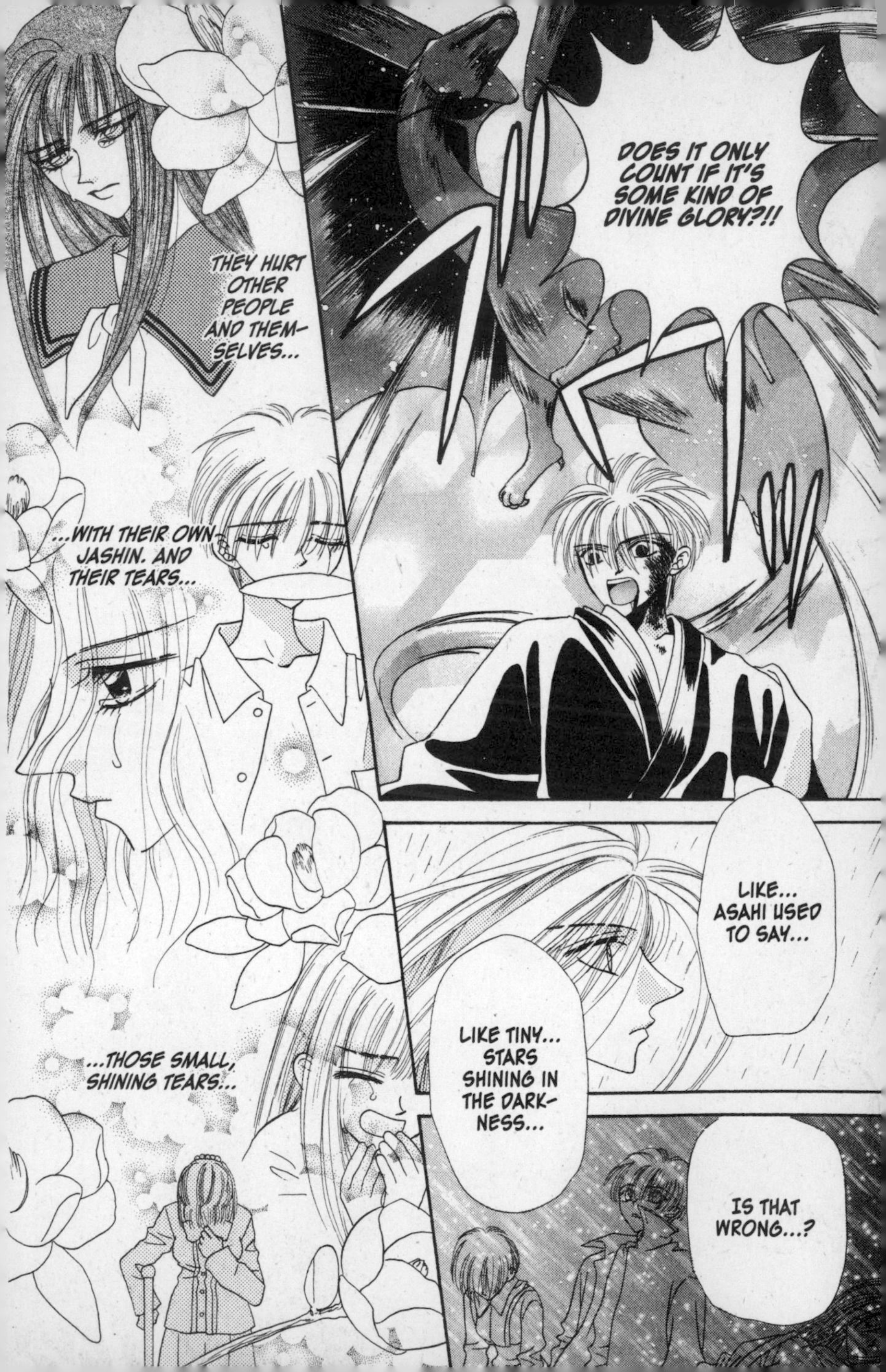
DOES IT ONLY COUNT IF IT'S SOME KIND OF DIVINE GLORY?!!
LIKE... ASAHI USED TO SAY...
LIKE TINY... STARS SHINING IN THE DARK-NESS...
IS THAT WRONG...?
THEY HURT OTHER PEOPLE AND THEM-SELVES...
...WITH THEIR OWN JASHIN. AND THEIR TEARS...
...THOSE SMALL, SHINING TEARS...

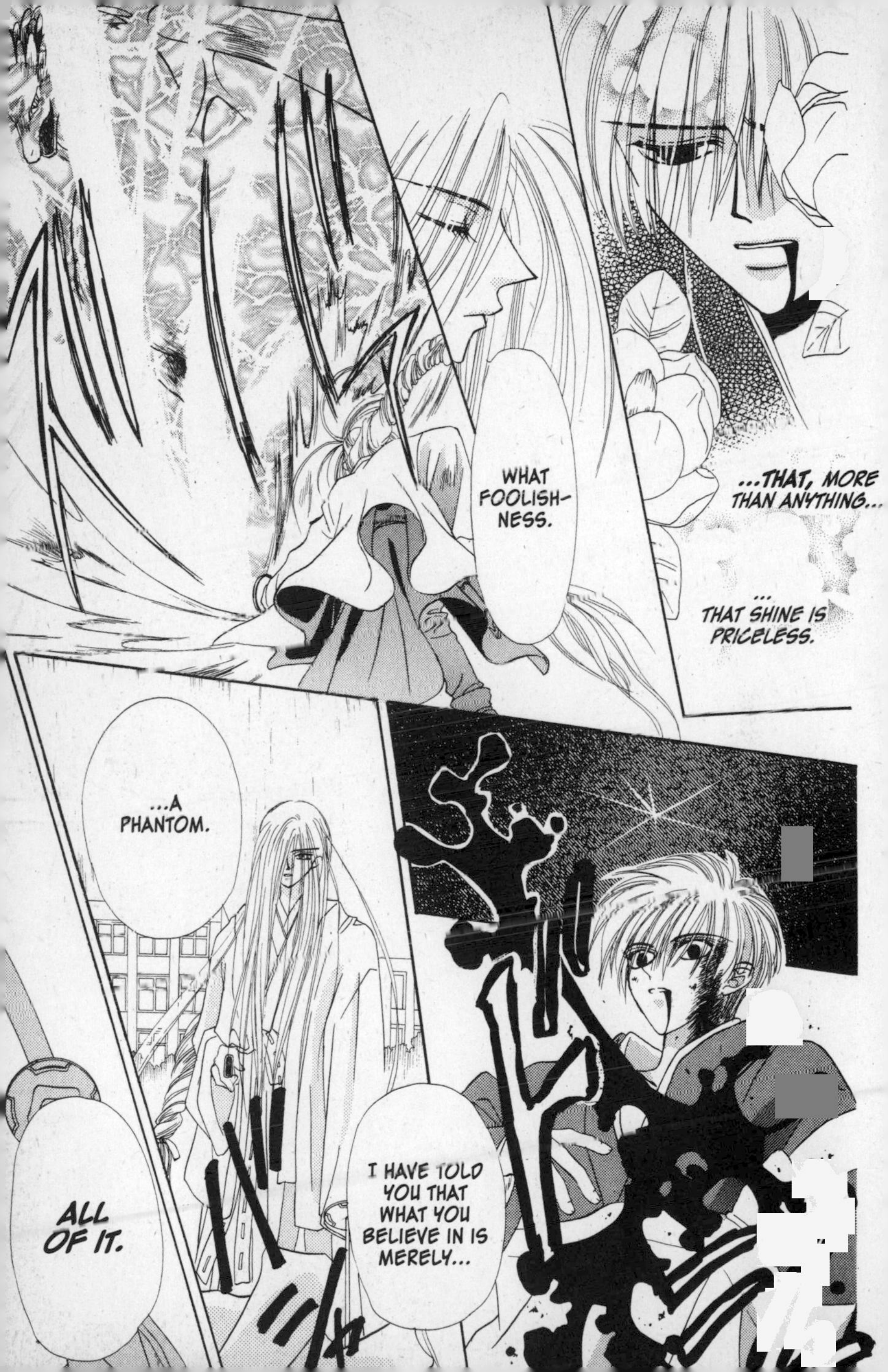
...THAT, MORE THAN ANYTHING...
... THAT SHINE IS PRICELESS.
WHAT FOOLISHNESS.
I HAVE TOLD YOU THAT WHAT YOU BELIEVE IN IS MERELY...
...A PHANTOM.
ALL OF IT.

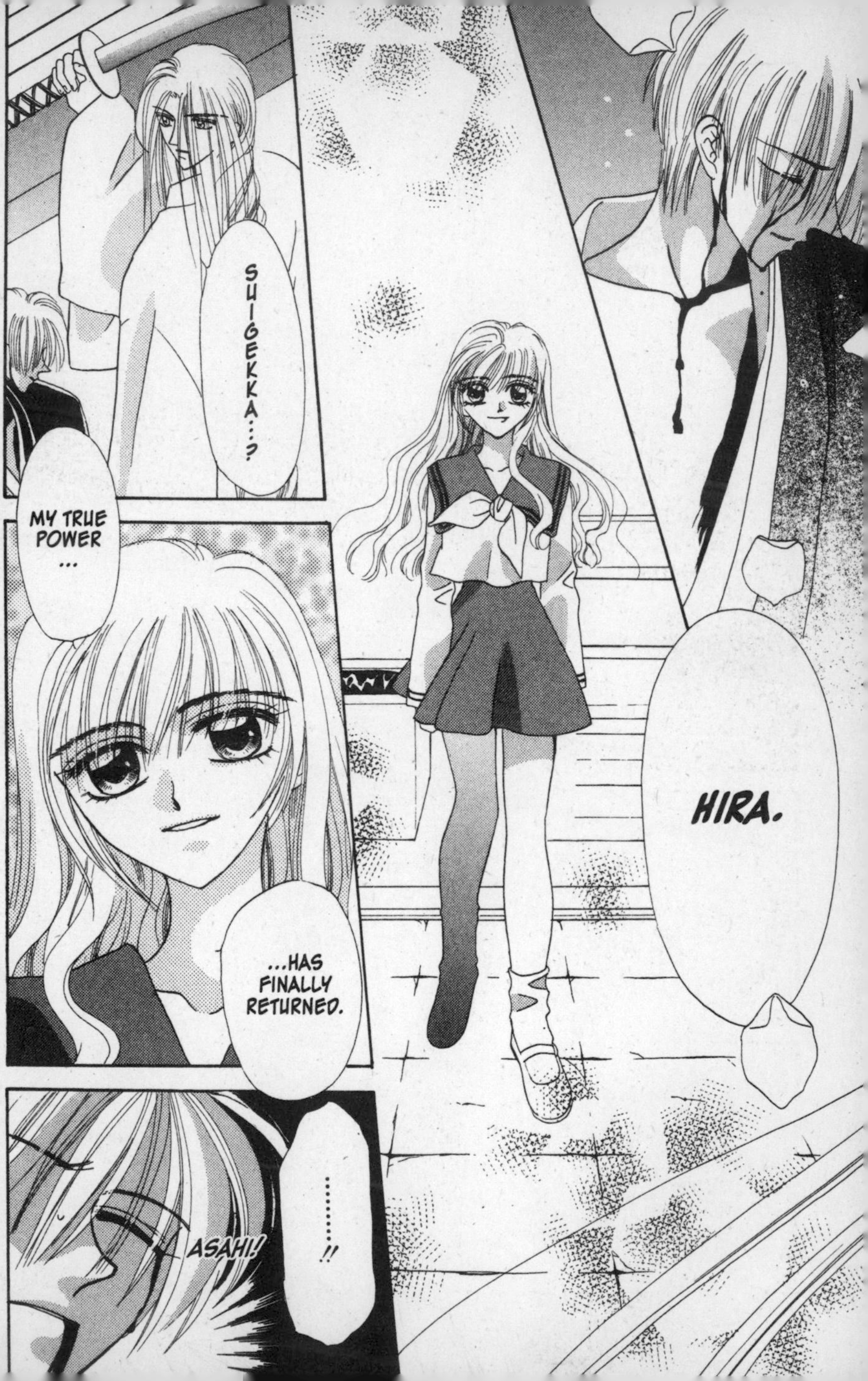
HIRA.
SUIGEKKA...?
MY TRUE POWER ...
...HAS FINALLY RETURNED.
......!!
ASAHI!

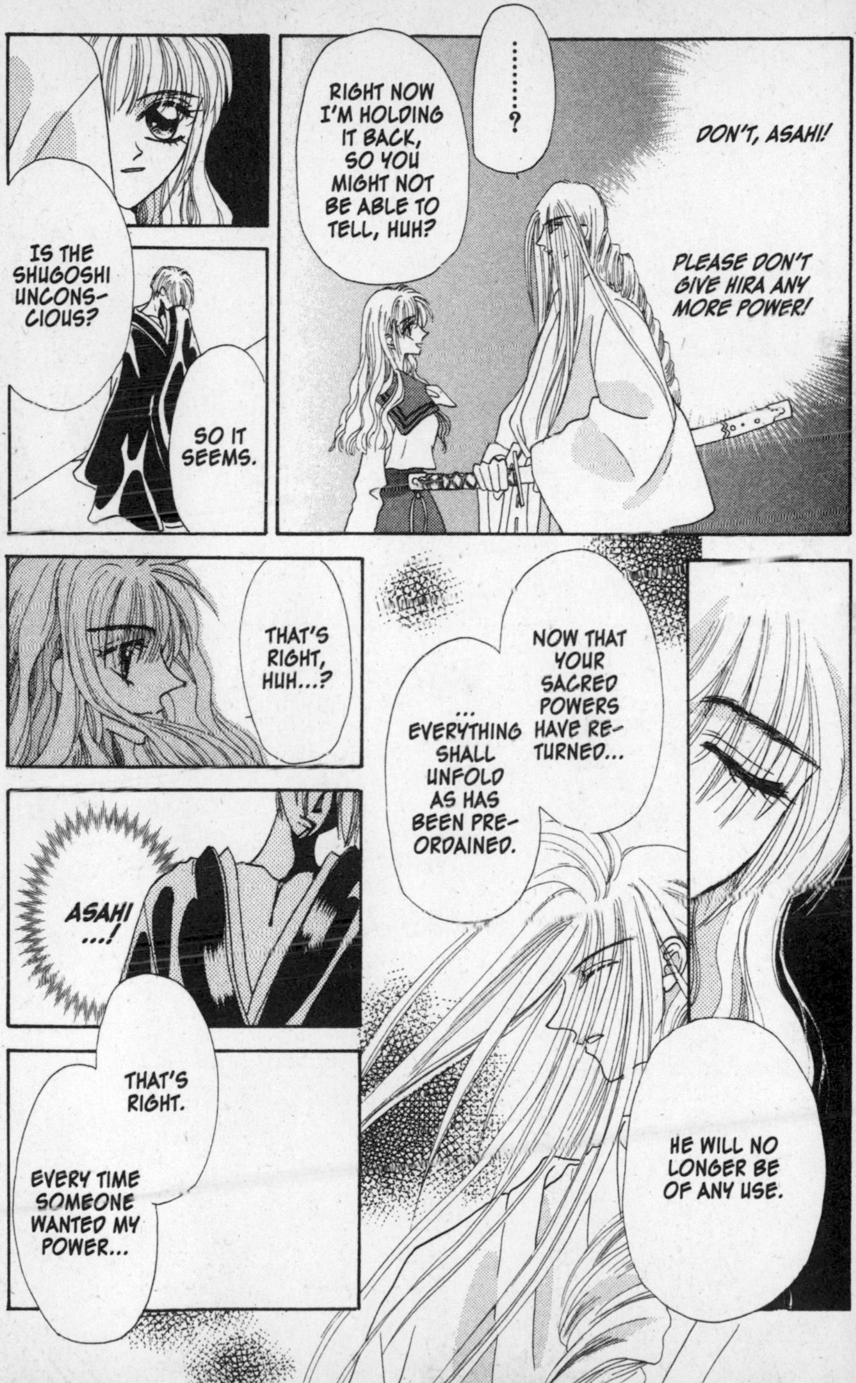
......?
DON'T, ASAHI!
RIGHT NOW I'M HOLDING IT BACK, SO YOU MIGHT NOT BE ABLE TO TELL, HUH?
PLEASE DON'T GIVE HIRA ANY MORE POWER!
IS THE SHUGOSHI UNCONSCIOUS?
SO IT SEEMS.
NOW THAT YOUR SACRED POWERS HAVE RETURNED...
...EVERYTHING SHALL UNFOLD AS HAS BEEN PREORDAINED.
HE WILL NO LONGER BE OF ANY USE.
THAT'S RIGHT, HUH...?
ASAHI ...!
THAT'S RIGHT.
EVERY TIME SOMEONE WANTED MY POWER...

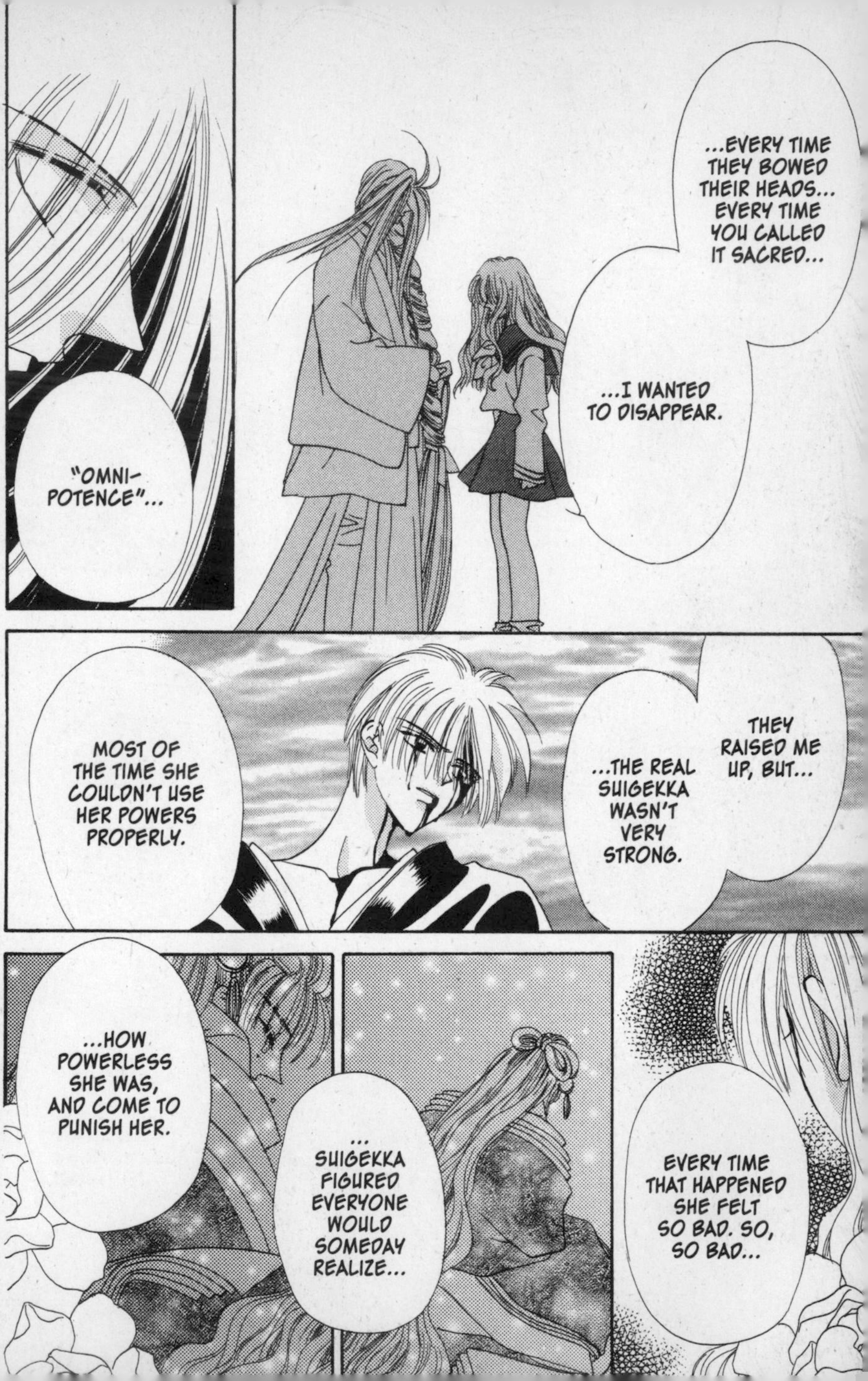
...EVERY TIME THEY BOWED THEIR HEADS... EVERY TIME YOU CALLED IT SACRED...
...I WANTED TO DISAPPEAR.
"OMNI-POTENCE"...
THEY RAISED ME UP, BUT...
...THE REAL SUIGEKKA WASN'T VERY STRONG.
MOST OF THE TIME SHE COULDN'T USE HER POWERS PROPERLY.
EVERY TIME THAT HAPPENED SHE FELT SO BAD. SO, SO BAD...
...SUIGEKKA FIGURED EVERYONE WOULD SOMEDAY REALIZE...
...HOW POWERLESS SHE WAS, AND COME TO PUNISH HER.

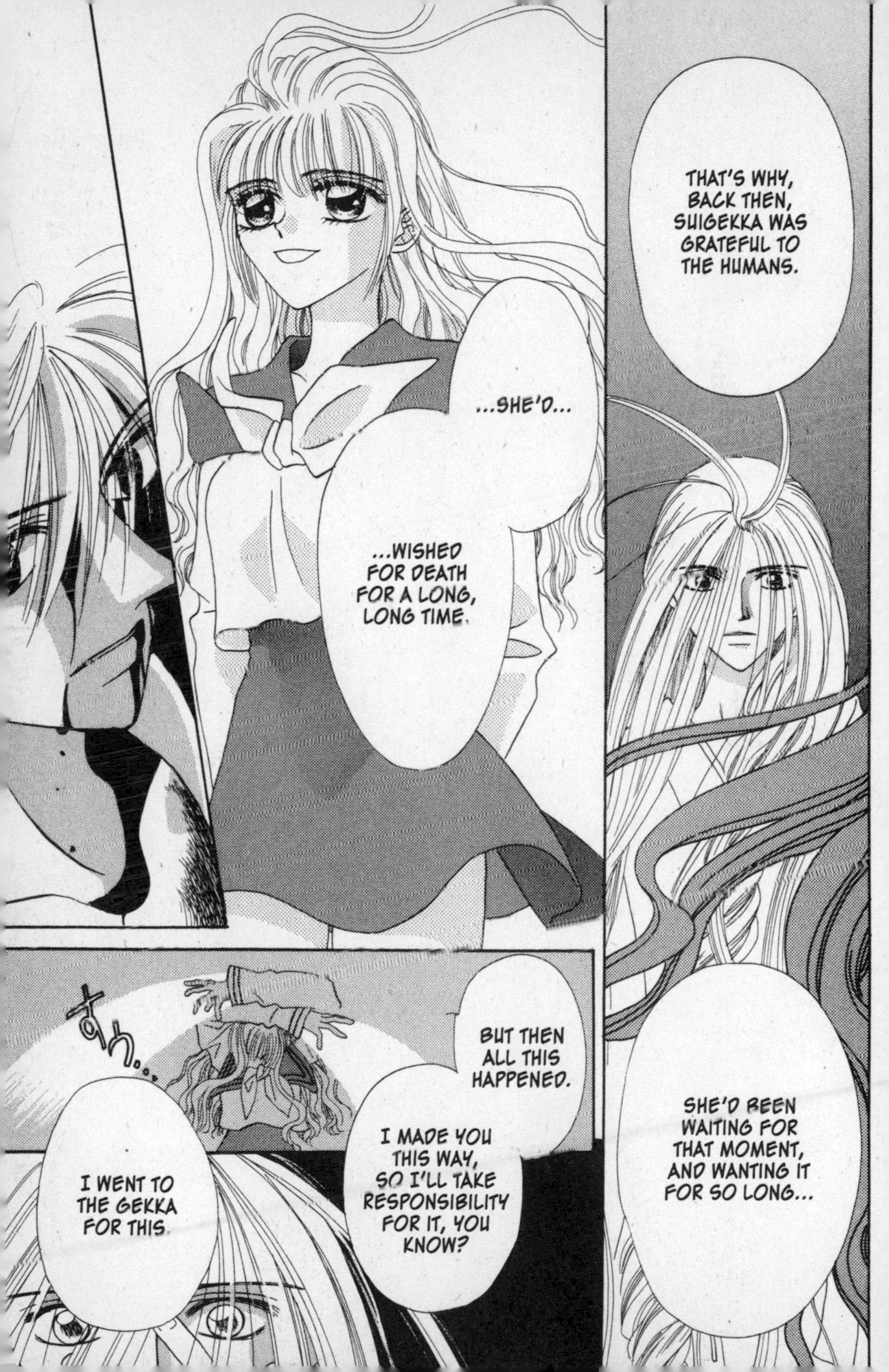
THAT'S WHY, BACK THEN, SUIGEKKA WAS GRATEFUL TO THE HUMANS.
SHE'D BEEN WAITING FOR THAT MOMENT, AND WANTING IT FOR SO LONG...
...SHE'D...
...WISHED FOR DEATH FOR A LONG, LONG TIME.
すん...
BUT THEN ALL THIS HAPPENED.
I MADE YOU THIS WAY, SO I'LL TAKE RESPONSIBILITY FOR IT, YOU KNOW?
I WENT TO THE GEKKA FOR THIS.

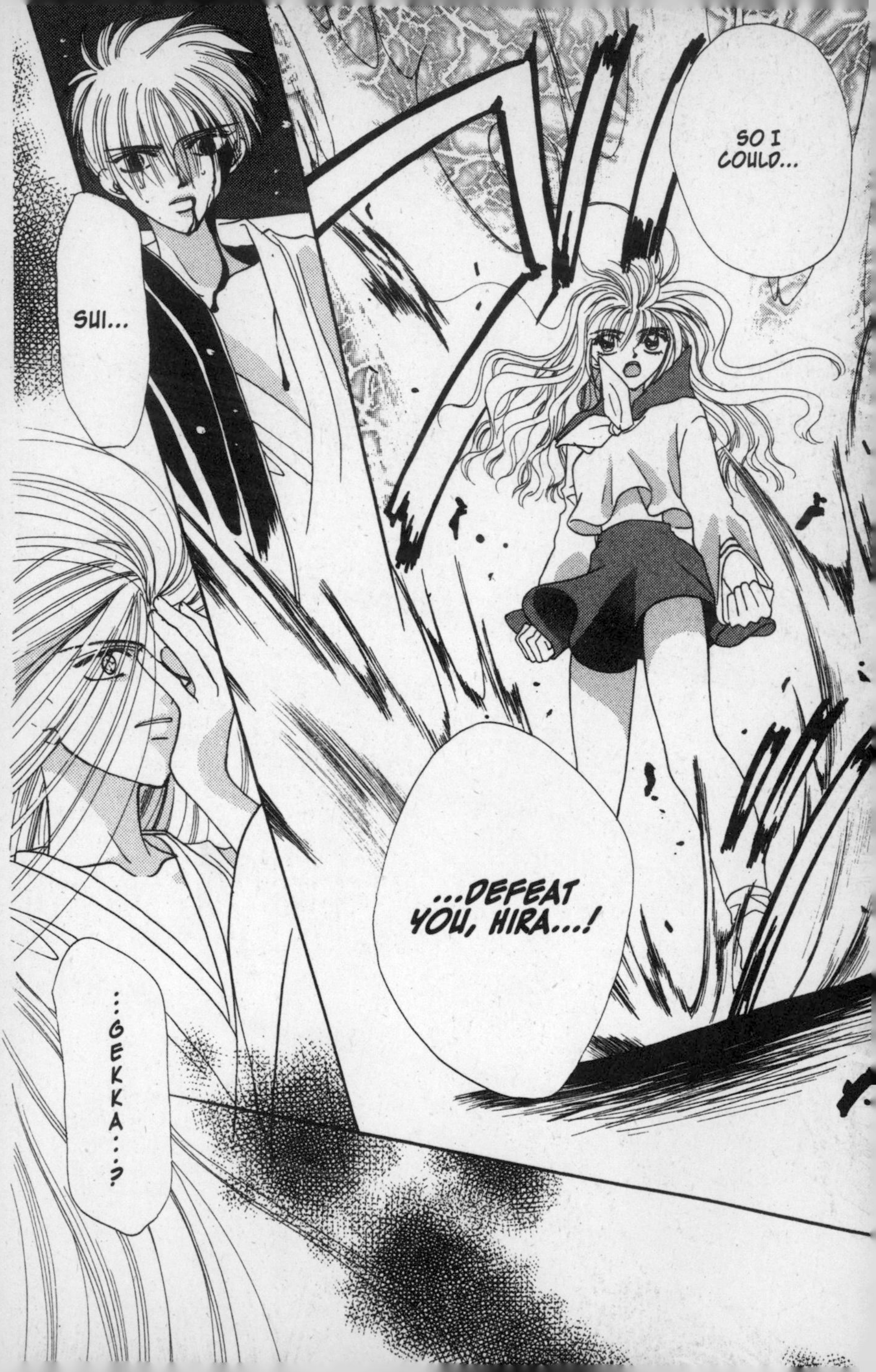
SO I COULD...
...DEFEAT YOU, HIRA...!
SUI...
...GEKKA...?

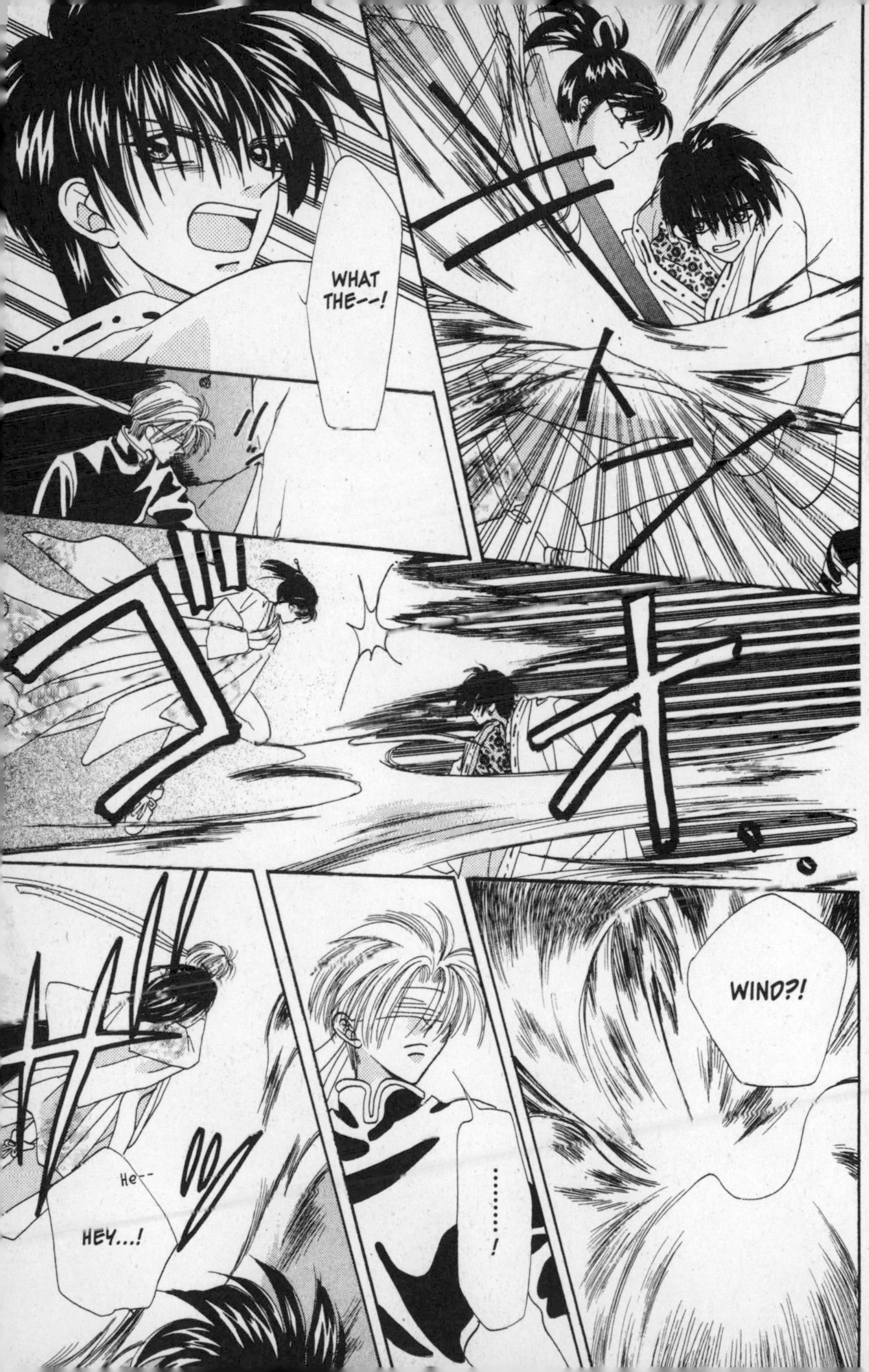
WHAT THE--!
WIND?!
......!
He--
HEY...!

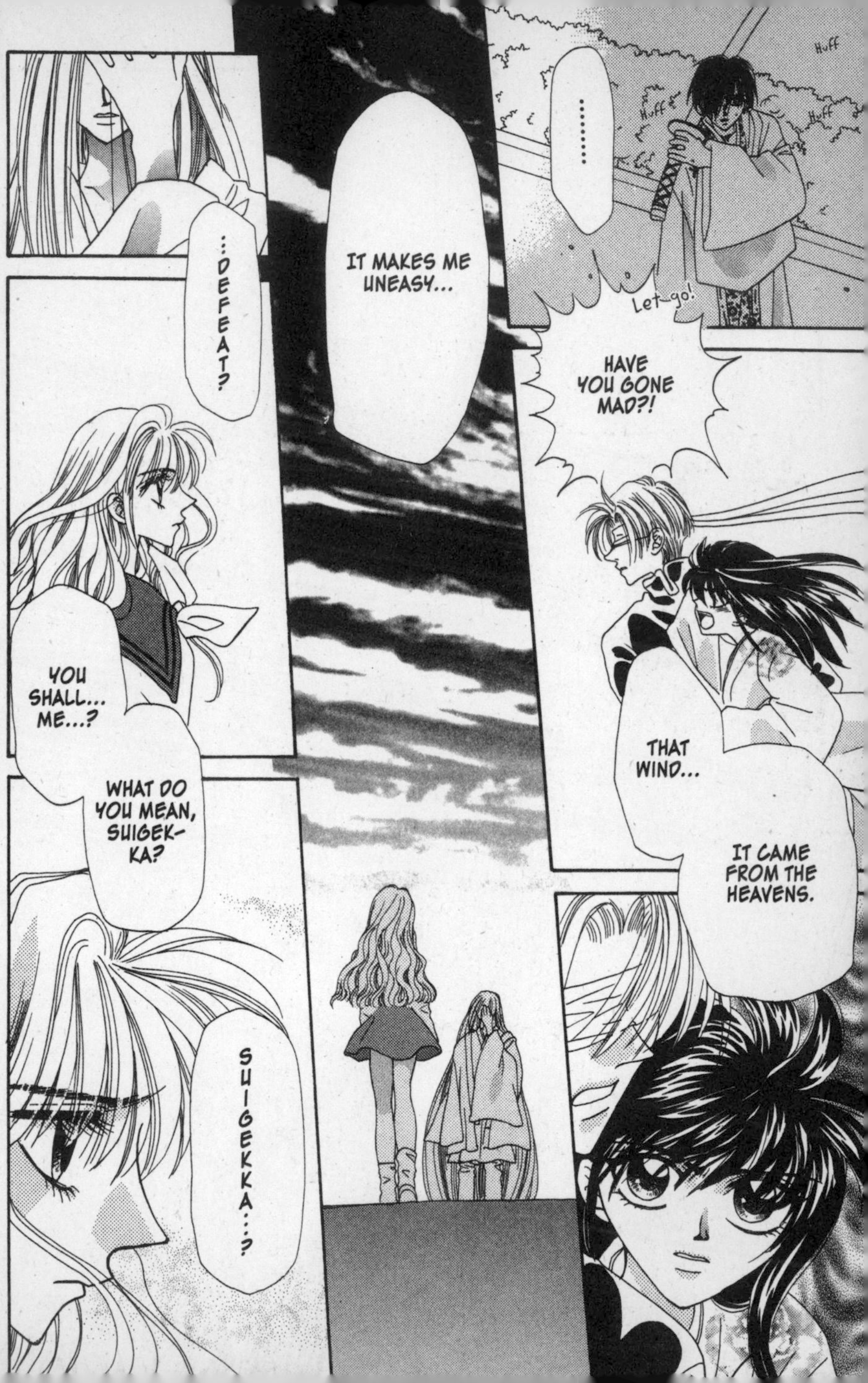
......
Huff
Huff
Huff
Let go!
HAVE YOU GONE MAD?!
THAT WIND...
IT CAME FROM THE HEAVENS.
IT MAKES ME UNEASY...
...DEFEAT?
YOU SHALL... ME...?
WHAT DO YOU MEAN, SUIGEK-KA?
SUIGEKKA...?

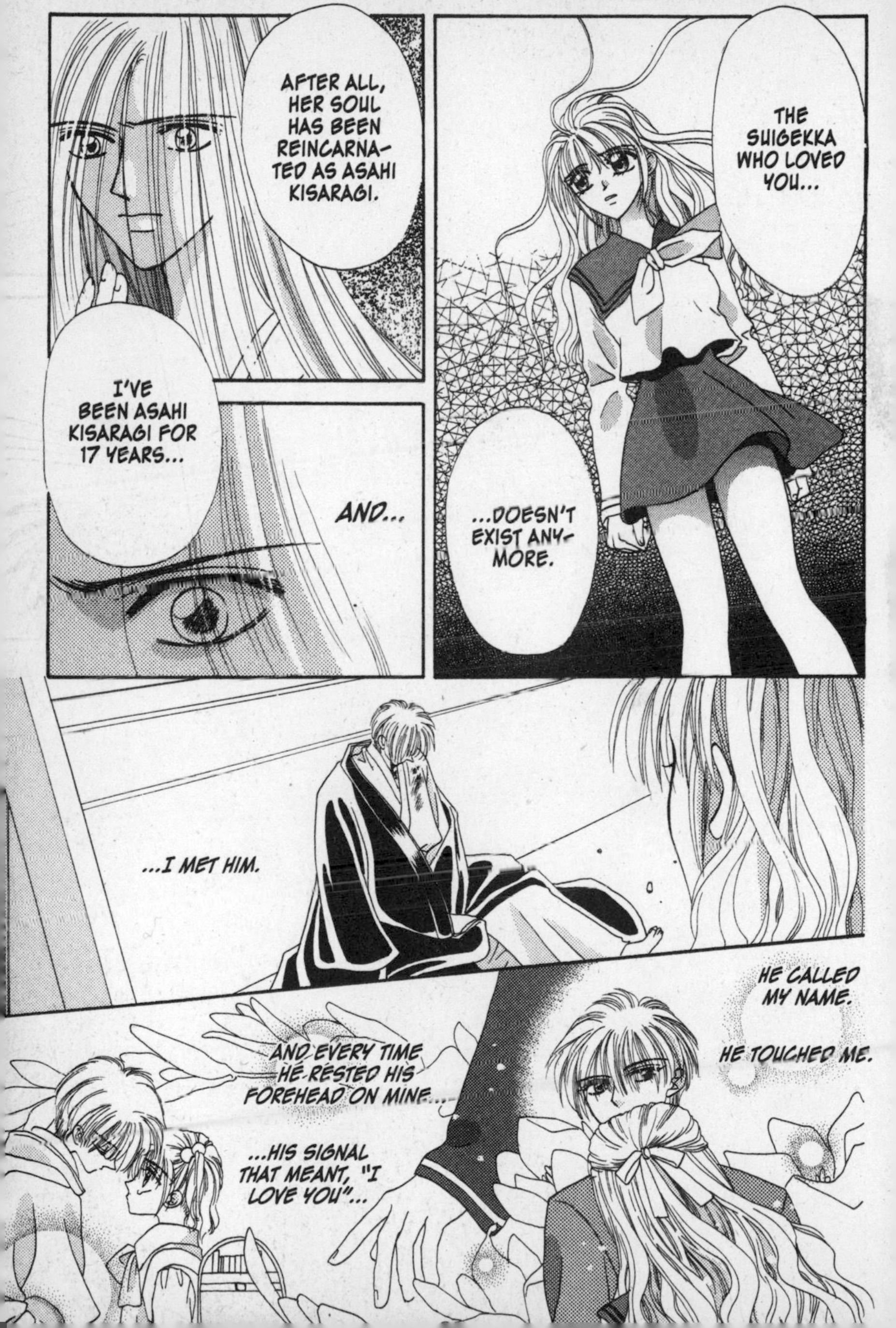
THE SUIGEKKA WHO LOVED YOU...
...DOESN'T EXIST ANYMORE.
AFTER ALL, HER SOUL HAS BEEN REINCARNATED AS ASAHI KISARAGI.
I'VE BEEN ASAHI KISARAGI FOR 17 YEARS...
AND...
...I MET HIM.
HE CALLED MY NAME.
HE TOUCHED ME.
AND EVERY TIME HE RESTED HIS FOREHEAD ON MINE...
...HIS SIGNAL THAT MEANT, "I LOVE YOU"...

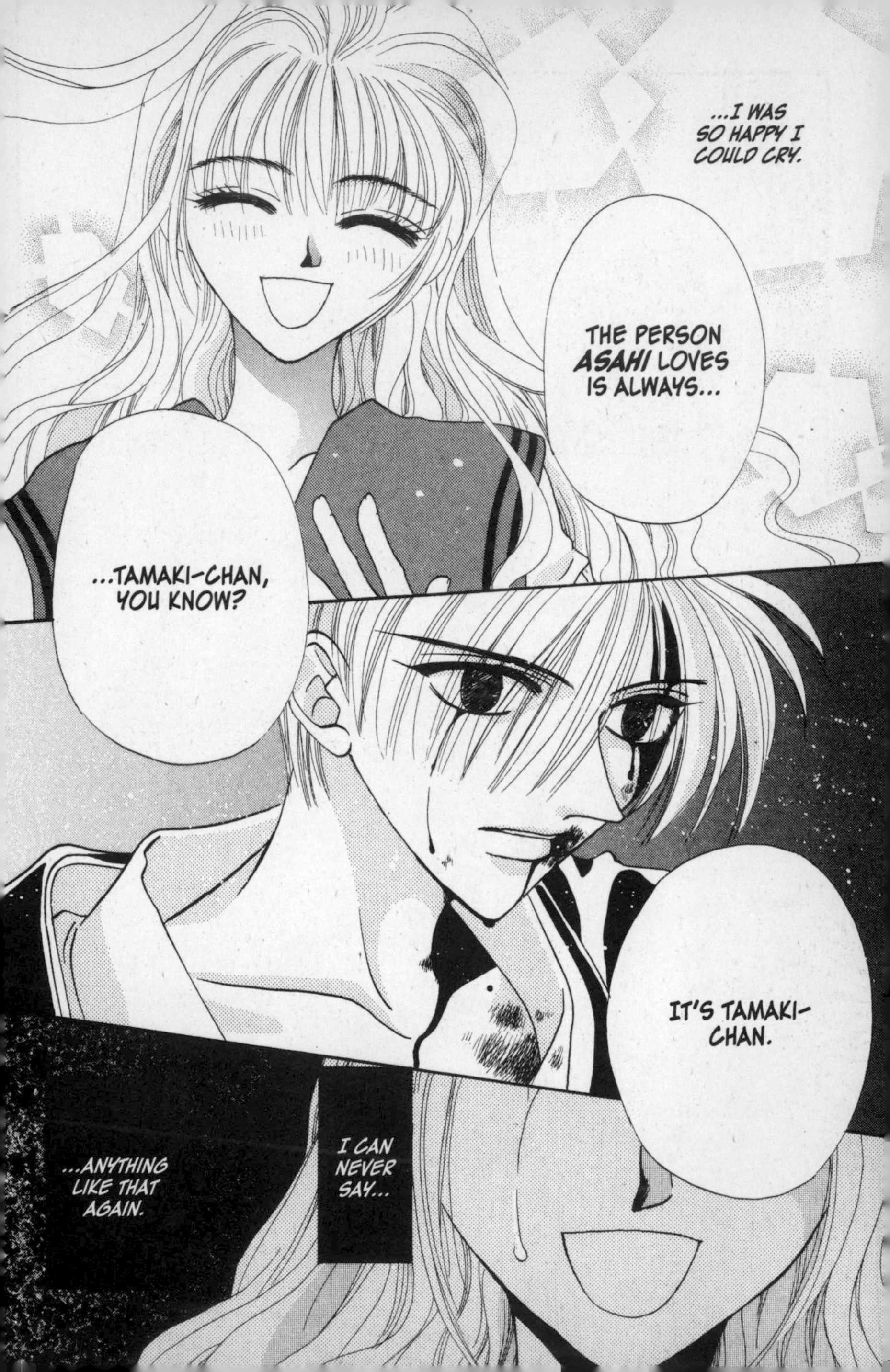
...I WAS SO HAPPY I COULD CRY.
THE PERSON ASAHI LOVES IS ALWAYS...
...TAMAKI-CHAN, YOU KNOW?
IT'S TAMAKI-CHAN.
I CAN NEVER SAY...
...ANYTHING LIKE THAT AGAIN.

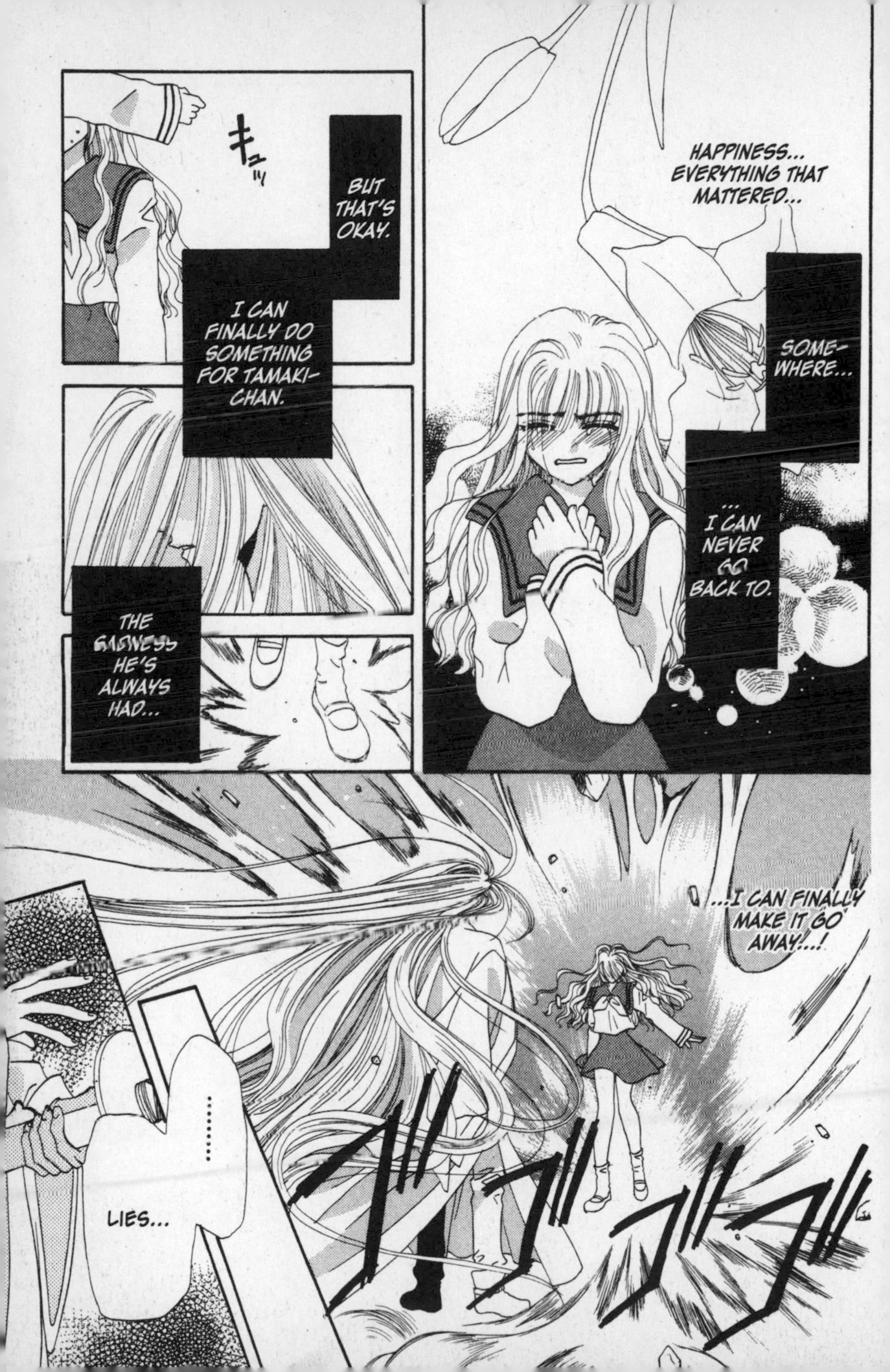
HAPPINESS... EVERYTHING THAT MATTERED...
SOME-WHERE...
... I CAN NEVER GO BACK TO.
キュッ
BUT THAT'S OKAY.
I CAN FINALLY DO SOMETHING FOR TAMAKI-CHAN.
THE SADNESS HE'S ALWAYS HAD...
...I CAN FINALLY MAKE IT GO AWAY...!
......
LIES...

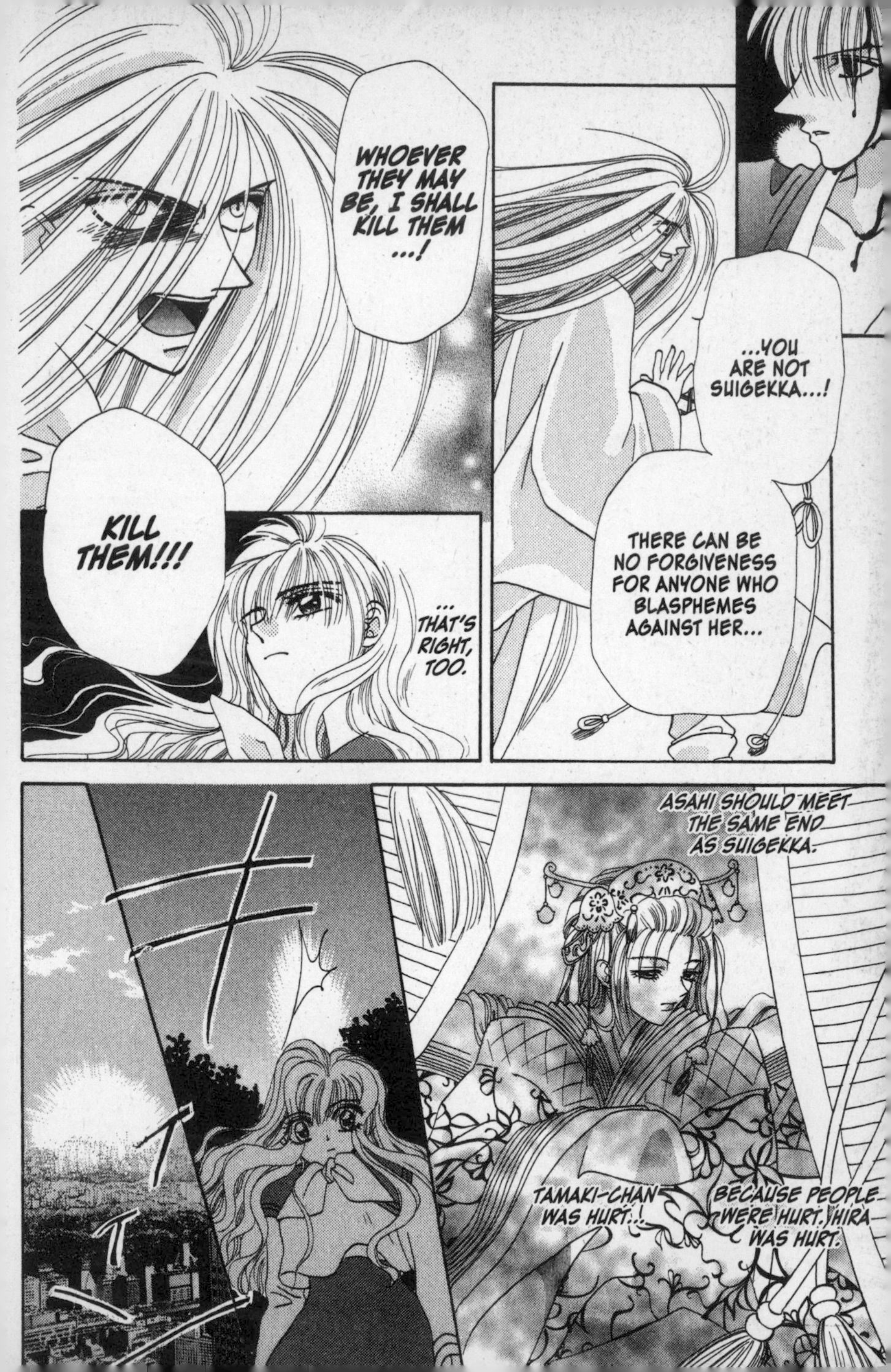
...YOU ARE NOT SUIGEKKA...!
THERE CAN BE NO FORGIVENESS FOR ANYONE WHO BLASPHEMES AGAINST HER...
WHOEVER THEY MAY BE, I SHALL KILL THEM ...!
KILL THEM!!!
... THAT'S RIGHT, TOO.
ASAHI SHOULD MEET THE SAME END AS SUIGEKKA.
BECAUSE PEOPLE WERE HURT, HIRA WAS HURT.
TAMAKI-CHAN WAS HURT...!

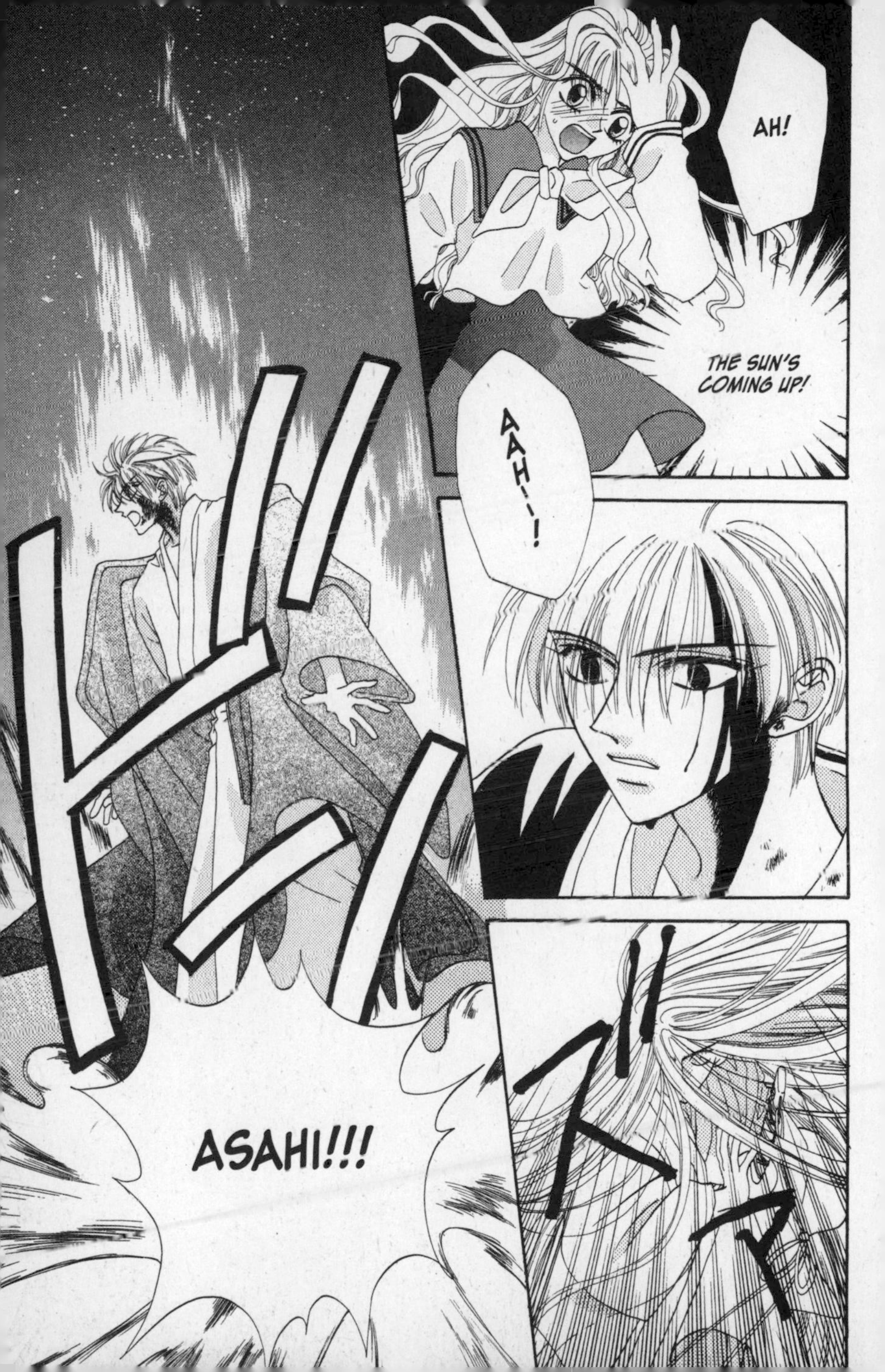

AH!
THE SUN'S COMING UP!
AAH...!
ASAHI!!!

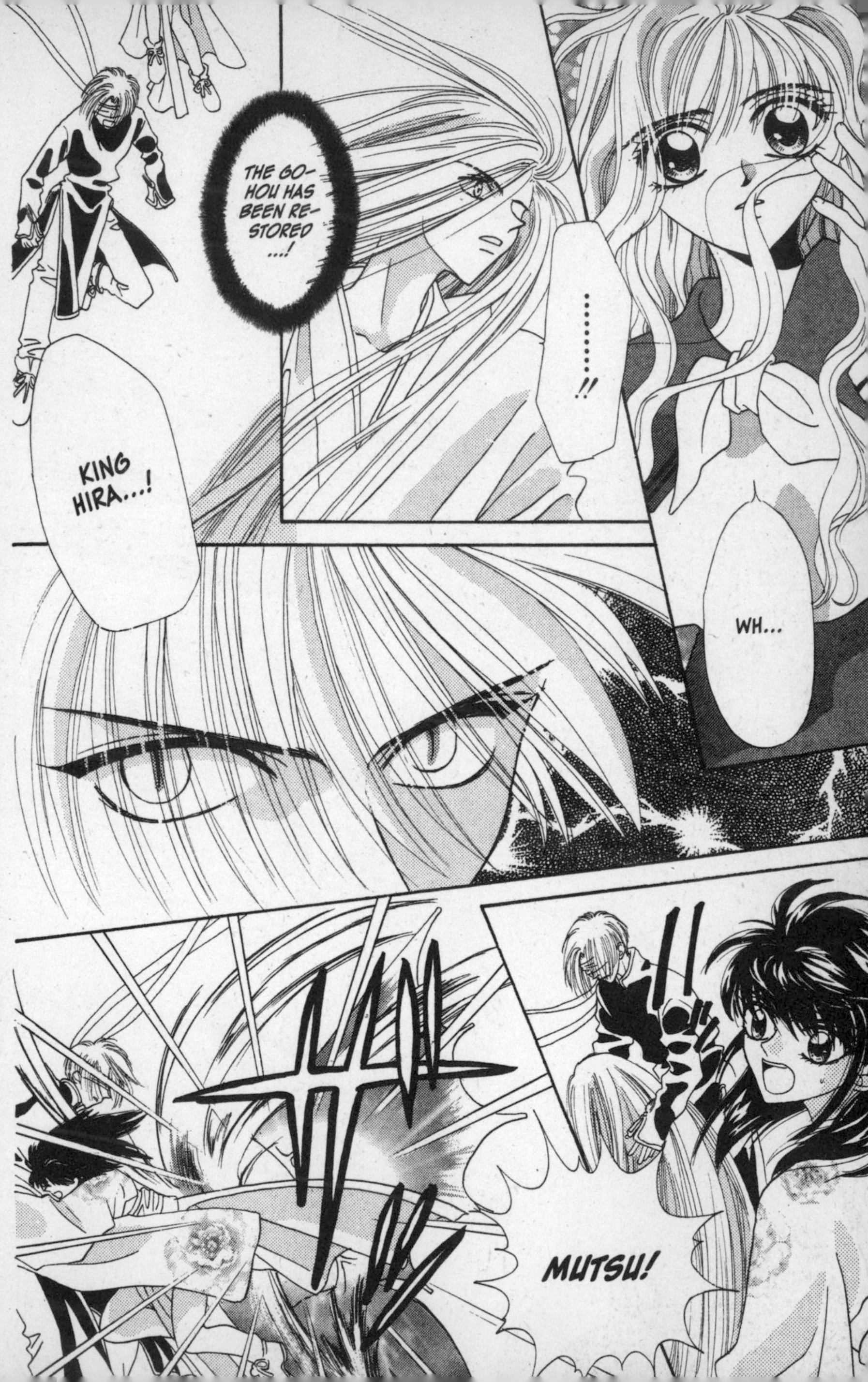
......!!
THE GO-HOU HAS BEEN RE-STORED ...!
KING HIRA...!
WH...
MUTSU!

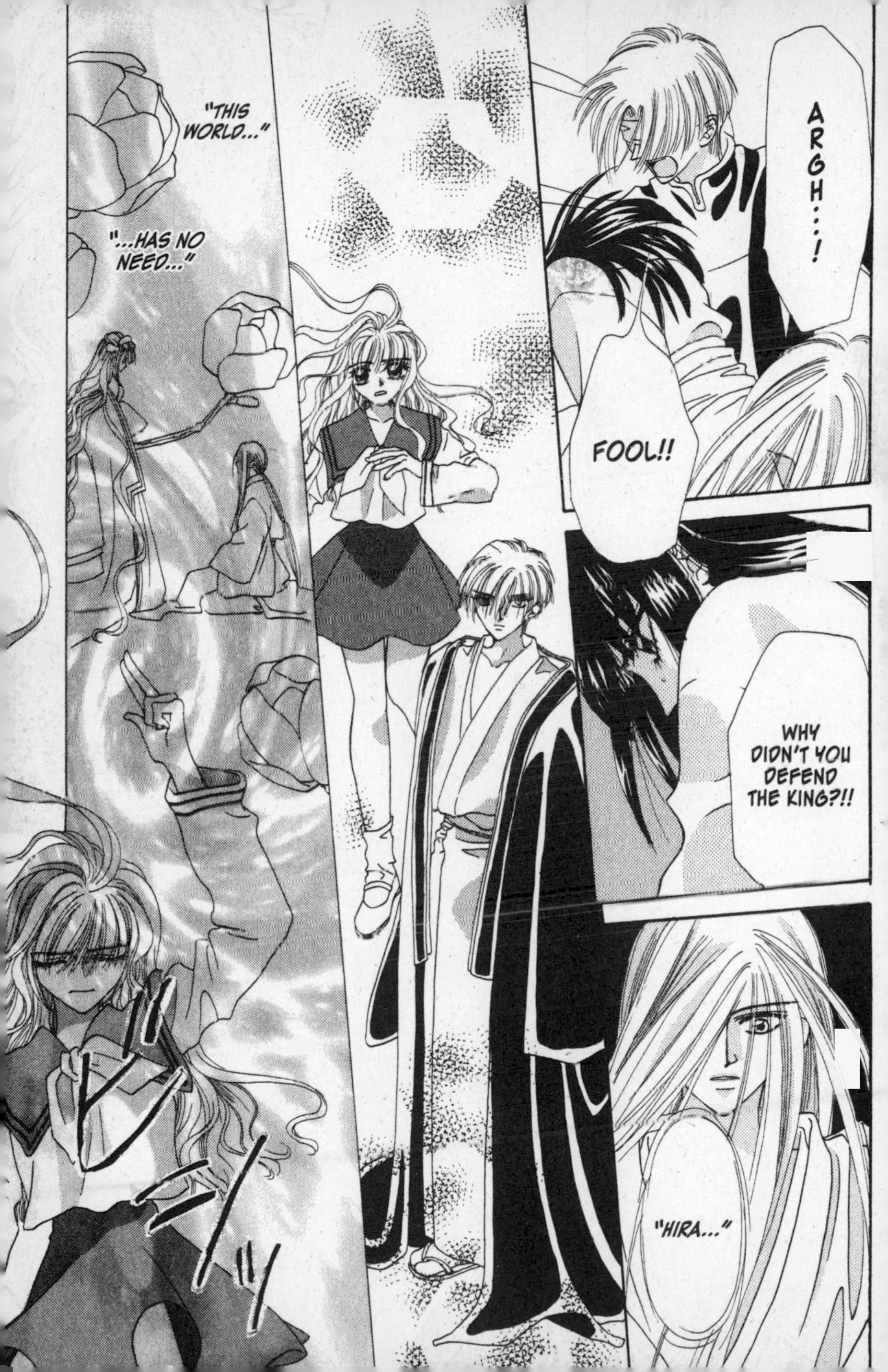
ARGH...!
FOOL!!
WHY DIDN'T YOU DEFEND THE KING?!!
"HIRA..."
"THIS WORLD..."
"...HAS NO NEED..."

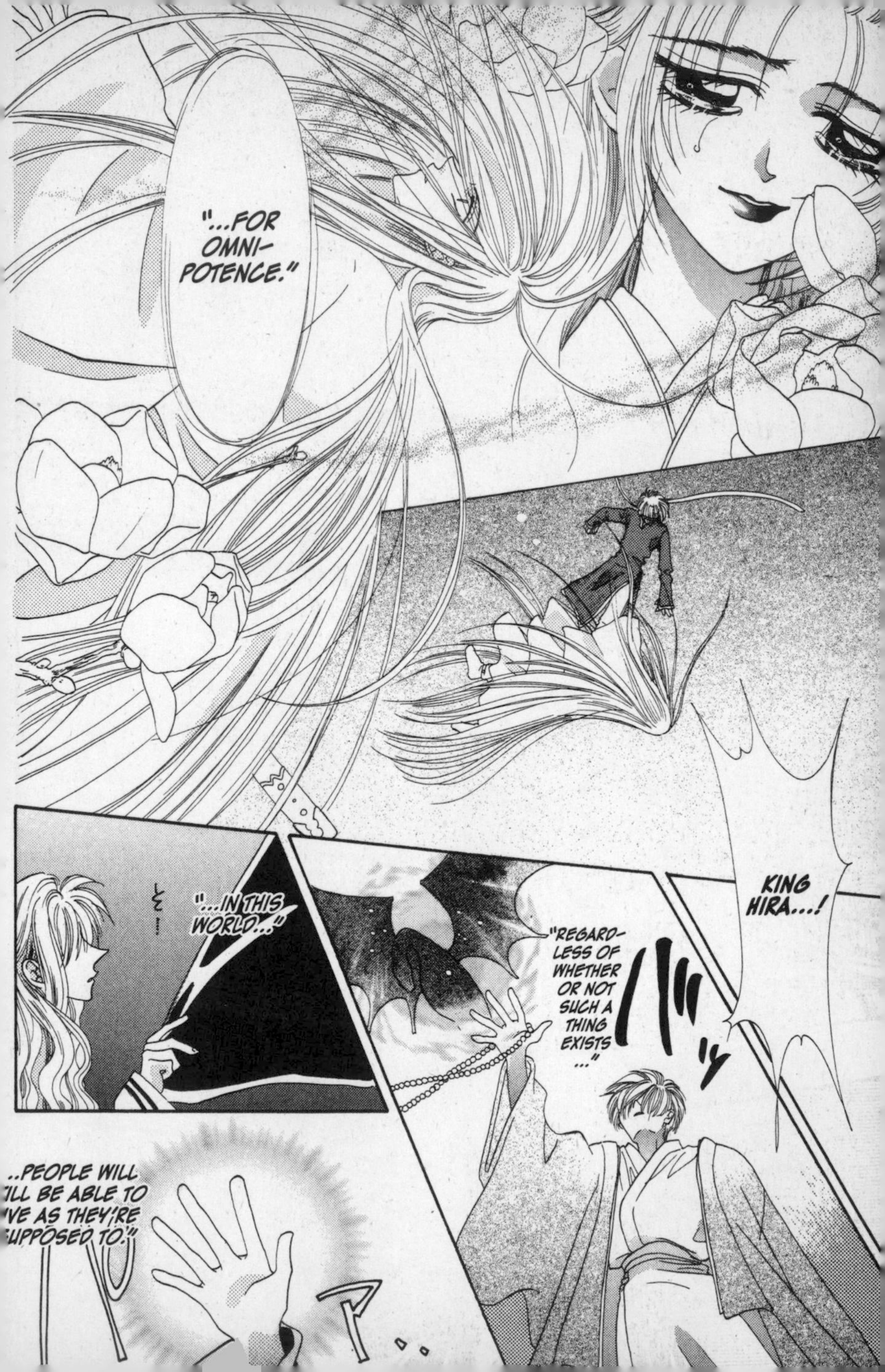
"...FOR OMNI-POTENCE."
KING HIRA...!
"REGARDLESS OF WHETHER OR NOT SUCH A THING EXISTS..."
"...IN THIS WORLD..."
...PEOPLE WILL
ILL BE ABLE TO
VE AS THEY'RE
UPPOSED TO."

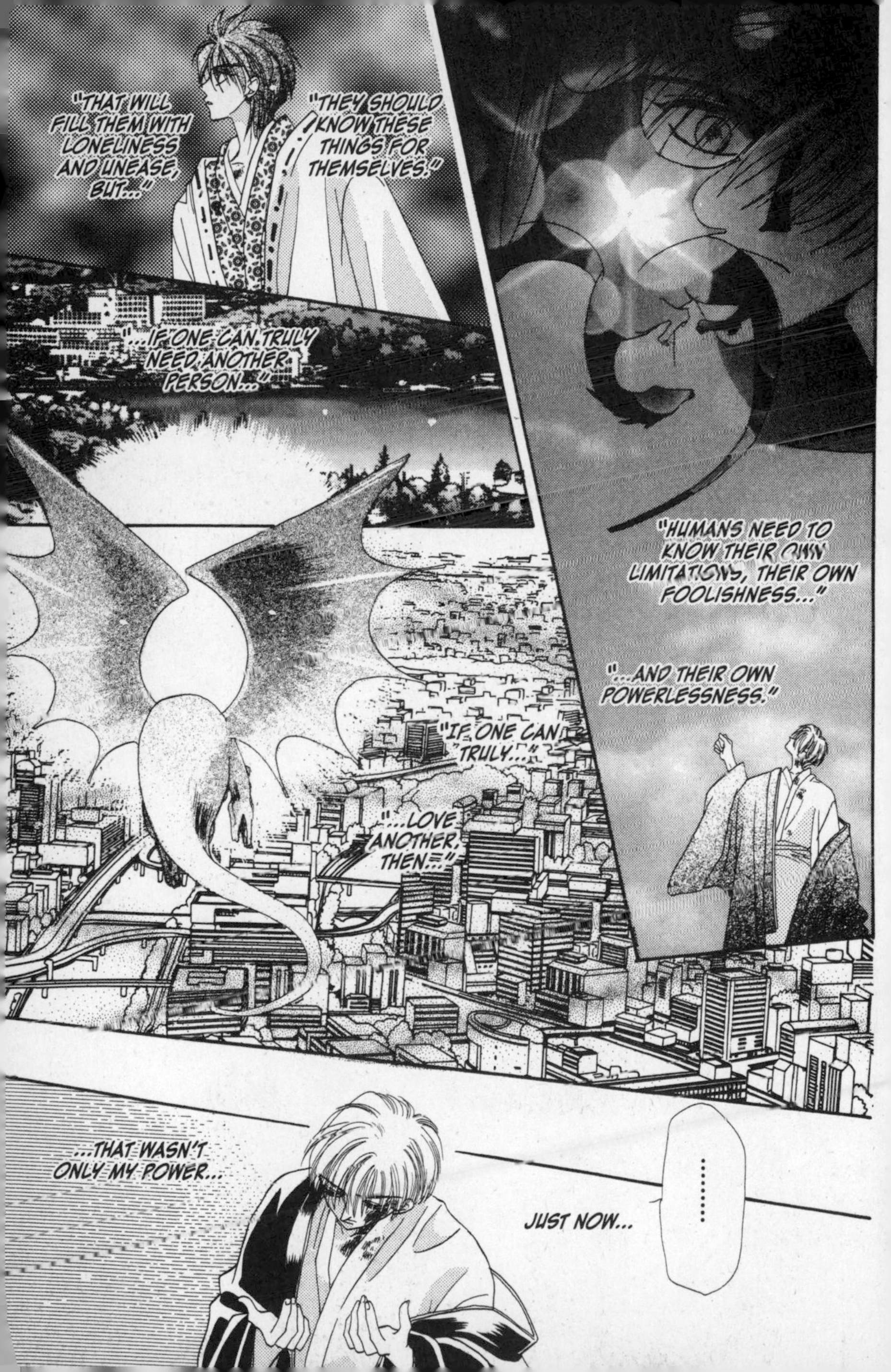
"HUMANS NEED TO KNOW THEIR OWN LIMITATIONS, THEIR OWN FOOLISHNESS..."
"...AND THEIR OWN POWERLESSNESS."
"THEY SHOULD KNOW THESE THINGS FOR THEMSELVES."
"THAT WILL FILL THEM WITH LONELINESS AND UNEASE, BUT..."
"...IF ONE CAN TRULY NEED ANOTHER PERSON..."
"IF ONE CAN TRULY..."
"...LOVE ANOTHER, THEN..."
......
JUST NOW...
...THAT WASN'T ONLY MY POWER...

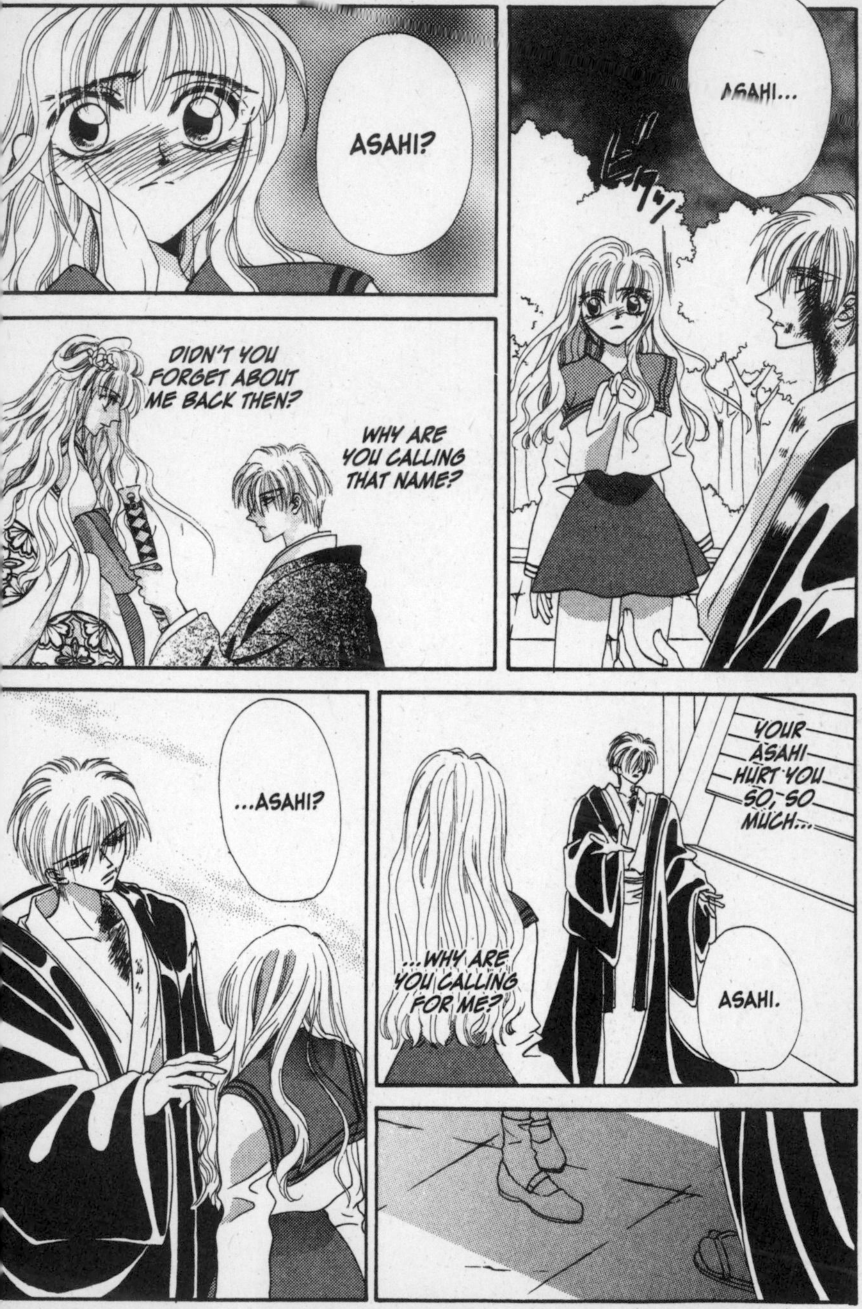
ASAHI...
ASAHI?
DIDN'T YOU FORGET ABOUT ME BACK THEN?
WHY ARE YOU CALLING THAT NAME?
YOUR ASAHI HURT YOU SO, SO MUCH...
ASAHI.
...WHY ARE YOU CALLING FOR ME?
...ASAHI?

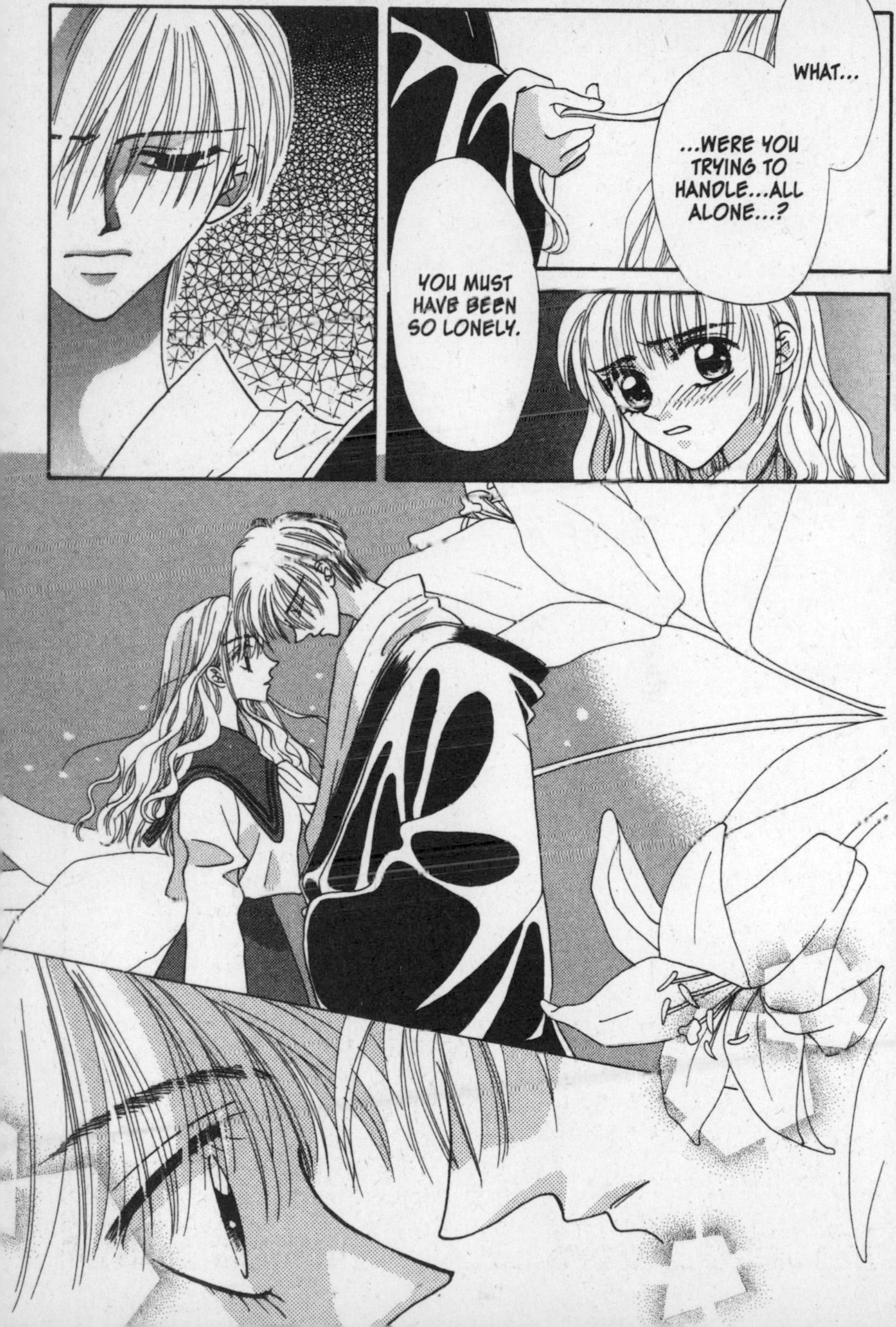
WHAT...
...WERE YOU TRYING TO HANDLE...ALL ALONE...?
YOU MUST HAVE BEEN SO LONELY.

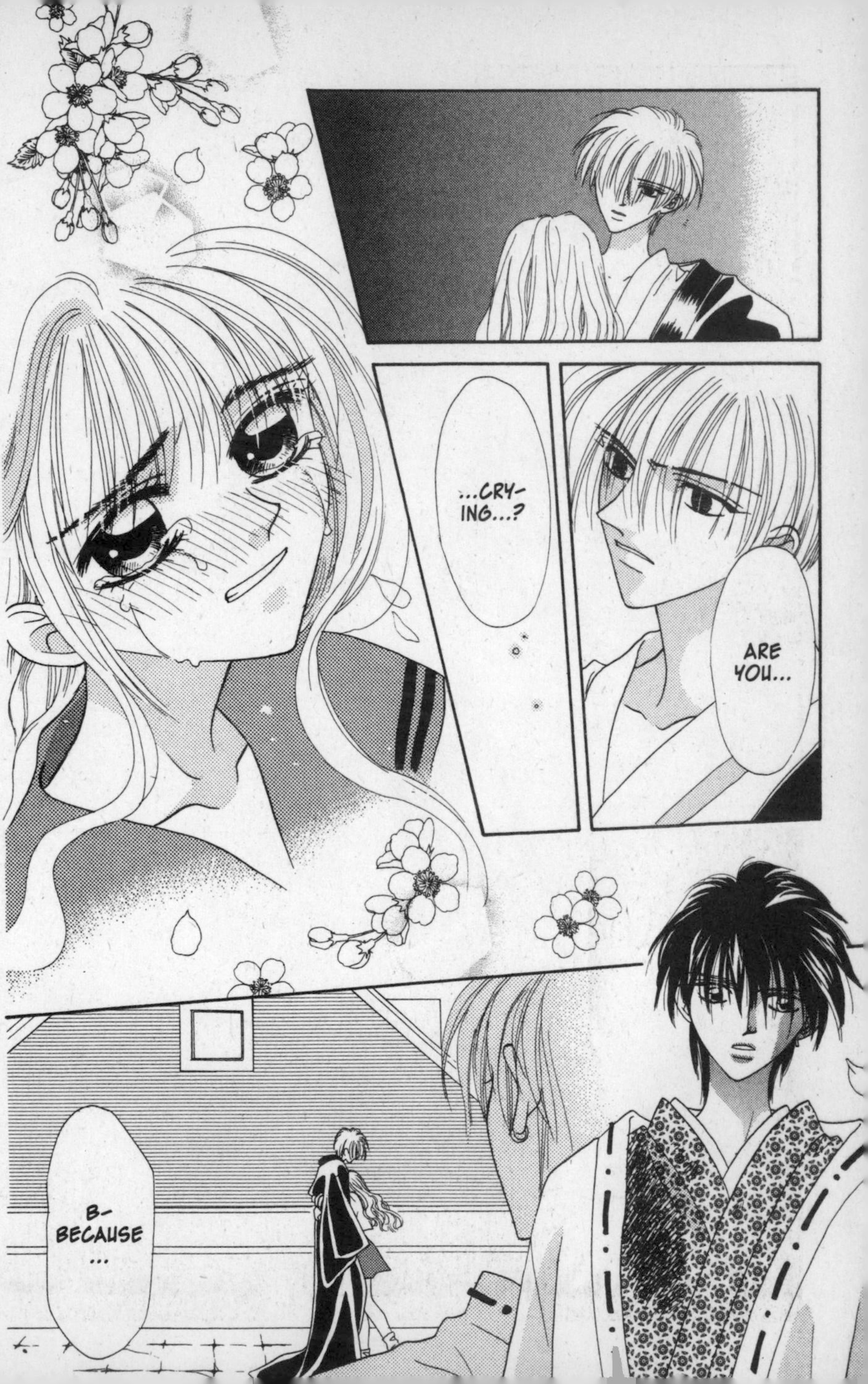
ARE YOU...
...CRY-ING...?
B-BECAUSE ...

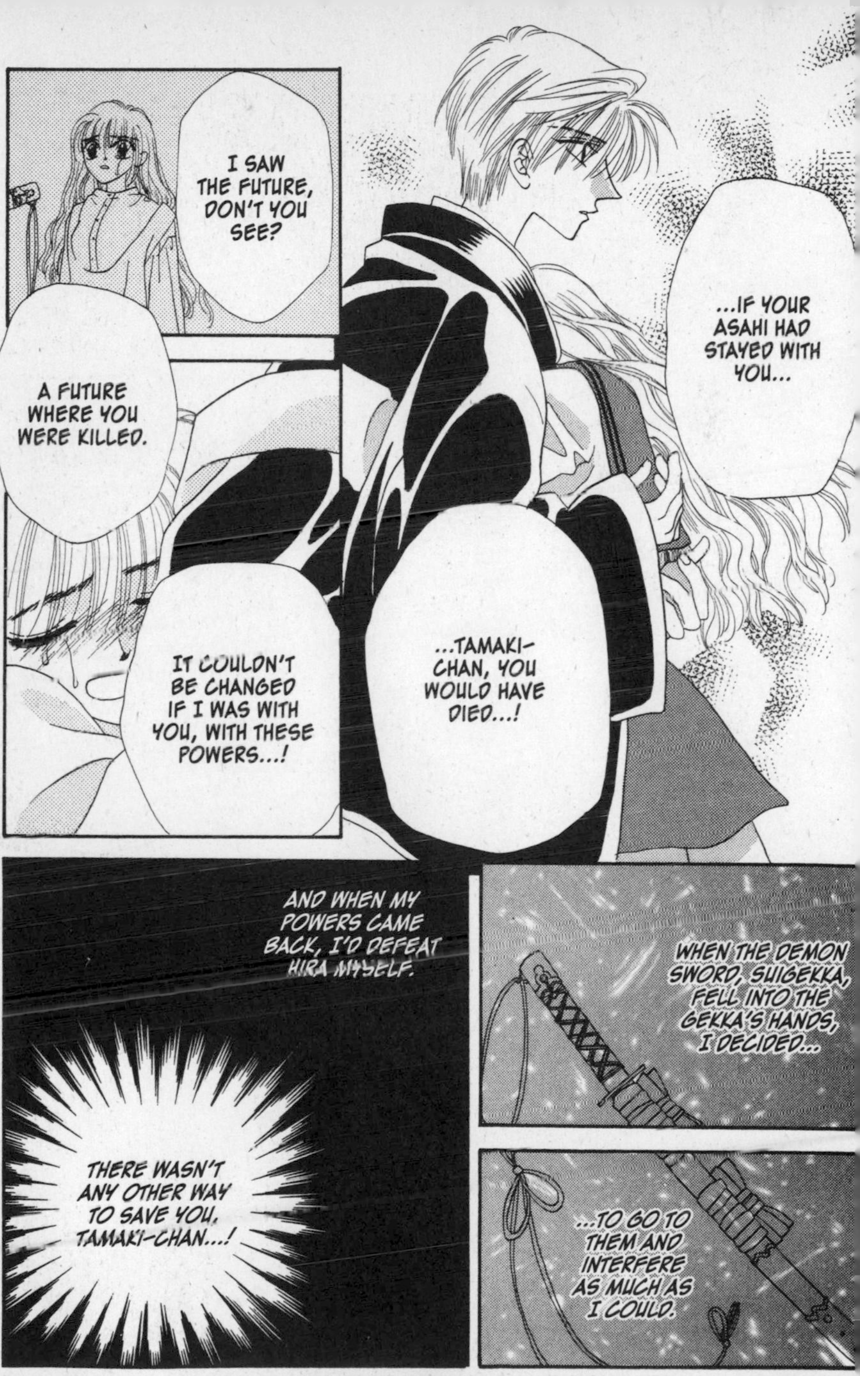

...IF YOUR ASAHI HAD STAYED WITH YOU...
...TAMAKI-CHAN, YOU WOULD HAVE DIED...!
I SAW THE FUTURE, DON'T YOU SEE?
A FUTURE WHERE YOU WERE KILLED.
IT COULDN'T BE CHANGED IF I WAS WITH YOU, WITH THESE POWERS...!
WHEN THE DEMON SWORD, SUIGEKKA, FELL INTO THE GEKKA'S HANDS, I DECIDED...
...TO GO TO THEM AND INTERFERE AS MUCH AS I COULD.
AND WHEN MY POWERS CAME BACK, I'D DEFEAT HIRA MYSELF.
THERE WASN'T ANY OTHER WAY TO SAVE YOU, TAMAKI-CHAN...!

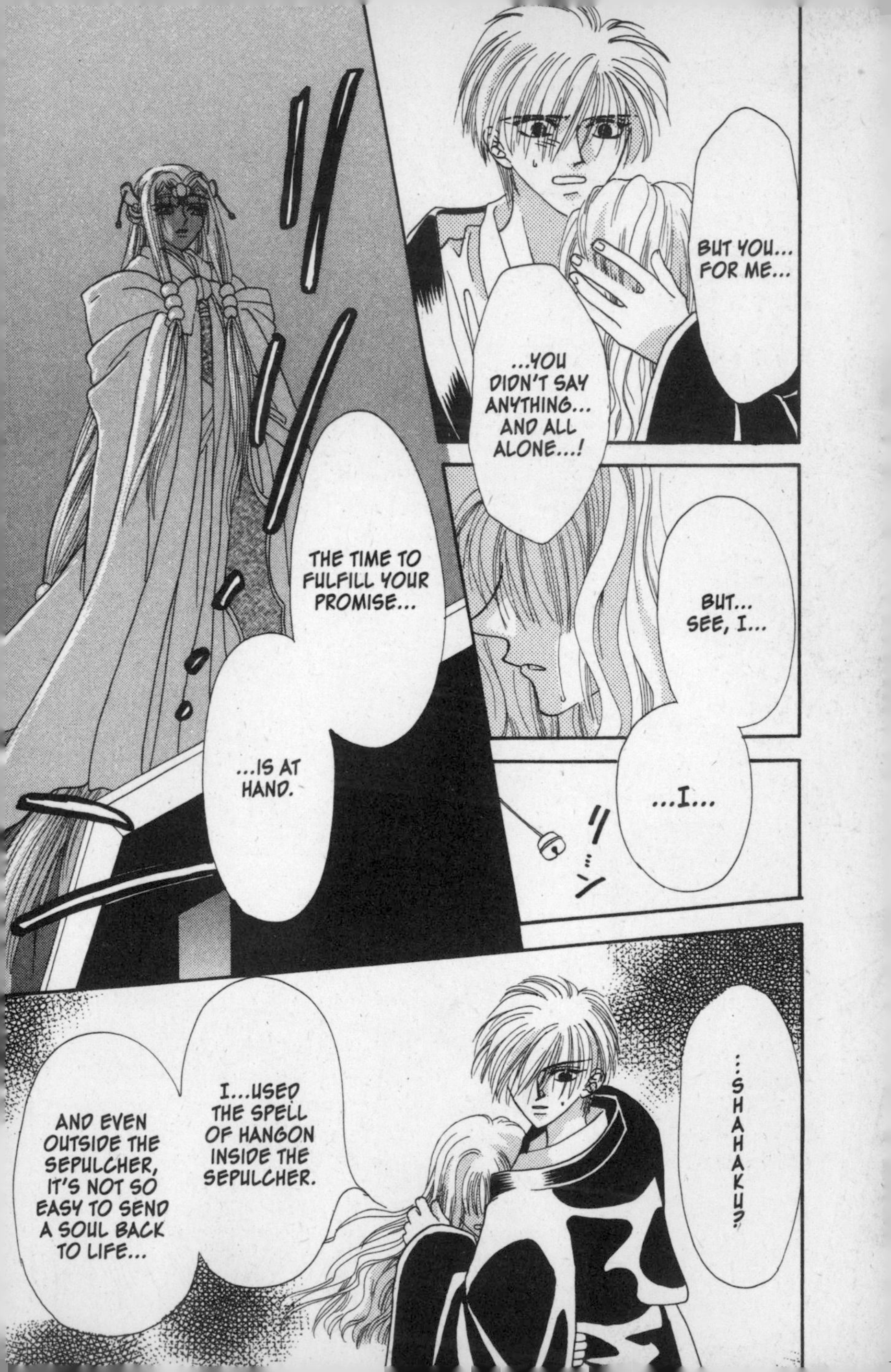
BUT YOU... FOR ME...
...YOU DIDN'T SAY ANYTHING... AND ALL ALONE...!
BUT... SEE, I...
...I...
THE TIME TO FULFILL YOUR PROMISE...
...IS AT HAND.
...SHAHAKU?
I...USED THE SPELL OF HANGON INSIDE THE SEPULCHER.
AND EVEN OUTSIDE THE SEPULCHER, IT'S NOT SO EASY TO SEND A SOUL BACK TO LIFE...

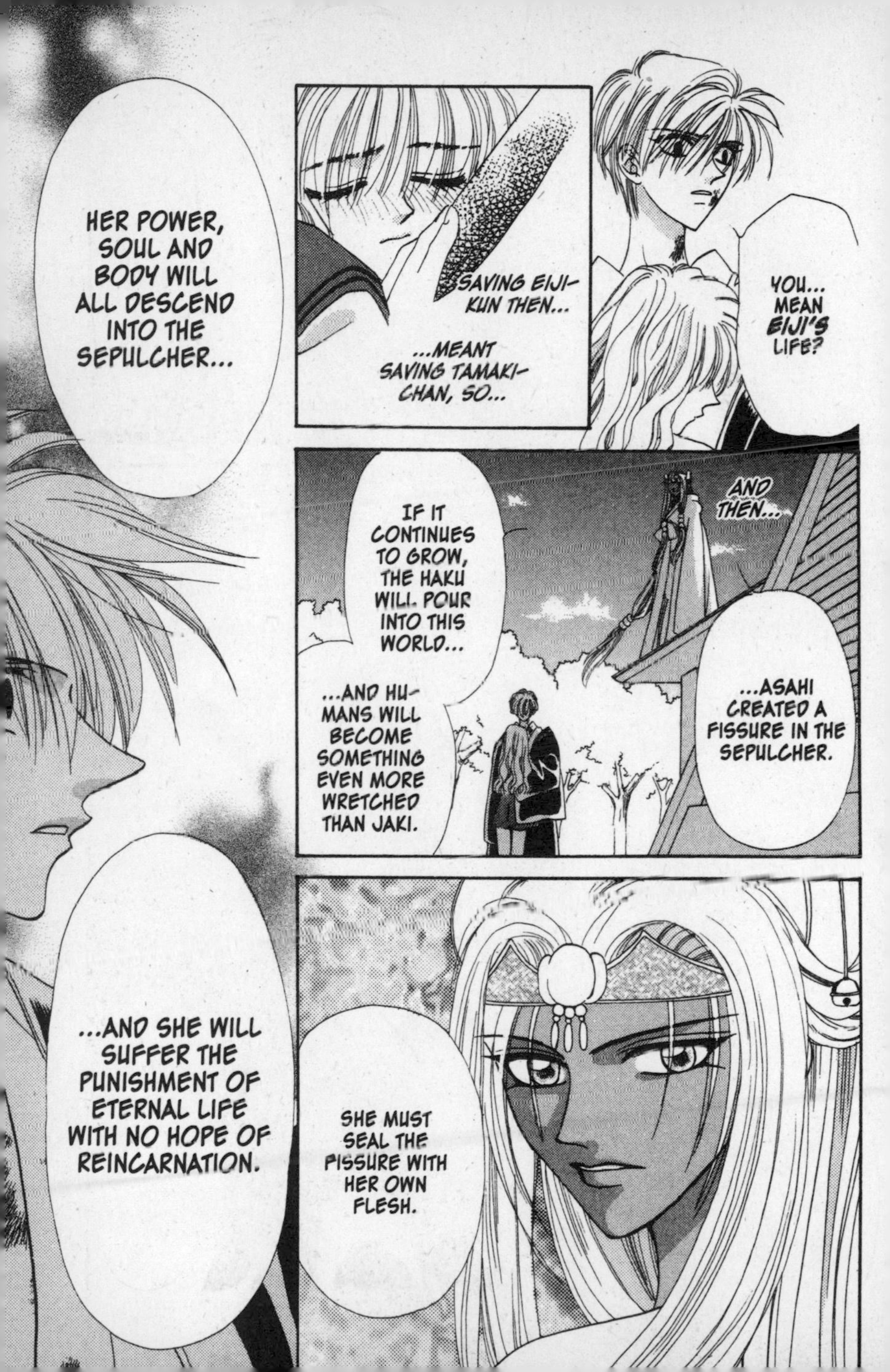
YOU... MEAN EIJI'S LIFE?
SAVING EIJI-KUN THEN...
...MEANT SAVING TAMAKI-CHAN, SO...
AND THEN...
...ASAHI CREATED A FISSURE IN THE SEPULCHER.
IF IT CONTINUES TO GROW, THE HAKU WILL POUR INTO THIS WORLD...
...AND HUMANS WILL BECOME SOMETHING EVEN MORE WRETCHED THAN JAKI.
SHE MUST SEAL THE FISSURE WITH HER OWN FLESH.
HER POWER, SOUL AND BODY WILL ALL DESCEND INTO THE SEPULCHER...
...AND SHE WILL SUFFER THE PUNISHMENT OF ETERNAL LIFE WITH NO HOPE OF REINCARNATION.

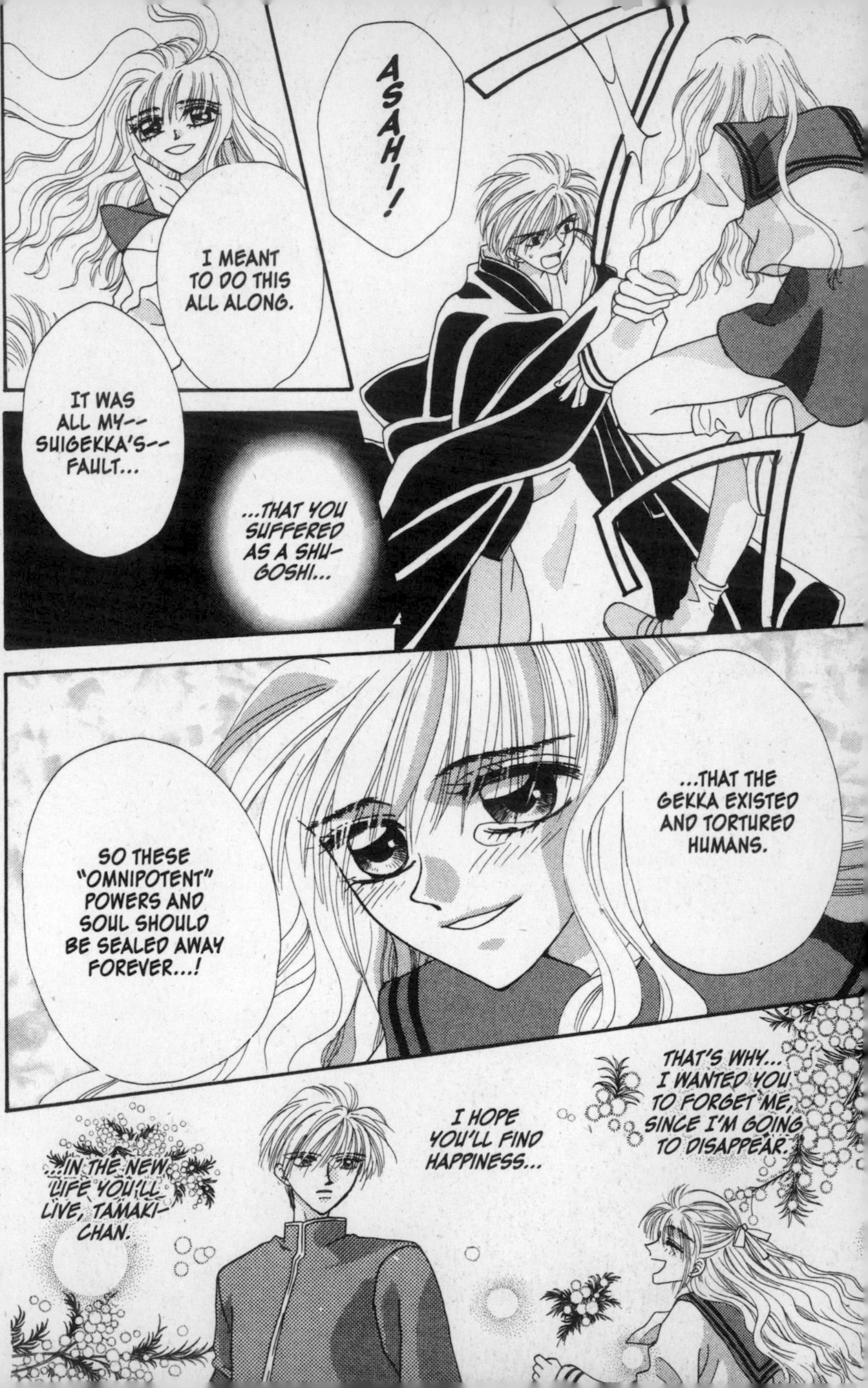
ASAHI!
I MEANT TO DO THIS ALL ALONG.
IT WAS ALL MY-- SUIGEKKA'S-- FAULT...
...THAT YOU SUFFERED AS A SHUGOSHI...
...THAT THE GEKKA EXISTED AND TORTURED HUMANS.
SO THESE "OMNIPOTENT" POWERS AND SOUL SHOULD BE SEALED AWAY FOREVER...!
THAT'S WHY... I WANTED YOU TO FORGET ME, SINCE I'M GOING TO DISAPPEAR.
I HOPE YOU'LL FIND HAPPINESS...
...IN THE NEW LIFE YOU'LL LIVE, TAMAKI-CHAN.

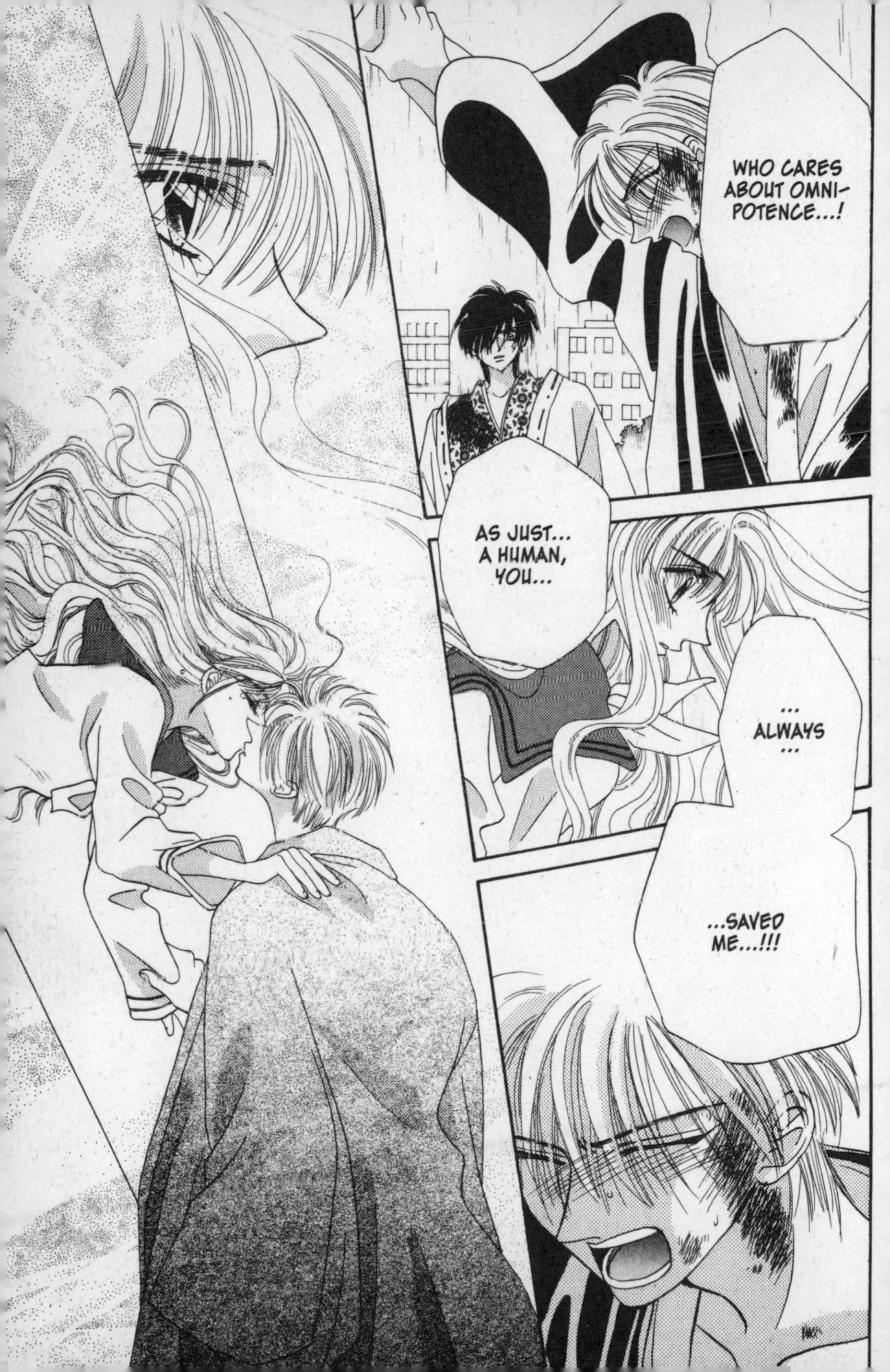
WHO CARES ABOUT OMNI-POTENCE...!
AS JUST... A HUMAN, YOU...
... ALWAYS ...
...SAVED ME...!!!

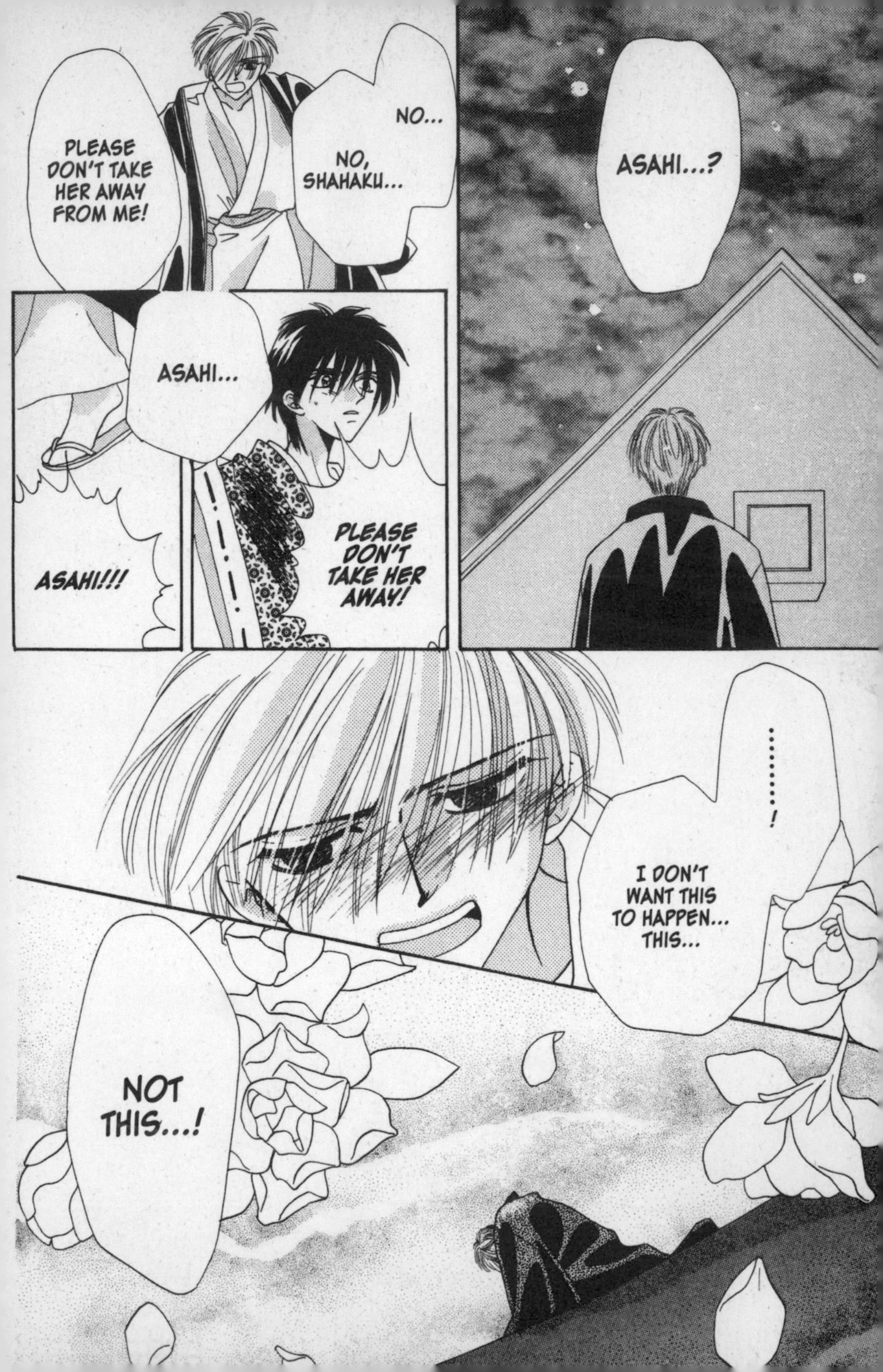
ASAHI...?
NO...
NO, SHAHAKU...
PLEASE DON'T TAKE HER AWAY FROM ME!
ASAHI...
PLEASE DON'T TAKE HER AWAY!
ASAHI!!!
......!
I DON'T WANT THIS TO HAPPEN... THIS...
NOT THIS...!

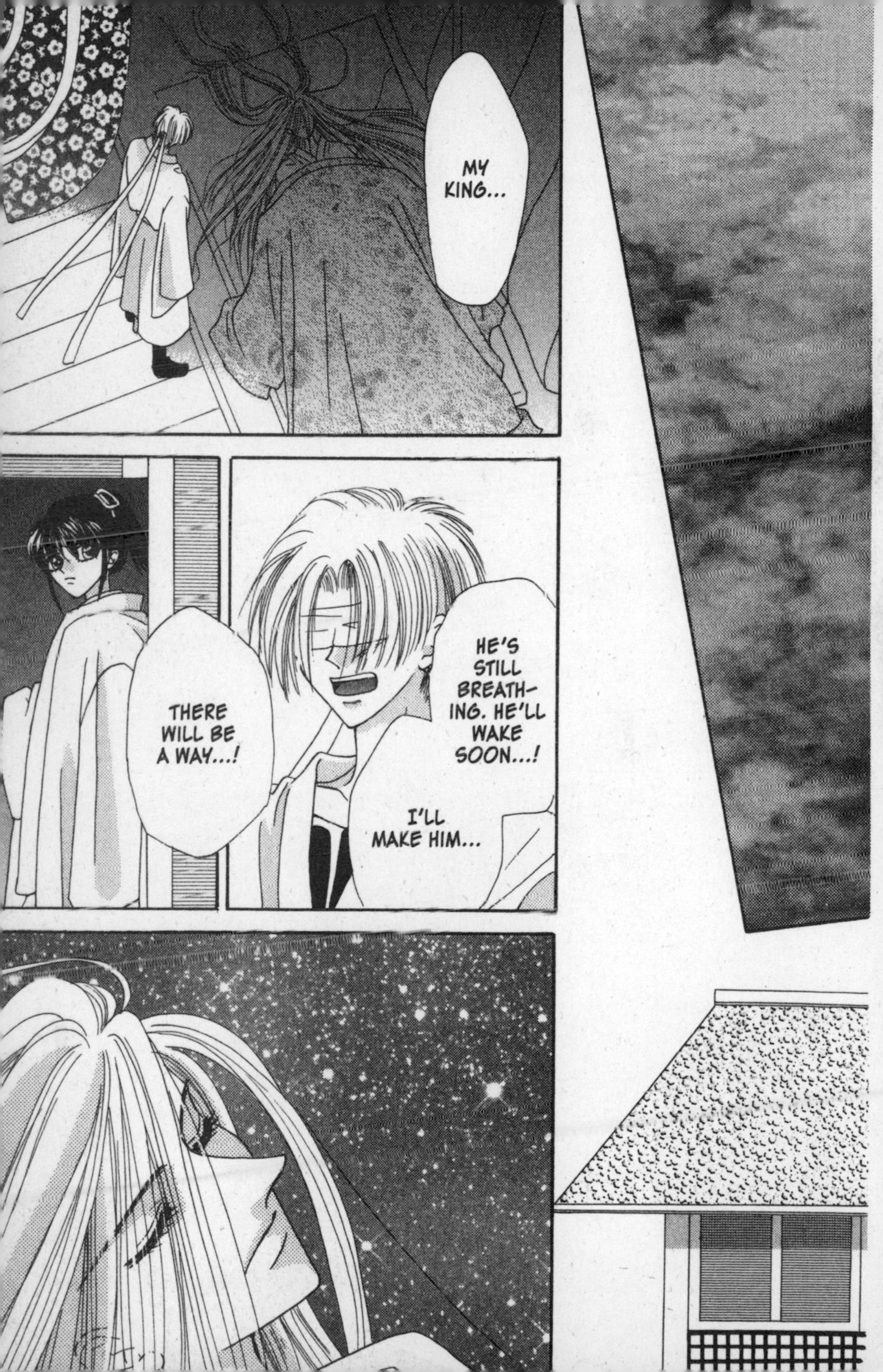
MY KING...
HE'S STILL BREATHING. HE'LL WAKE SOON...!
I'LL MAKE HIM...
THERE WILL BE A WAY...!

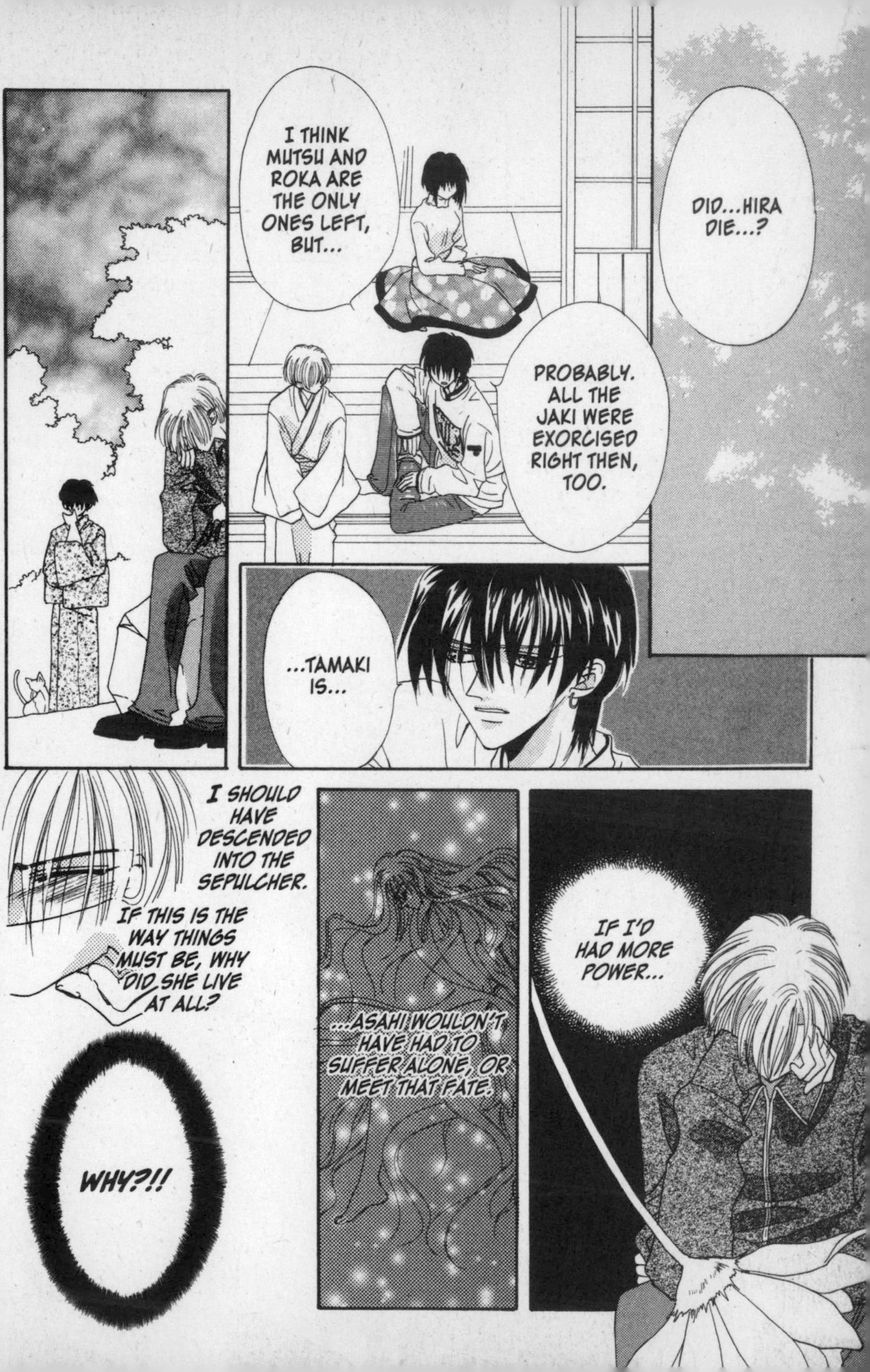
DID...HIRA DIE...?
I THINK MUTSU AND ROKA ARE THE ONLY ONES LEFT, BUT...
PROBABLY. ALL THE JAKI WERE EXORCISED RIGHT THEN, TOO.
...TAMAKI IS...
IF I'D HAD MORE POWER...
...ASAHI WOULDN'T HAVE HAD TO SUFFER ALONE, OR MEET THAT FATE.
I SHOULD HAVE DESCENDED INTO THE SEPULCHER.
IF THIS IS THE WAY THINGS MUST BE, WHY DID SHE LIVE AT ALL?
WHY?!!

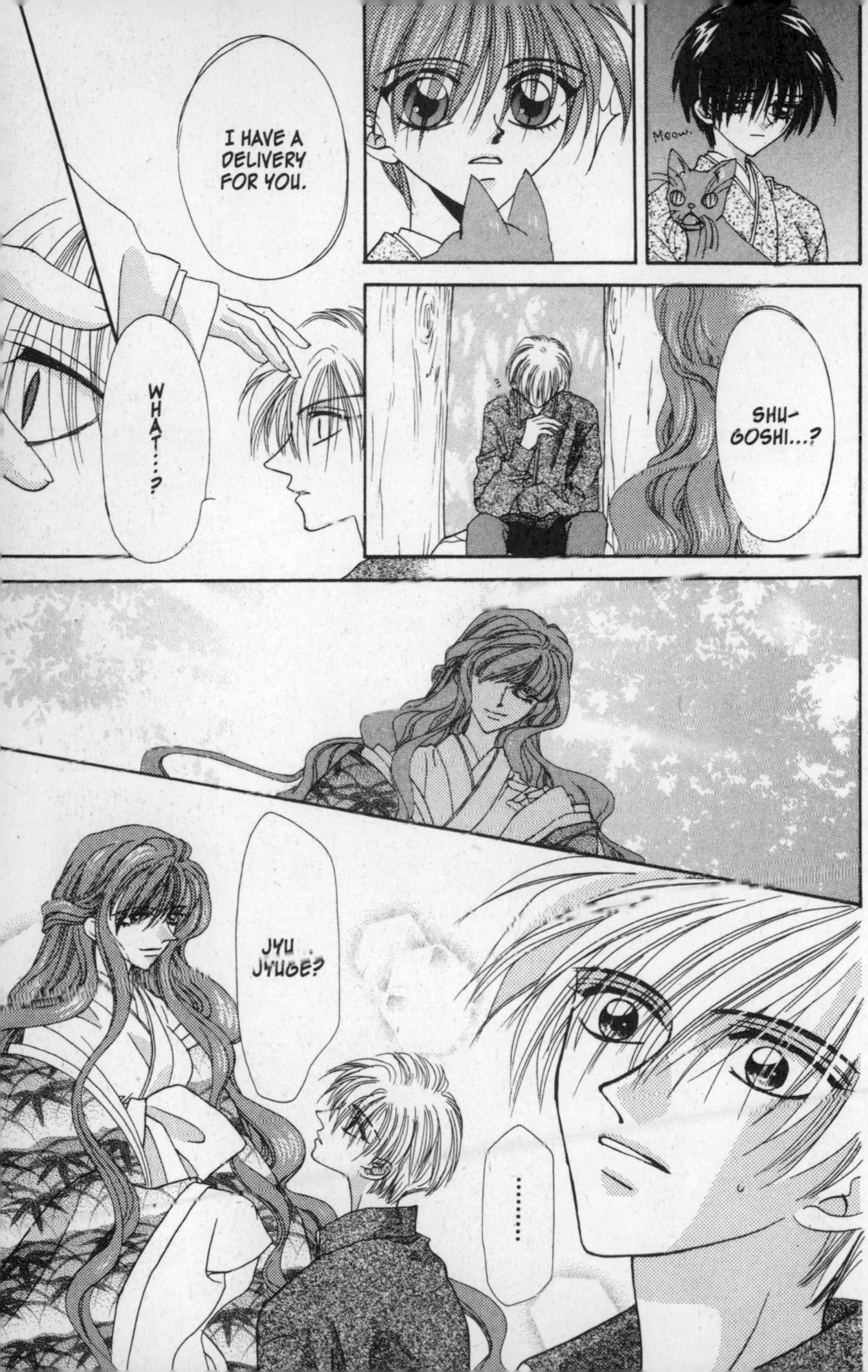
Meow.
SHU-GOSHI...?
I HAVE A DELIVERY FOR YOU.
WHAT...?
JYU... JYUGE?
......

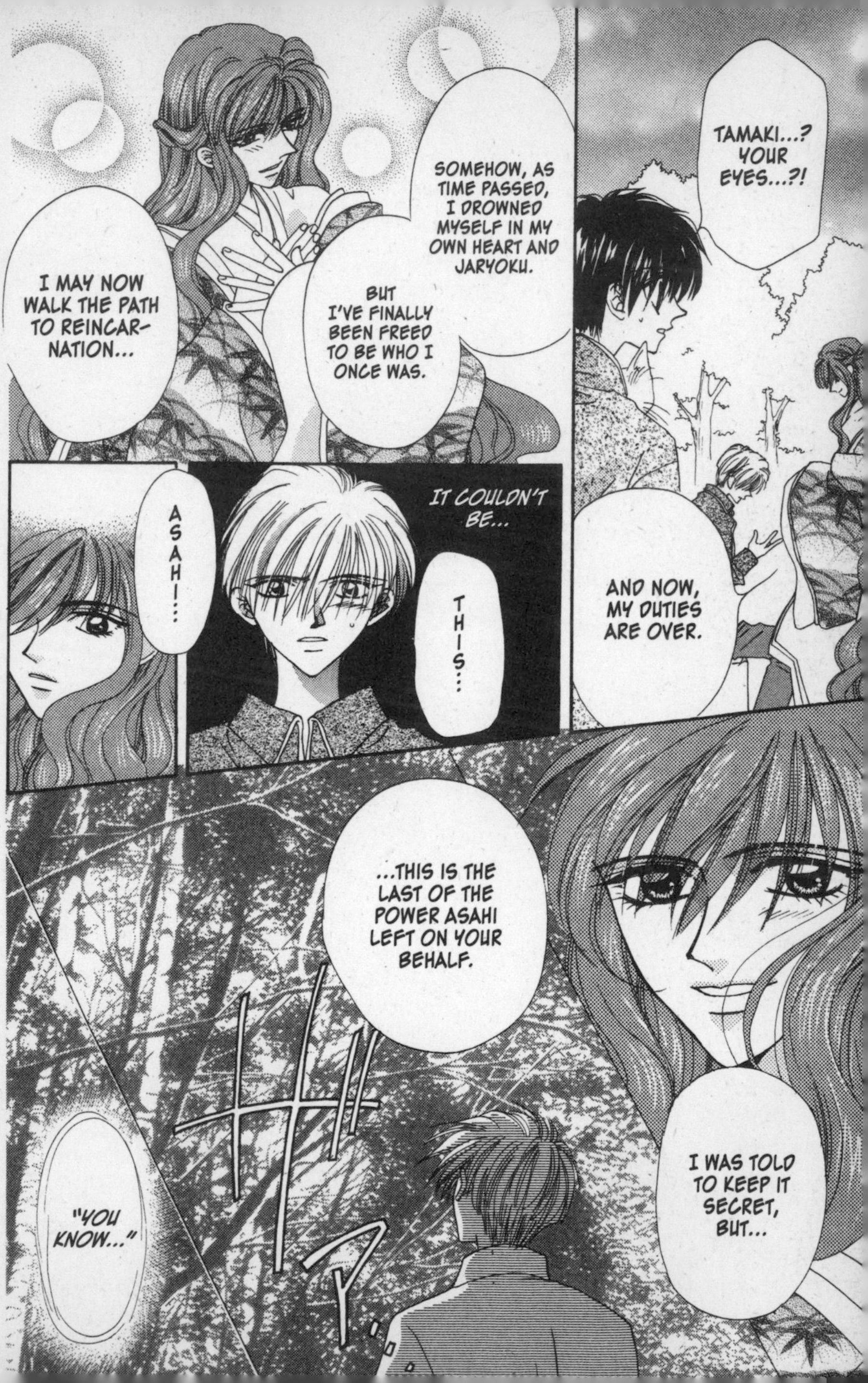
TAMAKI...? YOUR EYES...?!
AND NOW, MY DUTIES ARE OVER.
SOMEHOW, AS TIME PASSED, I DROWNED MYSELF IN MY OWN HEART AND JARYOKU.
BUT I'VE FINALLY BEEN FREED TO BE WHO I ONCE WAS.
I MAY NOW WALK THE PATH TO REINCAR-NATION...
IT COULDN'T BE...
THIS...
ASAHI...
I WAS TOLD TO KEEP IT SECRET, BUT...
...THIS IS THE LAST OF THE POWER ASAHI LEFT ON YOUR BEHALF.
"YOU KNOW..."

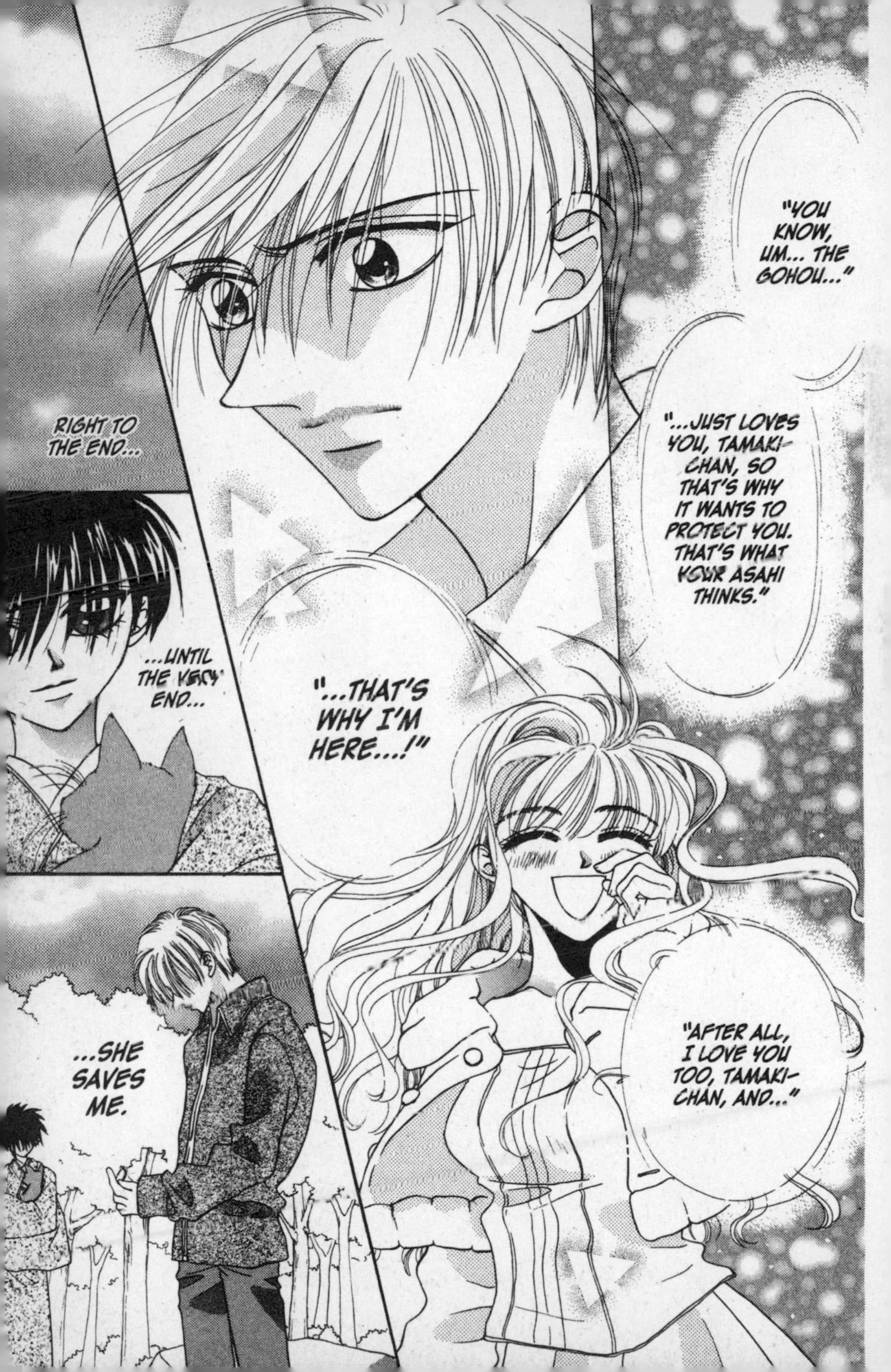
"YOU KNOW, UM... THE GOHOU..."
"...JUST LOVES YOU, TAMAKI-CHAN, SO THAT'S WHY IT WANTS TO PROTECT YOU. THAT'S WHAT YOUR ASAHI THINKS."
"AFTER ALL, I LOVE YOU TOO, TAMAKI-CHAN, AND..."
"...THAT'S WHY I'M HERE...!"
RIGHT TO THE END...
...UNTIL THE VERY END...
...SHE SAVES ME.

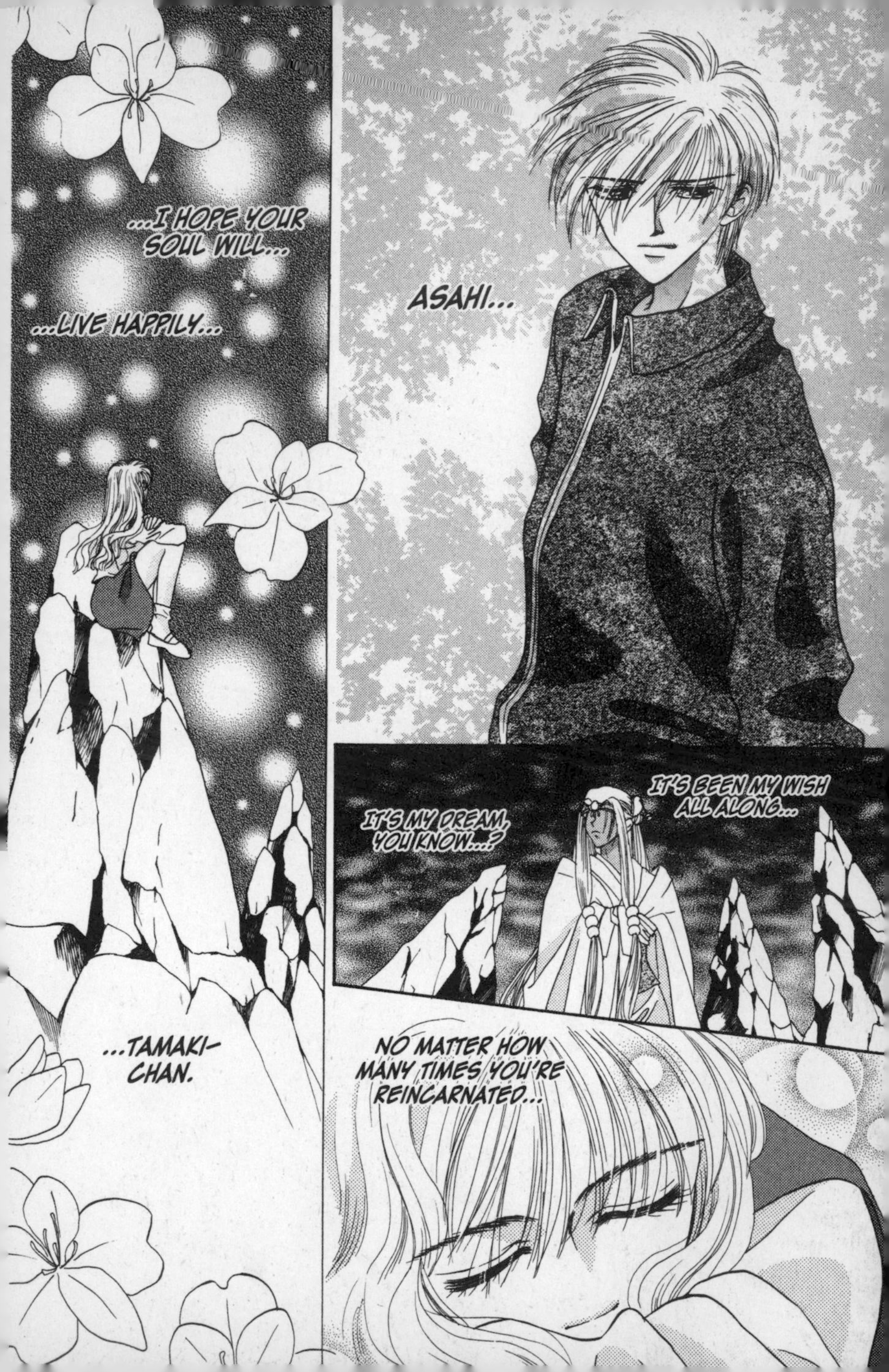
ASAHI...
IT'S BEEN MY WISH ALL ALONG...
IT'S MY DREAM, YOU KNOW...?
NO MATTER HOW MANY TIMES YOU'RE REINCARNATED...
...I HOPE YOUR SOUL WILL...
...LIVE HAPPILY...
...TAMAKI-CHAN.

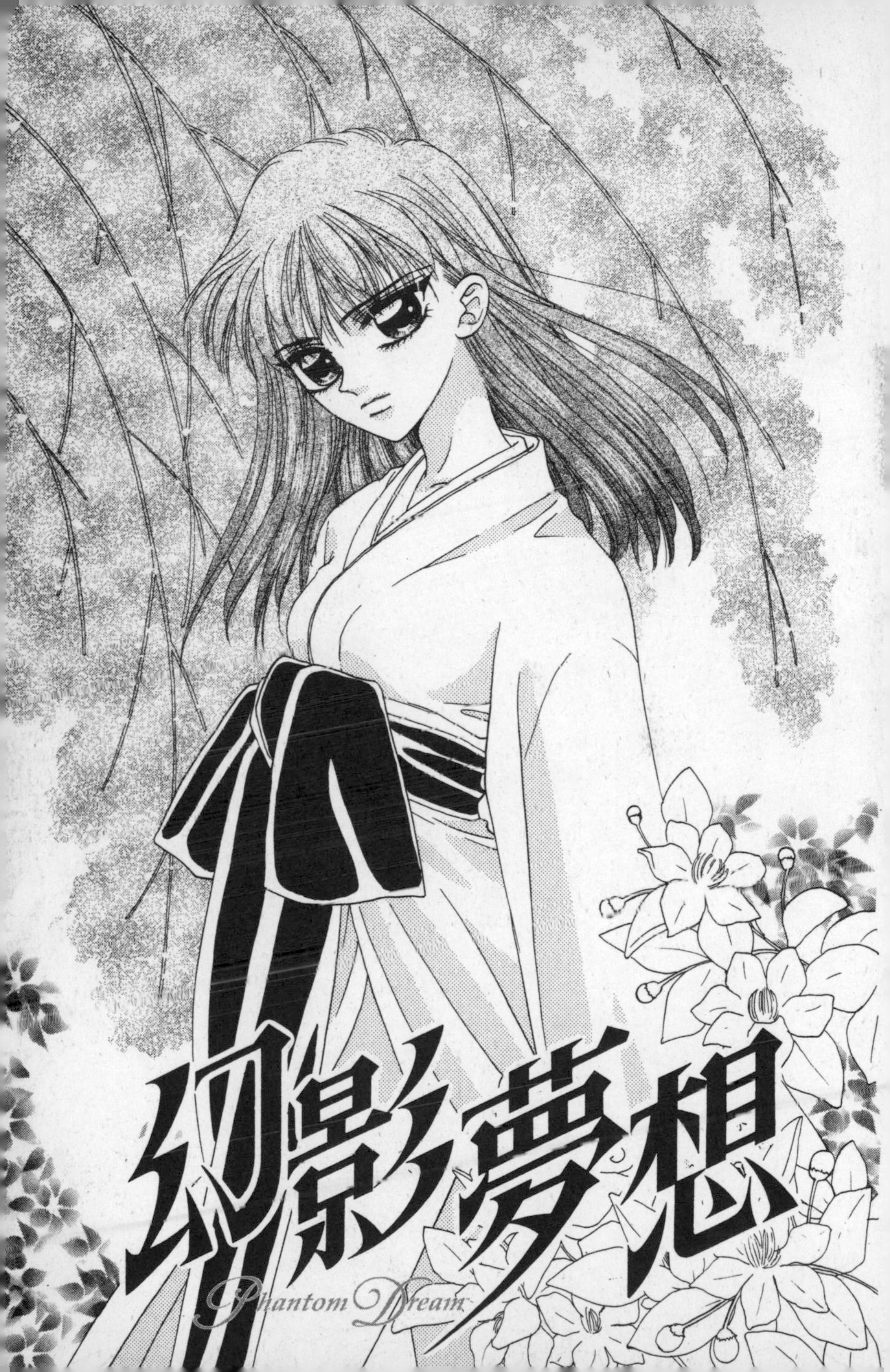
幻影夢想
Phantom Dream

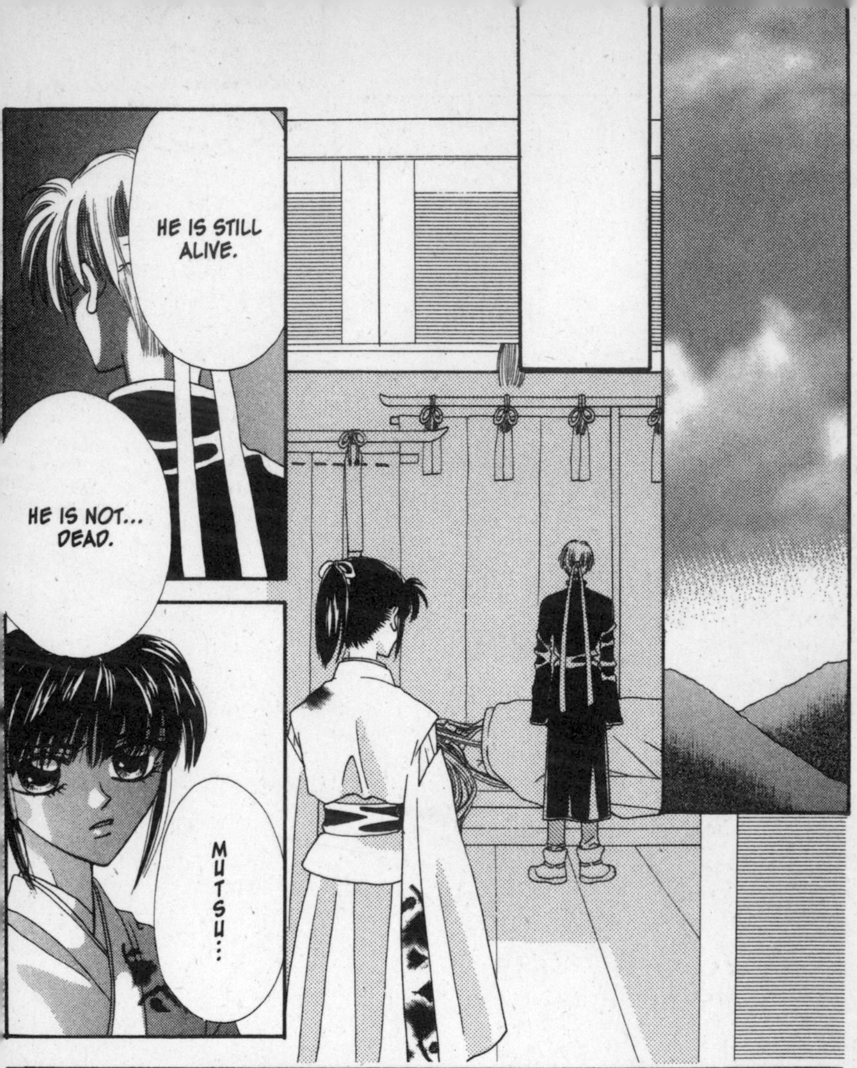
HE IS STILL ALIVE.
HE IS NOT... DEAD.
MUTSU...

ULTRA SPECIAL *THINGS THAT DON'T MATTER III*

When I sketch him at first, I draw Mutsu's full face, but... am I the only one thinks that it just doesn't look like Mutsu if his eyes aren't covered? I get the feeling that a surprising number of people support Roka (not just that she was popular). Still, ***DREAM*** is full of people with one-sided loves, isn't it? The only people who're still alive and return each other's feelings are Tamaki and Asahi, but they're separated...

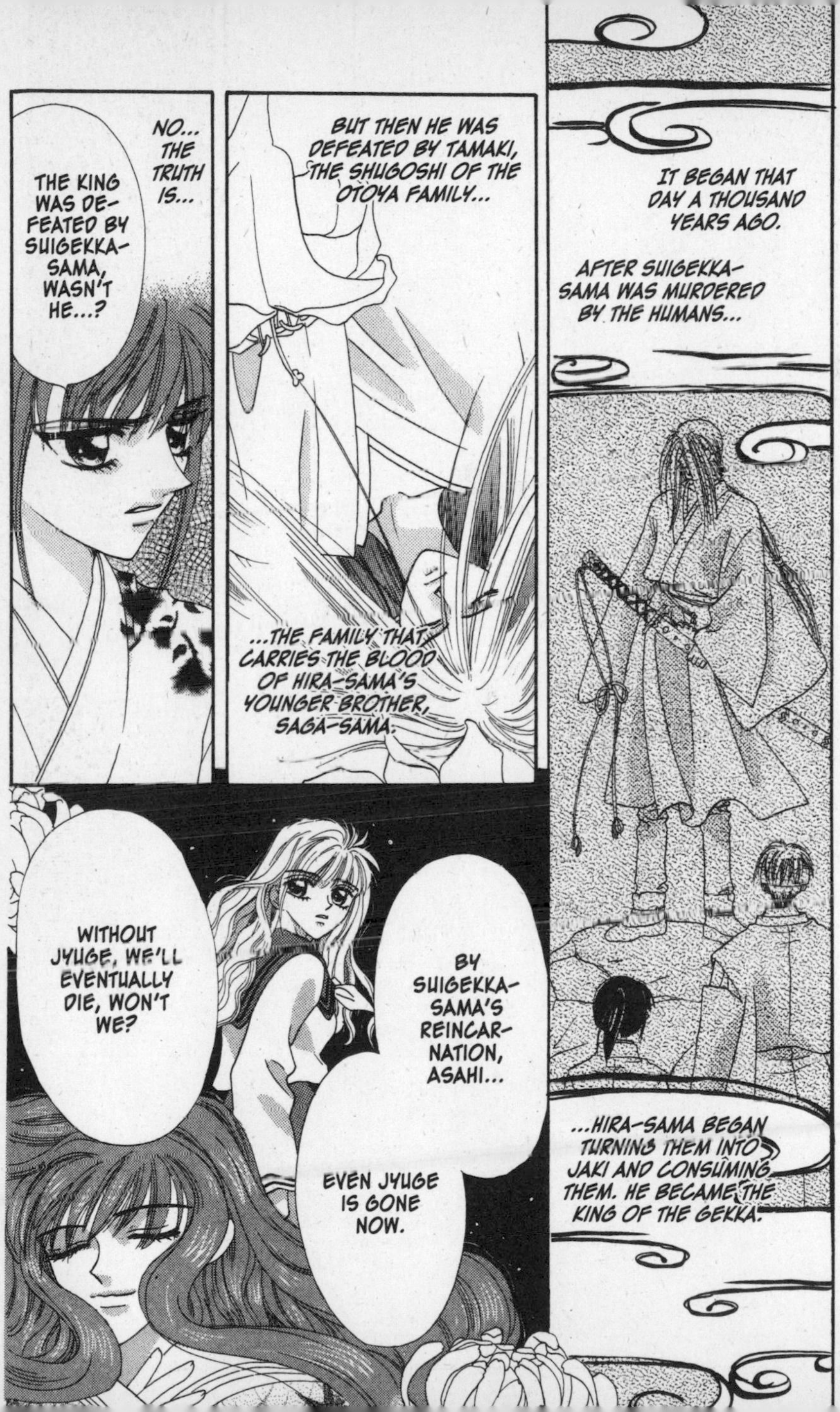
IT BEGAN THAT DAY A THOUSAND YEARS AGO.
AFTER SUIGEKKA-SAMA WAS MURDERED BY THE HUMANS...
...HIRA-SAMA BEGAN TURNING THEM INTO JAKI AND CONSUMING THEM. HE BECAME THE KING OF THE GEKKA.
BUT THEN HE WAS DEFEATED BY TAMAKI, THE SHUGOSHI OF THE OTOYA FAMILY...
...THE FAMILY THAT CARRIES THE BLOOD OF HIRA-SAMA'S YOUNGER BROTHER, SAGA-SAMA.
NO... THE TRUTH IS...
THE KING WAS DEFEATED BY SUIGEKKA-SAMA, WASN'T HE...?
BY SUIGEKKA-SAMA'S REINCARNATION, ASAHI...
EVEN JYUGE IS GONE NOW.
WITHOUT JYUGE, WE'LL EVENTUALLY DIE, WON'T WE?

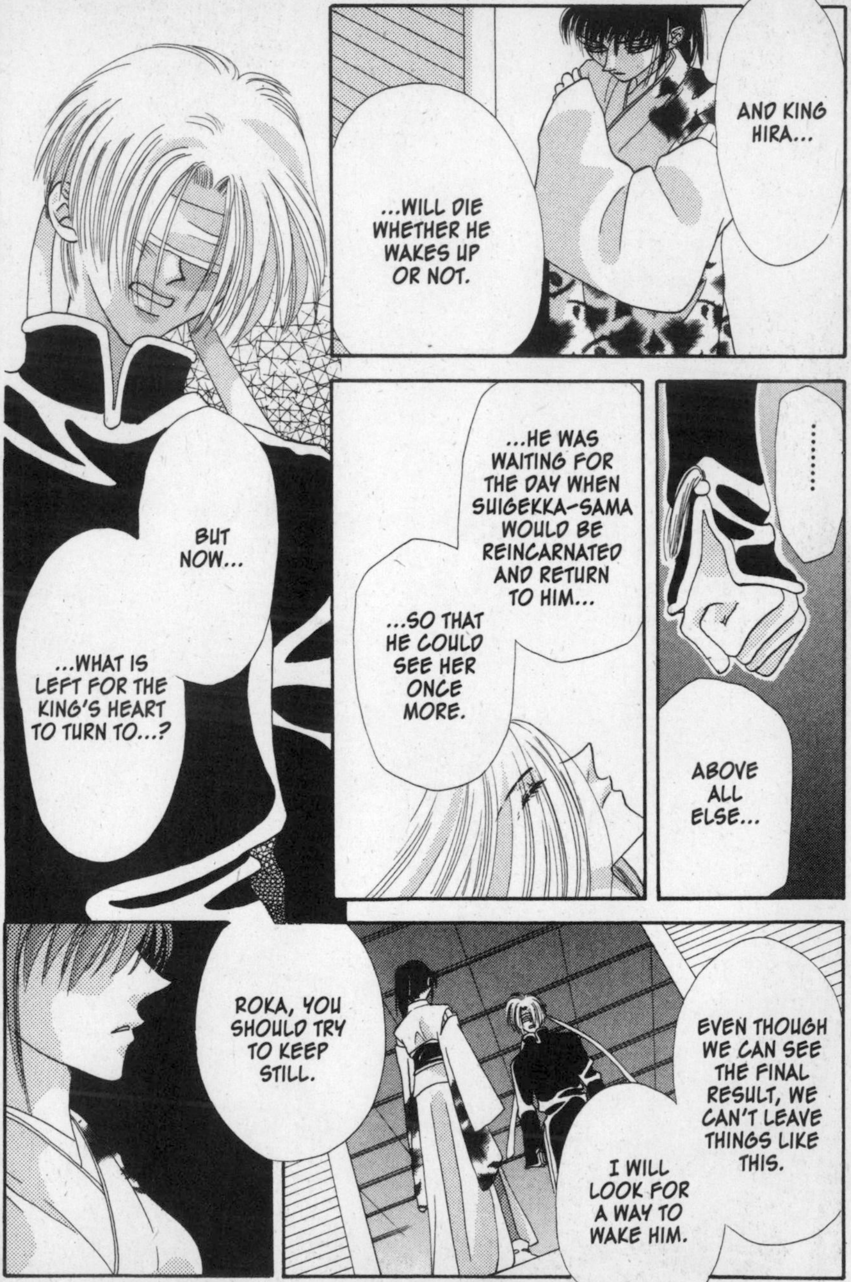
AND KING HIRA...
...WILL DIE WHETHER HE WAKES UP OR NOT.
......
ABOVE ALL ELSE...
...HE WAS WAITING FOR THE DAY WHEN SUIGEKKA-SAMA WOULD BE REINCARNATED AND RETURN TO HIM...
...SO THAT HE COULD SEE HER ONCE MORE.
BUT NOW...
...WHAT IS LEFT FOR THE KING'S HEART TO TURN TO...?
EVEN THOUGH WE CAN SEE THE FINAL RESULT, WE CAN'T LEAVE THINGS LIKE THIS.
I WILL LOOK FOR A WAY TO WAKE HIM.
ROKA, YOU SHOULD TRY TO KEEP STILL.

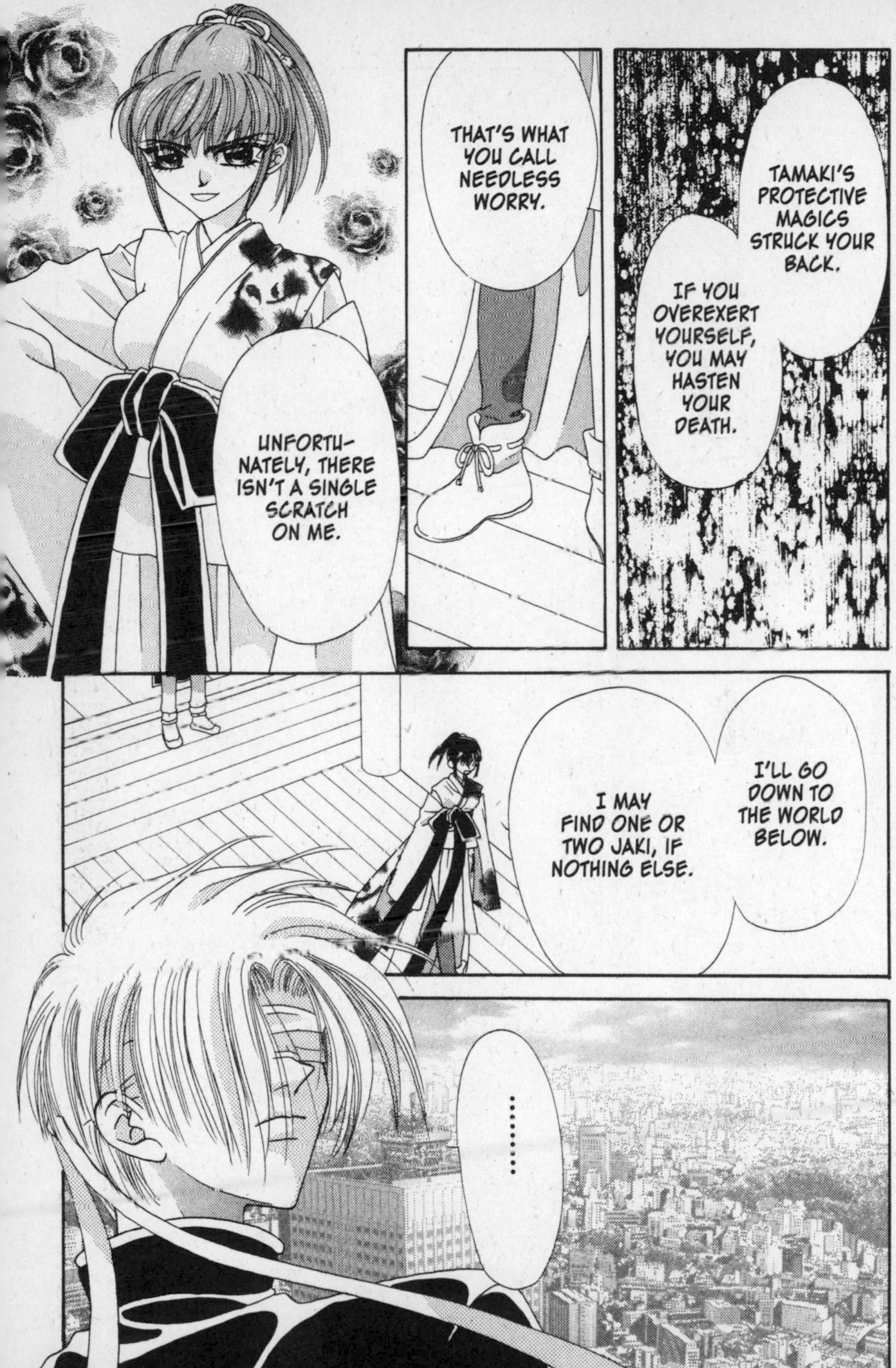
TAMAKI'S PROTECTIVE MAGICS STRUCK YOUR BACK.
IF YOU OVEREXERT YOURSELF, YOU MAY HASTEN YOUR DEATH.
THAT'S WHAT YOU CALL NEEDLESS WORRY.
UNFORTU-NATELY, THERE ISN'T A SINGLE SCRATCH ON ME.
I'LL GO DOWN TO THE WORLD BELOW.
I MAY FIND ONE OR TWO JAKI, IF NOTHING ELSE.
....

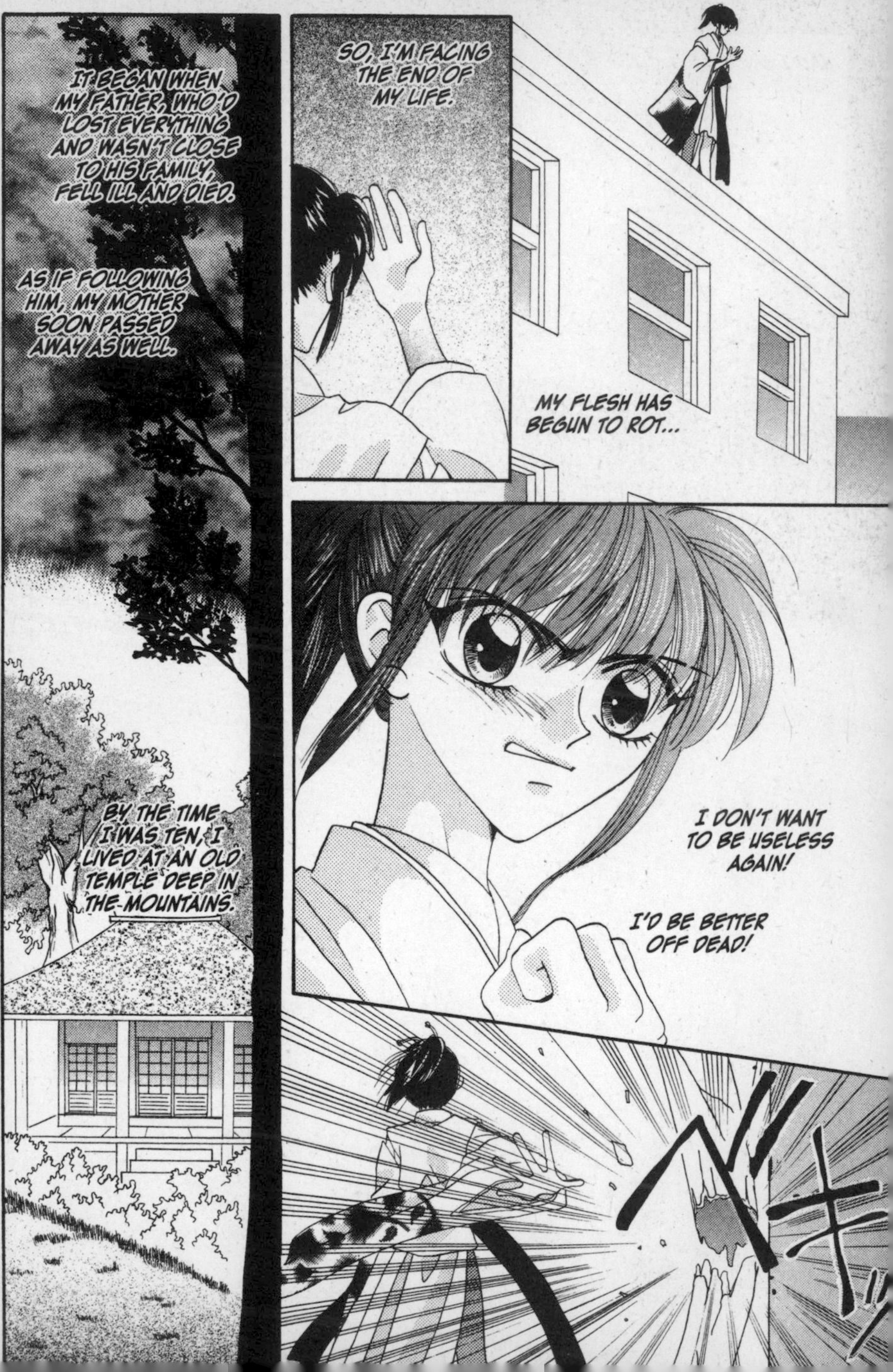
MY FLESH HAS BEGUN TO ROT...
SO, I'M FACING THE END OF MY LIFE.
I DON'T WANT TO BE USELESS AGAIN!
I'D BE BETTER OFF DEAD!
IT BEGAN WHEN MY FATHER, WHO'D LOST EVERYTHING AND WASN'T CLOSE TO HIS FAMILY, FELL ILL AND DIED.
AS IF FOLLOWING HIM, MY MOTHER SOON PASSED AWAY AS WELL.
BY THE TIME I WAS TEN, I LIVED AT AN OLD TEMPLE DEEP IN THE MOUNTAINS.

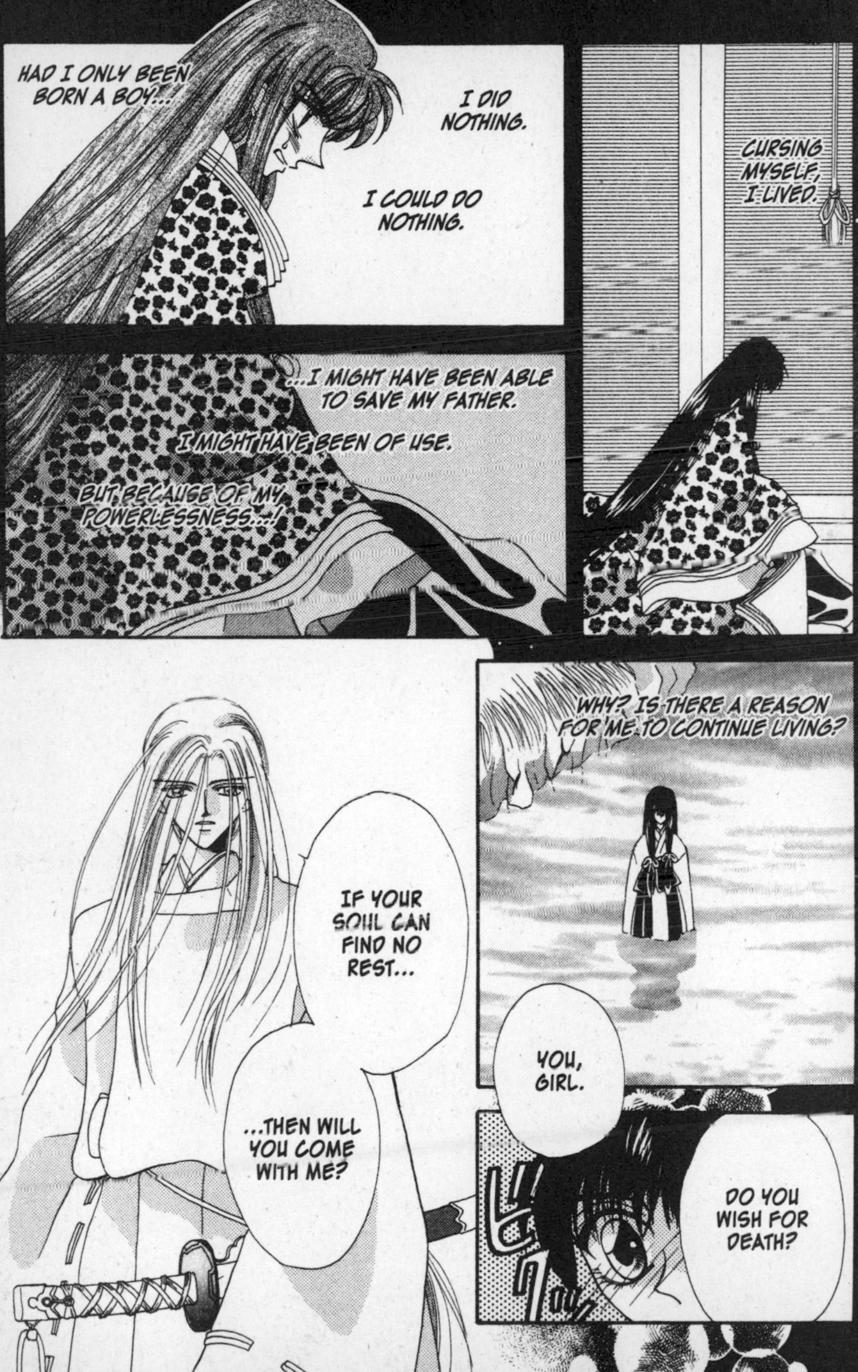
CURSING MYSELF, I LIVED.
I DID NOTHING.
I COULD DO NOTHING.
HAD I ONLY BEEN BORN A BOY...
...I MIGHT HAVE BEEN ABLE TO SAVE MY FATHER.
I MIGHT HAVE BEEN OF USE.
BUT BECAUSE OF MY POWERLESSNESS...!
WHY? IS THERE A REASON FOR ME TO CONTINUE LIVING?
YOU, GIRL.
DO YOU WISH FOR DEATH?
IF YOUR SOUL CAN FIND NO REST...
...THEN WILL YOU COME WITH ME?

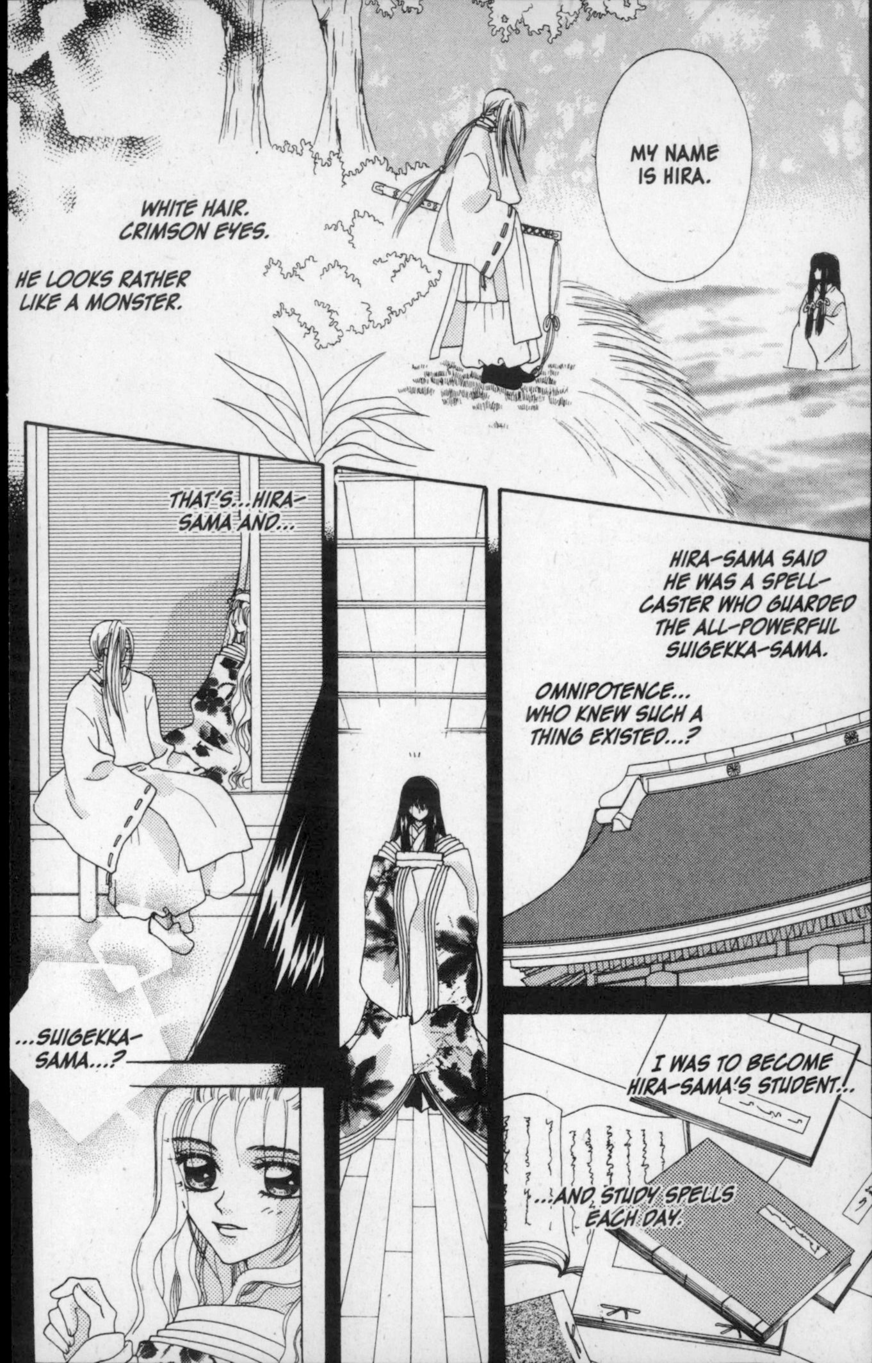
MY NAME IS HIRA.
WHITE HAIR. CRIMSON EYES.
HE LOOKS RATHER LIKE A MONSTER.
HIRA-SAMA SAID HE WAS A SPELL-CASTER WHO GUARDED THE ALL-POWERFUL SUIGEKKA-SAMA.
OMNIPOTENCE... WHO KNEW SUCH A THING EXISTED...?
I WAS TO BECOME HIRA-SAMA'S STUDENT...
...AND STUDY SPELLS EACH DAY.
THAT'S...HIRA-SAMA AND...
...SUIGEKKA-SAMA...?

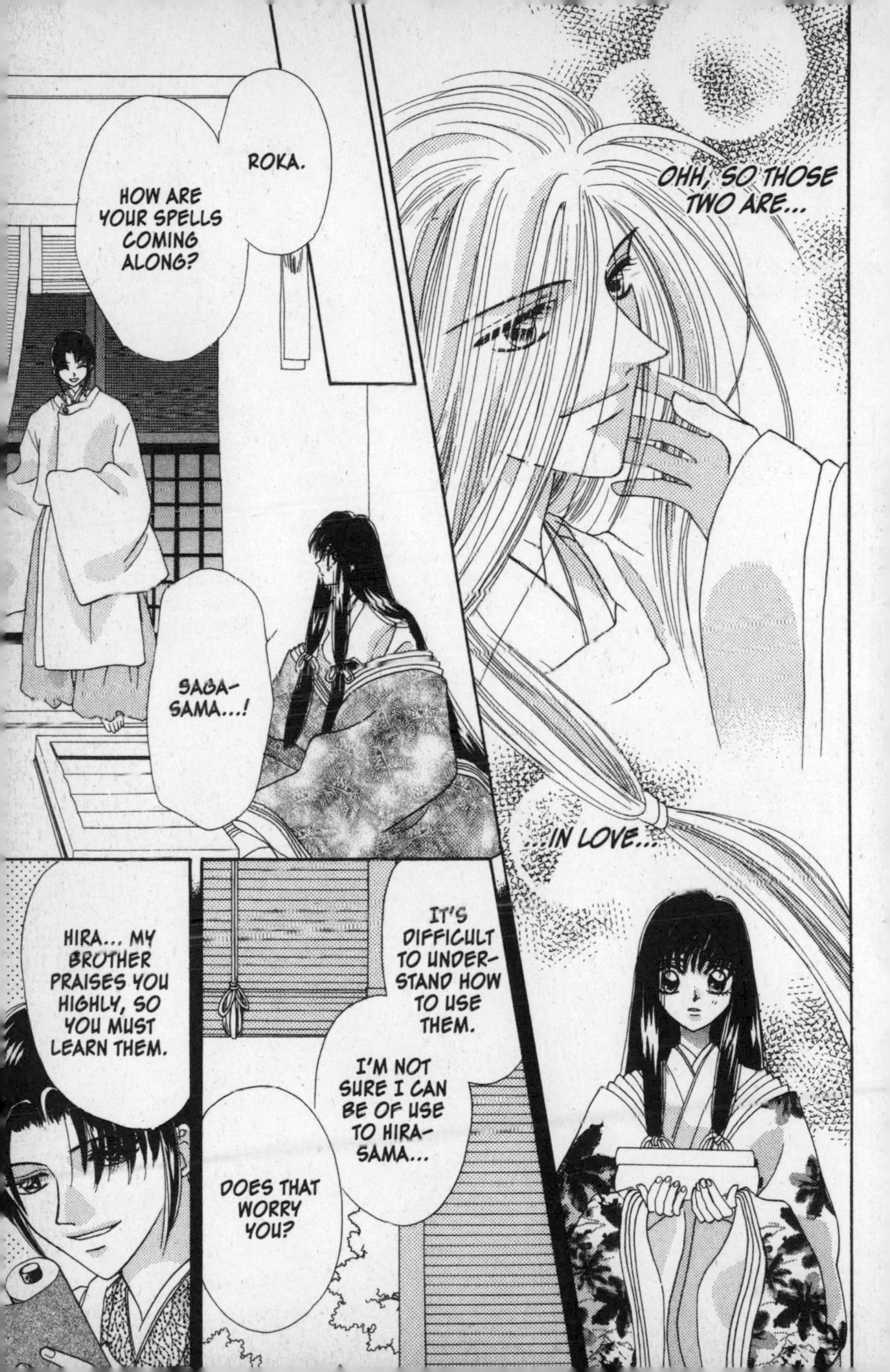
OHH, SO THOSE TWO ARE...
...IN LOVE...
ROKA.
HOW ARE YOUR SPELLS COMING ALONG?
SAGA-SAMA...!
IT'S DIFFICULT TO UNDER-STAND HOW TO USE THEM.
I'M NOT SURE I CAN BE OF USE TO HIRA-SAMA...
DOES THAT WORRY YOU?
HIRA... MY BROTHER PRAISES YOU HIGHLY, SO YOU MUST LEARN THEM.

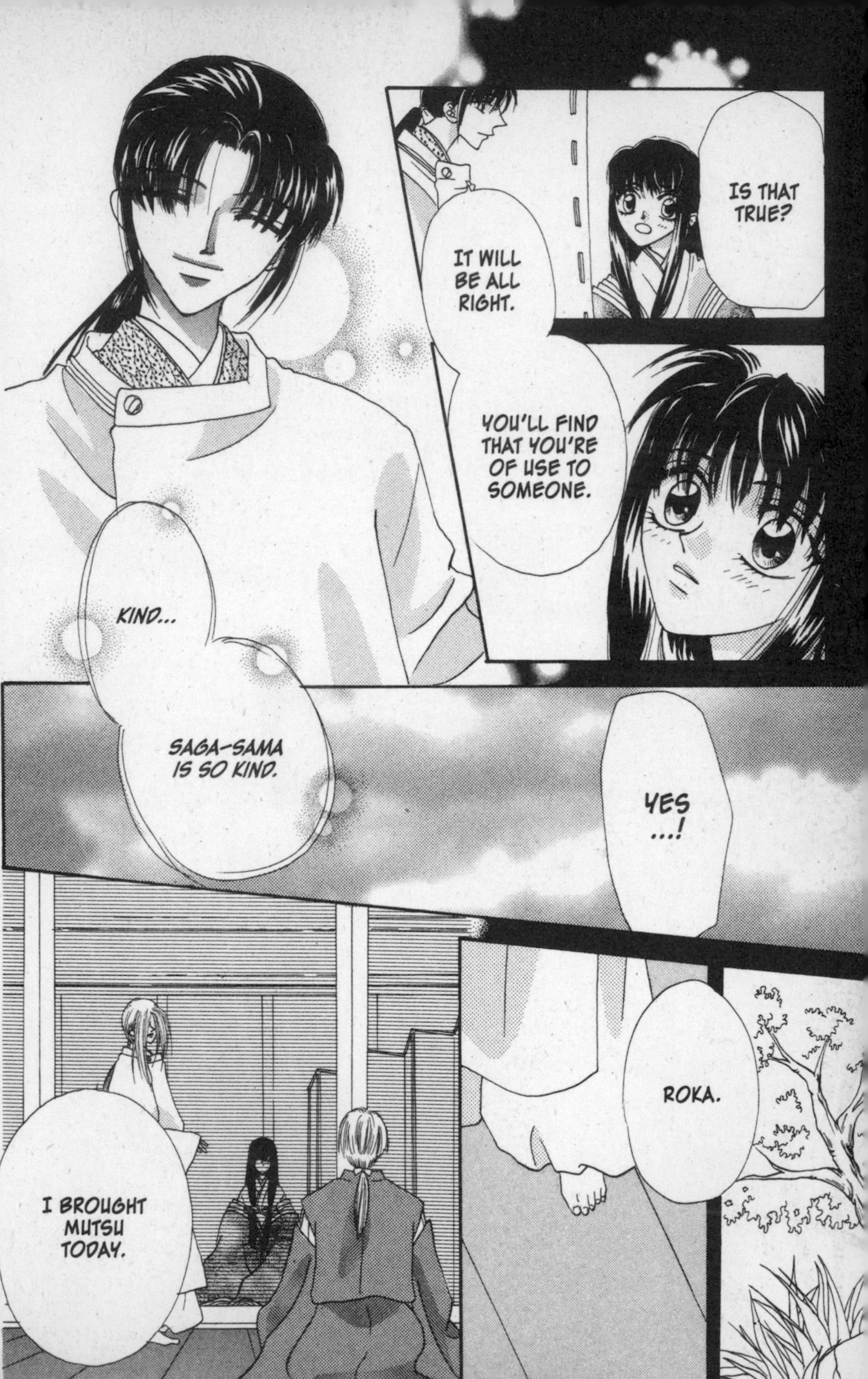
IS THAT TRUE?
IT WILL BE ALL RIGHT.
YOU'LL FIND THAT YOU'RE OF USE TO SOMEONE.
KIND...
SAGA-SAMA IS SO KIND.
YES ...!
ROKA.
I BROUGHT MUTSU TODAY.

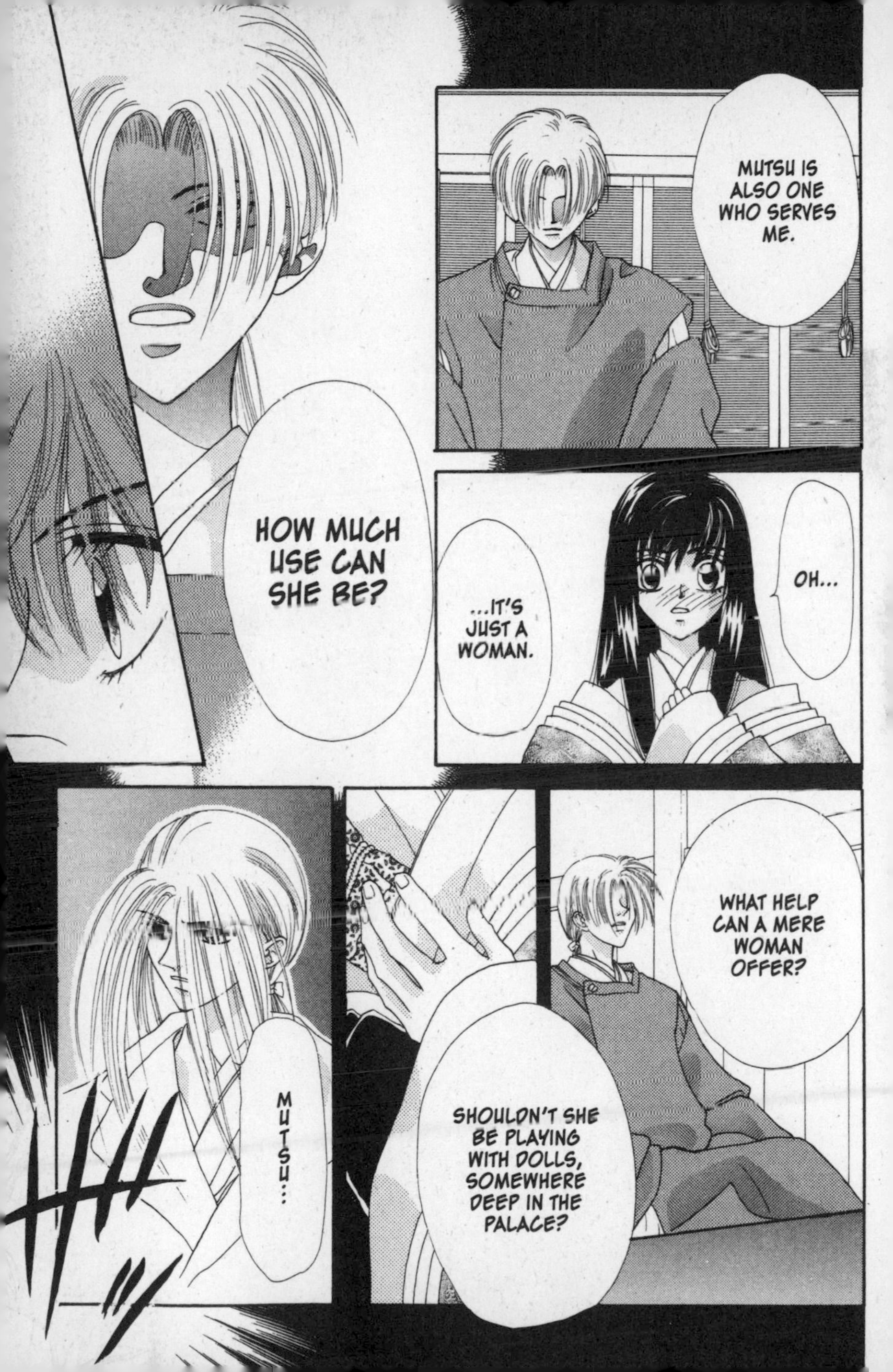
MUTSU IS ALSO ONE WHO SERVES ME.
OH...
...IT'S JUST A WOMAN.
HOW MUCH USE CAN SHE BE?
WHAT HELP CAN A MERE WOMAN OFFER?
SHOULDN'T SHE BE PLAYING WITH DOLLS, SOMEWHERE DEEP IN THE PALACE?
MUTSU...

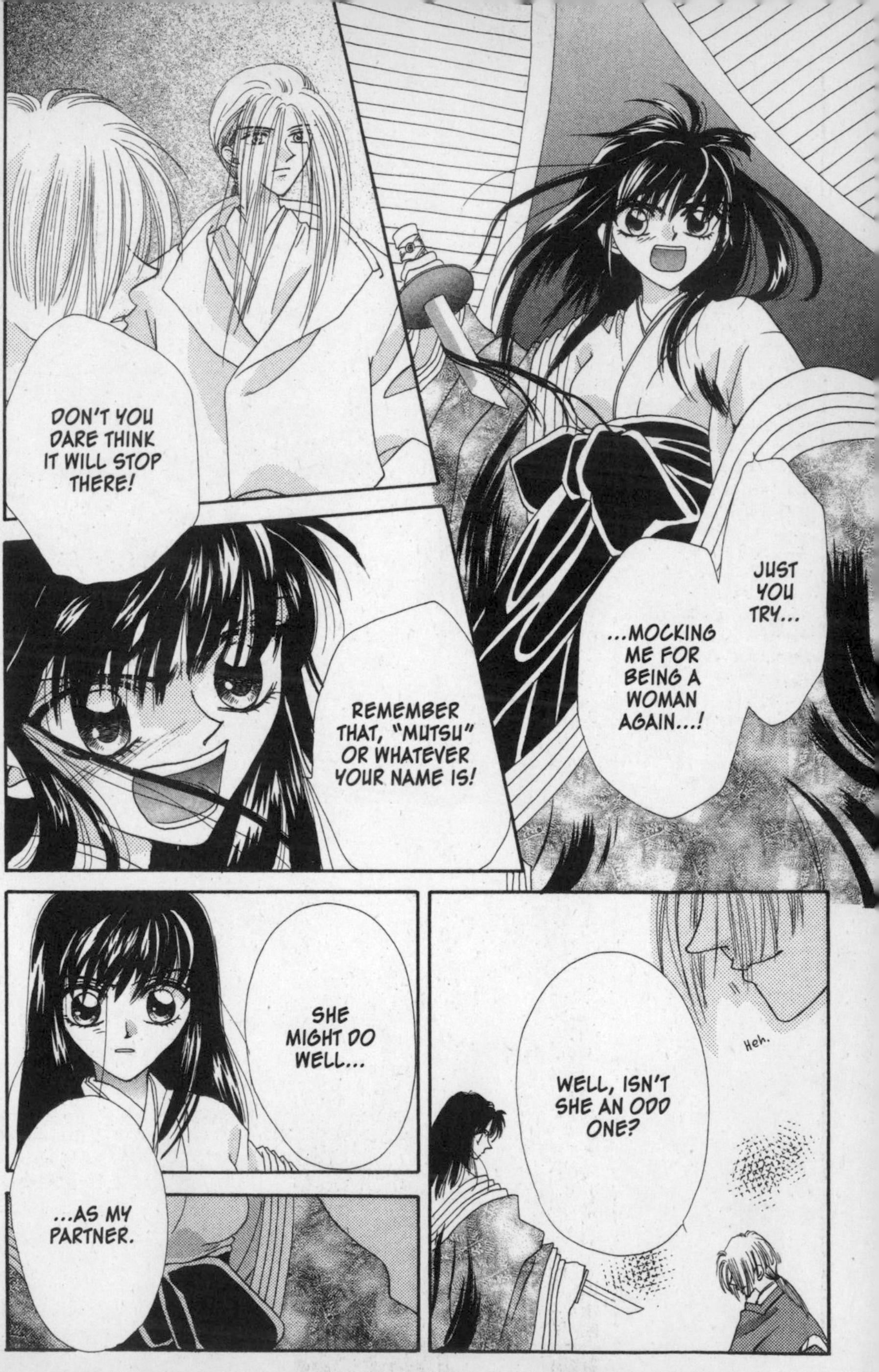
JUST YOU TRY...
...MOCKING ME FOR BEING A WOMAN AGAIN...!
DON'T YOU DARE THINK IT WILL STOP THERE!
REMEMBER THAT, "MUTSU" OR WHATEVER YOUR NAME IS!
Heh.
WELL, ISN'T SHE AN ODD ONE?
SHE MIGHT DO WELL...
...AS MY PARTNER.

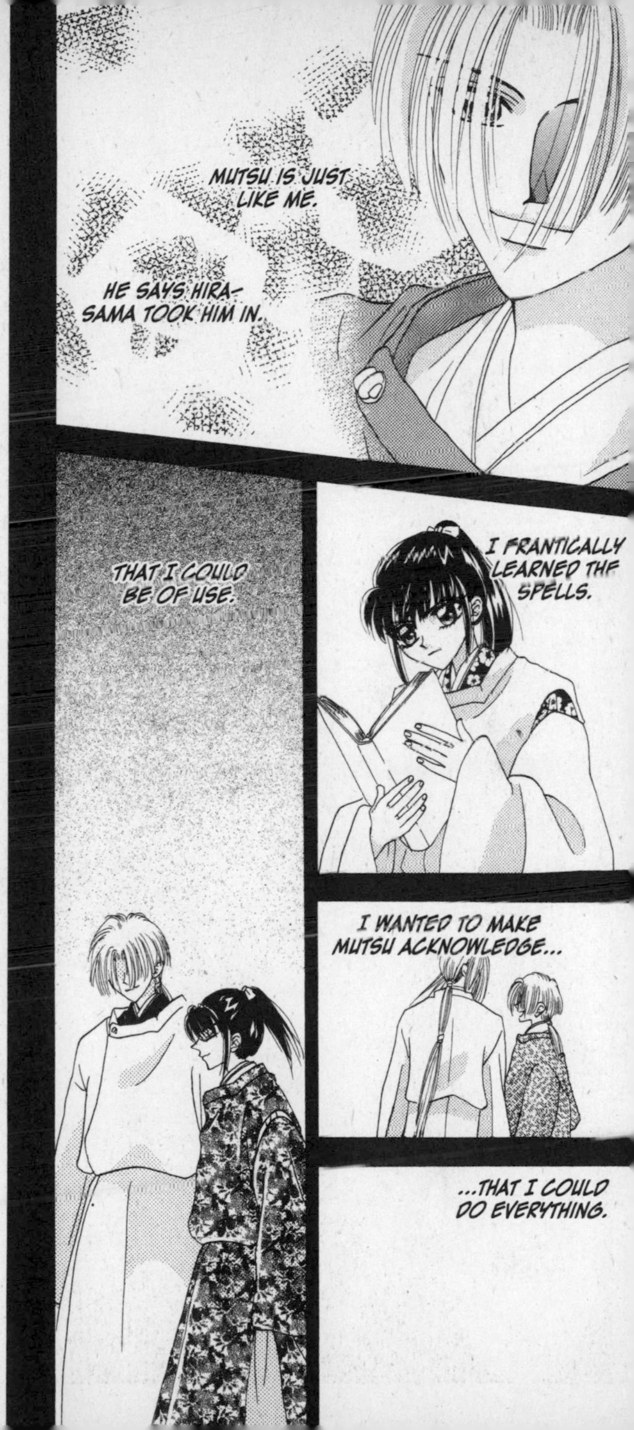
MUTSU IS JUST LIKE ME.
HE SAYS HIRA-SAMA TOOK HIM IN.
I FRANTICALLY LEARNED THE SPELLS.
I WANTED TO MAKE MUTSU ACKNOWLEDGE...
...THAT I COULD DO EVERYTHING.
THAT I COULD BE OF USE.

Scroll Five

Right now the games I'm playing are Kowloon's Gate, I.Q. and PaRappa the Rapper. "COOL" is pretty hard. I'm waiting for Final Fantasy Tactics, Biohazard 2 and Front Mission 2. Thinking about Front...the one before this one amazed me. The ending's direction was cool, wasn't it? Sakata-san was surprisingly old. Stuff like that. (laughs) Looks so young, though. Yan was invincible alone, and that felt good. Although Yan's too strong, so I beat everyone on my own. First Sutan Davuru no Arashi. Of course, mostly I have FF. ♥ It's hard to play Kowloon because I get motion sick. The enemies aren't good, either, and the fields run by, and the ground makes me go "ugh..." a little. (As you can see, I gave up censoring the names.) The movement in games keeps getting more realistic, but... please, not that. Games support my soul!

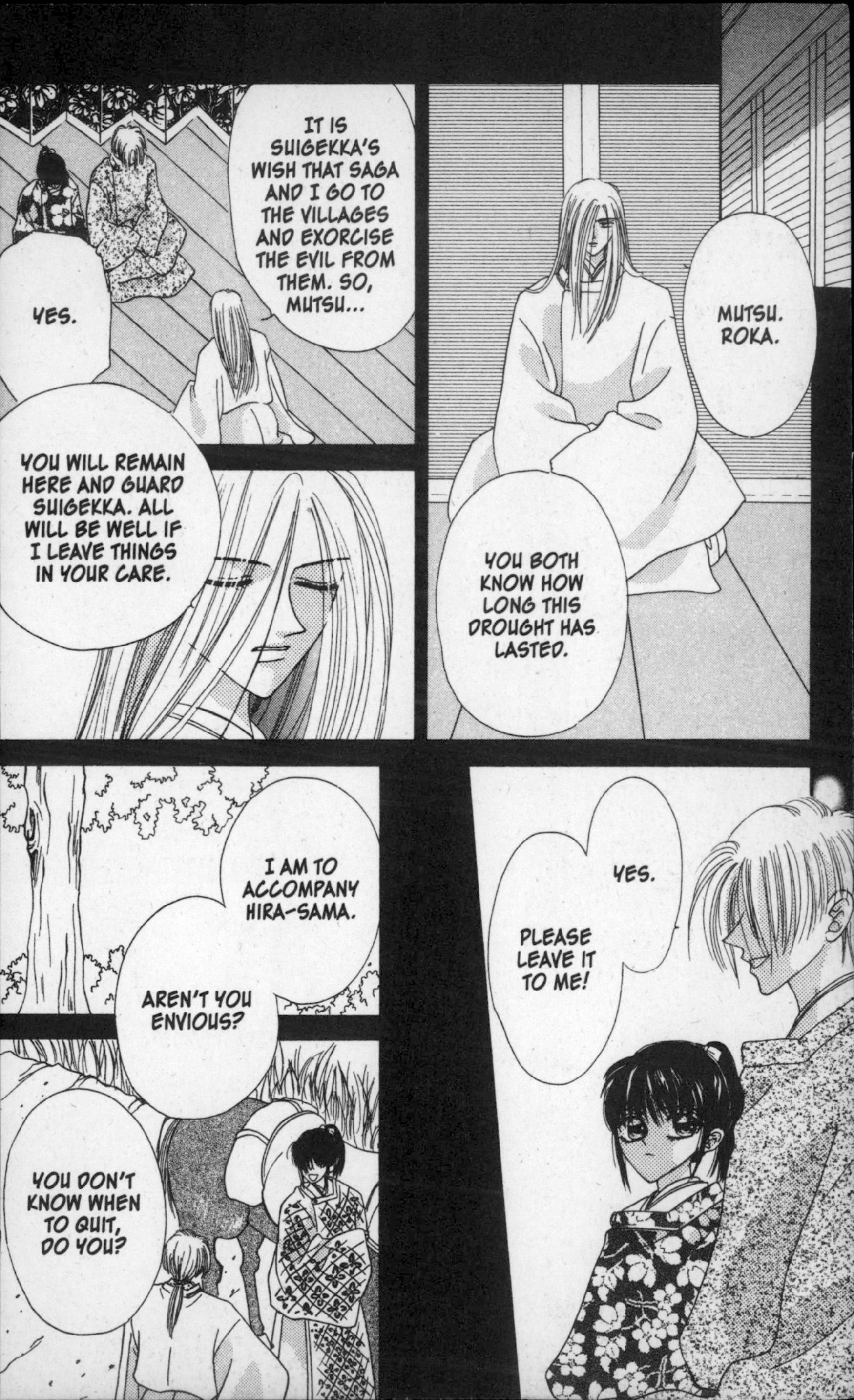
MUTSU. ROKA.
YOU BOTH KNOW HOW LONG THIS DROUGHT HAS LASTED.
IT IS SUIGEKKA'S WISH THAT SAGA AND I GO TO THE VILLAGES AND EXORCISE THE EVIL FROM THEM. SO, MUTSU...
YES.
YOU WILL REMAIN HERE AND GUARD SUIGEKKA. ALL WILL BE WELL IF I LEAVE THINGS IN YOUR CARE.
YES.
PLEASE LEAVE IT TO ME!
I AM TO ACCOMPANY HIRA-SAMA.
AREN'T YOU ENVIOUS?
YOU DON'T KNOW WHEN TO QUIT, DO YOU?

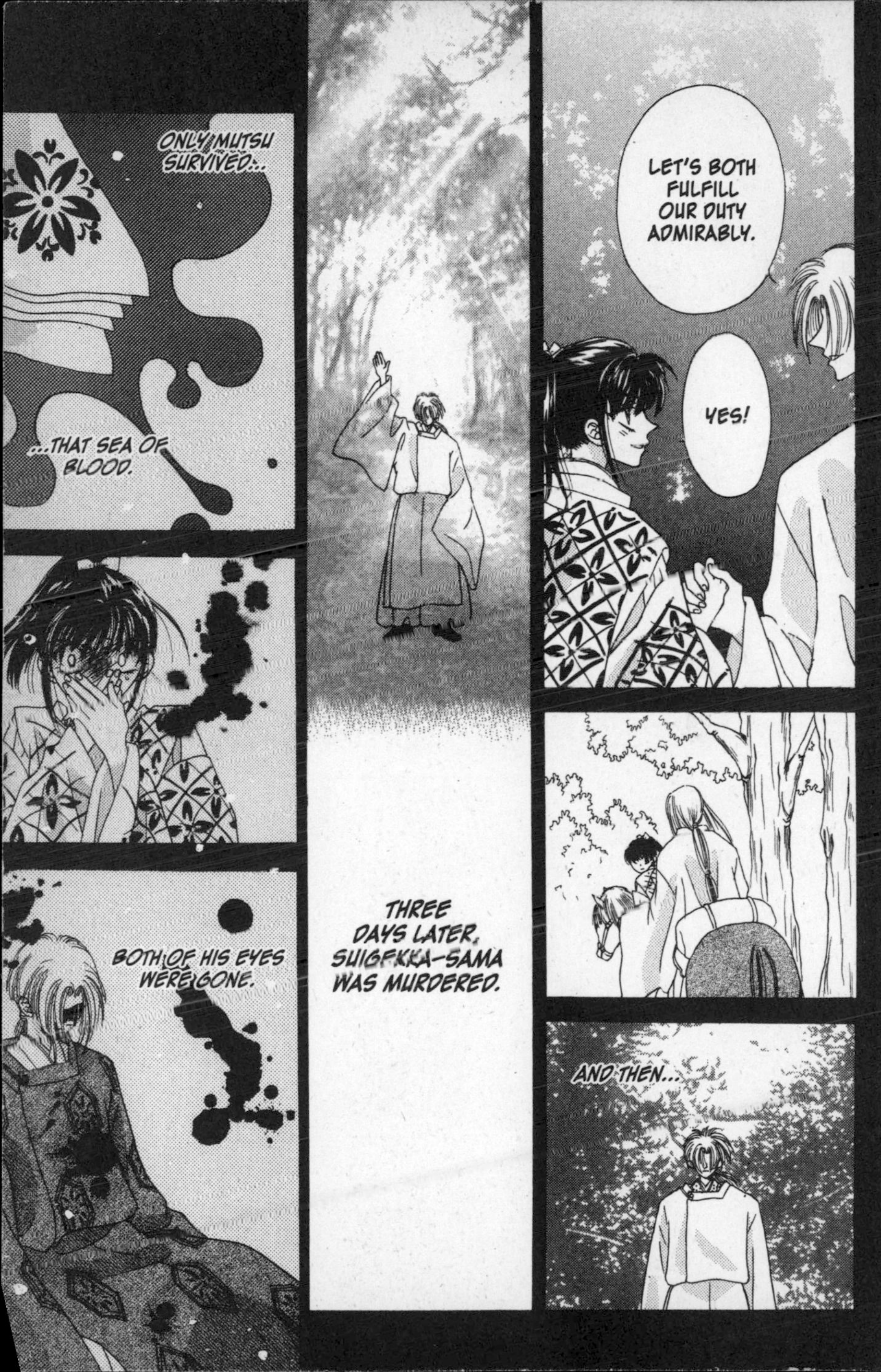
LET'S BOTH FULFILL OUR DUTY ADMIRABLY.
YES!
AND THEN...
THREE DAYS LATER, SUIGEKKA-SAMA WAS MURDERED.
ONLY MUTSU SURVIVED...
...THAT SEA OF BLOOD.
BOTH OF HIS EYES WERE GONE.

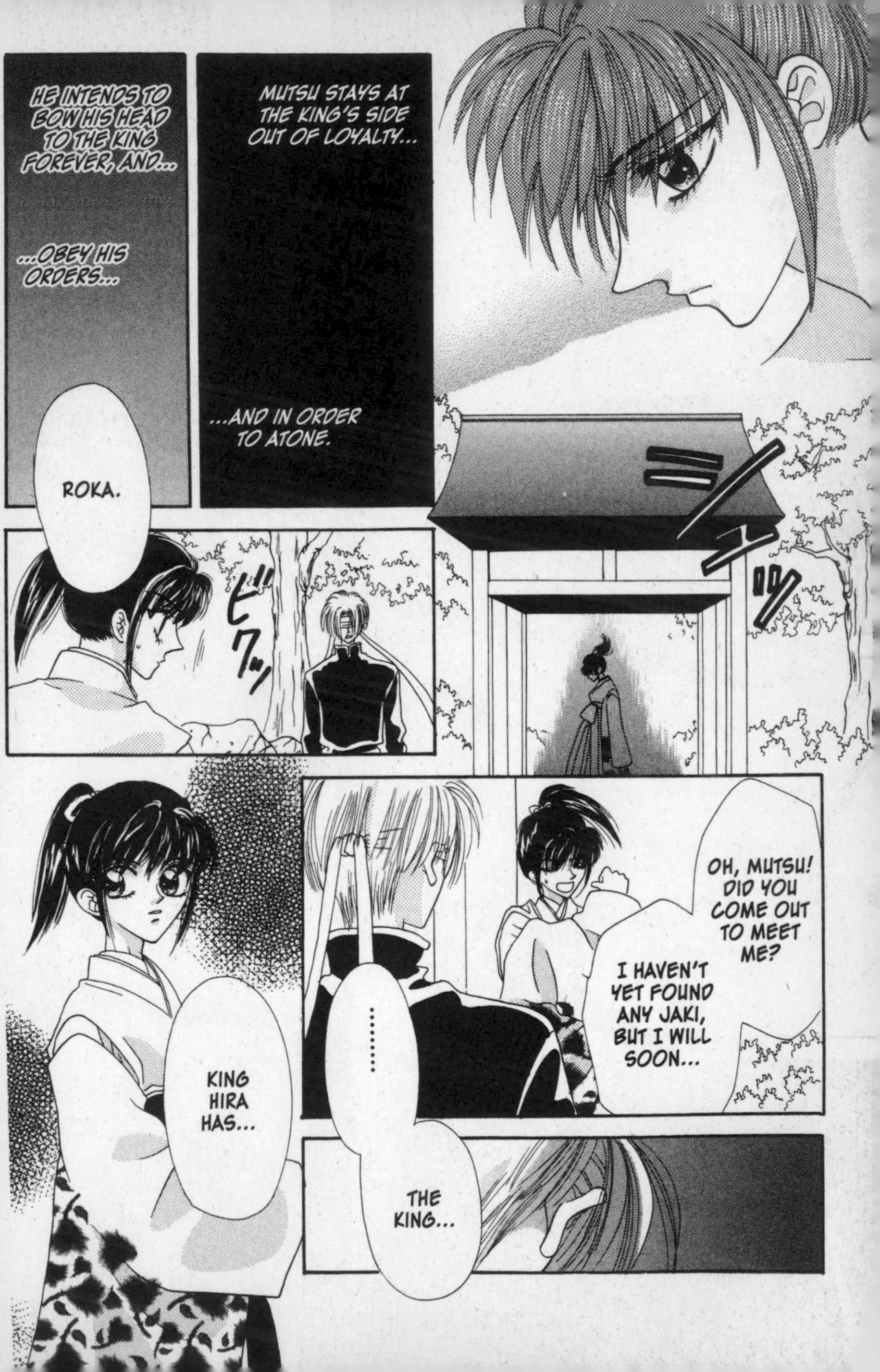
MUTSU STAYS AT THE KING'S SIDE OUT OF LOYALTY...
...AND IN ORDER TO ATONE.
HE INTENDS TO BOW HIS HEAD TO THE KING FOREVER, AND...
...OBEY HIS ORDERS...
ROKA.
ビクッ
OH, MUTSU! DID YOU COME OUT TO MEET ME?
I HAVEN'T YET FOUND ANY JAKI, BUT I WILL SOON...
......
THE KING...
KING HIRA HAS...

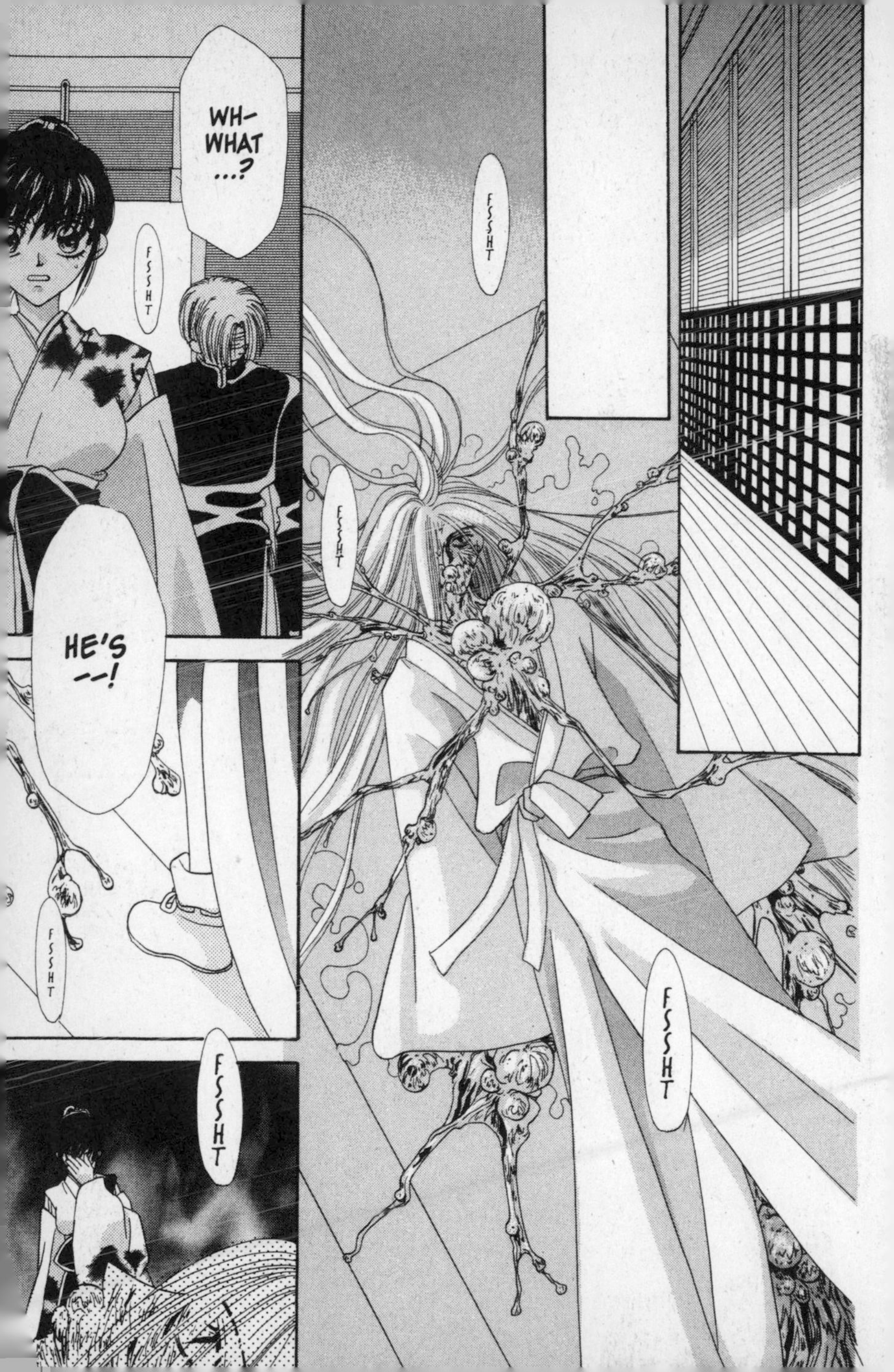
FSSHT
FSSHT
FSSHT
WH- WHAT ...?
FSSHT
HE'S --!
FSSHT
FSSHT

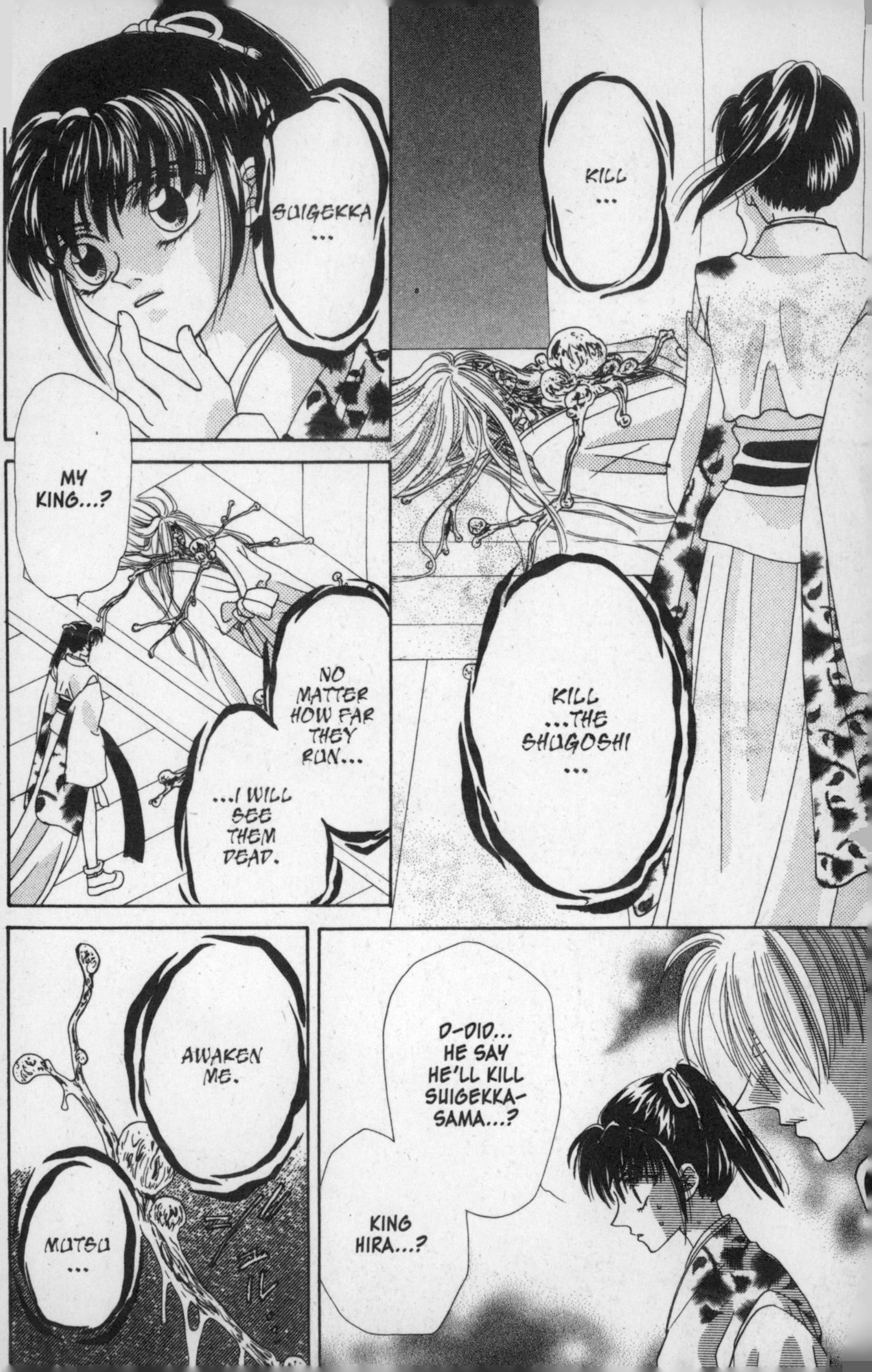
KILL ...
KILL ...THE SHUGOSHI ...
SUIGEKKA ...
MY KING...?
NO MATTER HOW FAR THEY RUN...
...I WILL SEE THEM DEAD.
D-DID... HE SAY HE'LL KILL SUIGEKKA-SAMA...?
KING HIRA...?
AWAKEN ME.
MUTSU ...

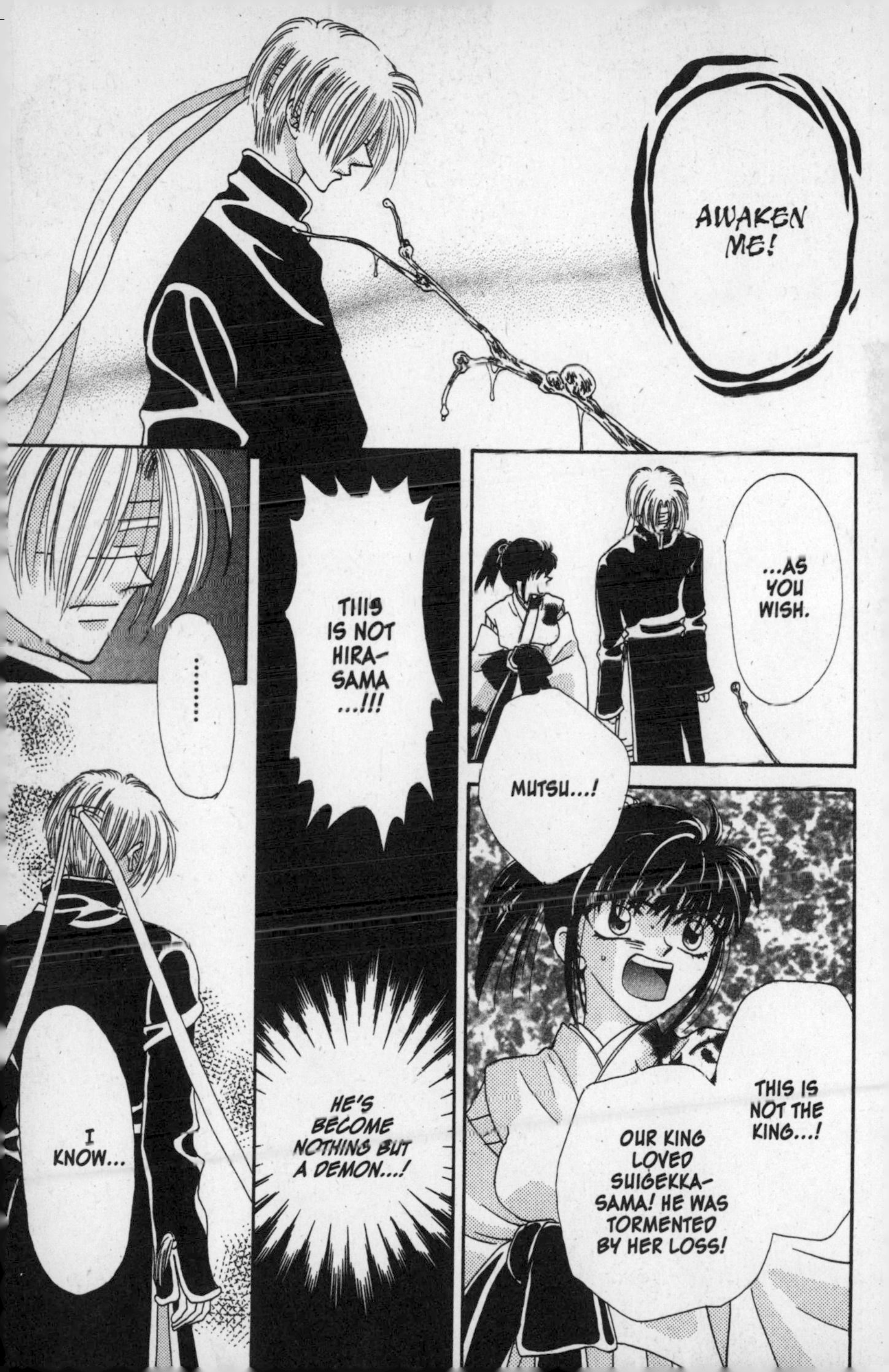
AWAKEN ME!
...AS YOU WISH.
MUTSU...!
THIS IS NOT THE KING...!
OUR KING LOVED SUIGEKKA-SAMA! HE WAS TORMENTED BY HER LOSS!
THIS IS NOT HIRA-SAMA...!!!
HE'S BECOME NOTHING BUT A DEMON...!
....
I KNOW...

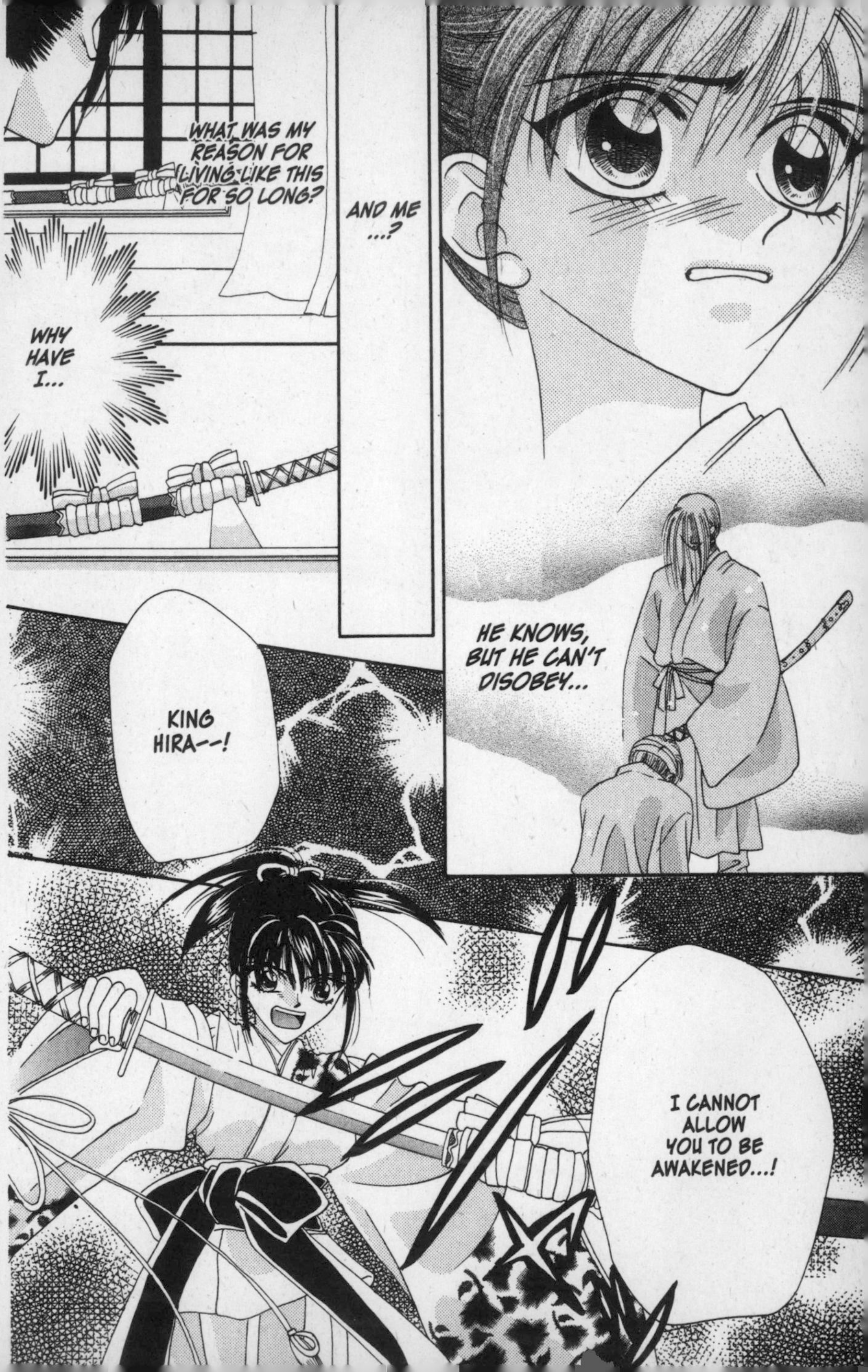
HE KNOWS, BUT HE CAN'T DISOBEY...
AND ME ...?
WHAT WAS MY REASON FOR LIVING LIKE THIS FOR SO LONG?
WHY HAVE I...
KING HIRA--!
I CANNOT ALLOW YOU TO BE AWAKENED...!

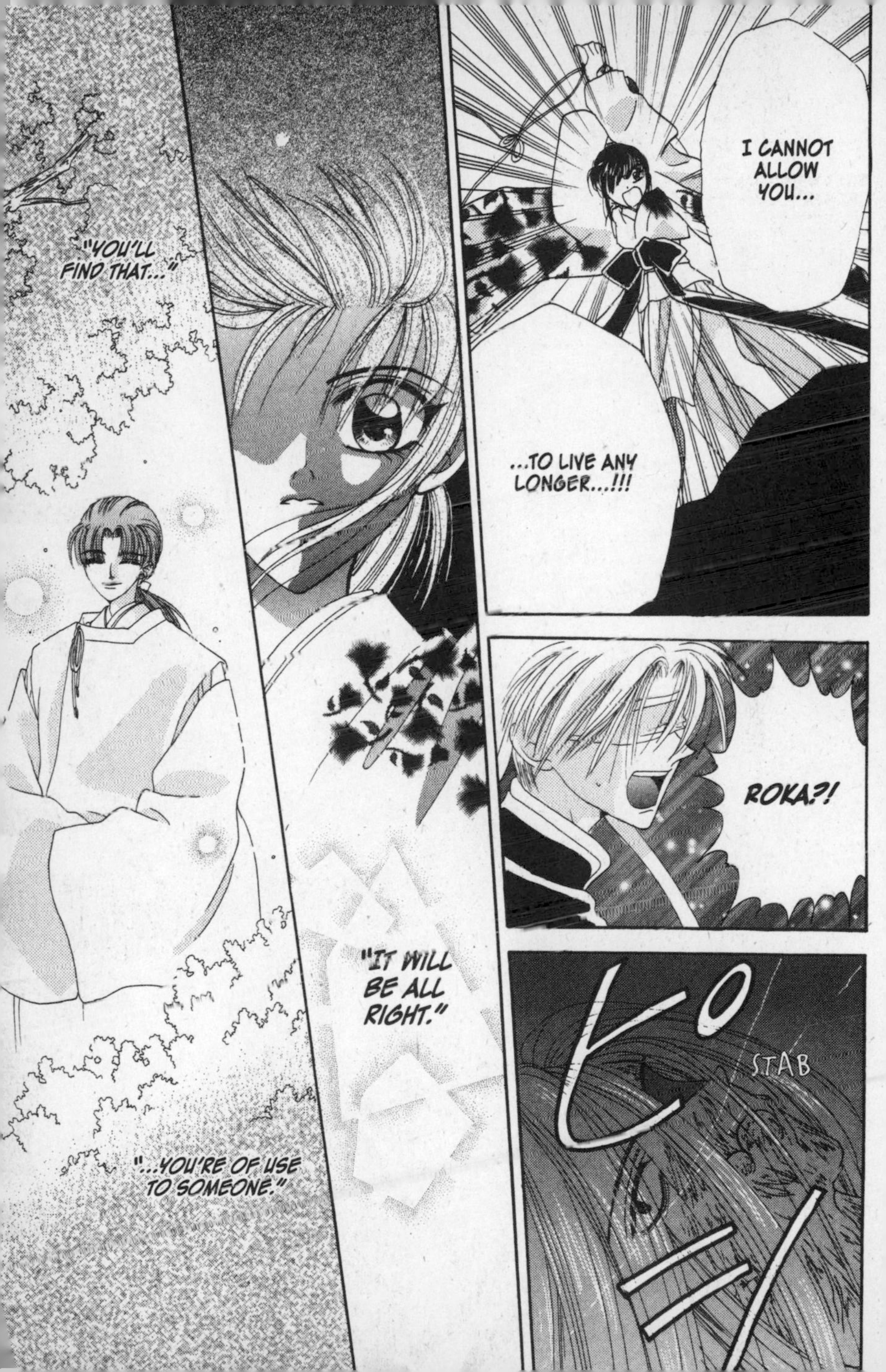
I CANNOT ALLOW YOU...
...TO LIVE ANY LONGER...!!!
ROKA?!
STAB
"IT WILL BE ALL RIGHT."
"YOU'LL FIND THAT..."
"...YOU'RE OF USE TO SOMEONE."

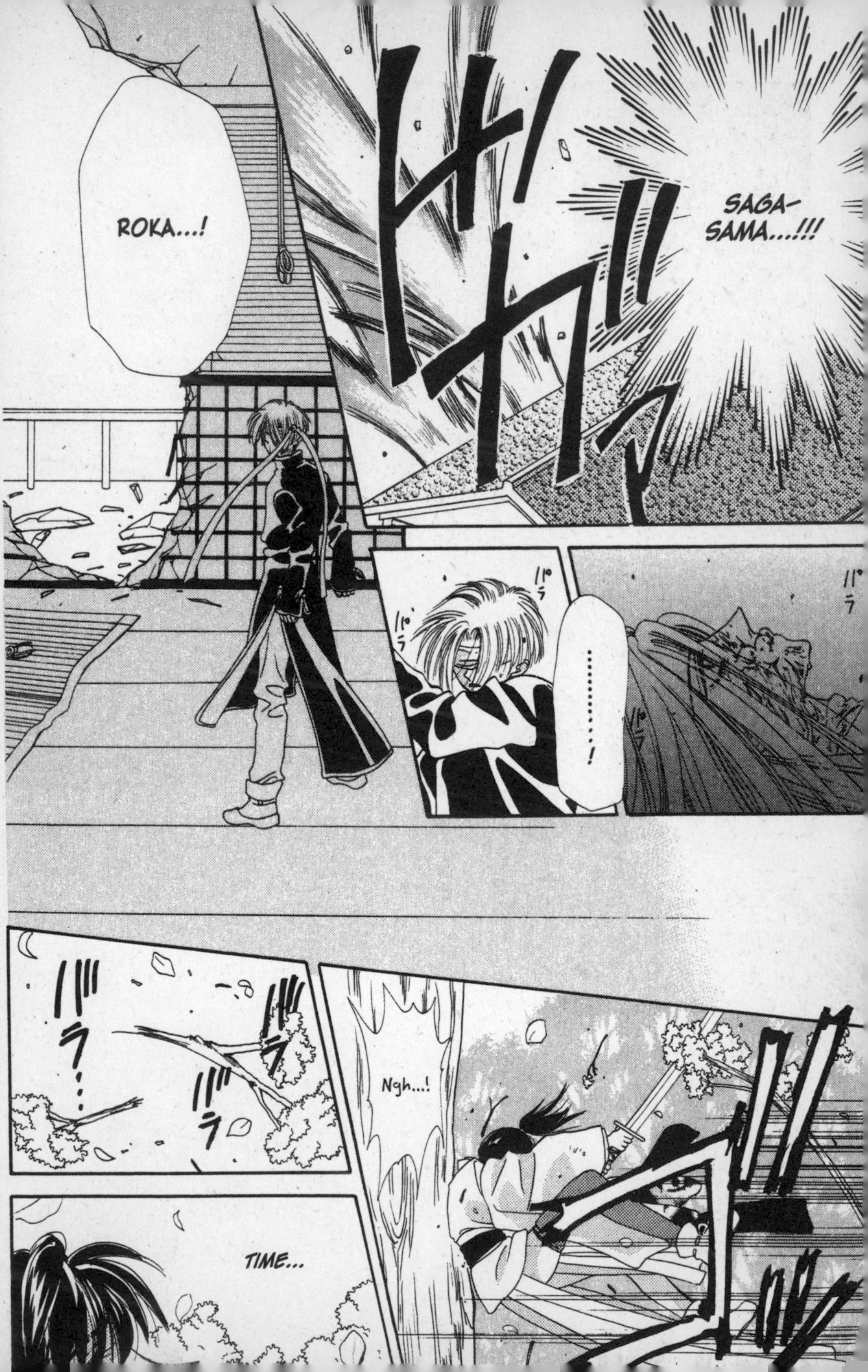

SAGA-SAMA...!!!
......!
ROKA...!
Ngh...!
TIME...

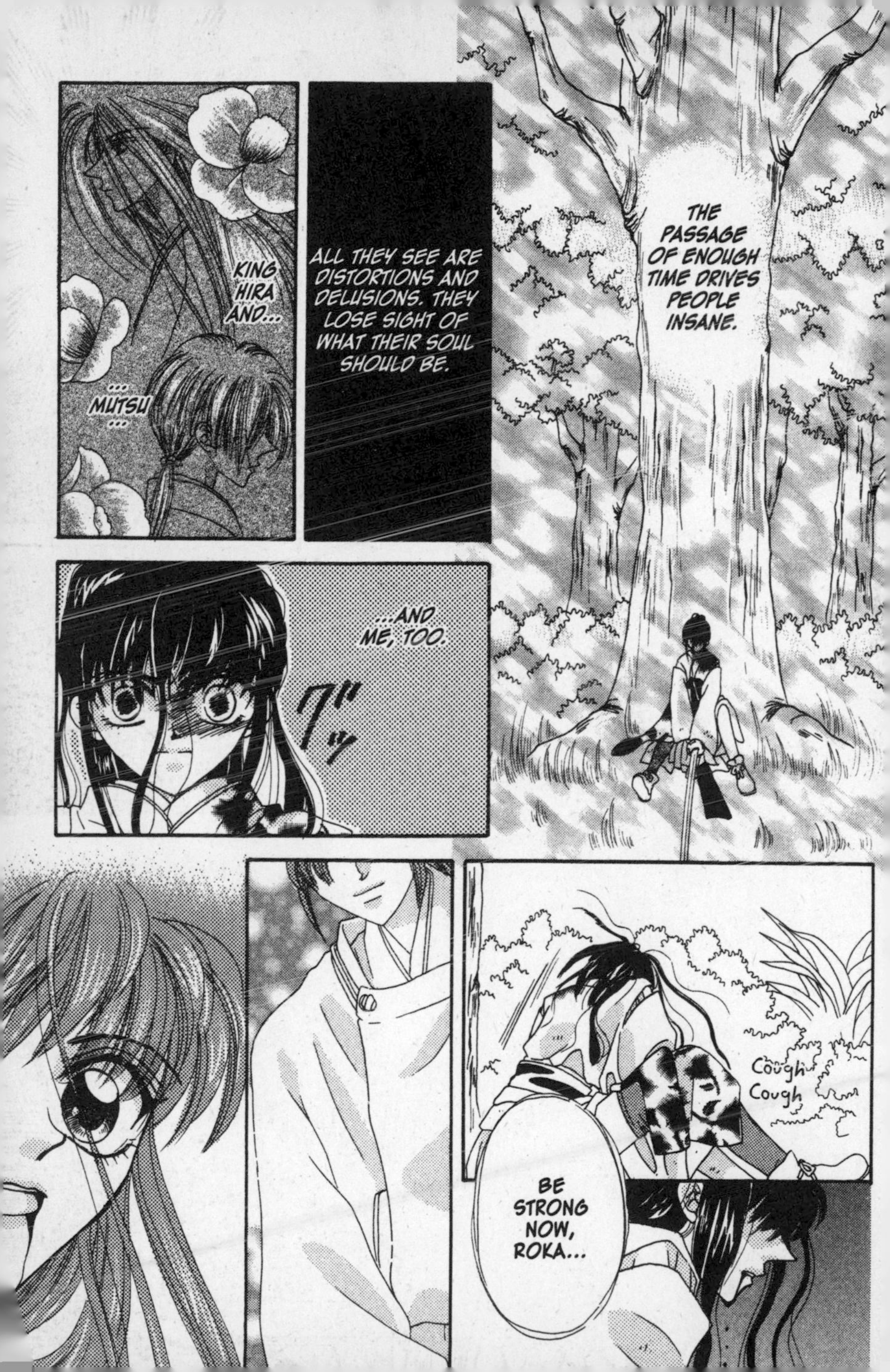
THE PASSAGE OF ENOUGH TIME DRIVES PEOPLE INSANE.
ALL THEY SEE ARE DISTORTIONS AND DELUSIONS. THEY LOSE SIGHT OF WHAT THEIR SOUL SHOULD BE.
KING HIRA AND...
...MUTSU...
...AND ME, TOO.
Cough Cough
BE STRONG NOW, ROKA...

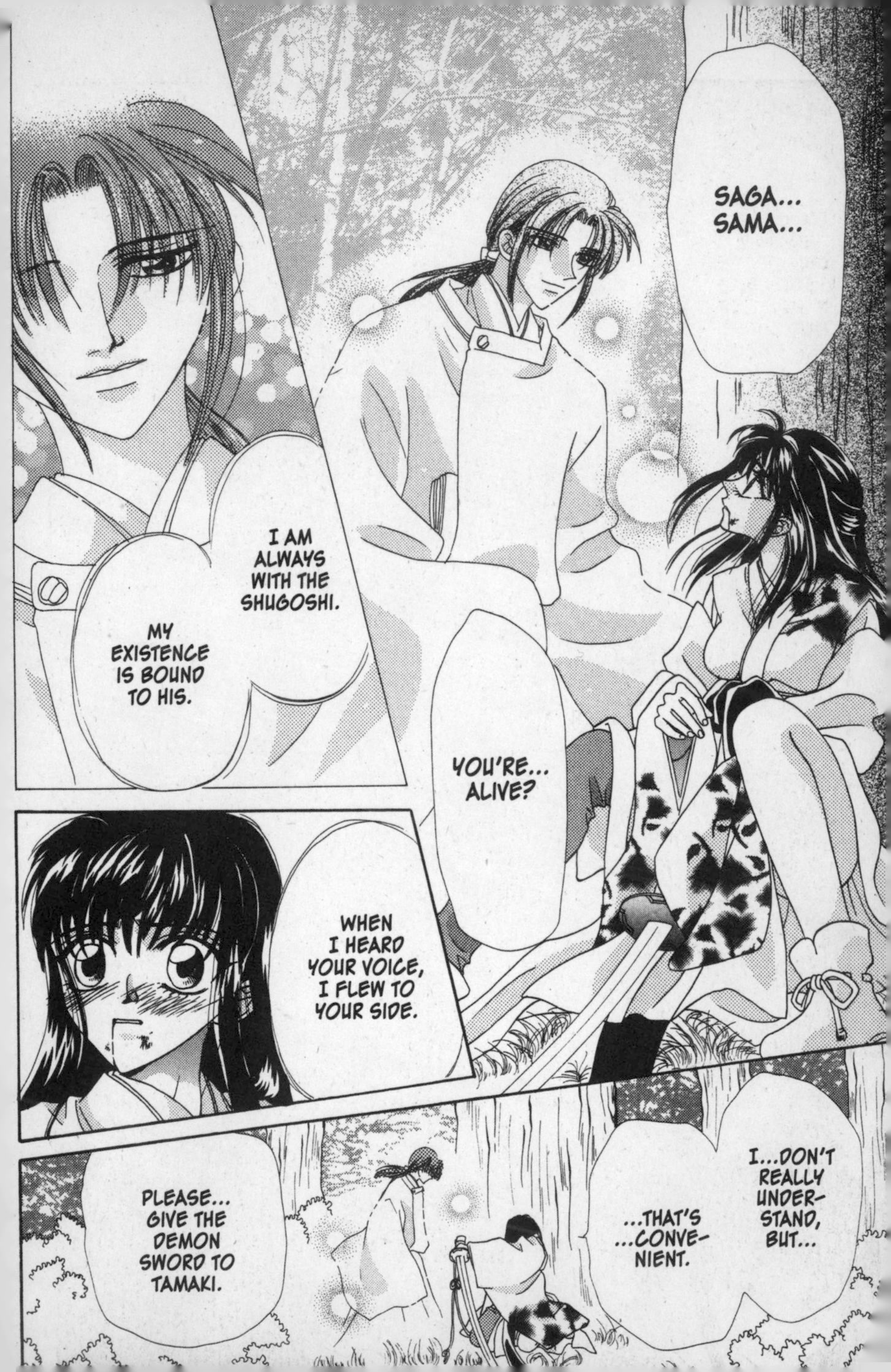
SAGA... SAMA...
YOU'RE... ALIVE?
I AM ALWAYS WITH THE SHUGOSHI.
MY EXISTENCE IS BOUND TO HIS.
WHEN I HEARD YOUR VOICE, I FLEW TO YOUR SIDE.
I...DON'T REALLY UNDER-STAND, BUT...
...THAT'S ...CONVE-NIENT.
PLEASE... GIVE THE DEMON SWORD TO TAMAKI.

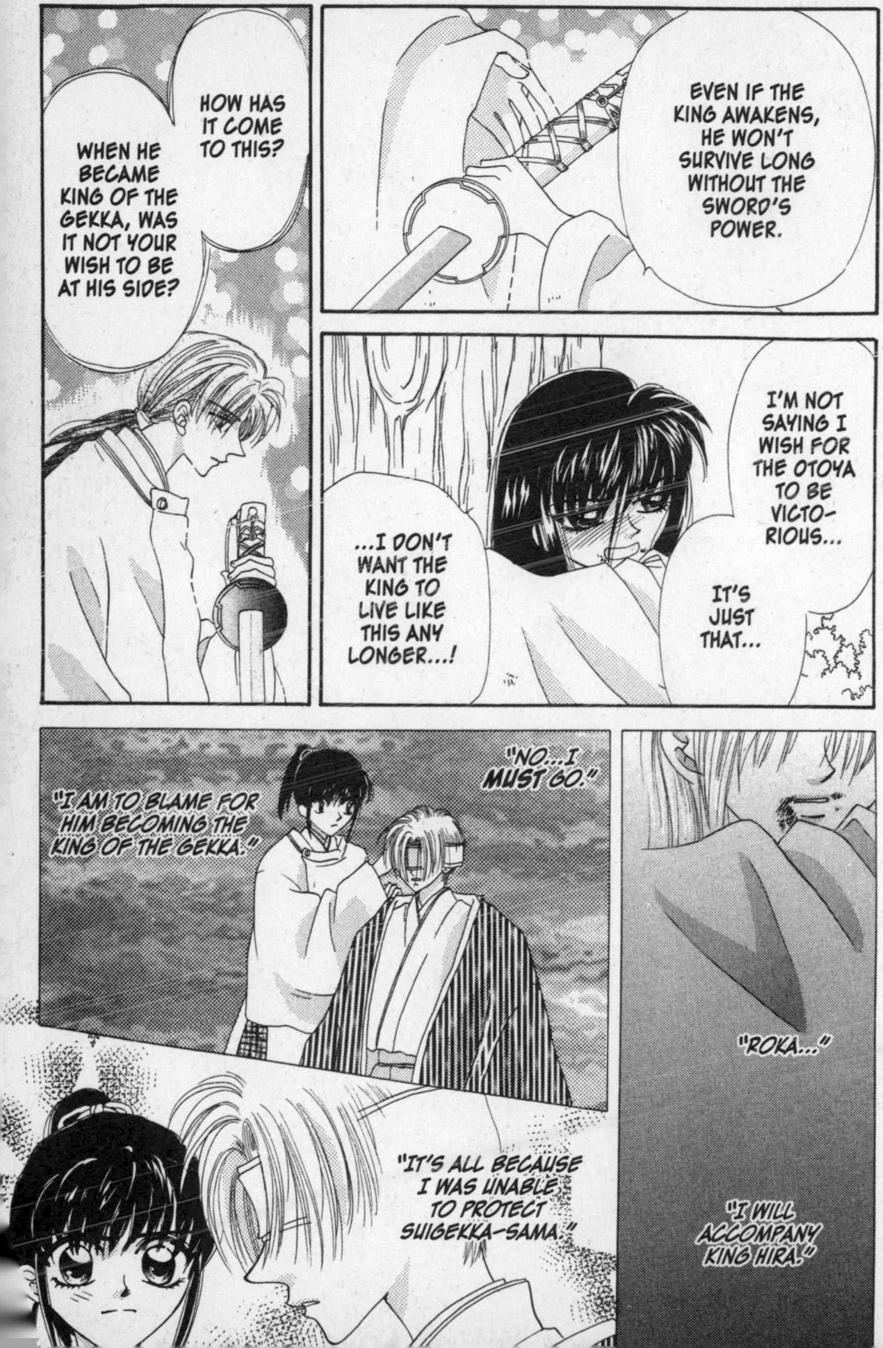
EVEN IF THE KING AWAKENS, HE WON'T SURVIVE LONG WITHOUT THE SWORD'S POWER.
I'M NOT SAYING I WISH FOR THE OTOYA TO BE VICTO-RIOUS...
IT'S JUST THAT...
...I DON'T WANT THE KING TO LIVE LIKE THIS ANY LONGER...!
HOW HAS IT COME TO THIS?
WHEN HE BECAME KING OF THE GEKKA, WAS IT NOT YOUR WISH TO BE AT HIS SIDE?
"ROKA..."
"I WILL ACCOMPANY KING HIRA."
"NO...I MUST GO."
"I AM TO BLAME FOR HIM BECOMING THE KING OF THE GEKKA."
"IT'S ALL BECAUSE I WAS UNABLE TO PROTECT SUIGEKKA-SAMA."

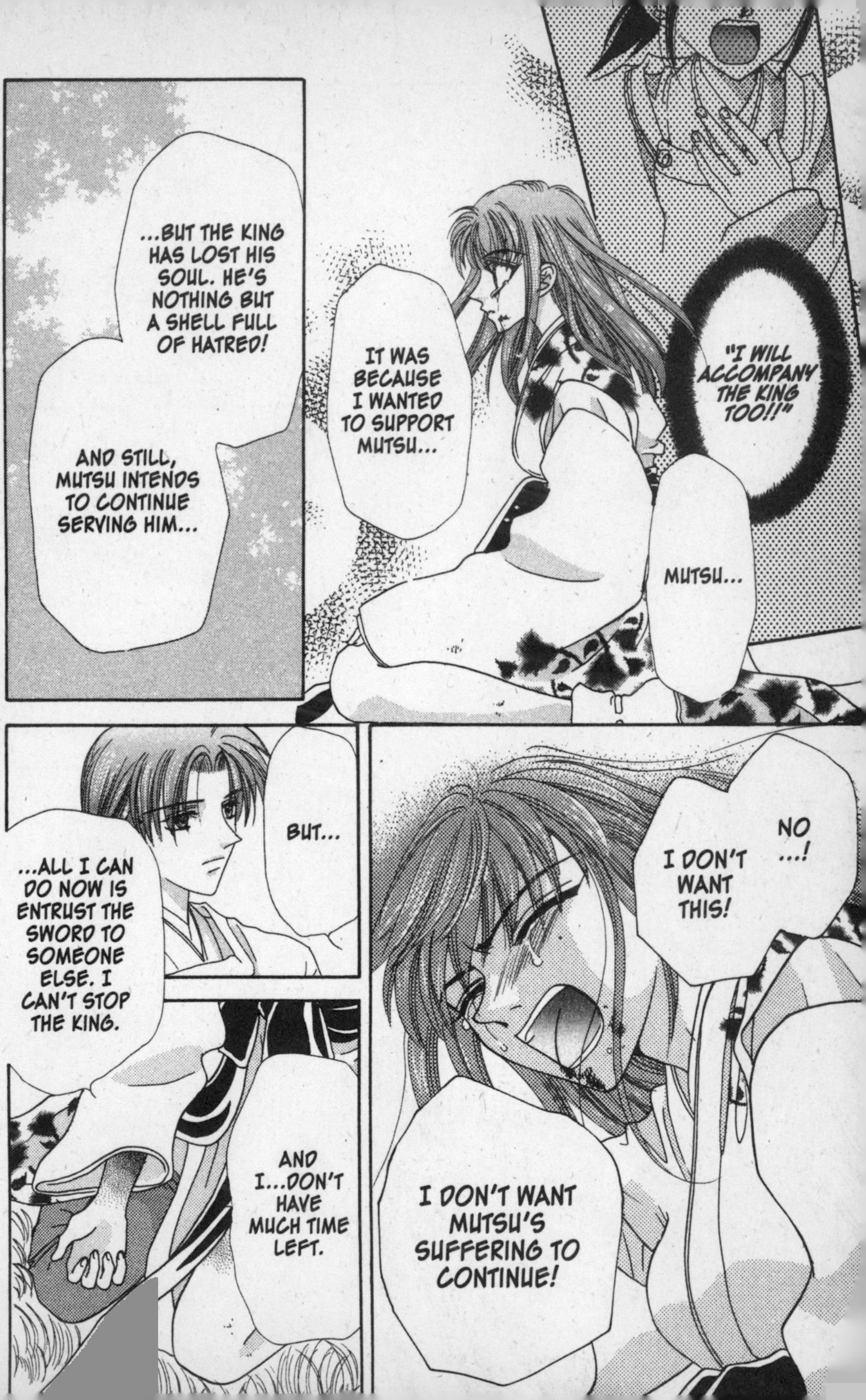
"I WILL ACCOMPANY THE KING TOO!!"
MUTSU...
IT WAS BECAUSE I WANTED TO SUPPORT MUTSU...
...BUT THE KING HAS LOST HIS SOUL. HE'S NOTHING BUT A SHELL FULL OF HATRED!
AND STILL, MUTSU INTENDS TO CONTINUE SERVING HIM...
NO ...!
I DON'T WANT THIS!
I DON'T WANT MUTSU'S SUFFERING TO CONTINUE!
BUT...
...ALL I CAN DO NOW IS ENTRUST THE SWORD TO SOMEONE ELSE. I CAN'T STOP THE KING.
AND I...DON'T HAVE MUCH TIME LEFT.

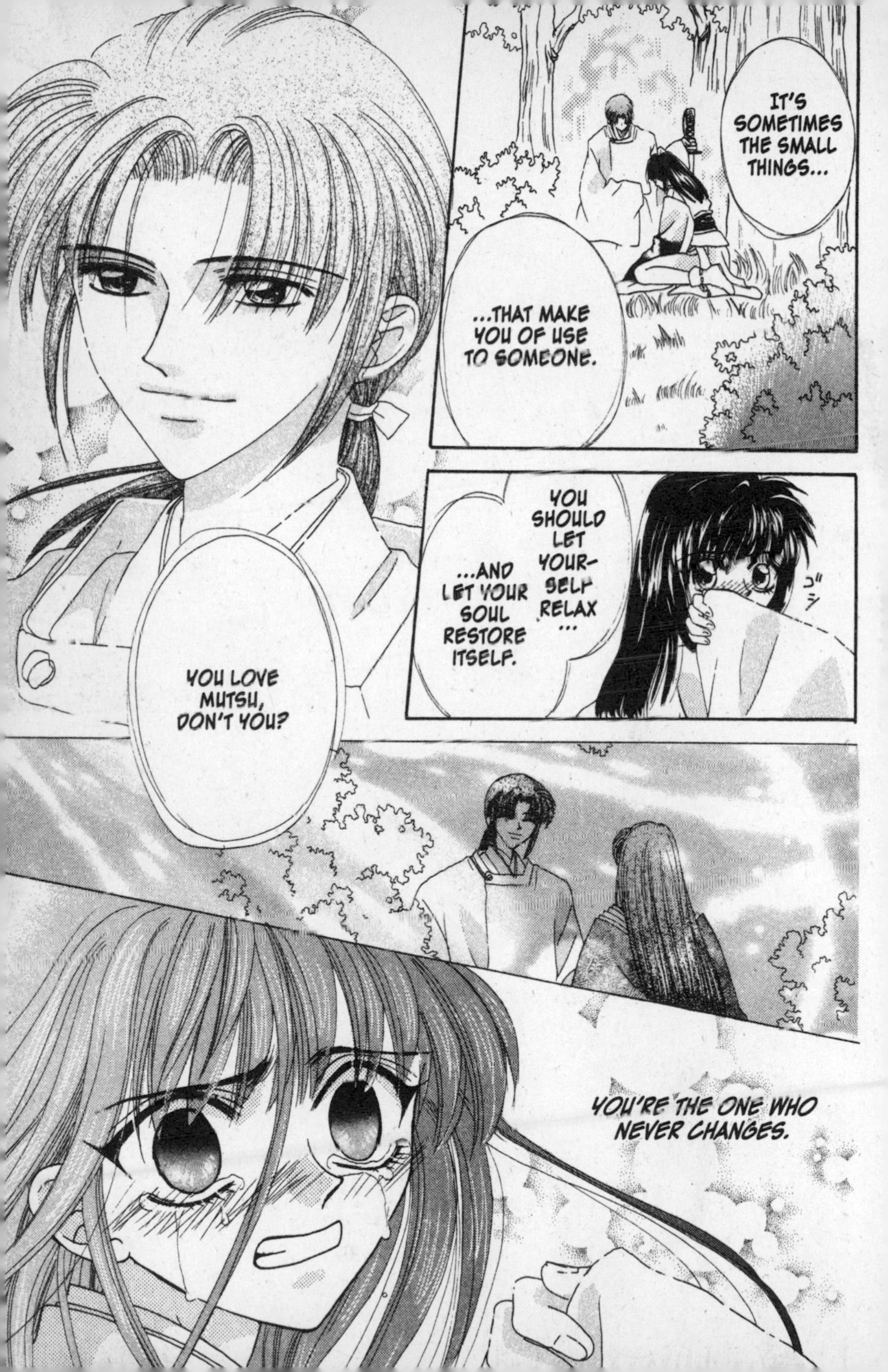
IT'S SOMETIMES THE SMALL THINGS...
...THAT MAKE YOU OF USE TO SOMEONE.
YOU SHOULD LET YOURSELF RELAX...
...AND LET YOUR SOUL RESTORE ITSELF.
ゴシ
YOU LOVE MUTSU, DON'T YOU?
YOU'RE THE ONE WHO NEVER CHANGES.

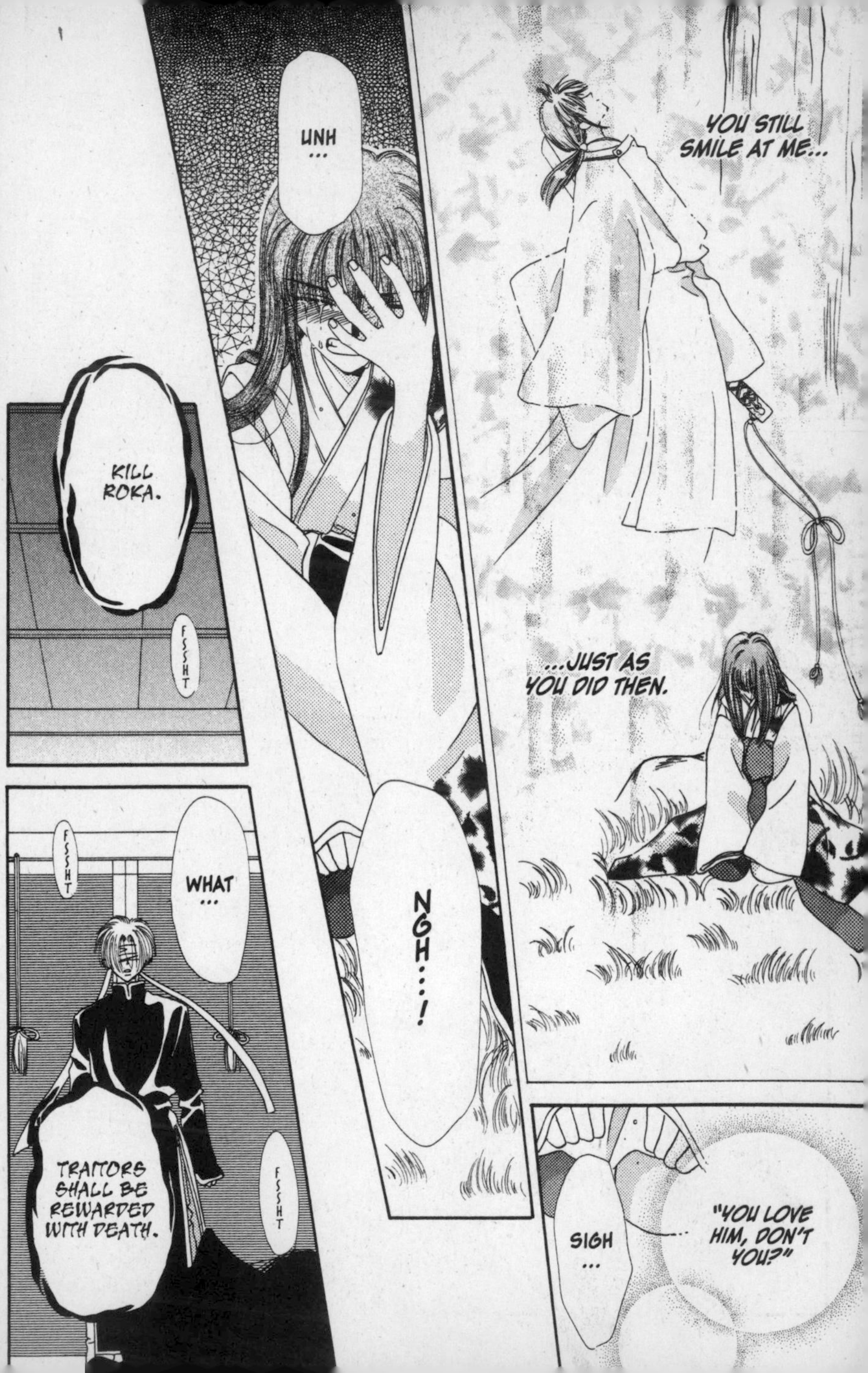
YOU STILL SMILE AT ME...
...JUST AS YOU DID THEN.
"YOU LOVE HIM, DON'T YOU?"
SIGH...
UNH...
NGH...!
KILL ROKA.
FSSHT
FSSHT
WHAT...
TRAITORS SHALL BE REWARDED WITH DEATH.
FSSHT

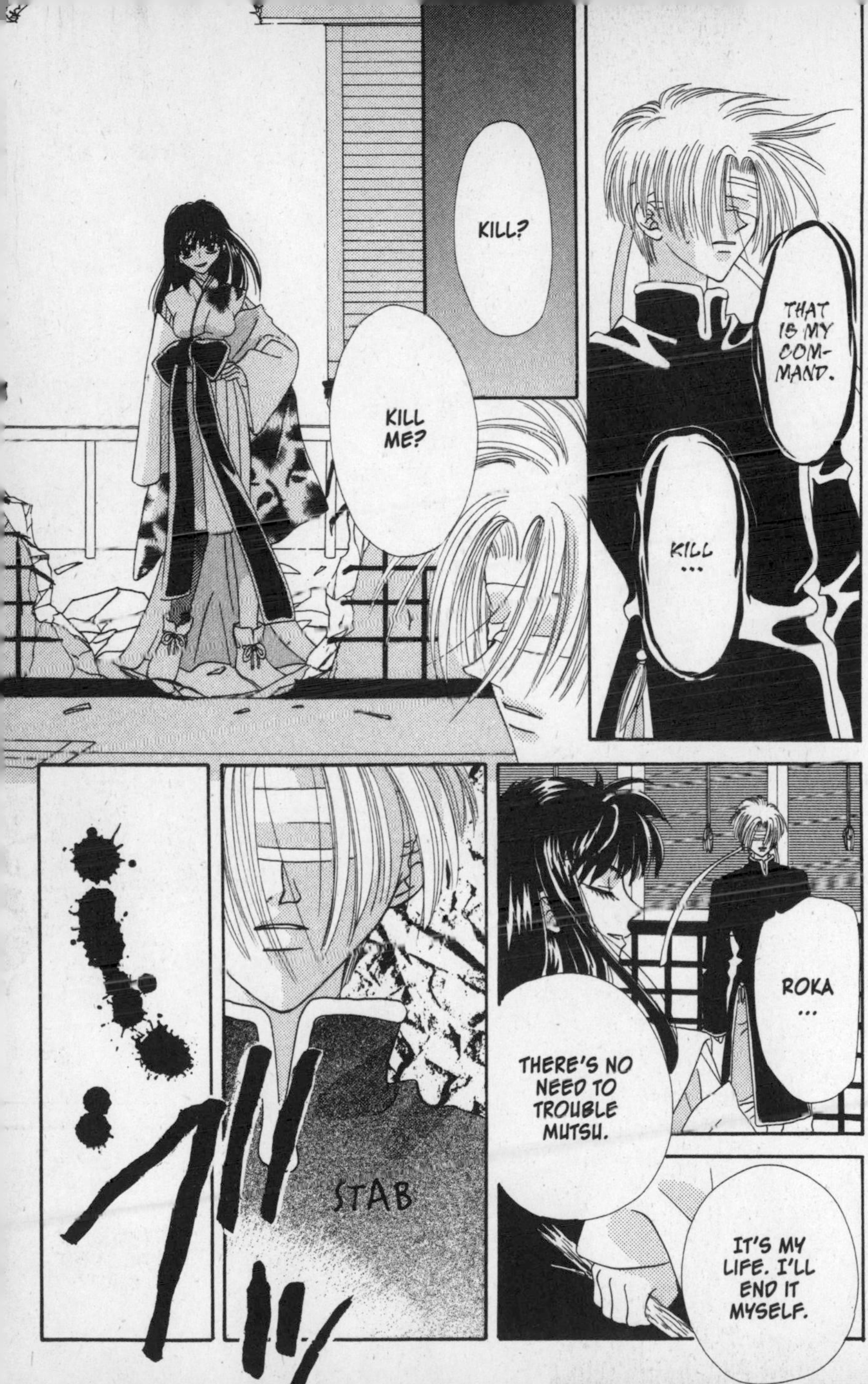
THAT IS MY COM-MAND.
KILL ...
KILL?
KILL ME?
ROKA ...
THERE'S NO NEED TO TROUBLE MUTSU.
IT'S MY LIFE. I'LL END IT MYSELF.
STAB

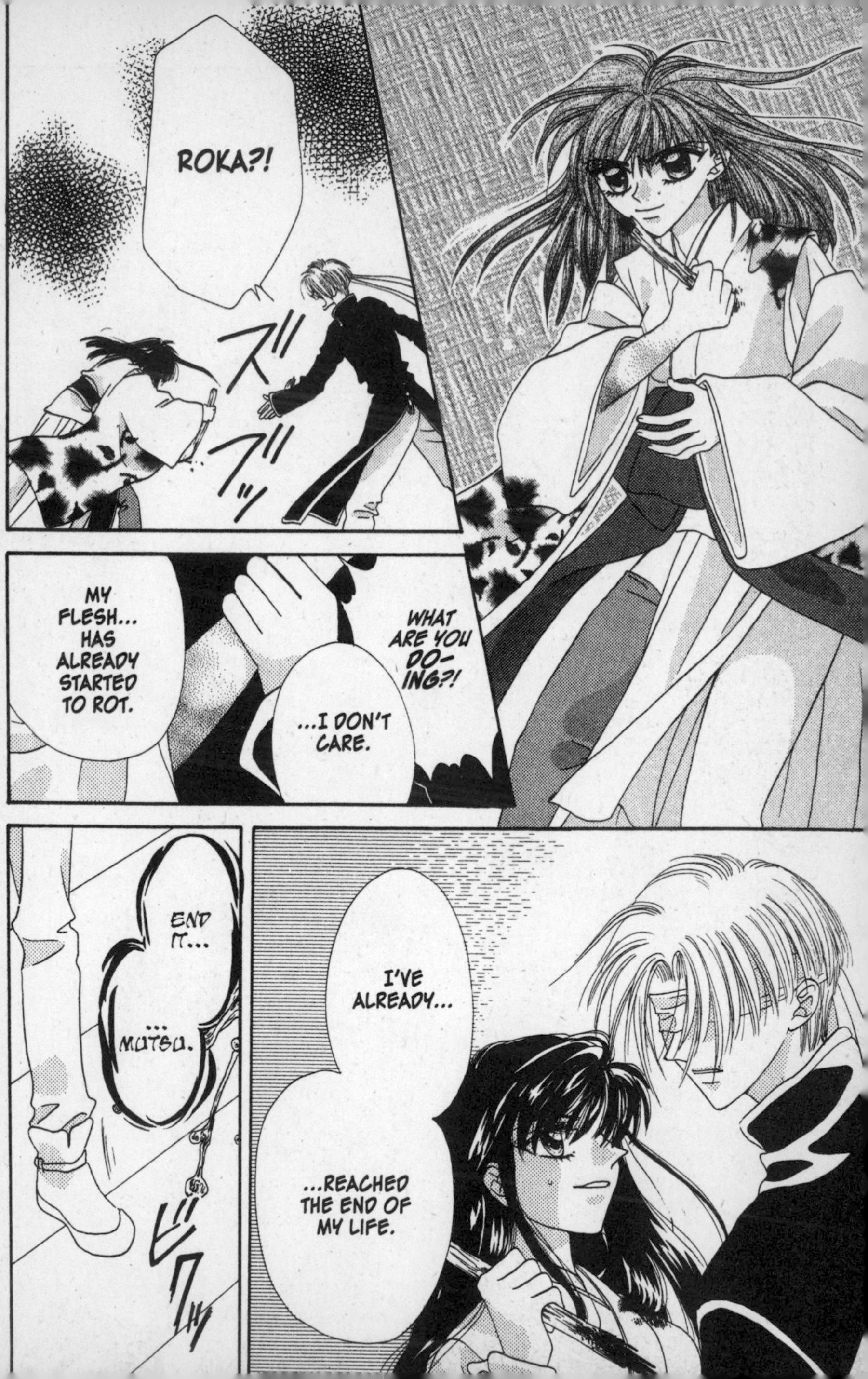
ROKA?!
ズズッ
WHAT ARE YOU DOING?!
MY FLESH... HAS ALREADY STARTED TO ROT.
...I DON'T CARE.
I'VE ALREADY...
...REACHED THE END OF MY LIFE.
END IT...
...MUTSU.
ビクッ

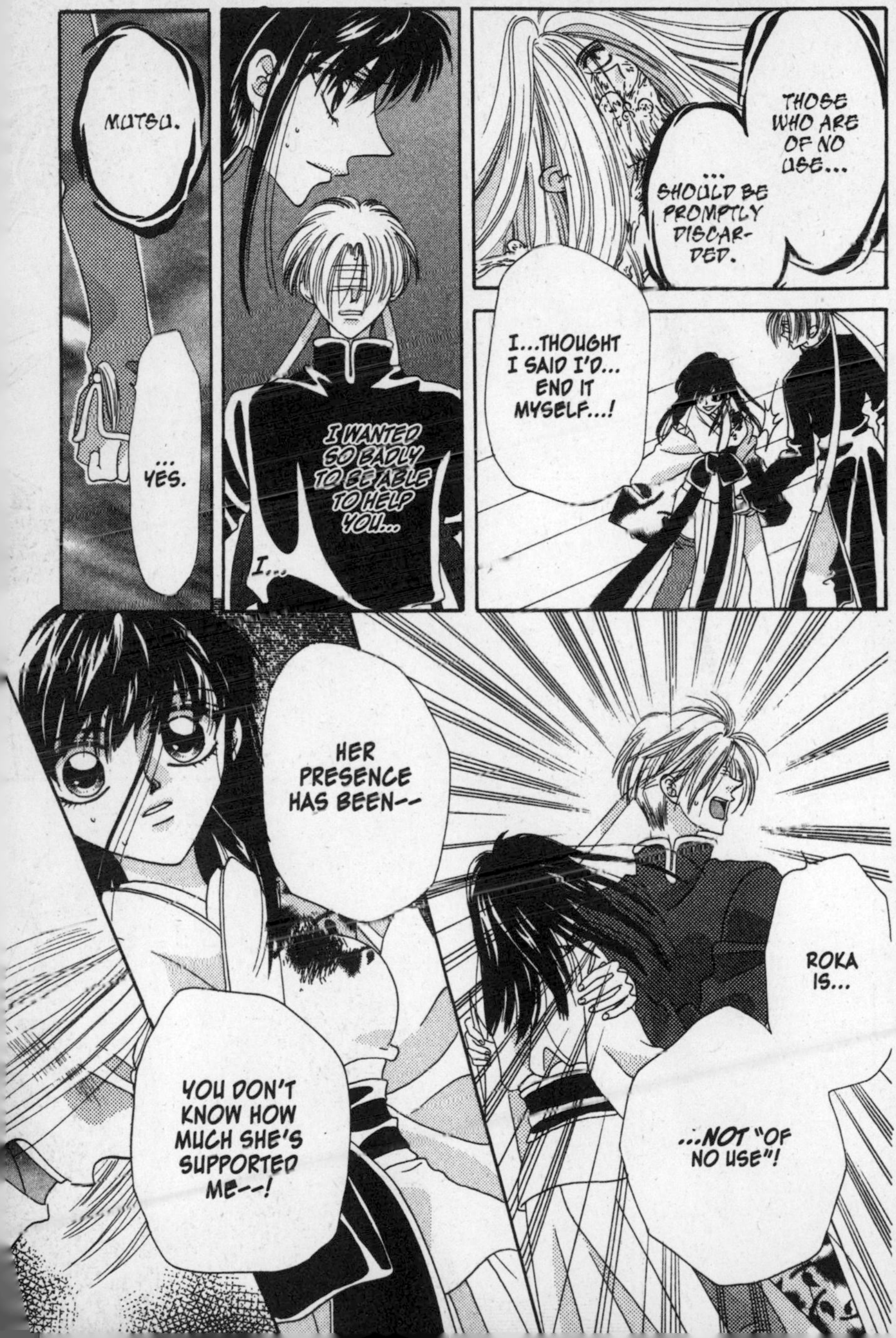
THOSE WHO ARE OF NO USE...
...SHOULD BE PROMPTLY DISCAR-DED.
I...THOUGHT I SAID I'D... END IT MYSELF...!
I WANTED SO BADLY TO BE ABLE TO HELP YOU...
I...
MUTSU.
...YES.
ROKA IS...
...NOT "OF NO USE"!
HER PRESENCE HAS BEEN--
YOU DON'T KNOW HOW MUCH SHE'S SUPPORTED ME--!

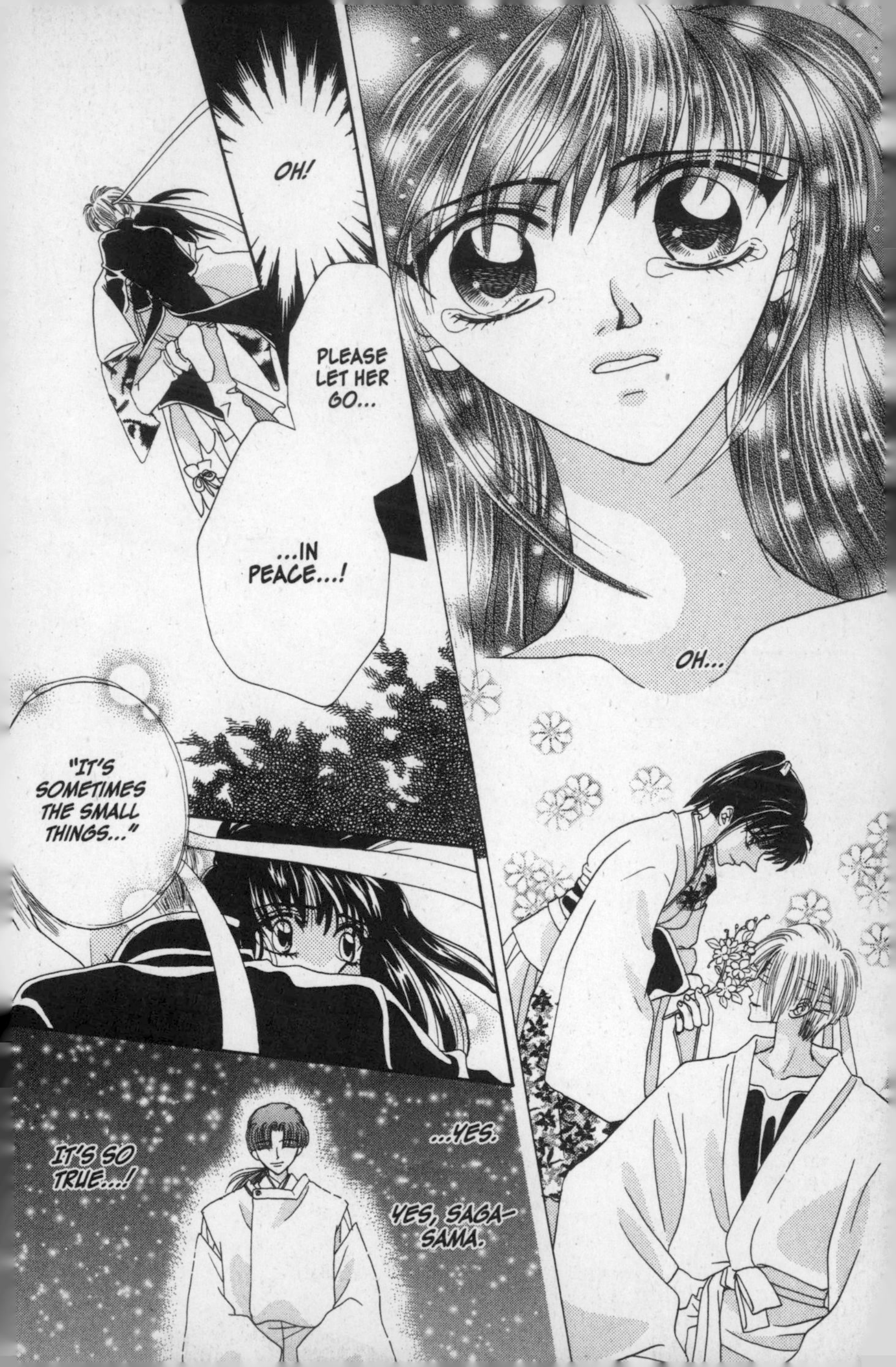
OH...
OH!
PLEASE LET HER GO...
...IN PEACE...!
"IT'S SOMETIMES THE SMALL THINGS..."
...YES.
YES, SAGA-SAMA.
IT'S SO TRUE...!

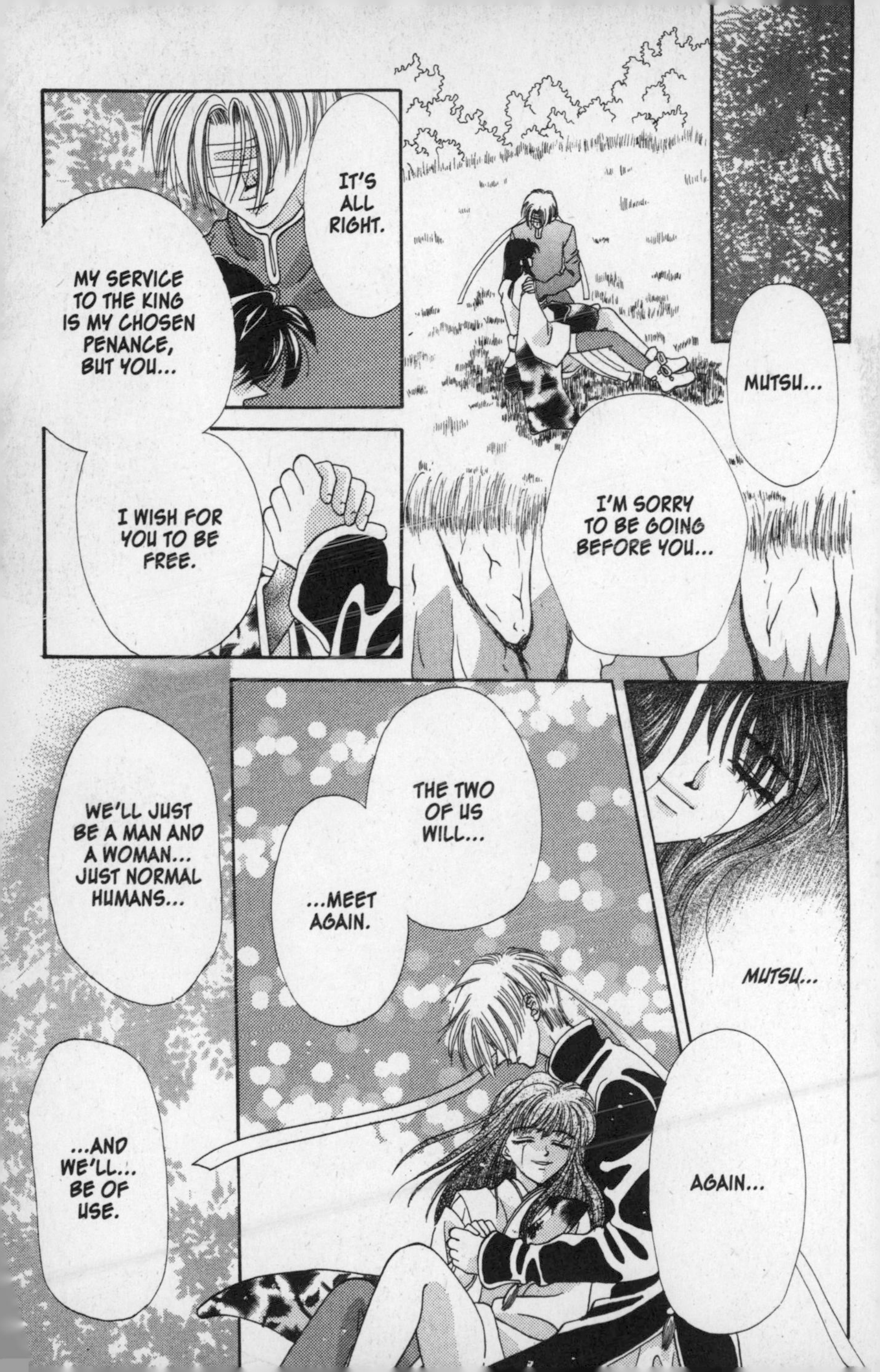
MUTSU...
I'M SORRY TO BE GOING BEFORE YOU...
IT'S ALL RIGHT.
MY SERVICE TO THE KING IS MY CHOSEN PENANCE, BUT YOU...
I WISH FOR YOU TO BE FREE.
MUTSU...
AGAIN...
THE TWO OF US WILL...
...MEET AGAIN.
WE'LL JUST BE A MAN AND A WOMAN... JUST NORMAL HUMANS...
...AND WE'LL... BE OF USE.

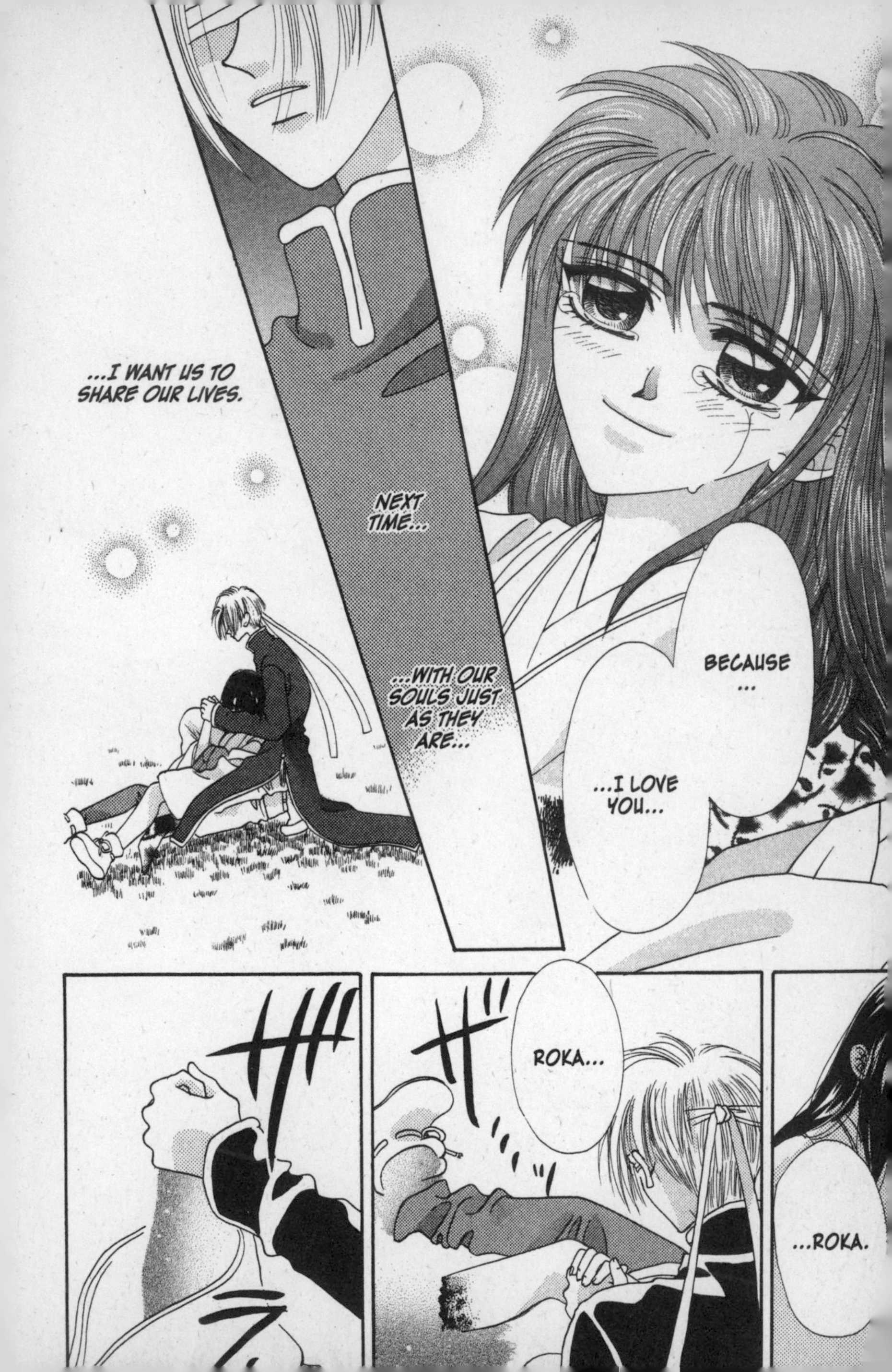
BECAUSE ...
...I LOVE YOU...
NEXT TIME...
...WITH OUR SOULS JUST AS THEY ARE...
...I WANT US TO SHARE OUR LIVES.
...ROKA.
ROKA...

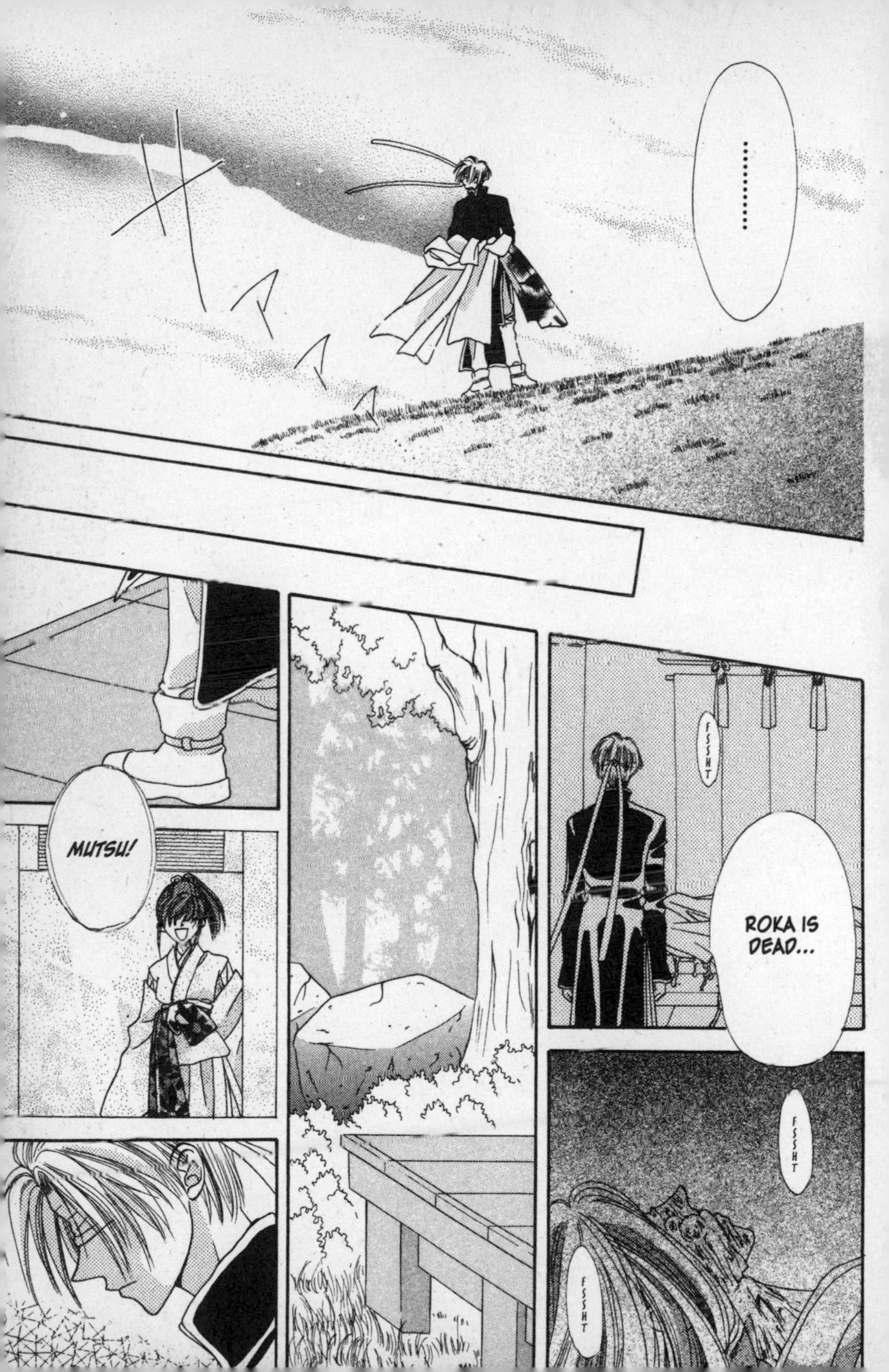
......
FSSHT
ROKA IS DEAD...
FSSHT
FSSHT
MUTSU!

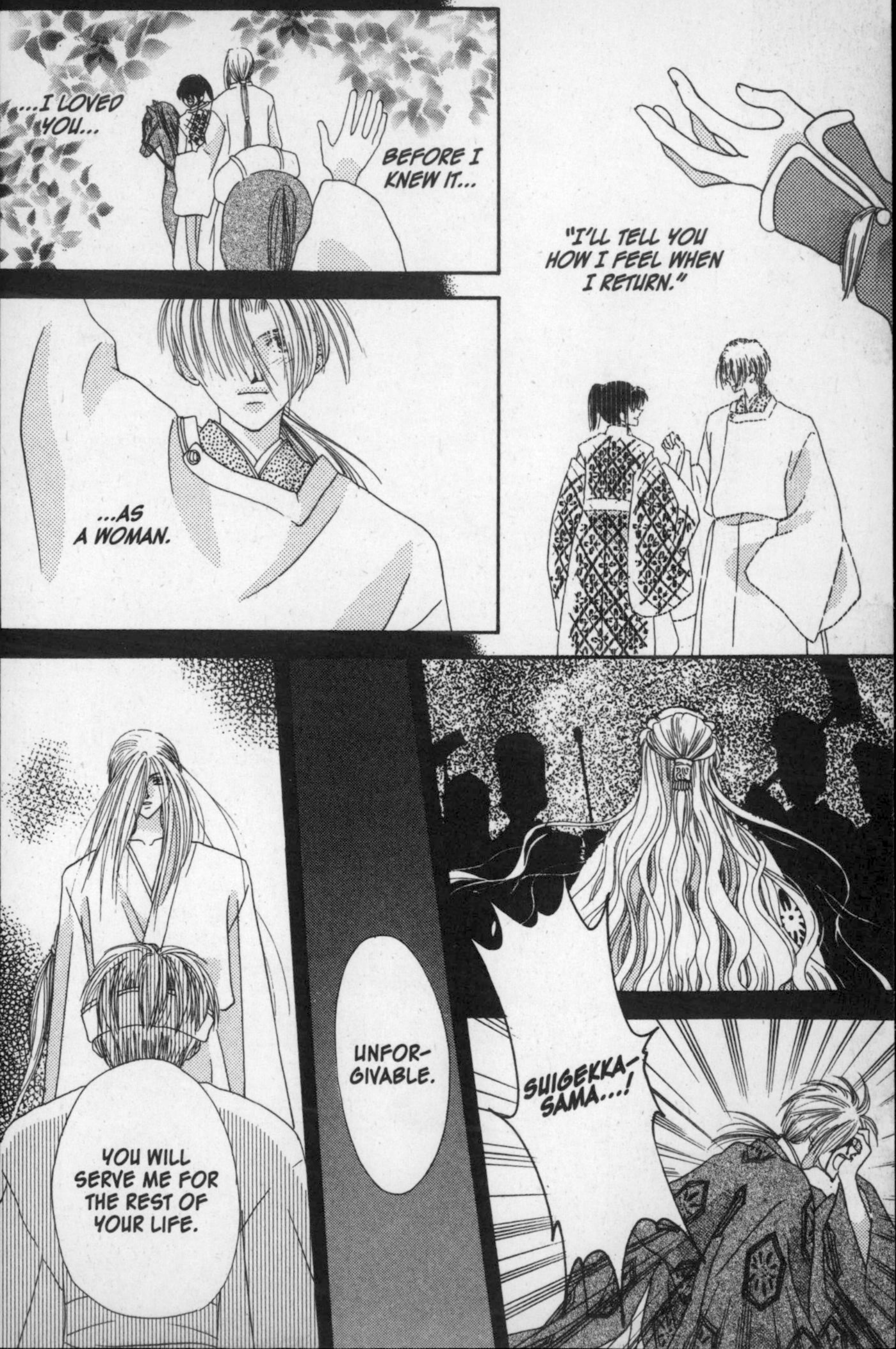
"I'LL TELL YOU HOW I FEEL WHEN I RETURN."
BEFORE I KNEW IT...
...I LOVED YOU...
...AS A WOMAN.
SUIGEKKA-SAMA...!
UNFORGIVABLE.
YOU WILL SERVE ME FOR THE REST OF YOUR LIFE.

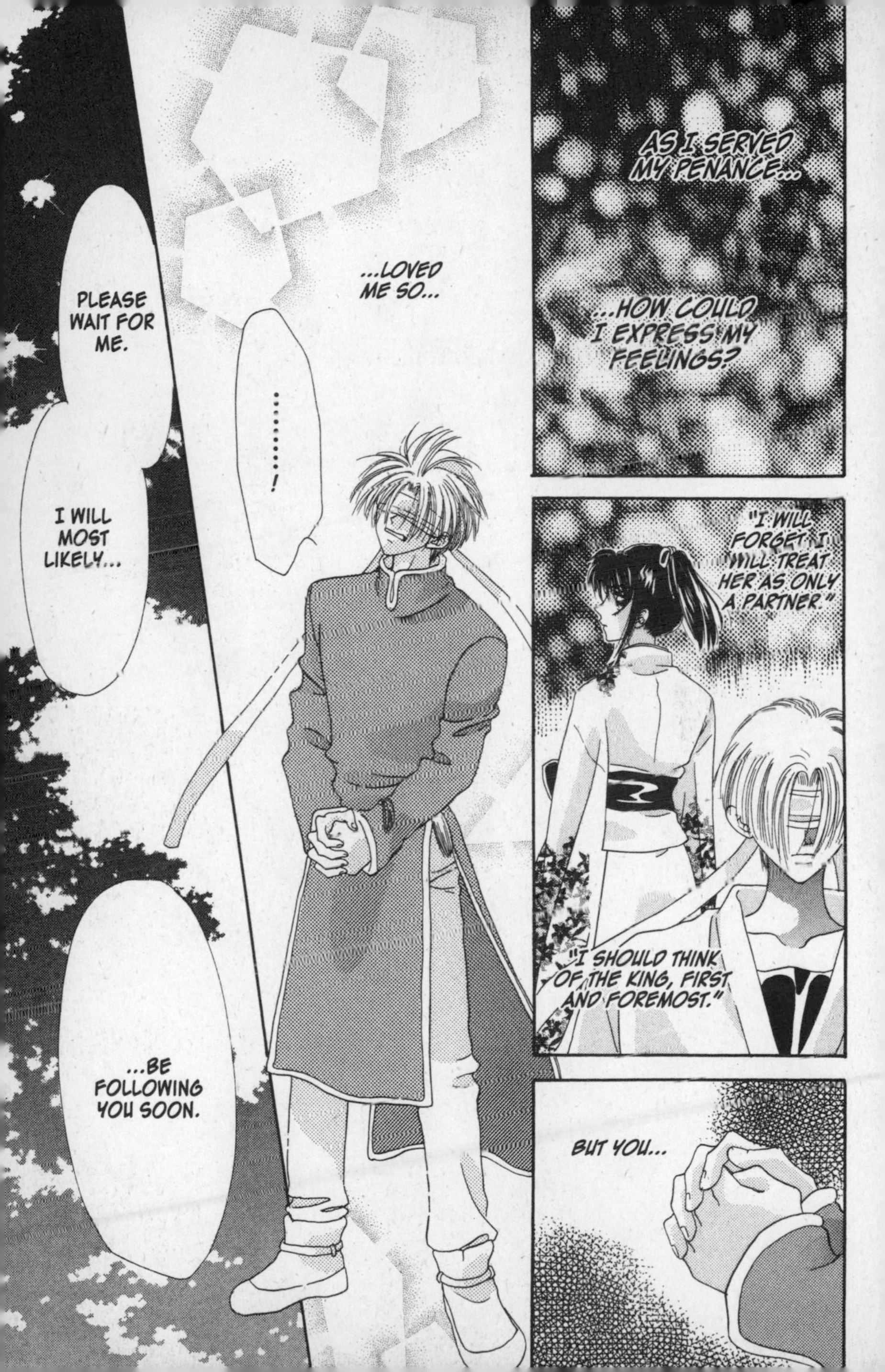
AS I SERVED MY PENANCE...
...HOW COULD I EXPRESS MY FEELINGS?
"I WILL FORGET. I WILL TREAT HER AS ONLY A PARTNER."
"I SHOULD THINK OF THE KING, FIRST AND FOREMOST."
BUT YOU...
...LOVED ME SO...
......!
PLEASE WAIT FOR ME.
I WILL MOST LIKELY...
...BE FOLLOWING YOU SOON.

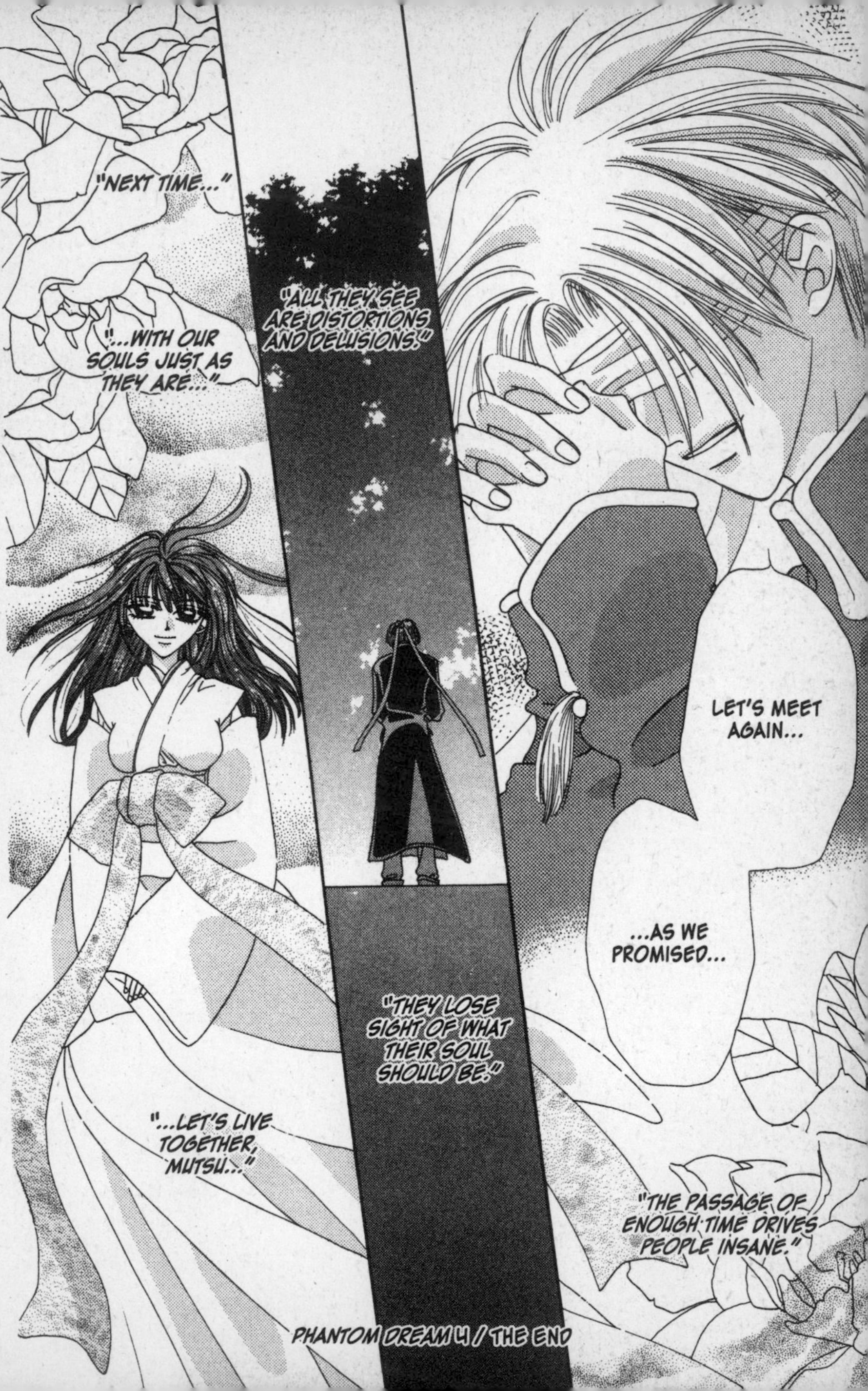
LET'S MEET AGAIN...
...AS WE PROMISED...
"THE PASSAGE OF ENOUGH TIME DRIVES PEOPLE INSANE."
"ALL THEY SEE ARE DISTORTIONS AND DELUSIONS."
"THEY LOSE SIGHT OF WHAT THEIR SOUL SHOULD BE."
"NEXT TIME..."
"...WITH OUR SOULS JUST AS THEY ARE..."
"...LET'S LIVE TOGETHER, MUTSU..."
PHANTOM DREAM 4 / THE END

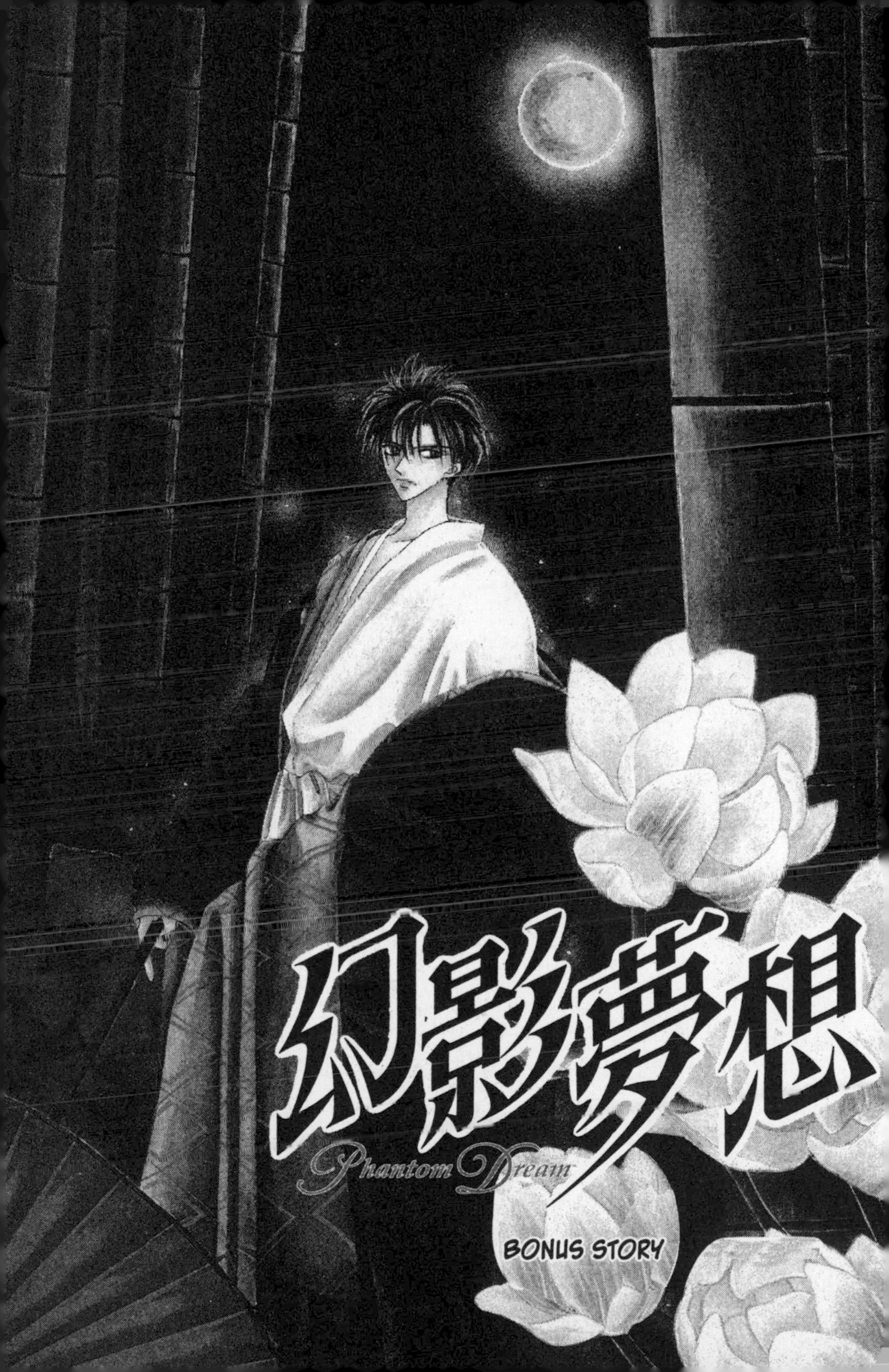
幻影夢想
Phantom Dream
BONUS STORY

UNEXPECTED AFTERWORD

I think I'm the only one who was sad that Jyuge never got to shine. (laughs) She was the poster child for what happens if you let jaki grow: you're taken over by your desires. It's a shame I didn't get to draw her as much as I wanted to. That's why I tried to draw her a lot at the end, see.

I'm so grateful to everyone!

Watanabe-sama
Nihongi-sama
Harada-sama
Araki-sama
Thank you for helping me with the manuscripts! I'm also indebted to my mother and my editor-sama.

To everyone who's read Dream, thank you! ♥
Right now I only have one volume left, and I'm very emotional about it. Please don't miss it! (laughs)

I'll see you again!

This was Natsuki Takaya.

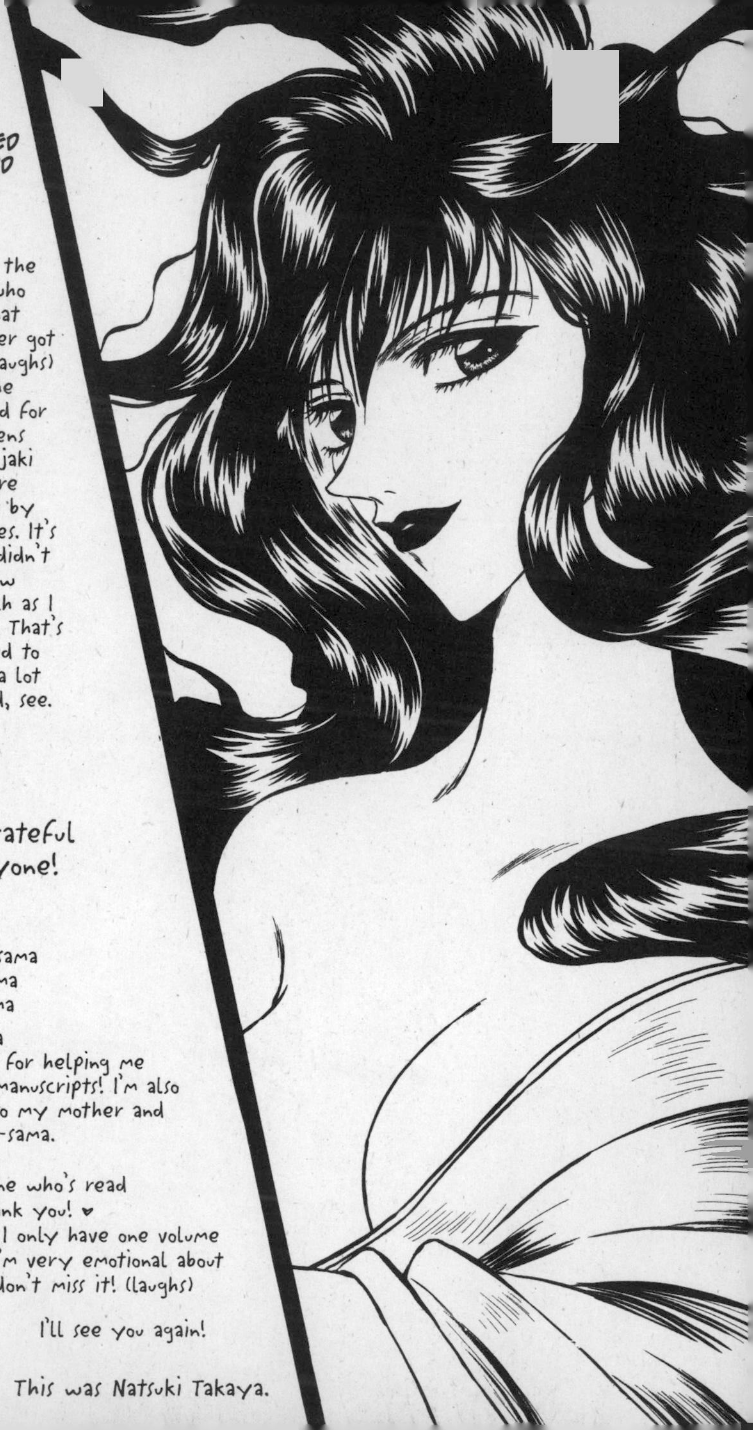

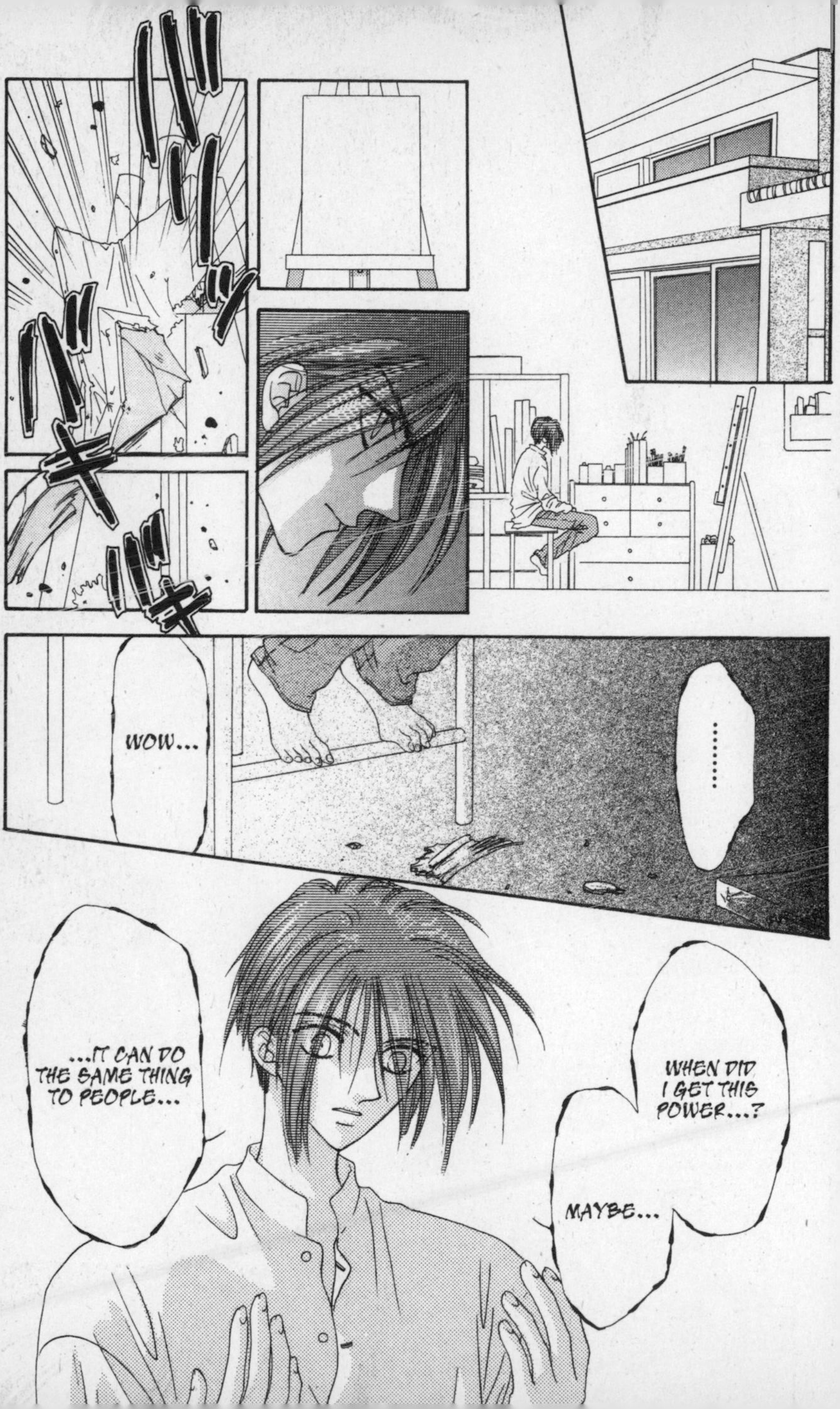
......
WOW...
WHEN DID I GET THIS POWER...?
MAYBE...
...IT CAN DO THE SAME THING TO PEOPLE...

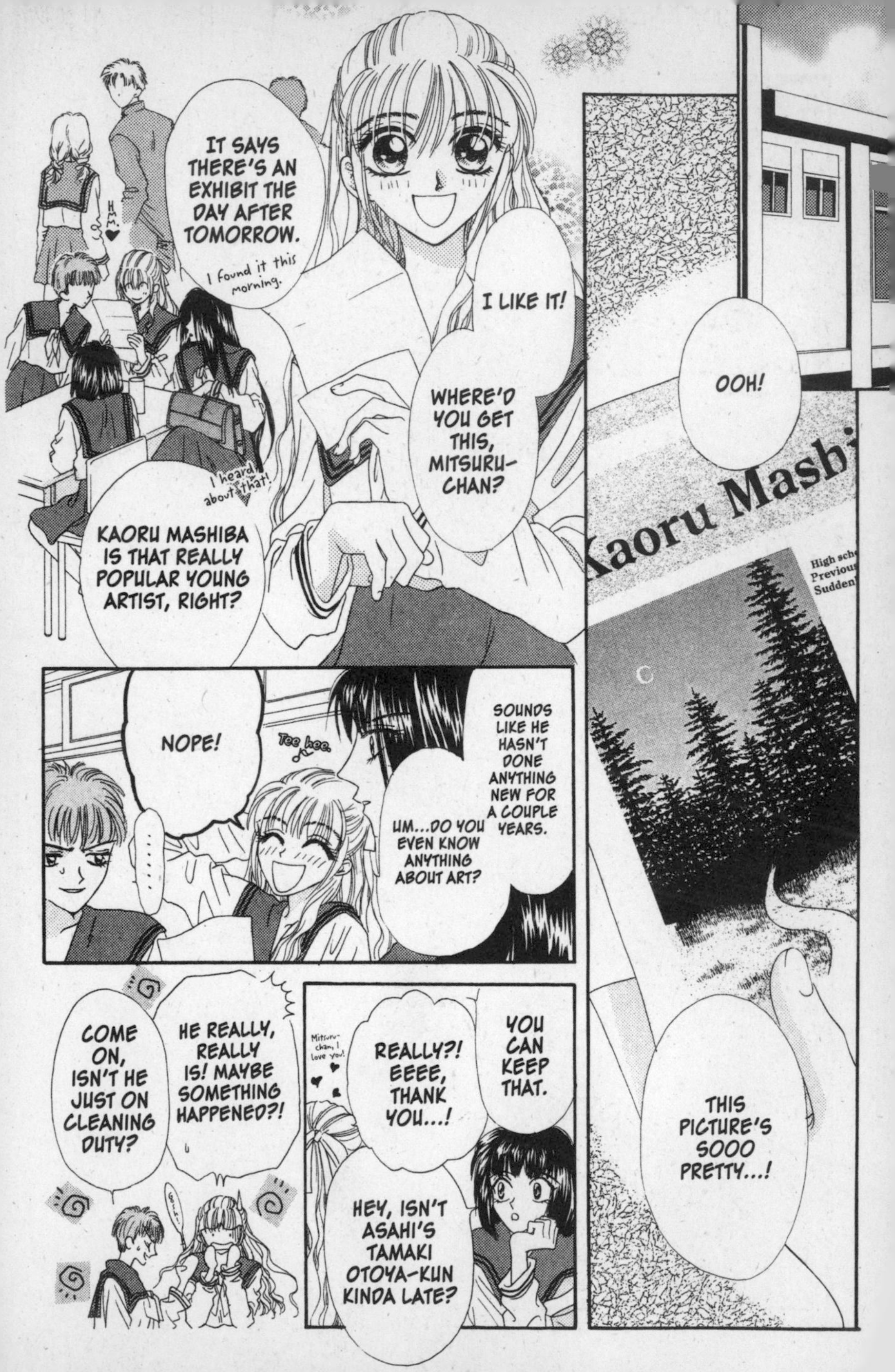
OOH!
Kaoru Mashi
High sch
Previou
Sudden
THIS PICTURE'S SOOO PRETTY...!
I LIKE IT!
WHERE'D YOU GET THIS, MITSURU-CHAN?
IT SAYS THERE'S AN EXHIBIT THE DAY AFTER TOMORROW.
I found it this morning.
HMM.♥
I heard about that!
KAORU MASHIBA IS THAT REALLY POPULAR YOUNG ARTIST, RIGHT?
SOUNDS LIKE HE HASN'T DONE ANYTHING NEW FOR A COUPLE YEARS.
UM...DO YOU EVEN KNOW ANYTHING ABOUT ART?
Tee hee.
NOPE!
......
YOU CAN KEEP THAT.
REALLY?! EEEE, THANK YOU...!
Mitsuru-chan, I love you!
HEY, ISN'T ASAHI'S TAMAKI OTOYA-KUN KINDA LATE?
HE REALLY, REALLY IS! MAYBE SOMETHING HAPPENED?!
COME ON, ISN'T HE JUST ON CLEANING DUTY?

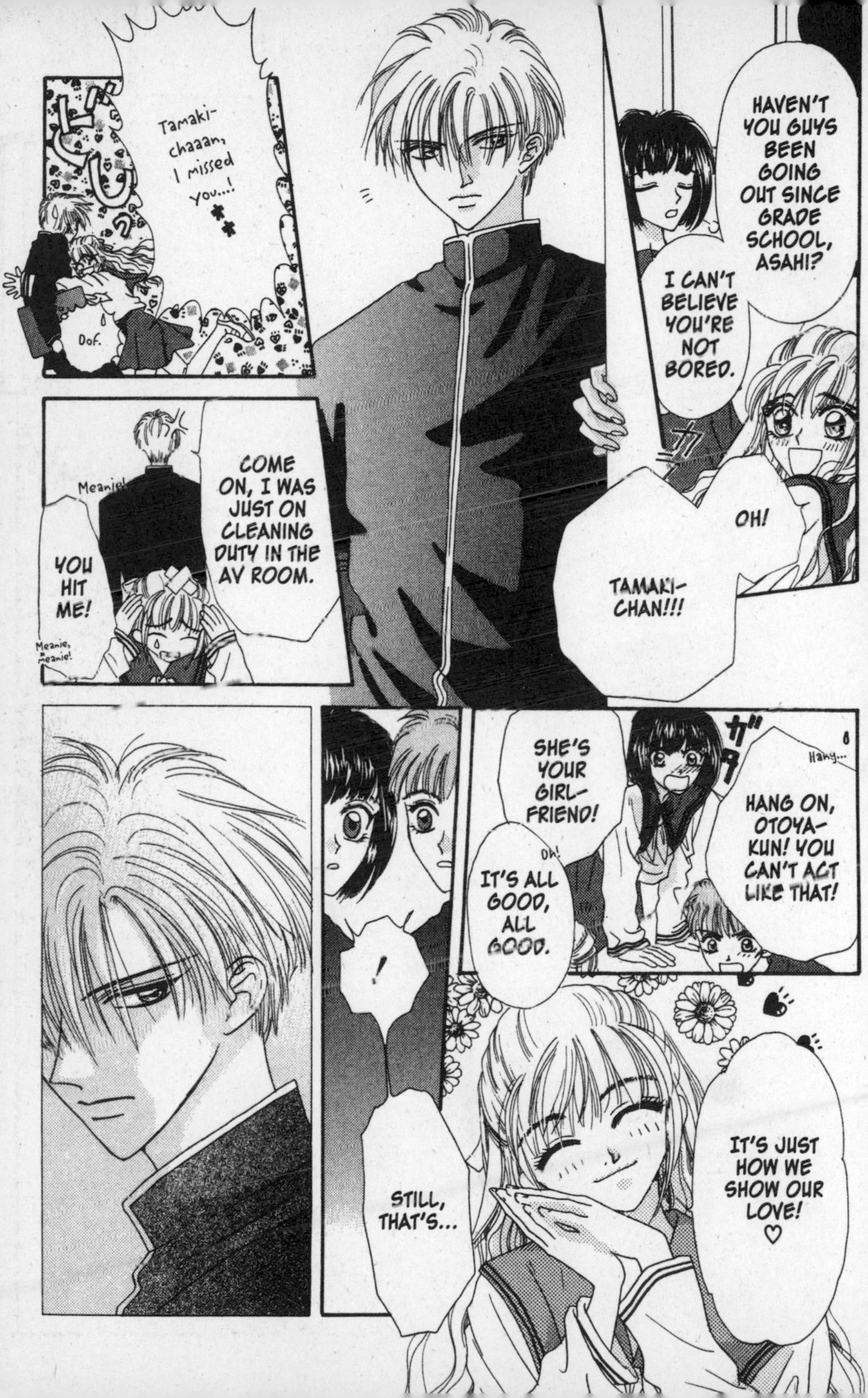
HAVEN'T YOU GUYS BEEN GOING OUT SINCE GRADE SCHOOL, ASAHI?
I CAN'T BELIEVE YOU'RE NOT BORED.
OH!
TAMAKI-CHAN!!!
Tamaki-chaaan, I missed you...!
Dof.
COME ON, I WAS JUST ON CLEANING DUTY IN THE AV ROOM.
Meanie!
YOU HIT ME!
Meanie, meanie!
Hang...
HANG ON, OTOYA-KUN! YOU CAN'T ACT LIKE THAT!
SHE'S YOUR GIRLFRIEND!
Oh!
IT'S ALL GOOD, ALL GOOD.
!
IT'S JUST HOW WE SHOW OUR LOVE! ♡
STILL, THAT'S...

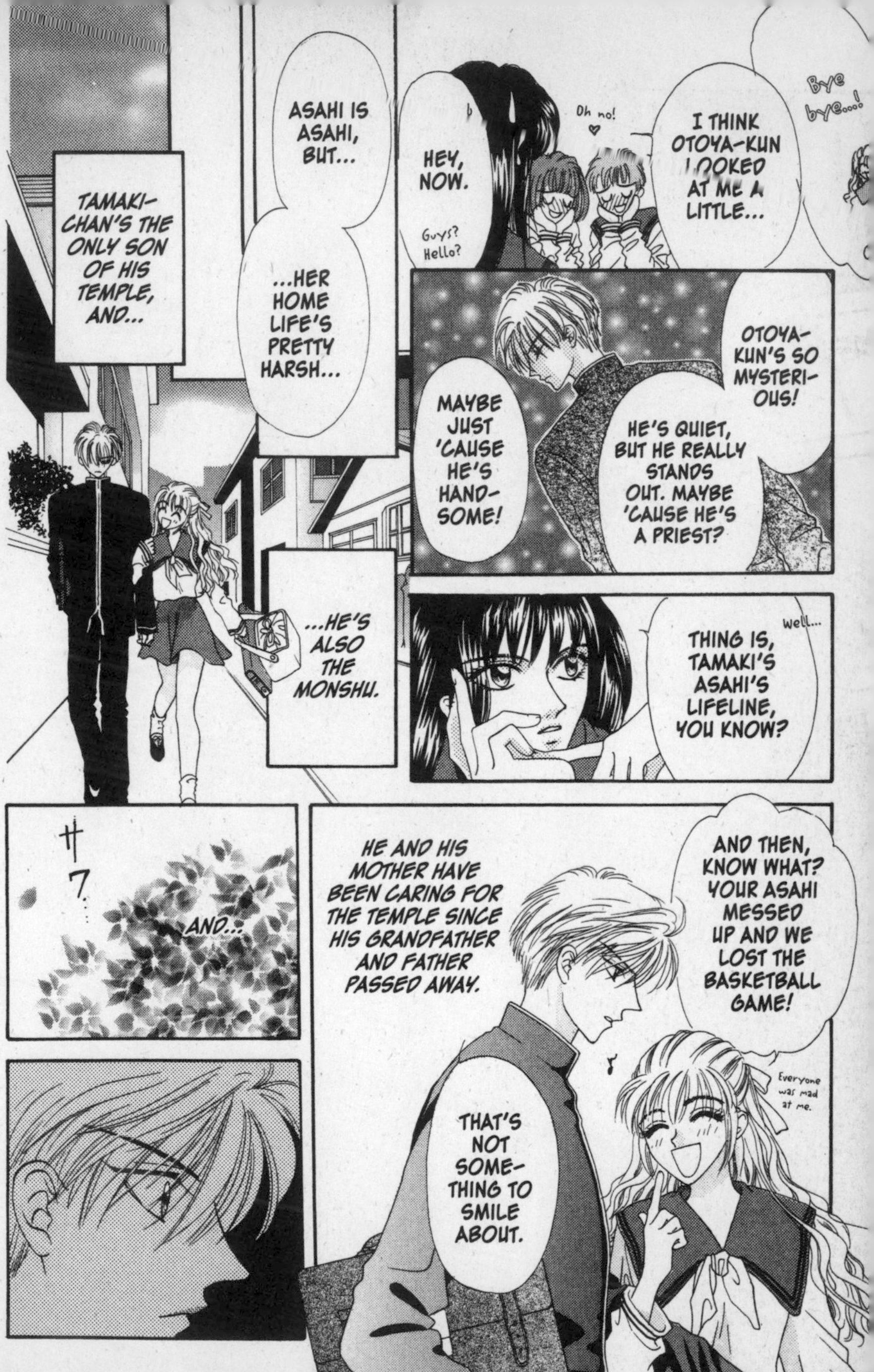
Bye bye...!
I THINK OTOYA-KUN LOOKED AT ME A LITTLE...
Oh no!
HEY, NOW.
Guys? Hello?
ASAHI IS ASAHI, BUT...
...HER HOME LIFE'S PRETTY HARSH...
OTOYA-KUN'S SO MYSTERIOUS!
HE'S QUIET, BUT HE REALLY STANDS OUT. MAYBE 'CAUSE HE'S A PRIEST?
MAYBE JUST 'CAUSE HE'S HANDSOME!
Well...
THING IS, TAMAKI'S ASAHI'S LIFELINE, YOU KNOW?
TAMAKI-CHAN'S THE ONLY SON OF HIS TEMPLE, AND...
...HE'S ALSO THE MONSHU.
AND THEN, KNOW WHAT? YOUR ASAHI MESSED UP AND WE LOST THE BASKETBALL GAME!
Everyone was mad at me.
HE AND HIS MOTHER HAVE BEEN CARING FOR THE TEMPLE SINCE HIS GRANDFATHER AND FATHER PASSED AWAY.
THAT'S NOT SOMETHING TO SMILE ABOUT.
AND...

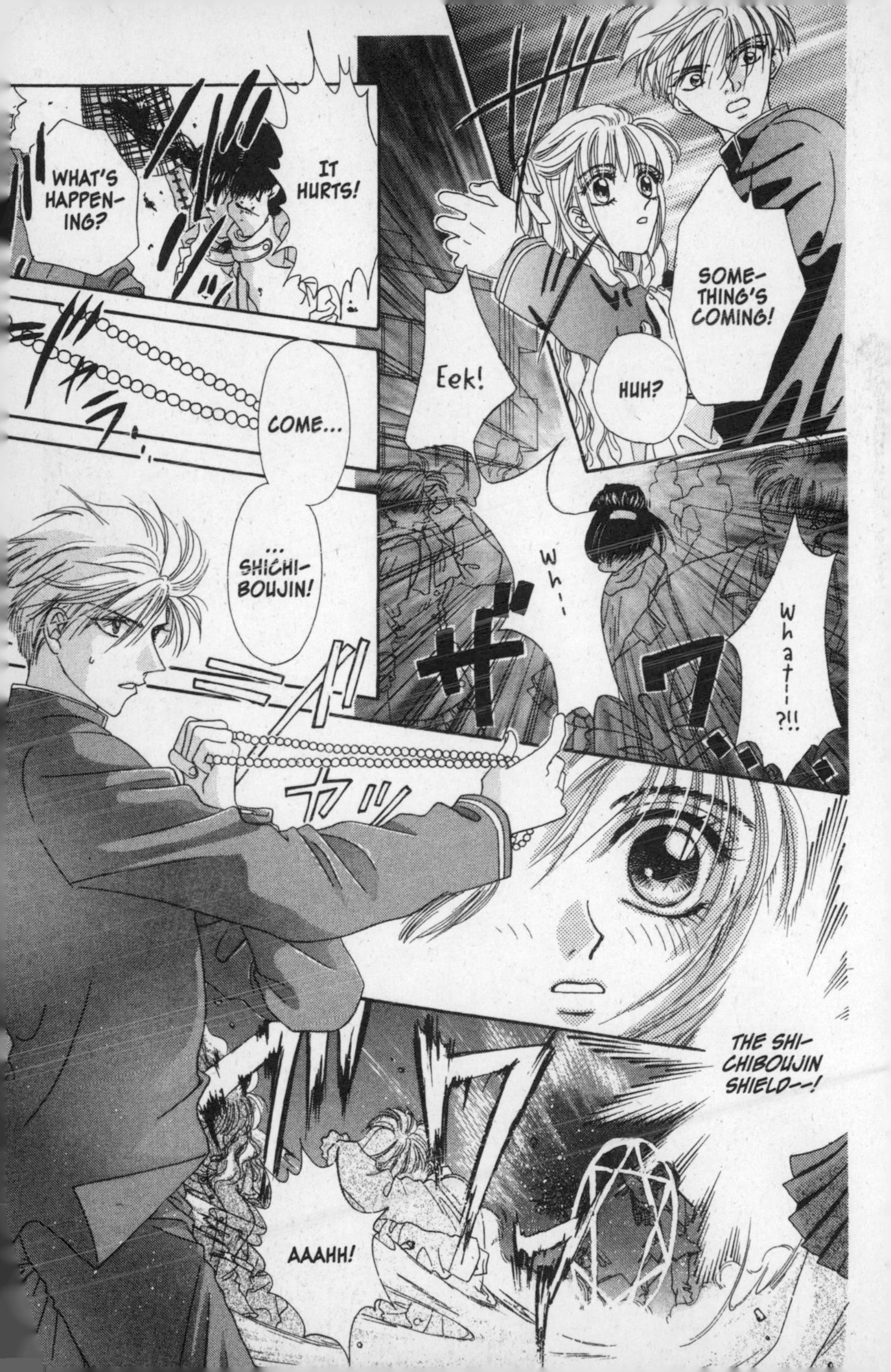
SOME-THING'S COMING!
HUH?
Eek!
IT HURTS!
WHAT'S HAPPEN-ING?
What--?!!
Wh--
COME...
...SHICHI-BOUJIN!
THE SHI-CHIBOUJIN SHIELD--!
AAAHH!

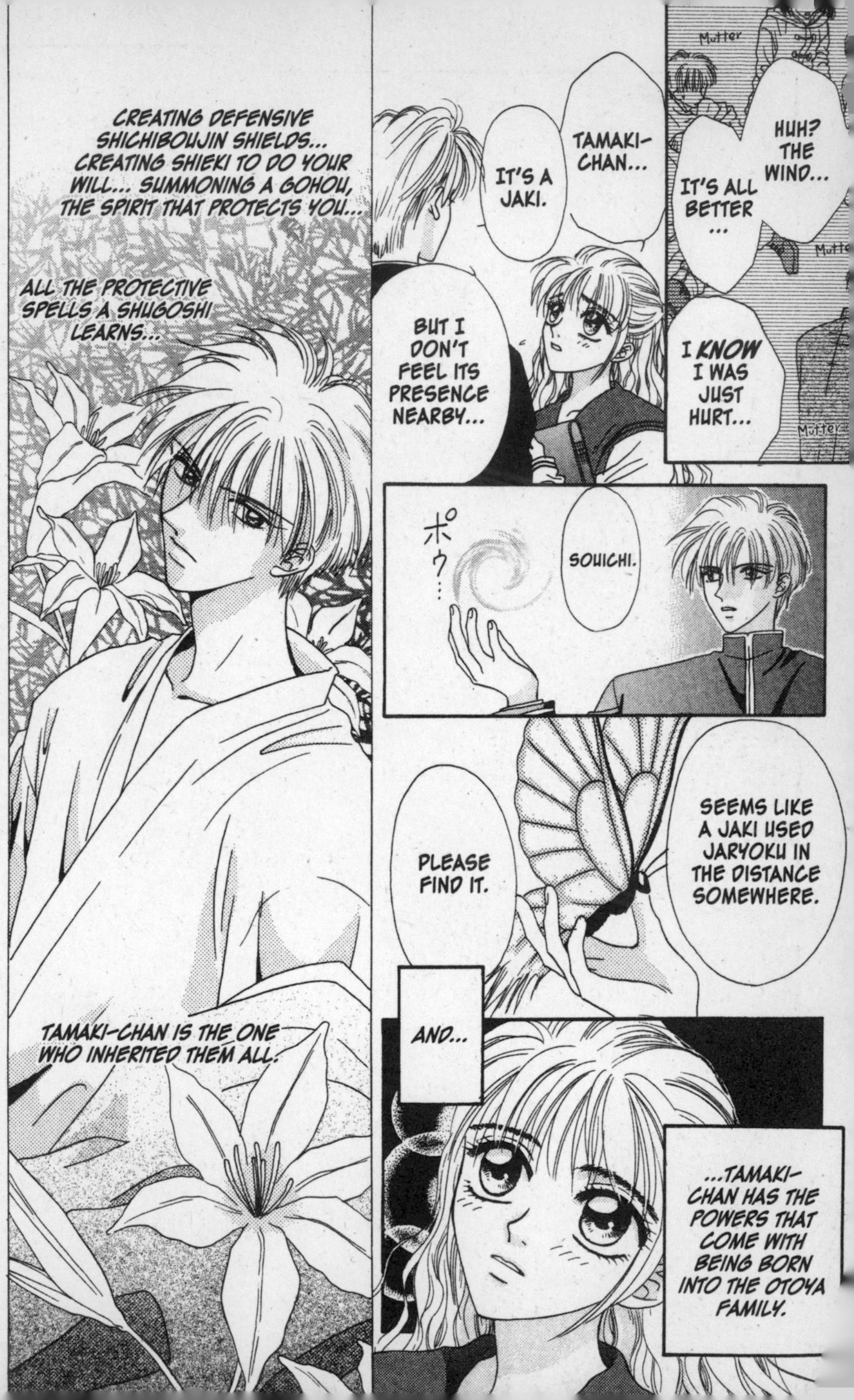
Mutter
HUH? THE WIND...
IT'S ALL BETTER...
I *KNOW* I WAS JUST HURT...
Mutter
Mutter
TAMAKI-CHAN...
IT'S A JAKI.
BUT I DON'T FEEL ITS PRESENCE NEARBY...
SOUICHI.
ポウ…
SEEMS LIKE A JAKI USED JARYOKU IN THE DISTANCE SOMEWHERE.
PLEASE FIND IT.
AND...
...TAMAKI-CHAN HAS THE POWERS THAT COME WITH BEING BORN INTO THE OTOYA FAMILY.
CREATING DEFENSIVE SHICHIBOUJIN SHIELDS... CREATING SHIEKI TO DO YOUR WILL... SUMMONING A GOHOU, THE SPIRIT THAT PROTECTS YOU...
ALL THE PROTECTIVE SPELLS A SHUGOSHI LEARNS...
TAMAKI-CHAN IS THE ONE WHO INHERITED THEM ALL.

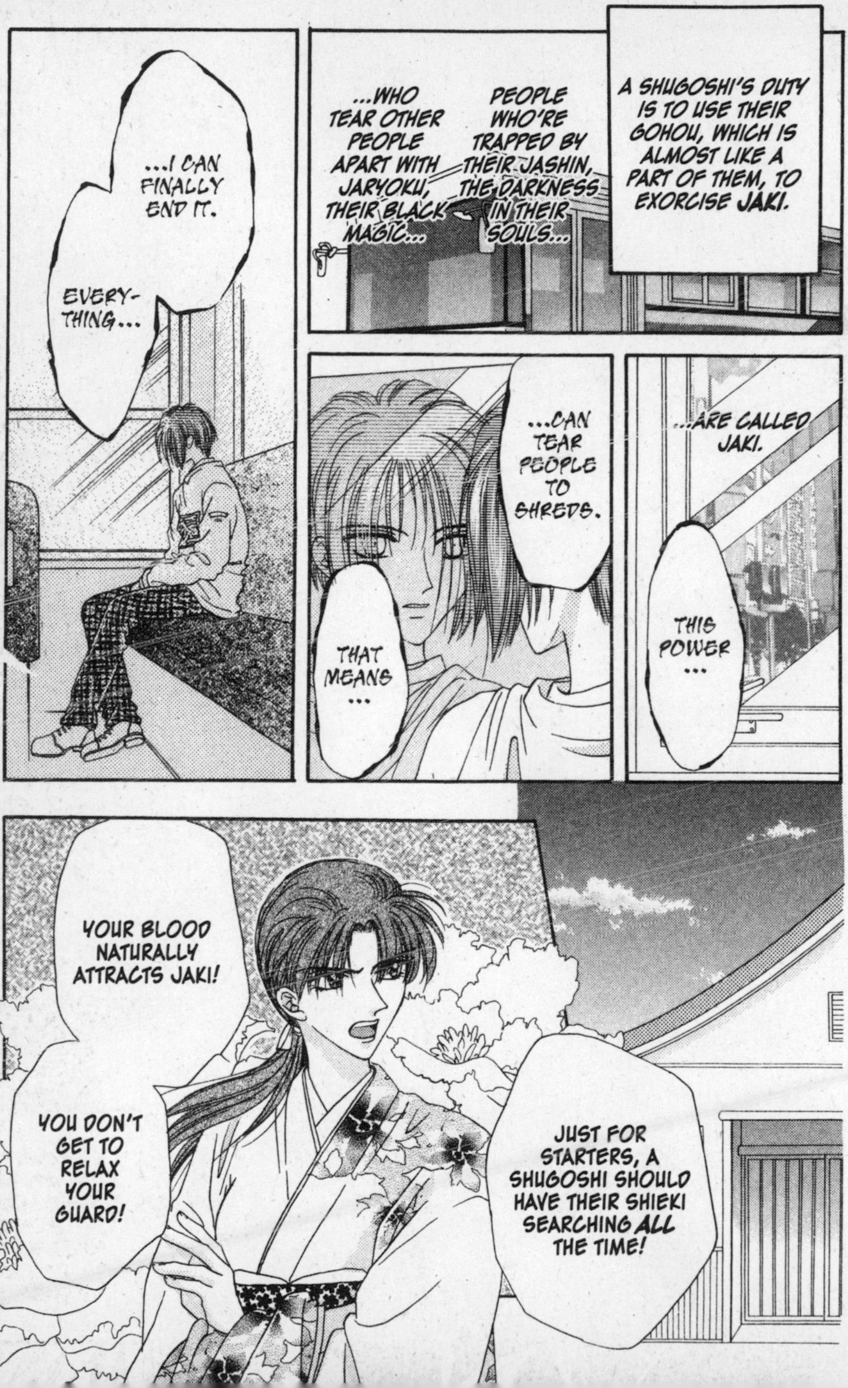

A SHUGOSHI'S DUTY IS TO USE THEIR GOHOU, WHICH IS ALMOST LIKE A PART OF THEM, TO EXORCISE **JAKI**.
PEOPLE WHO'RE TRAPPED BY THEIR JASHIN, THE DARKNESS IN THEIR SOULS...
...WHO TEAR OTHER PEOPLE APART WITH JARYOKU, THEIR BLACK MAGIC...
...ARE CALLED JAKI.
THIS POWER...
...CAN TEAR PEOPLE TO SHREDS.
THAT MEANS...
...I CAN FINALLY END IT.
EVERY-THING...
JUST FOR STARTERS, A SHUGOSHI SHOULD HAVE THEIR SHIEKI SEARCHING **ALL** THE TIME!
YOUR BLOOD NATURALLY ATTRACTS JAKI!
YOU DON'T GET TO RELAX YOUR GUARD!

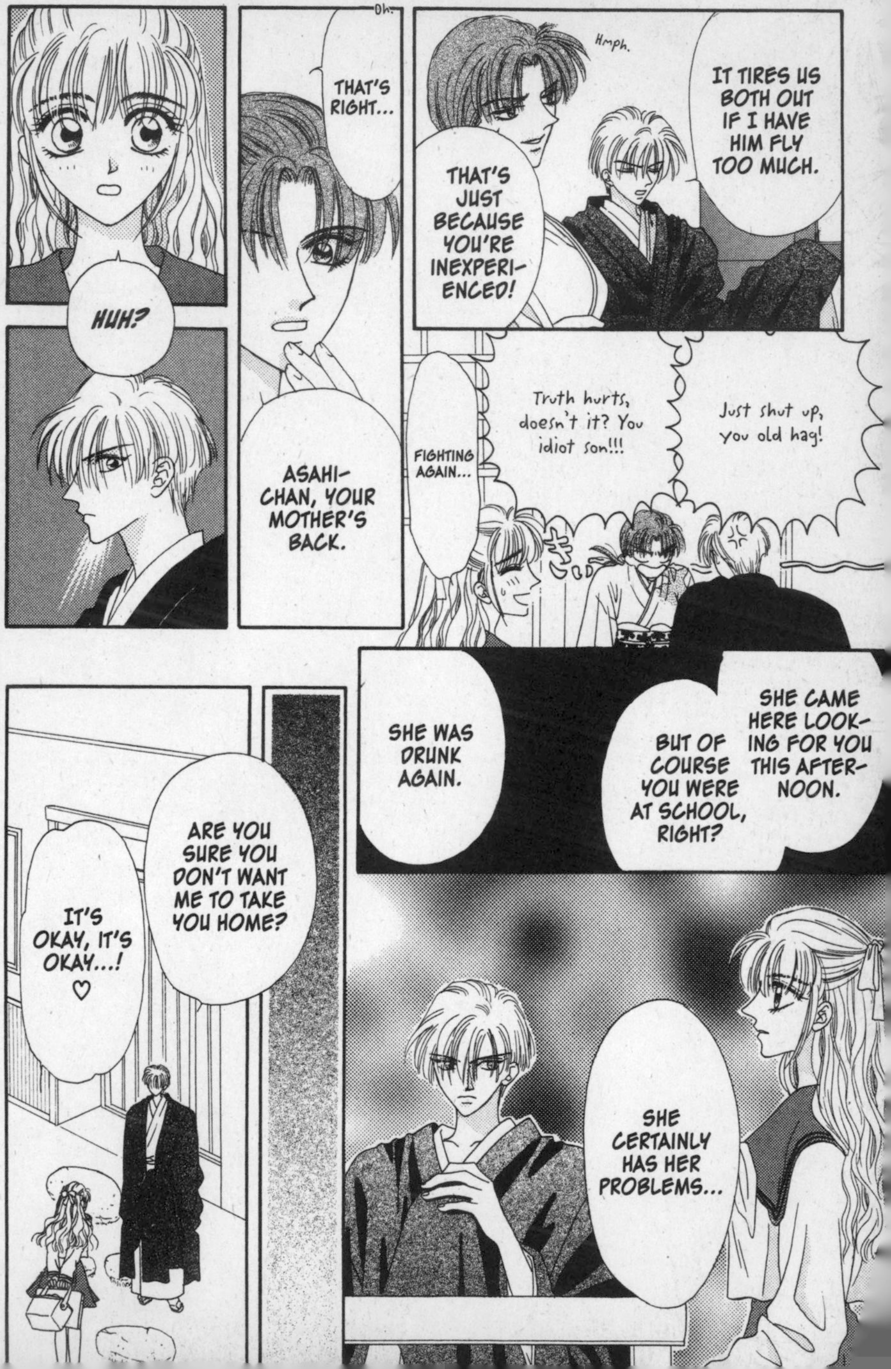

IT TIRES US BOTH OUT IF I HAVE HIM FLY TOO MUCH.
Hmph.
THAT'S JUST BECAUSE YOU'RE INEXPERIENCED!
Just shut up, you old hag!
Truth hurts, doesn't it? You idiot son!!!
FIGHTING AGAIN...
Oh.
THAT'S RIGHT...
ASAHI-CHAN, YOUR MOTHER'S BACK.
HUH?
SHE CAME HERE LOOKING FOR YOU THIS AFTERNOON.
BUT OF COURSE YOU WERE AT SCHOOL, RIGHT?
SHE WAS DRUNK AGAIN.
SHE CERTAINLY HAS HER PROBLEMS...
ARE YOU SURE YOU DON'T WANT ME TO TAKE YOU HOME?
IT'S OKAY, IT'S OKAY...! ♡

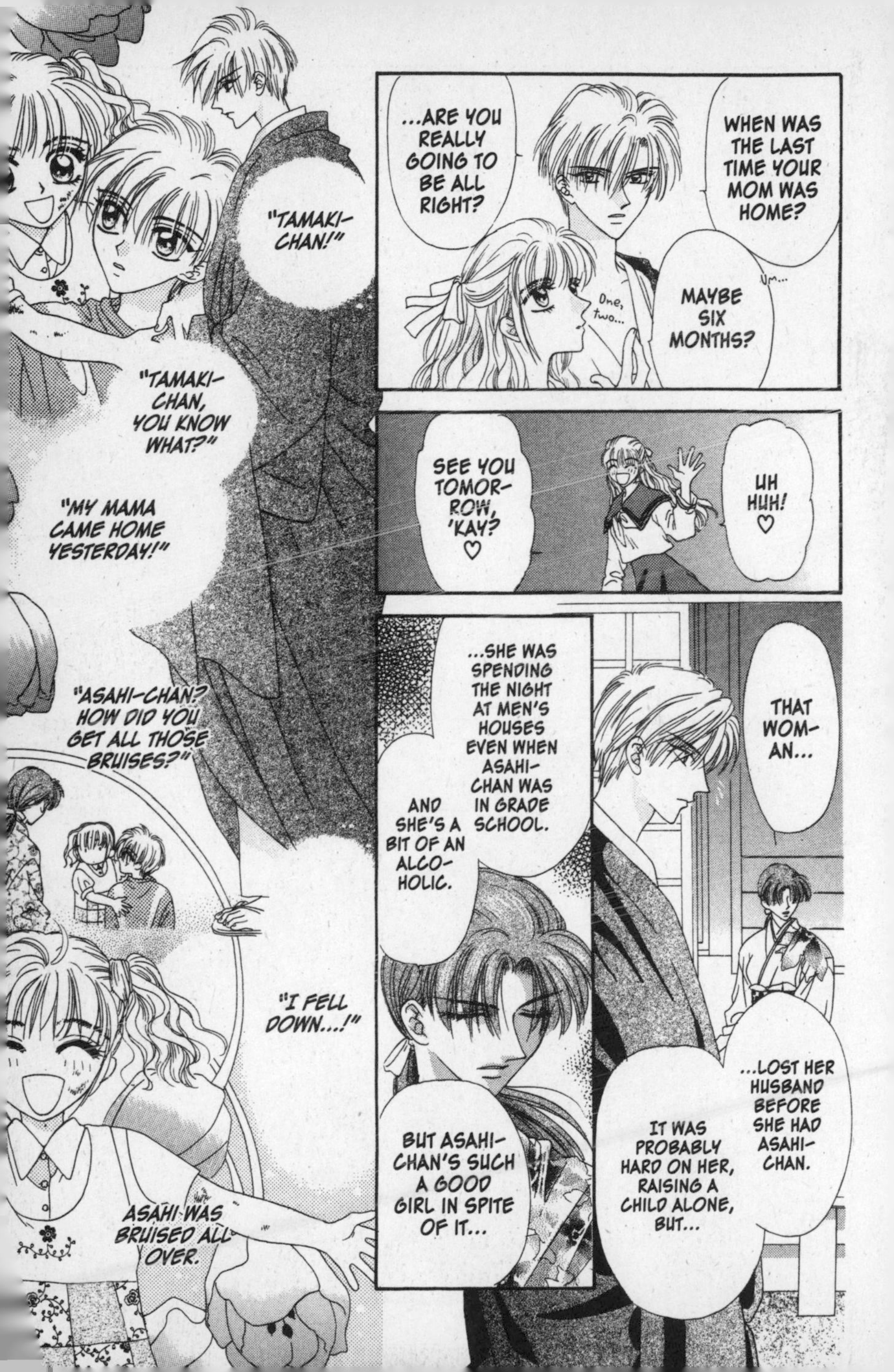
WHEN WAS THE LAST TIME YOUR MOM WAS HOME?
Um...
MAYBE SIX MONTHS?
One, two...
...ARE YOU REALLY GOING TO BE ALL RIGHT?
UH HUH! ♡
SEE YOU TOMORROW, 'KAY? ♡
THAT WOMAN...
...SHE WAS SPENDING THE NIGHT AT MEN'S HOUSES EVEN WHEN ASAHI-CHAN WAS IN GRADE SCHOOL.
AND SHE'S A BIT OF AN ALCOHOLIC.
...LOST HER HUSBAND BEFORE SHE HAD ASAHI-CHAN.
IT WAS PROBABLY HARD ON HER, RAISING A CHILD ALONE, BUT...
BUT ASAHI-CHAN'S SUCH A GOOD GIRL IN SPITE OF IT...
"TAMAKI-CHAN!"
"TAMAKI-CHAN, YOU KNOW WHAT?"
"MY MAMA CAME HOME YESTERDAY!"
"ASAHI-CHAN? HOW DID YOU GET ALL THOSE BRUISES?"
"I FELL DOWN...!"
ASAHI WAS BRUISED ALL OVER.

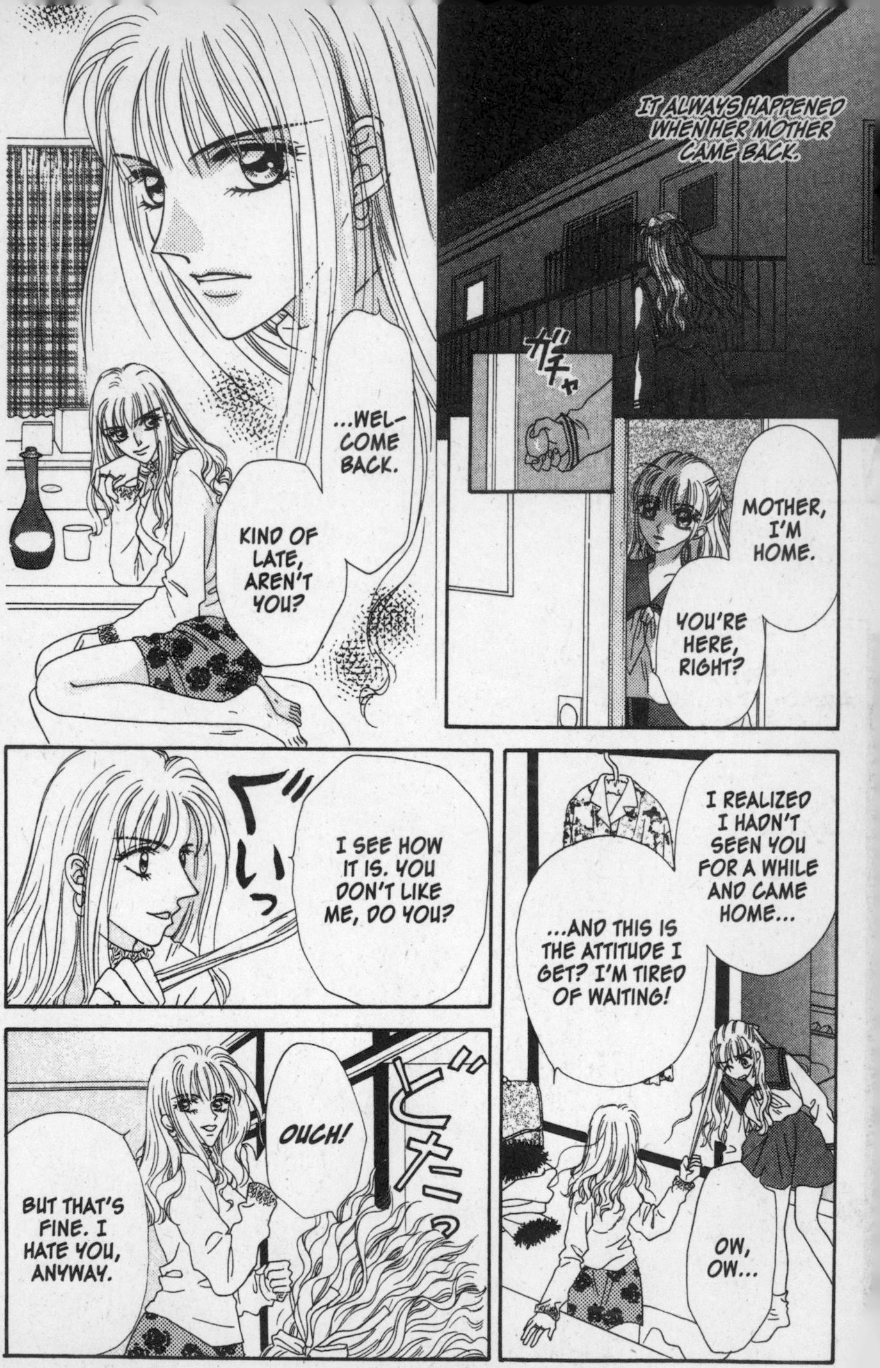
IT ALWAYS HAPPENED WHEN HER MOTHER CAME BACK.
ガチャ
MOTHER, I'M HOME.
YOU'RE HERE, RIGHT?
...WEL-COME BACK.
KIND OF LATE, AREN'T YOU?
I REALIZED I HADN'T SEEN YOU FOR A WHILE AND CAME HOME...
...AND THIS IS THE ATTITUDE I GET? I'M TIRED OF WAITING!
OW, OW...
ぐいっ
I SEE HOW IT IS. YOU DON'T LIKE ME, DO YOU?
ドサーっ
OUCH!
BUT THAT'S FINE. I HATE YOU, ANYWAY.

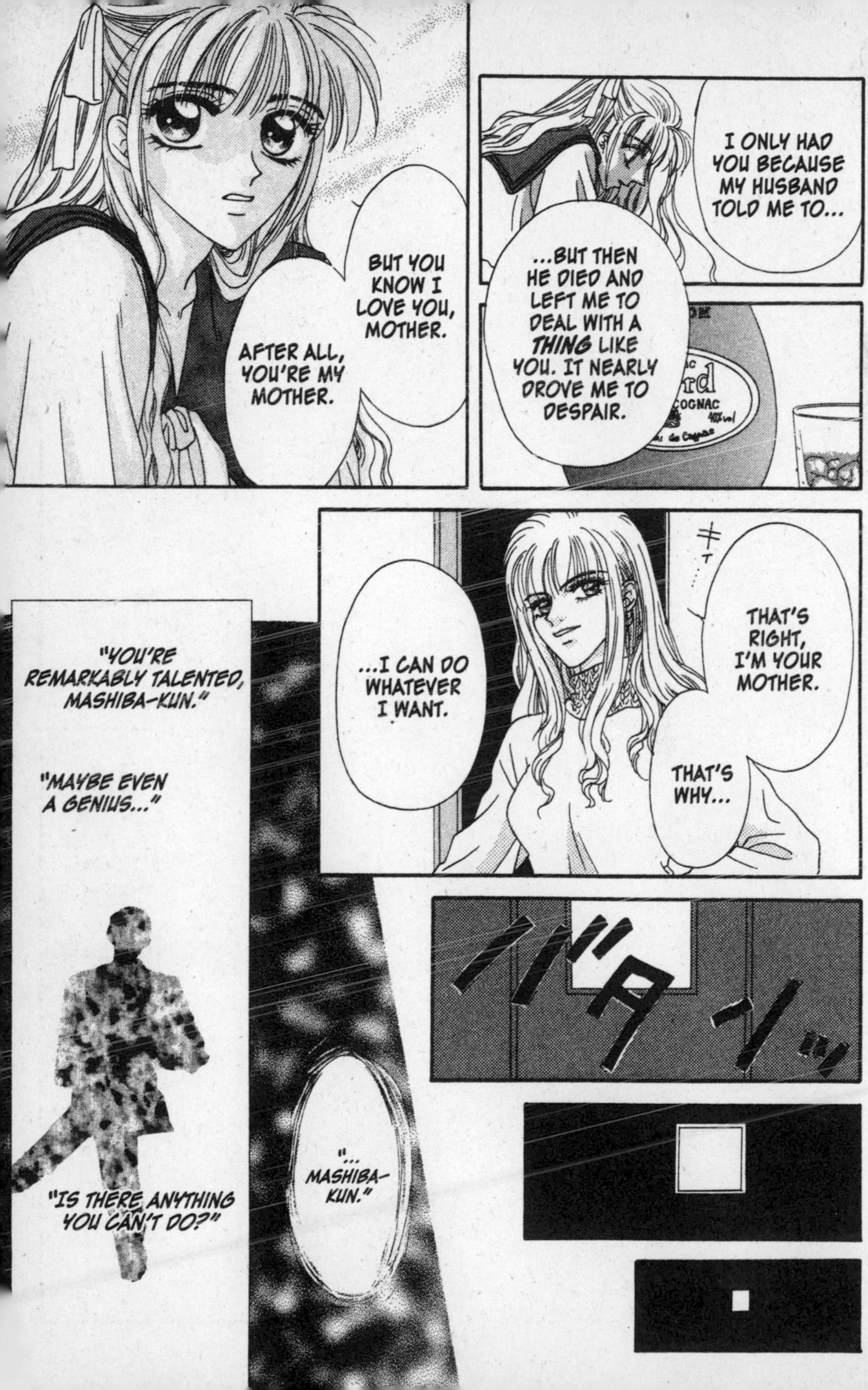
I ONLY HAD YOU BECAUSE MY HUSBAND TOLD ME TO...
...BUT THEN HE DIED AND LEFT ME TO DEAL WITH A *THING* LIKE YOU. IT NEARLY DROVE ME TO DESPAIR.
BUT YOU KNOW I LOVE YOU, MOTHER.
AFTER ALL, YOU'RE MY MOTHER.
THAT'S RIGHT, I'M YOUR MOTHER.
THAT'S WHY...
...I CAN DO WHATEVER I WANT.
バタンッ
"YOU'RE REMARKABLY TALENTED, MASHIBA-KUN."
"MAYBE EVEN A GENIUS..."
"... MASHIBA-KUN."
"IS THERE ANYTHING YOU CAN'T DO?"

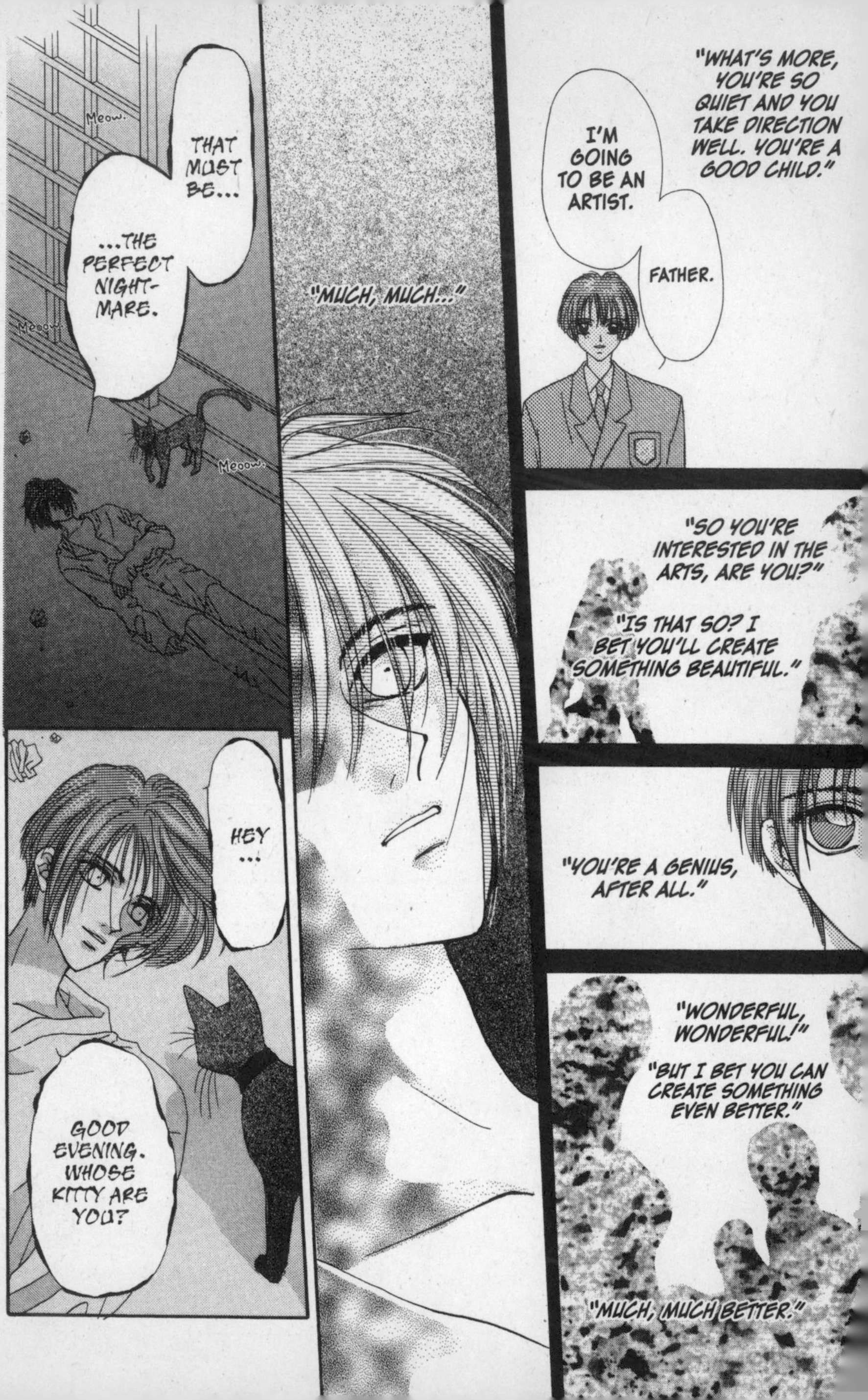
"WHAT'S MORE, YOU'RE SO QUIET AND YOU TAKE DIRECTION WELL. YOU'RE A GOOD CHILD."
I'M GOING TO BE AN ARTIST.
FATHER.
"SO YOU'RE INTERESTED IN THE ARTS, ARE YOU?"
"IS THAT SO? I BET YOU'LL CREATE SOMETHING BEAUTIFUL."
"YOU'RE A GENIUS, AFTER ALL."
"WONDERFUL, WONDERFUL!"
"BUT I BET YOU CAN CREATE SOMETHING EVEN BETTER."
"MUCH, MUCH BETTER."
"MUCH, MUCH..."
Meow.
THAT MUST BE...
...THE PERFECT NIGHT-MARE.
Meow.
Meow.
HEY...
GOOD EVENING. WHOSE KITTY ARE YOU?

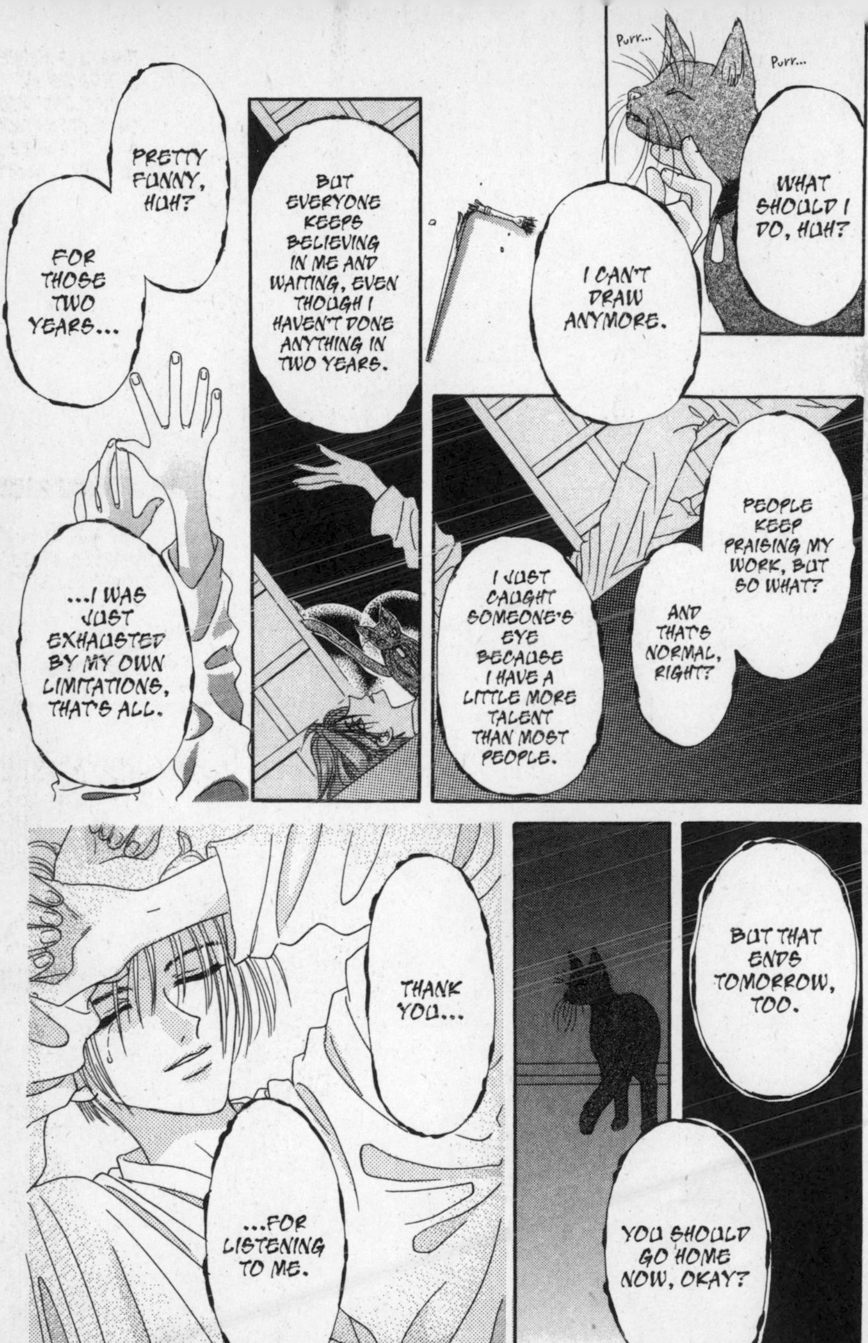
Purr...
Purr...
WHAT SHOULD I DO, HUH?
I CAN'T DRAW ANYMORE.
PEOPLE KEEP PRAISING MY WORK, BUT SO WHAT?
AND THAT'S NORMAL, RIGHT?
I JUST CAUGHT SOMEONE'S EYE BECAUSE I HAVE A LITTLE MORE TALENT THAN MOST PEOPLE.
BUT EVERYONE KEEPS BELIEVING IN ME AND WAITING, EVEN THOUGH I HAVEN'T DONE ANYTHING IN TWO YEARS.
PRETTY FUNNY, HUH?
FOR THOSE TWO YEARS...
...I WAS JUST EXHAUSTED BY MY OWN LIMITATIONS, THAT'S ALL.
BUT THAT ENDS TOMORROW, TOO.
YOU SHOULD GO HOME NOW, OKAY?
THANK YOU...
...FOR LISTENING TO ME.

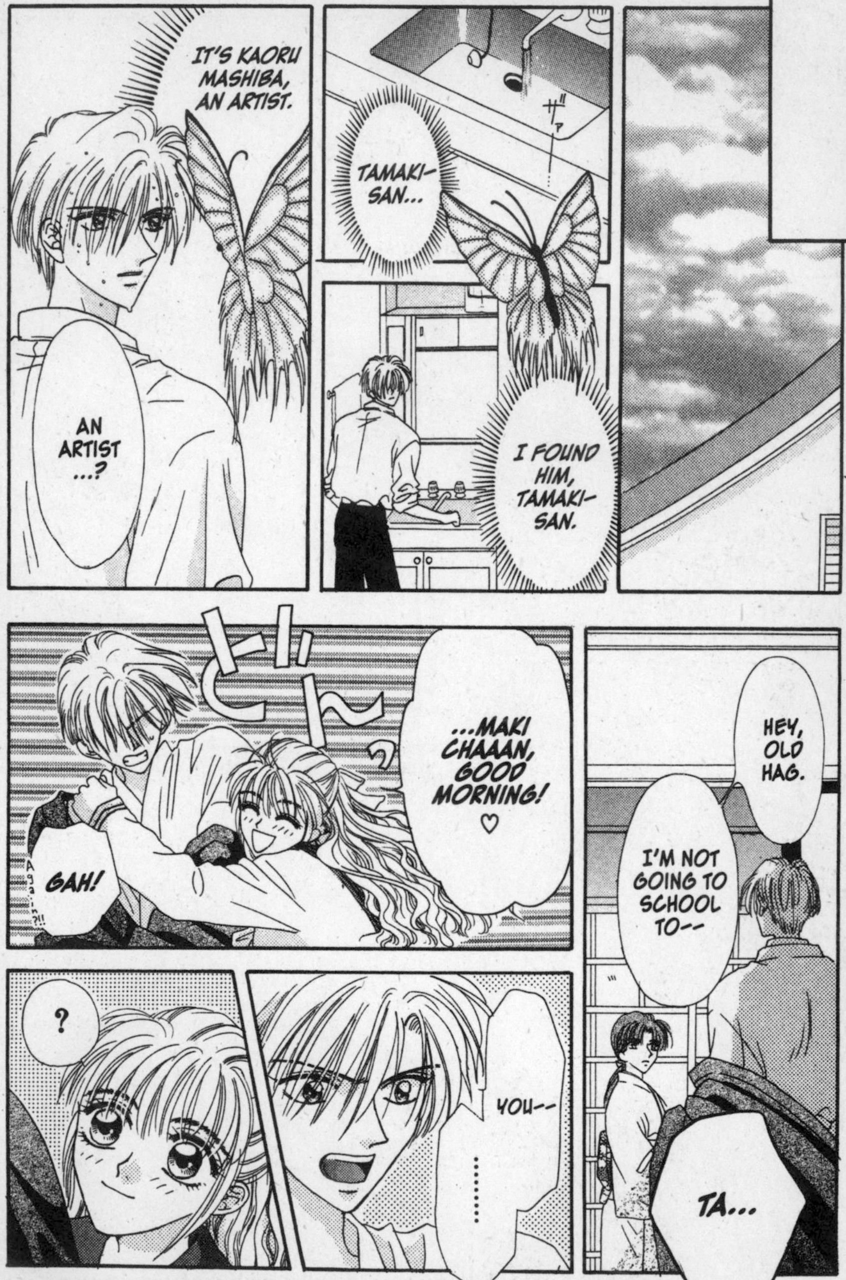
TAMAKI-SAN...
ザァ
I FOUND HIM, TAMAKI-SAN.
IT'S KAORU MASHIBA, AN ARTIST.
AN ARTIST ...?
HEY, OLD HAG.
I'M NOT GOING TO SCHOOL TO--
TA...
...MAKI CHAAAN, GOOD MORNING! ♡
GAH!
Aga..in?!!
YOU--
......
?

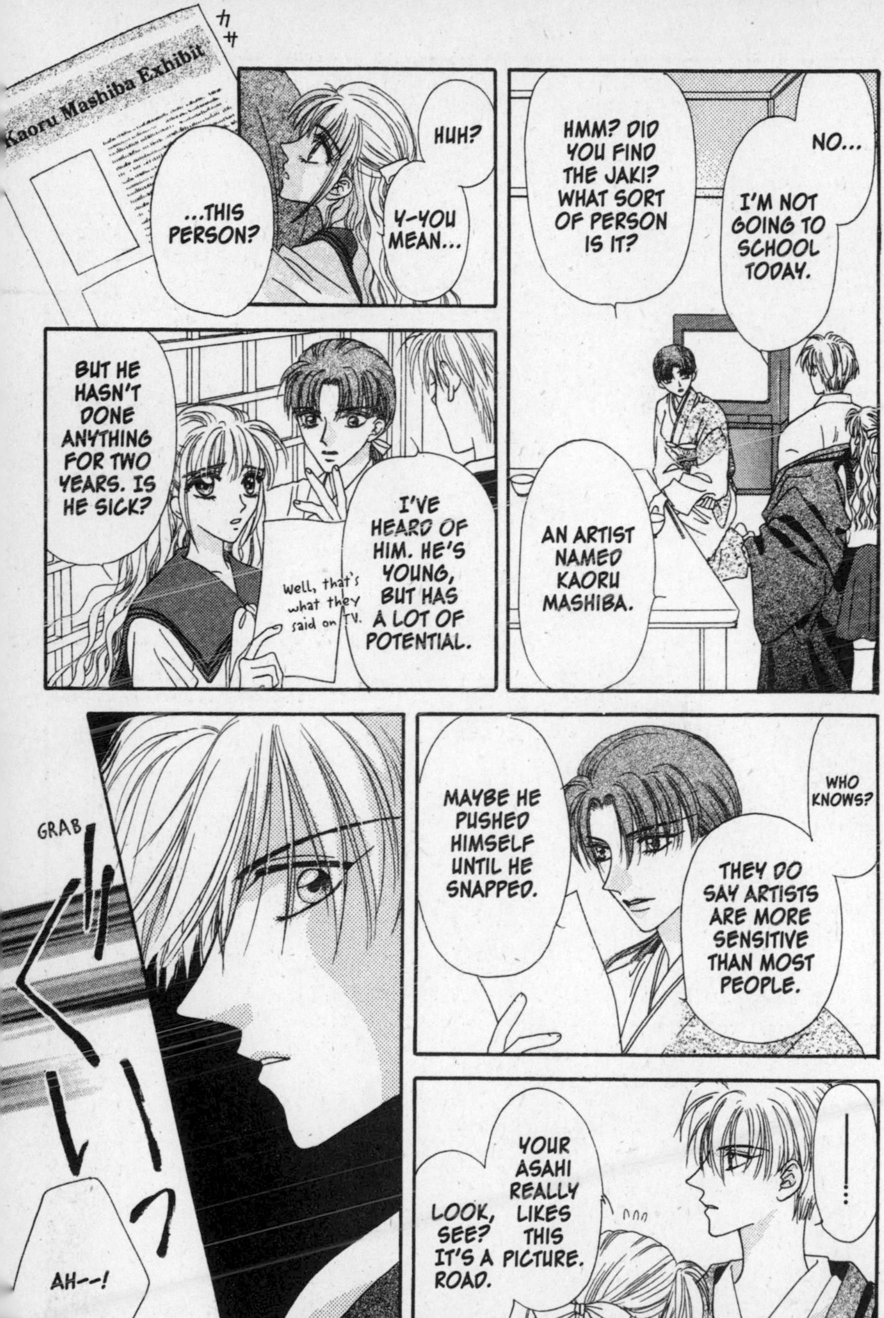
NO...
I'M NOT GOING TO SCHOOL TODAY.
HMM? DID YOU FIND THE JAKI? WHAT SORT OF PERSON IS IT?
AN ARTIST NAMED KAORU MASHIBA.
HUH?
Y-YOU MEAN...
...THIS PERSON?
Kaoru Mashiba Exhibit
I'VE HEARD OF HIM. HE'S YOUNG, BUT HAS A LOT OF POTENTIAL.
Well, that's what they said on TV.
BUT HE HASN'T DONE ANYTHING FOR TWO YEARS. IS HE SICK?
WHO KNOWS?
THEY DO SAY ARTISTS ARE MORE SENSITIVE THAN MOST PEOPLE.
MAYBE HE PUSHED HIMSELF UNTIL HE SNAPPED.
...!
YOUR ASAHI REALLY LIKES THIS PICTURE.
LOOK, SEE? IT'S A ROAD.
GRAB
AH--!

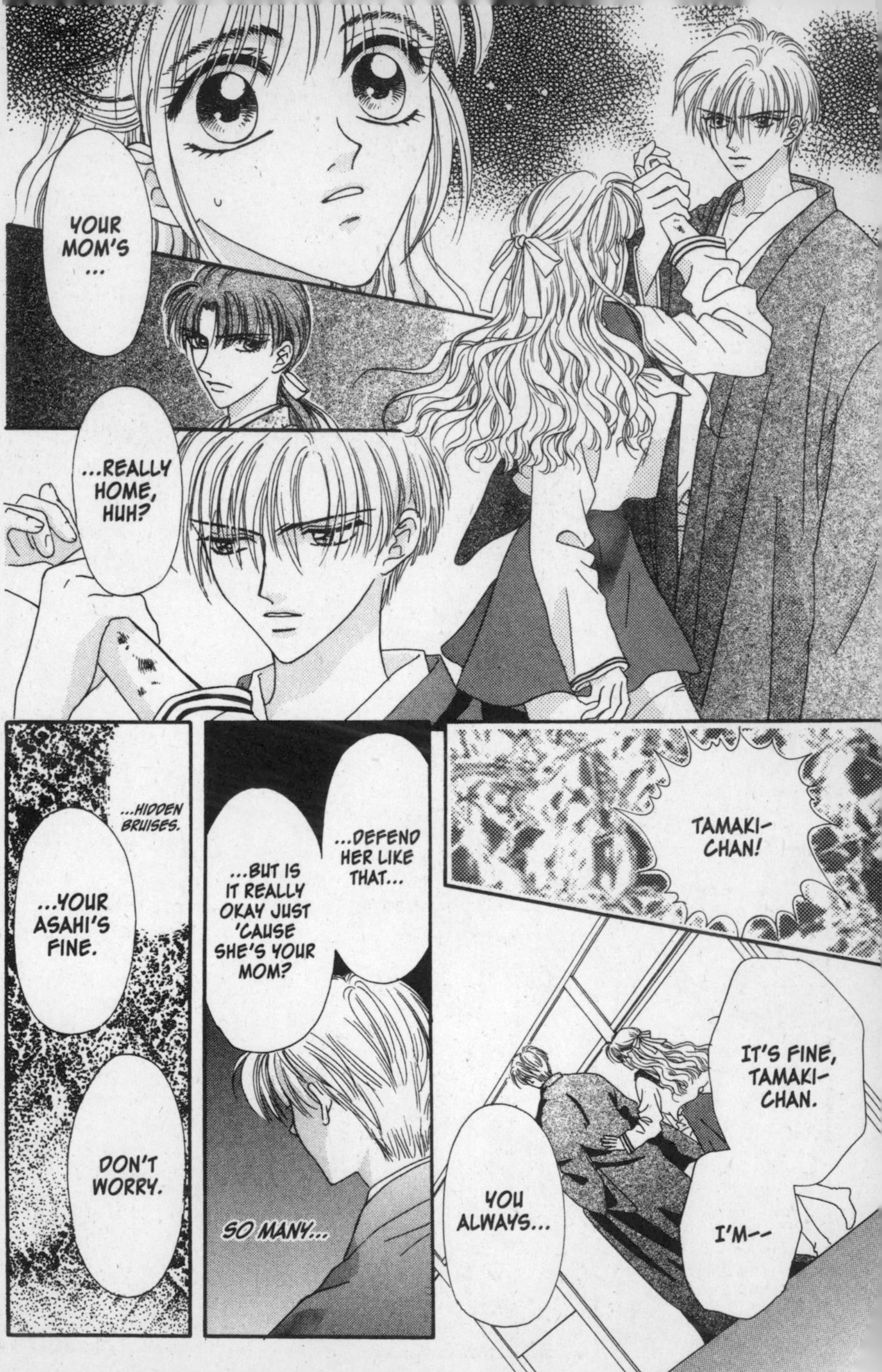
YOUR MOM'S ...
...REALLY HOME, HUH?
TAMAKI-CHAN!
IT'S FINE, TAMAKI-CHAN.
I'M--
YOU ALWAYS...
...DEFEND HER LIKE THAT...
...BUT IS IT REALLY OKAY JUST 'CAUSE SHE'S YOUR MOM?
SO MANY...
...HIDDEN BRUISES.
...YOUR ASAHI'S FINE.
DON'T WORRY.

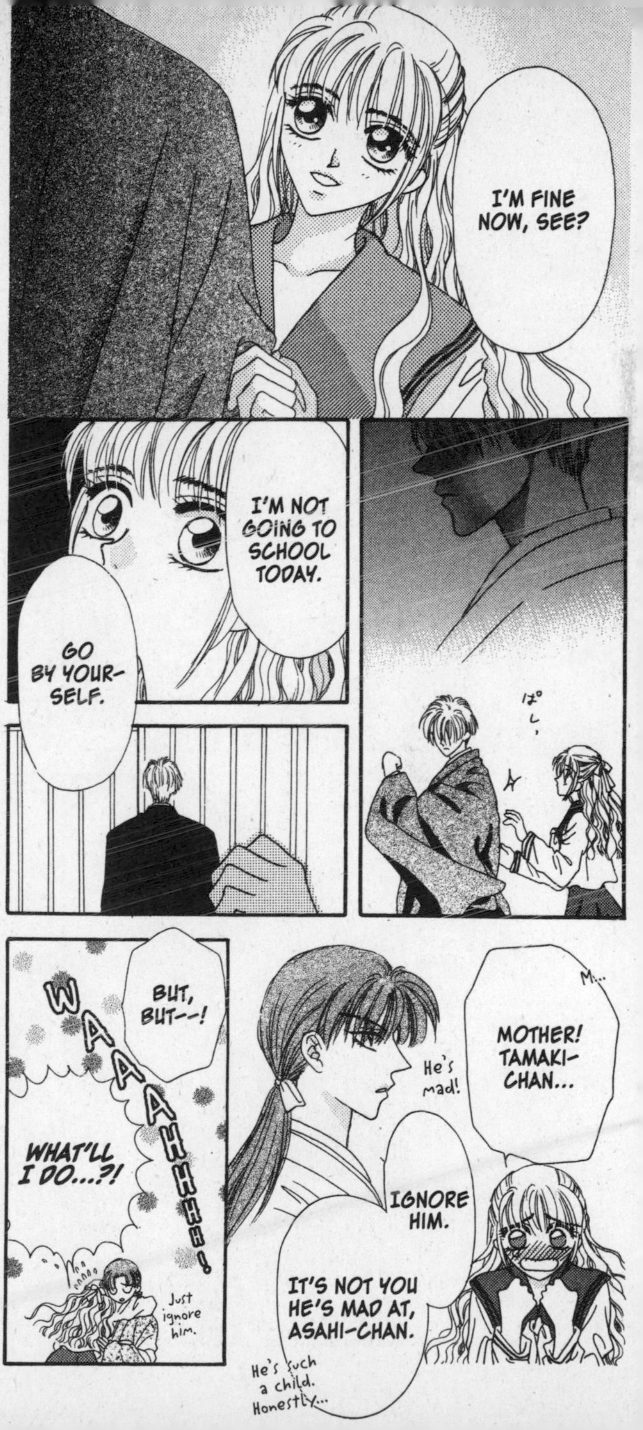
I'M FINE NOW, SEE?
ぱし
I'M NOT GOING TO SCHOOL TODAY.
GO BY YOURSELF.
M...
MOTHER! TAMAKI-CHAN...
He's mad!
IGNORE HIM.
IT'S NOT YOU HE'S MAD AT, ASAHI-CHAN.
He's such a child. Honestly...
BUT, BUT--!
WAAAAHHHHH!
WHAT'LL I DO...?!
Just ignore him.

Scroll Six

This story ran in the magazine. In terms of the storyline, it's set after Souichi's exorcism. The cat that visited Kaoru is really Kageha. Maybe no one noticed that, huh? (laughs) I was just playing around, though, so it's okay. I get the feeling a lot of people first heard about Dream through this story. Asahi and Kaname were popular right from the get-go with the main series, and... that was true this time, too. That's why people said things like, "I was so shocked" and "What happened, Asahi?" when they read the character introduction, which was full of words like "death" and "traitor." Even I--the writer!--thought, "So many things happened back then, but to Tamaki, it was a peaceful time, wasn't it?" People didn't like Asahi's mother (of course), but I really wanted to write about there being people who just don't or won't understand, no matter what. I don't know if Asahi's mom is lucky or unlucky in not realizing what she's missing...

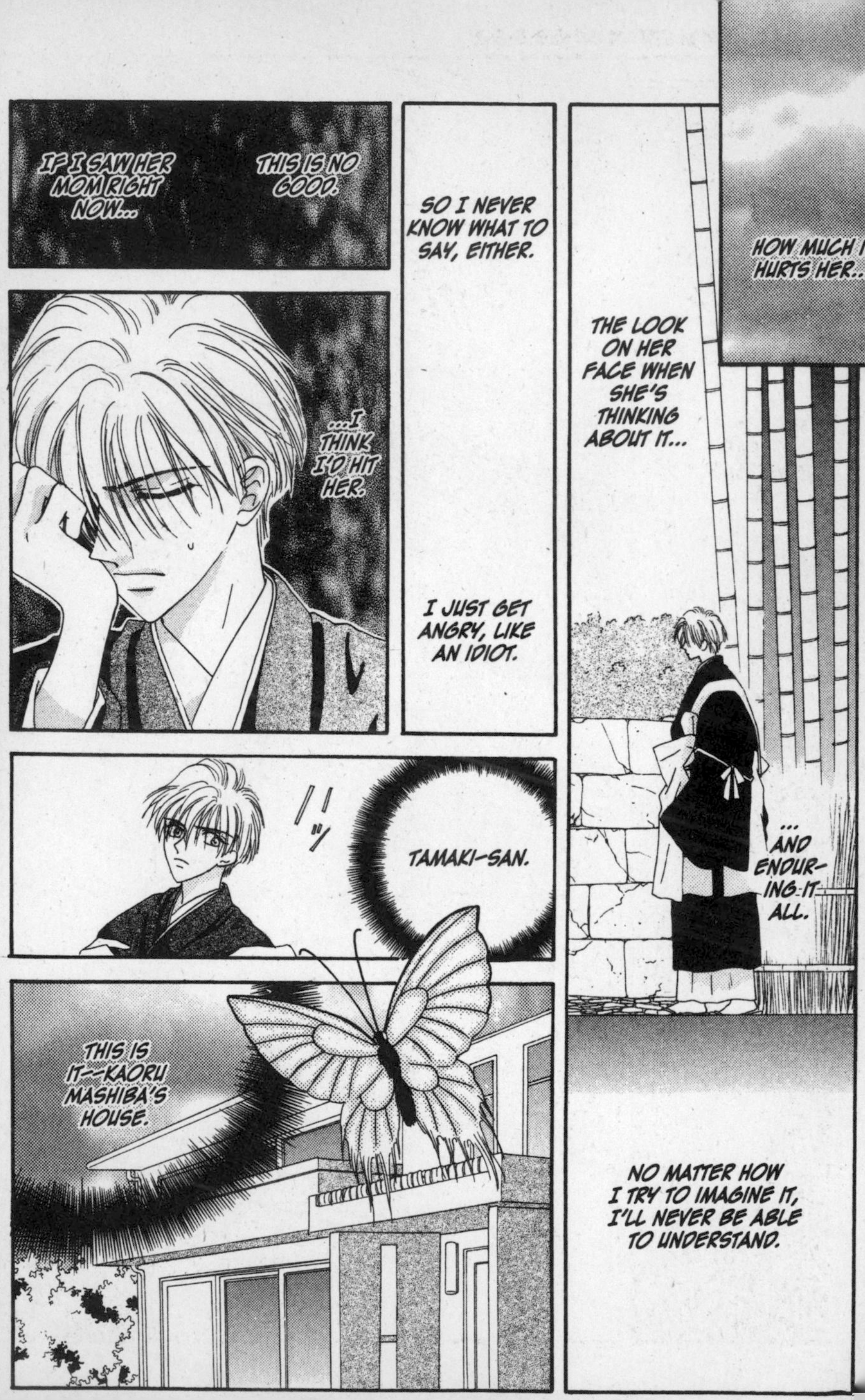
HOW MUCH IT HURTS HER...
THE LOOK ON HER FACE WHEN SHE'S THINKING ABOUT IT...
...AND ENDURING IT ALL.
NO MATTER HOW I TRY TO IMAGINE IT, I'LL NEVER BE ABLE TO UNDERSTAND.
SO I NEVER KNOW WHAT TO SAY, EITHER.
I JUST GET ANGRY, LIKE AN IDIOT.
THIS IS NO GOOD.
IF I SAW HER MOM RIGHT NOW...
...I THINK I'D HIT HER.
TAMAKI-SAN.
THIS IS IT--KAORU MASHIBA'S HOUSE.

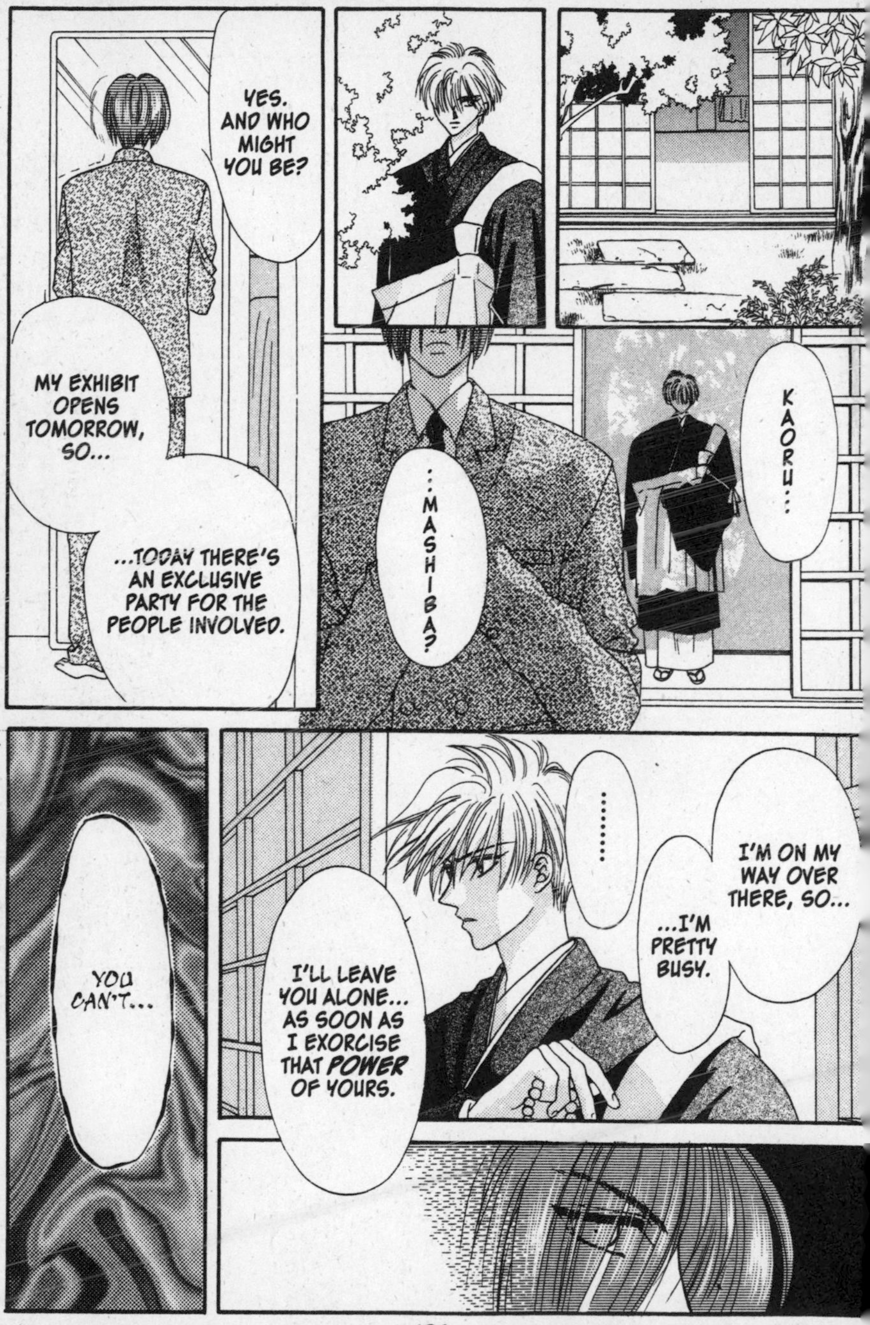
KAORU...
...MASHIBA?
YES. AND WHO MIGHT YOU BE?
MY EXHIBIT OPENS TOMORROW, SO...
...TODAY THERE'S AN EXCLUSIVE PARTY FOR THE PEOPLE INVOLVED.
I'M ON MY WAY OVER THERE, SO...
...I'M PRETTY BUSY.
......
I'LL LEAVE YOU ALONE... AS SOON AS I EXORCISE THAT *POWER* OF YOURS.
YOU CAN'T...

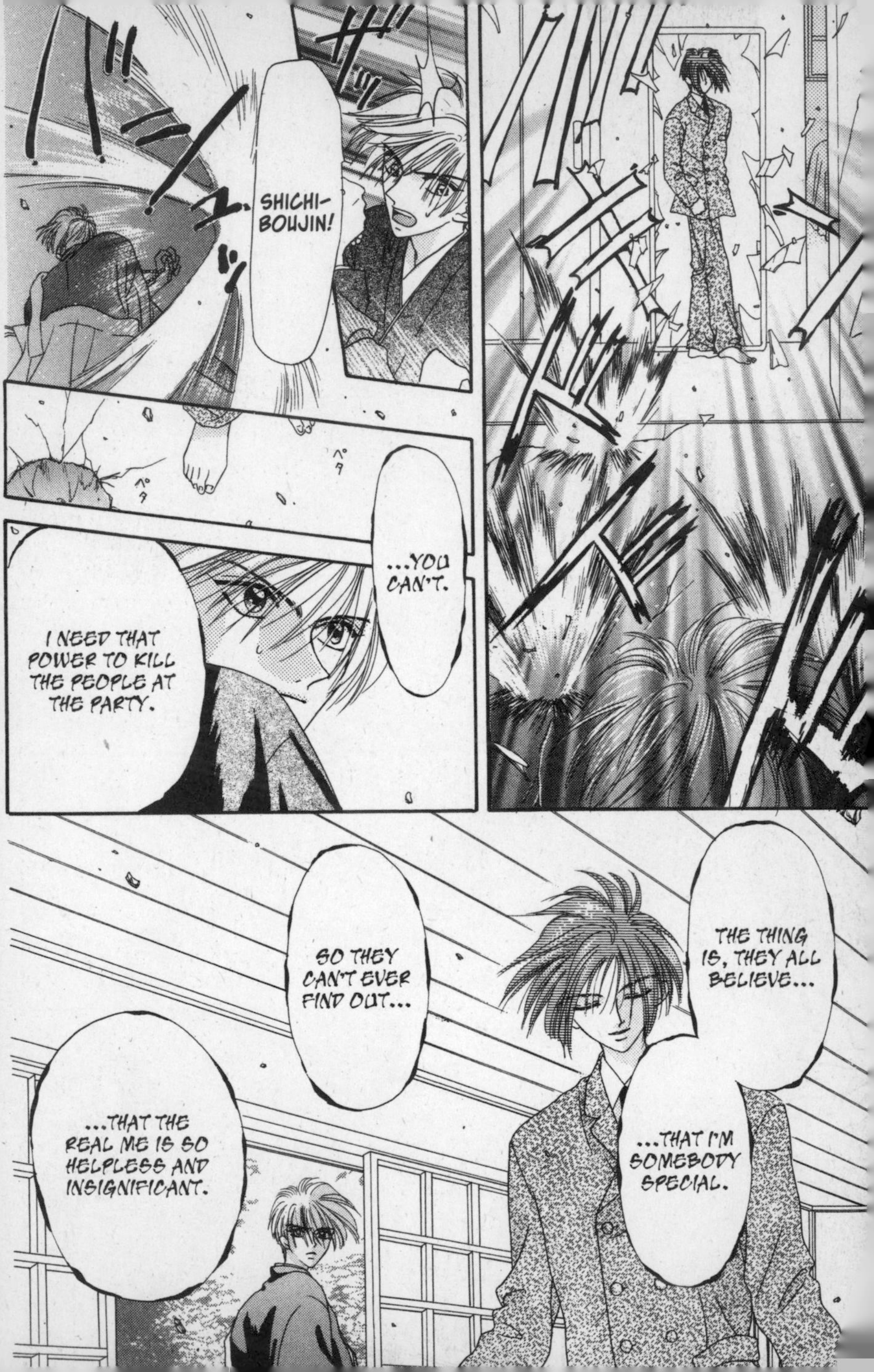
SHICHI-BOUJIN!
...YOU CAN'T.
I NEED THAT POWER TO KILL THE PEOPLE AT THE PARTY.
THE THING IS, THEY ALL BELIEVE...
...THAT I'M SOMEBODY SPECIAL.
SO THEY CAN'T EVER FIND OUT...
...THAT THE REAL ME IS SO HELPLESS AND INSIGNIFICANT.

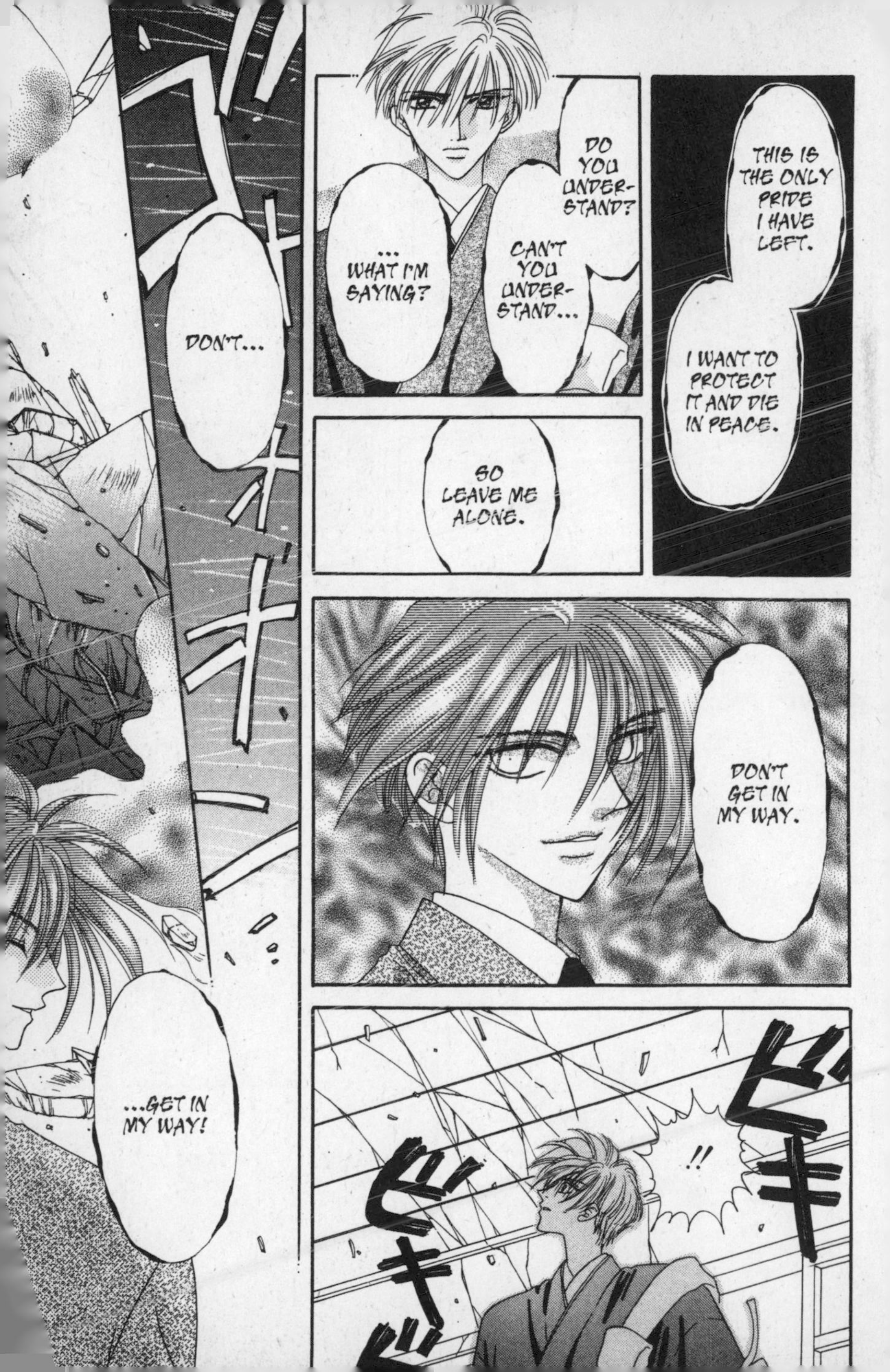
THIS IS THE ONLY PRIDE I HAVE LEFT.
I WANT TO PROTECT IT AND DIE IN PEACE.
DO YOU UNDERSTAND?
CAN'T YOU UNDERSTAND...
...WHAT I'M SAYING?
SO LEAVE ME ALONE.
DON'T GET IN MY WAY.
!!
DON'T...
...GET IN MY WAY!

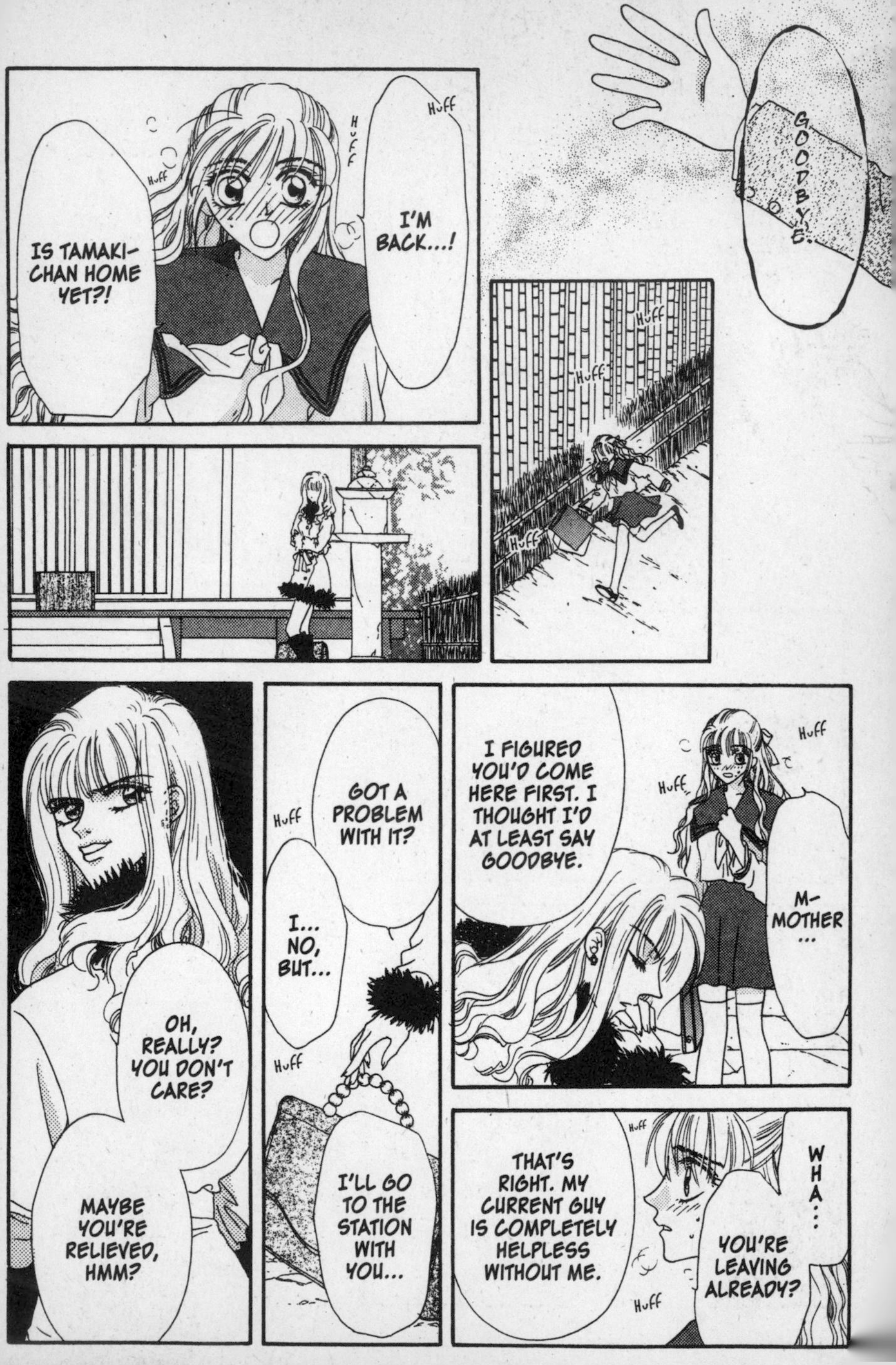
GOODBYE...
Huff
Huff
Huff
Huff
I'M BACK...!
Huff
Huff
IS TAMAKI-CHAN HOME YET?!
Huff
M-MOTHER...
Huff
I FIGURED YOU'D COME HERE FIRST. I THOUGHT I'D AT LEAST SAY GOODBYE.
WHA...
YOU'RE LEAVING ALREADY?
Huff
Huff
THAT'S RIGHT. MY CURRENT GUY IS COMPLETELY HELPLESS WITHOUT ME.
GOT A PROBLEM WITH IT?
Huff
I... NO, BUT...
Huff
I'LL GO TO THE STATION WITH YOU...
OH, REALLY? YOU DON'T CARE?
MAYBE YOU'RE RELIEVED, HMM?

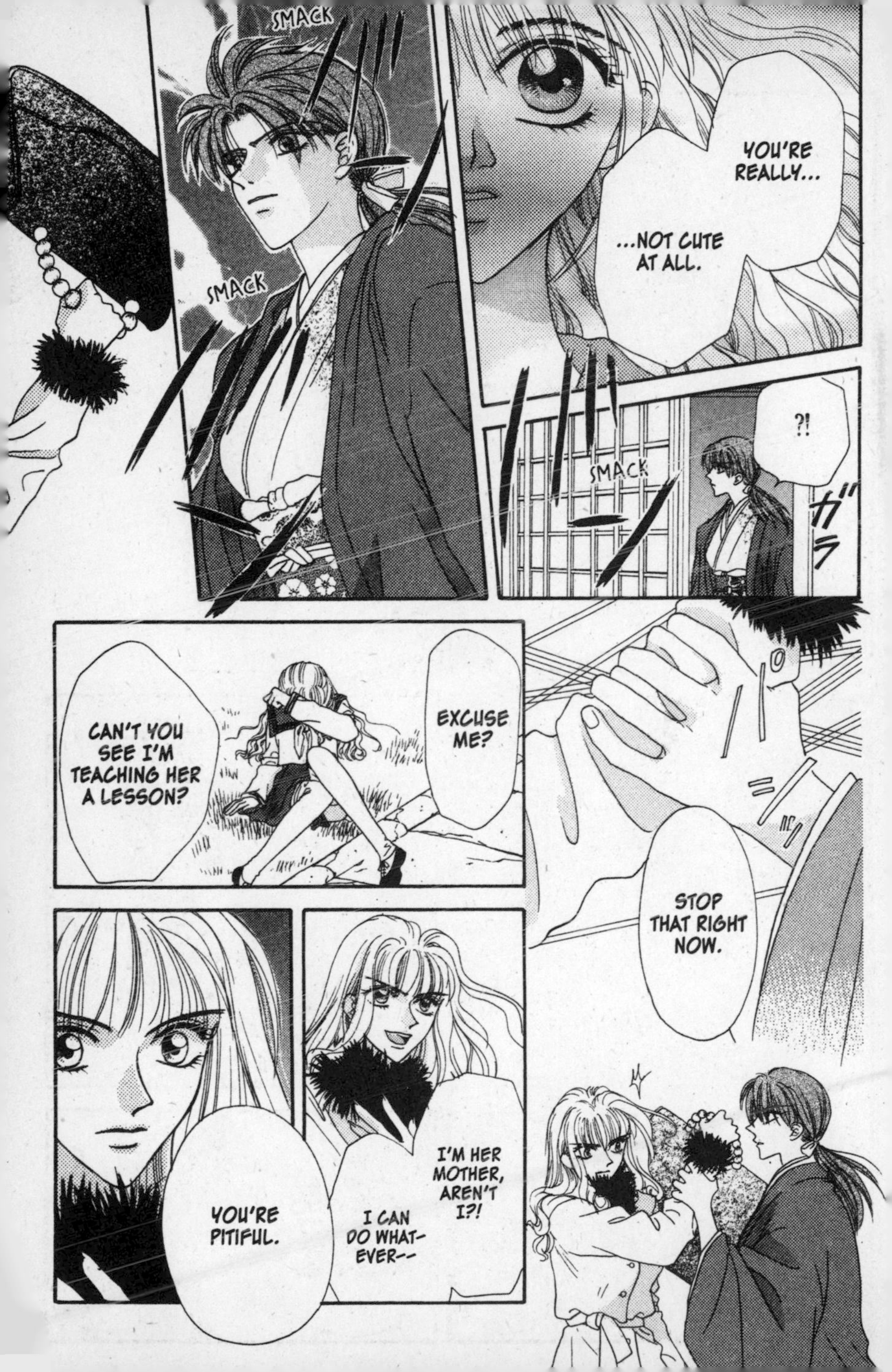
YOU'RE REALLY...
...NOT CUTE AT ALL.
?!
SMACK
ガラ
SMACK
SMACK
STOP THAT RIGHT NOW.
EXCUSE ME?
CAN'T YOU SEE I'M TEACHING HER A LESSON?
I'M HER MOTHER, AREN'T I?!
I CAN DO WHATEVER--
YOU'RE PITIFUL.

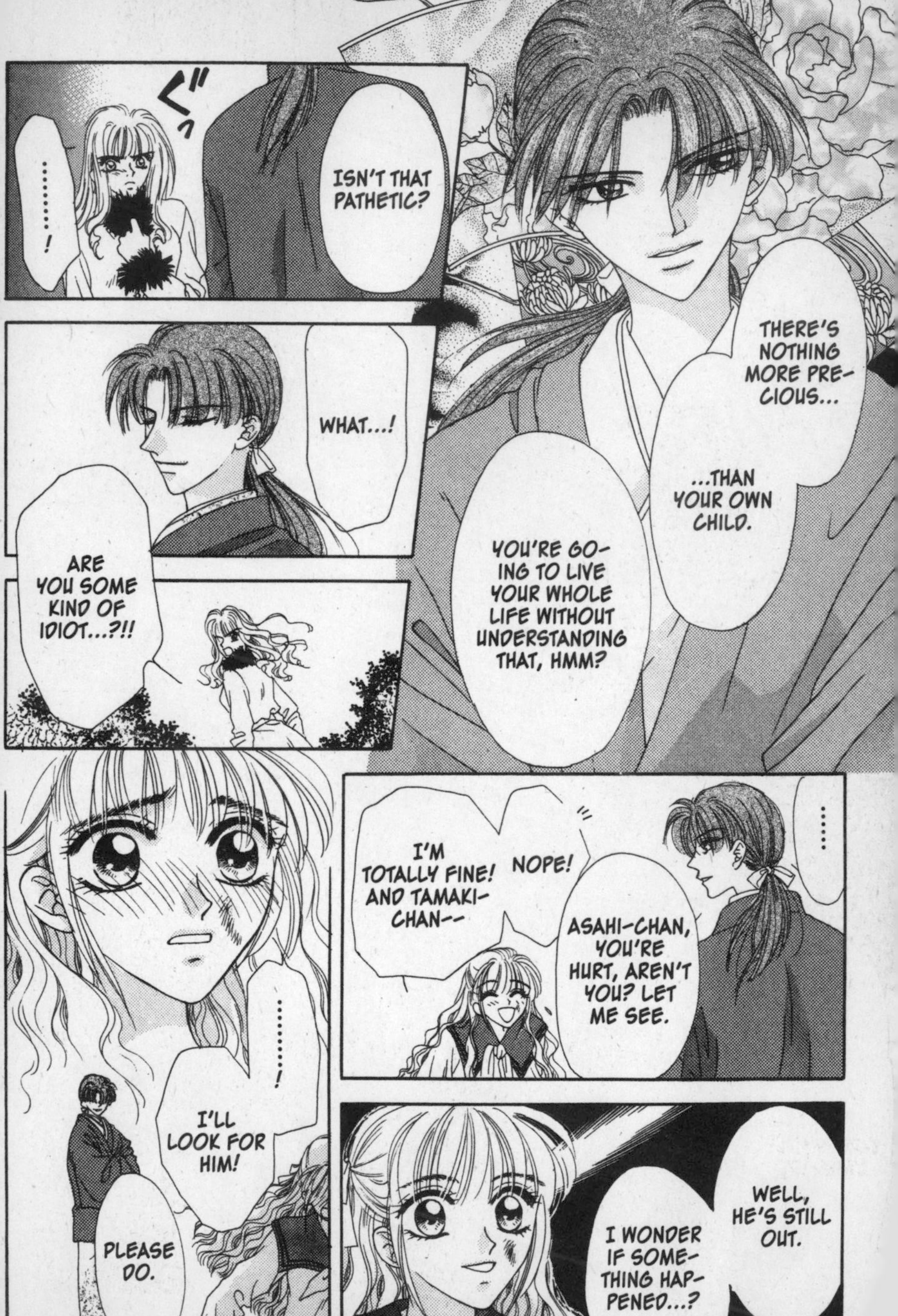

THERE'S NOTHING MORE PRECIOUS...
...THAN YOUR OWN CHILD.
YOU'RE GOING TO LIVE YOUR WHOLE LIFE WITHOUT UNDERSTANDING THAT, HMM?
ISN'T THAT PATHETIC?
......!
WHAT...!
ARE YOU SOME KIND OF IDIOT...?!!
......
ASAHI-CHAN, YOU'RE HURT, AREN'T YOU? LET ME SEE.
NOPE!
I'M TOTALLY FINE! AND TAMAKI-CHAN--
WELL, HE'S STILL OUT.
I WONDER IF SOMETHING HAPPENED...?
......!
I'LL LOOK FOR HIM!
PLEASE DO.

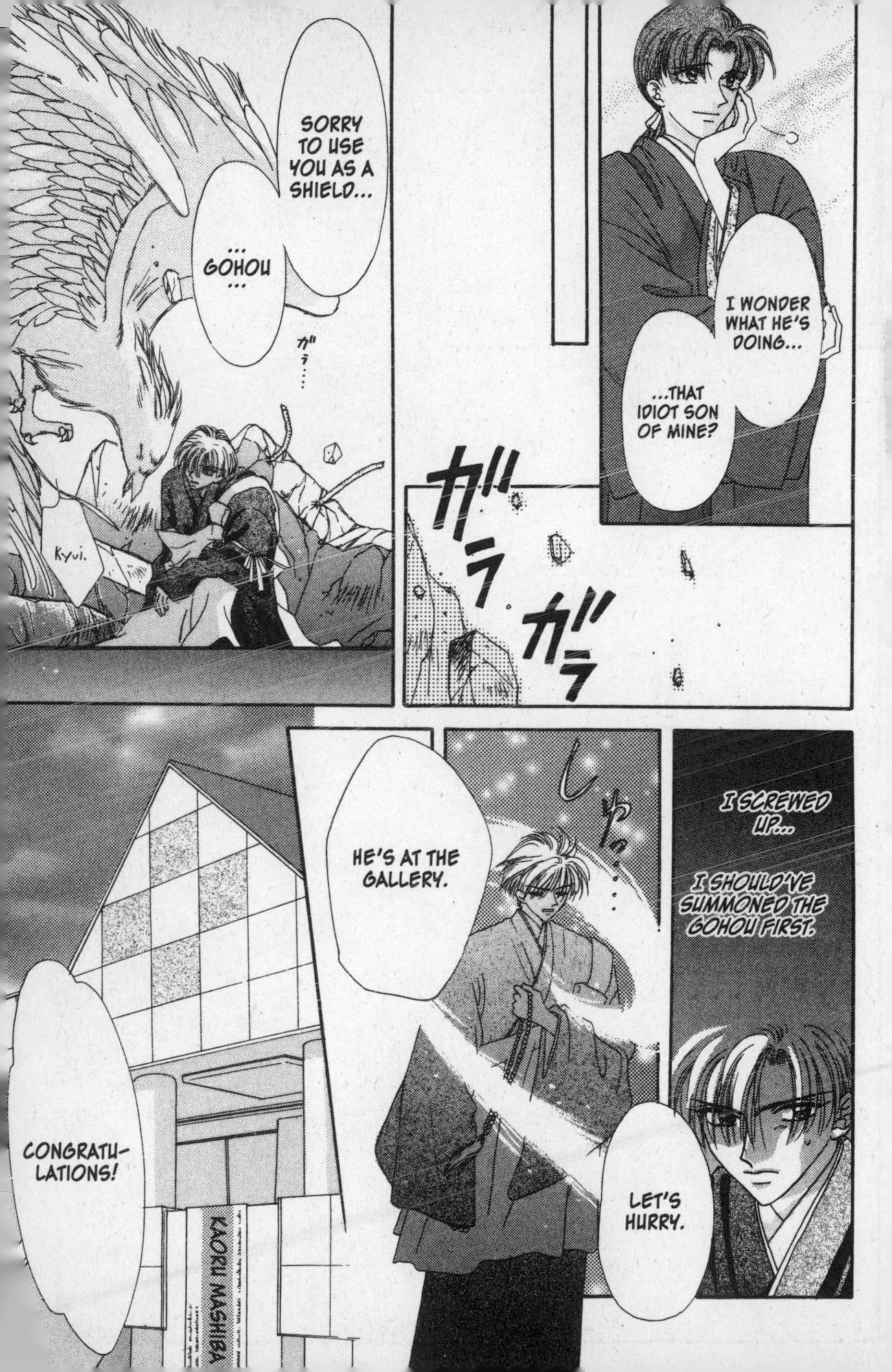
I WONDER WHAT HE'S DOING...
...THAT IDIOT SON OF MINE?
ガラガラ
SORRY TO USE YOU AS A SHIELD...
...GOHOU...
ガラ…
Kyui.
I SCREWED UP...
I SHOULD'VE SUMMONED THE GOHOU FIRST.
LET'S HURRY.
しゃっ…
HE'S AT THE GALLERY.
CONGRATU-LATIONS!
KAORU MASHIBA

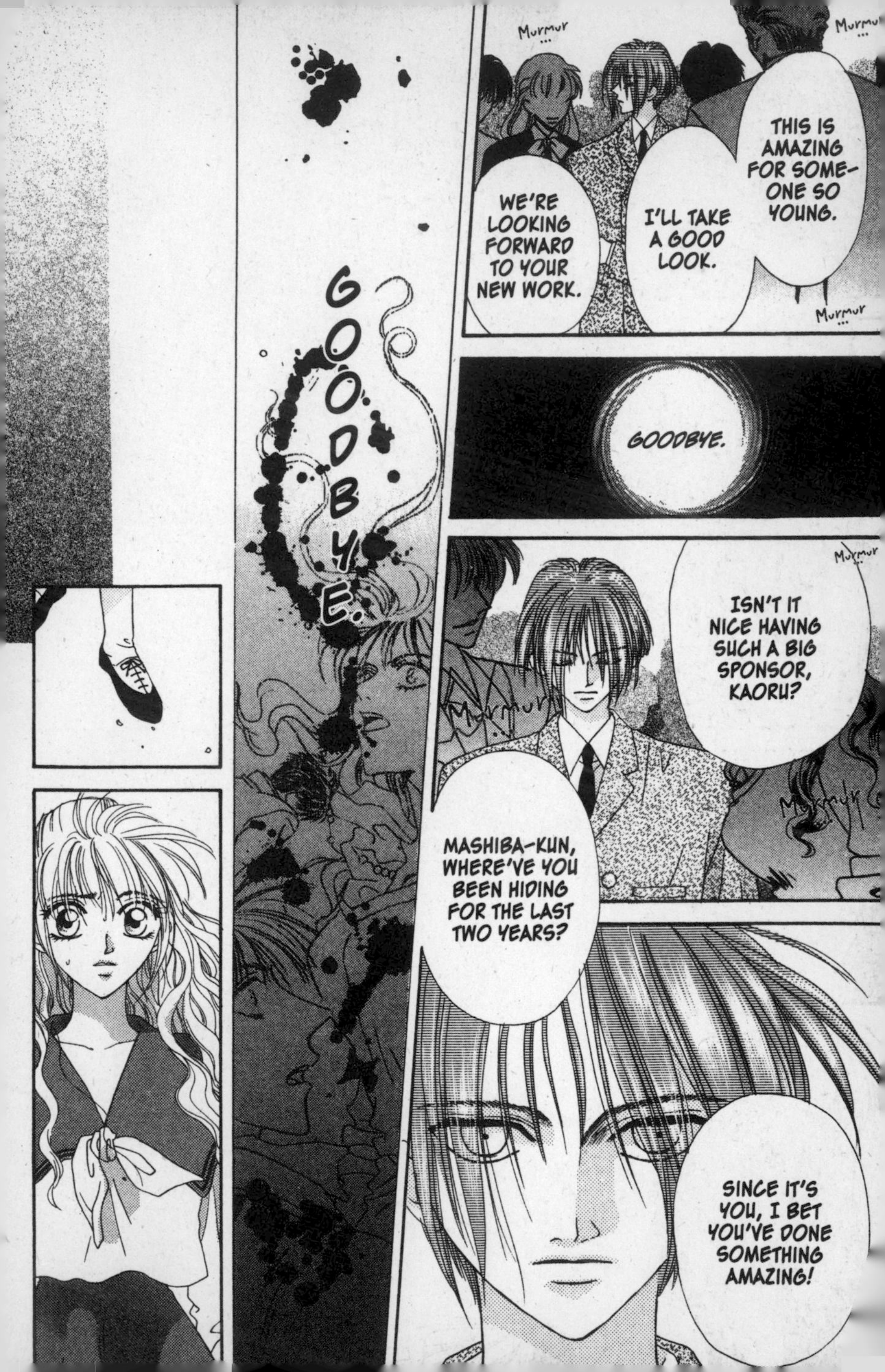
Murmur...
Murmur...
THIS IS AMAZING FOR SOME-ONE SO YOUNG.
I'LL TAKE A GOOD LOOK.
WE'RE LOOKING FORWARD TO YOUR NEW WORK.
Murmur...
GOODBYE.
Murmur...
ISN'T IT NICE HAVING SUCH A BIG SPONSOR, KAORU?
Murmur
Murmur
MASHIBA-KUN, WHERE'VE YOU BEEN HIDING FOR THE LAST TWO YEARS?
SINCE IT'S YOU, I BET YOU'VE DONE SOMETHING AMAZING!
GOODBYE.

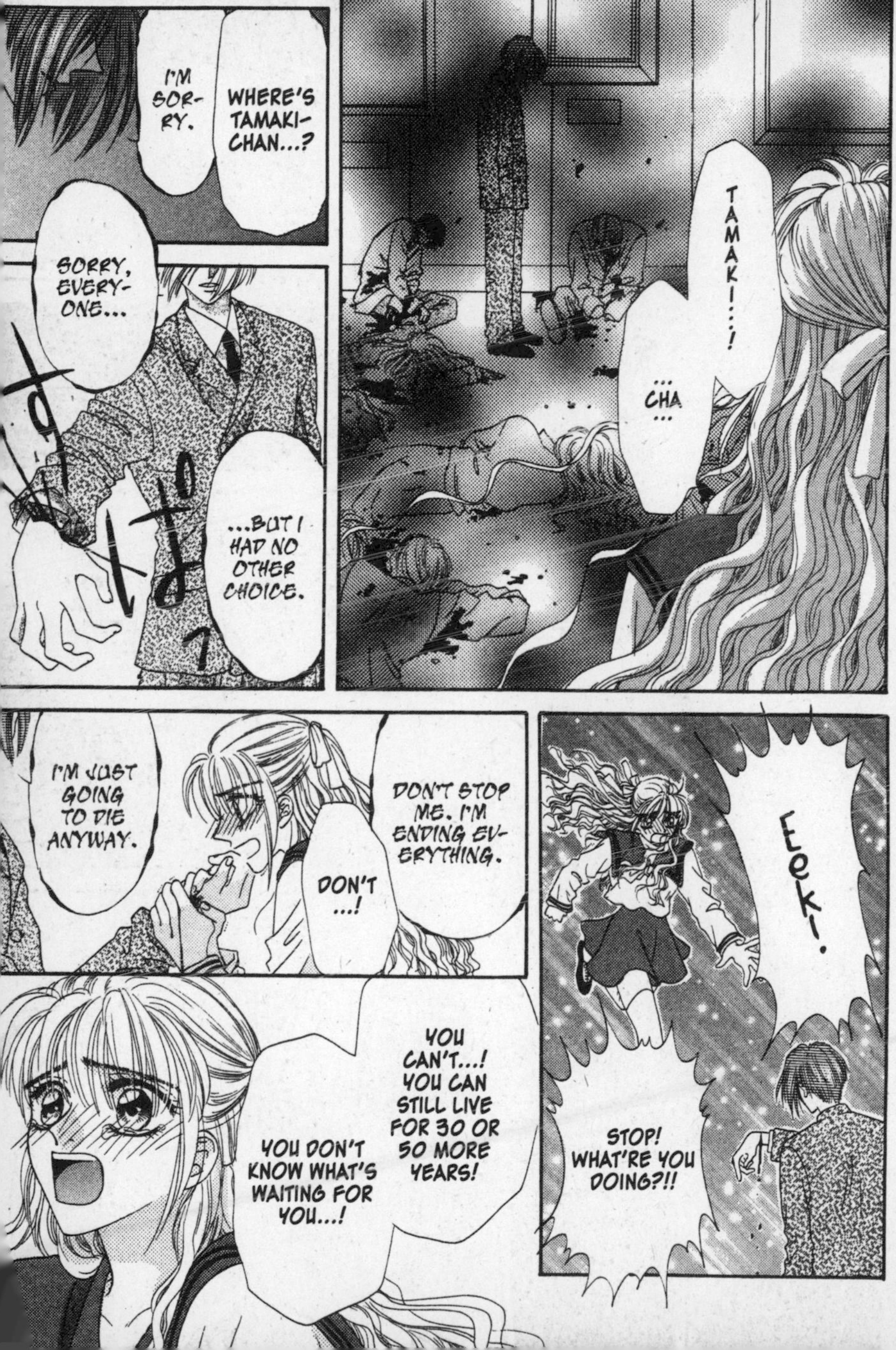
TAMAKI...!
...CHA...
WHERE'S TAMAKI-CHAN...?
I'M SORRY.
SORRY, EVERYONE...
...BUT I HAD NO OTHER CHOICE.
Eeki.
STOP! WHAT'RE YOU DOING?!!
DON'T STOP ME. I'M ENDING EVERYTHING.
DON'T...!
I'M JUST GOING TO DIE ANYWAY.
YOU CAN'T...! YOU CAN STILL LIVE FOR 30 OR 50 MORE YEARS!
YOU DON'T KNOW WHAT'S WAITING FOR YOU...!

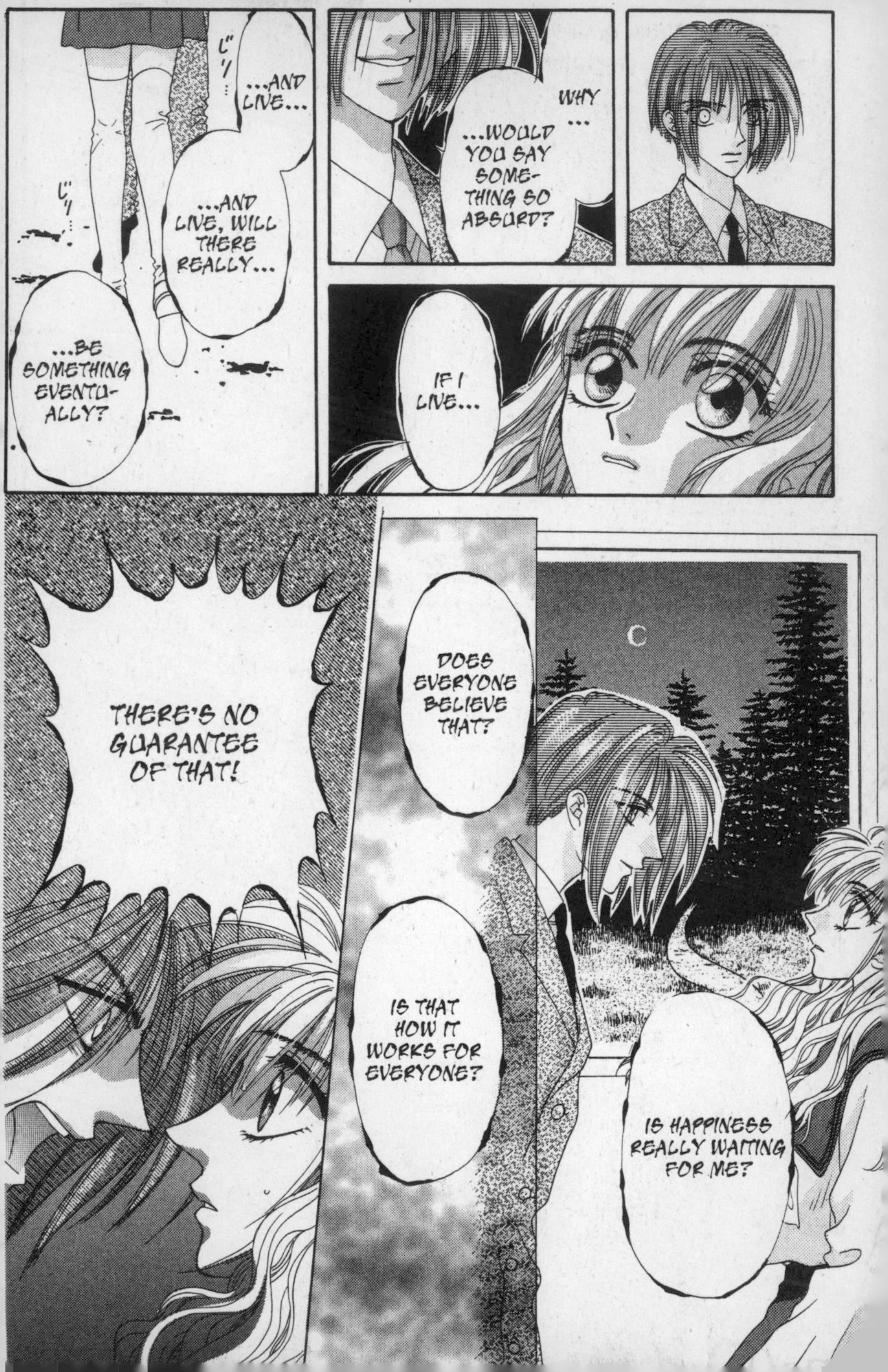
WHY ...
...WOULD YOU SAY SOMETHING SO ABSURD?
IF I LIVE...
...AND LIVE...
...AND LIVE, WILL THERE REALLY...
...BE SOMETHING EVENTUALLY?
IS HAPPINESS REALLY WAITING FOR ME?
DOES EVERYONE BELIEVE THAT?
IS THAT HOW IT WORKS FOR EVERYONE?
THERE'S NO GUARANTEE OF THAT!

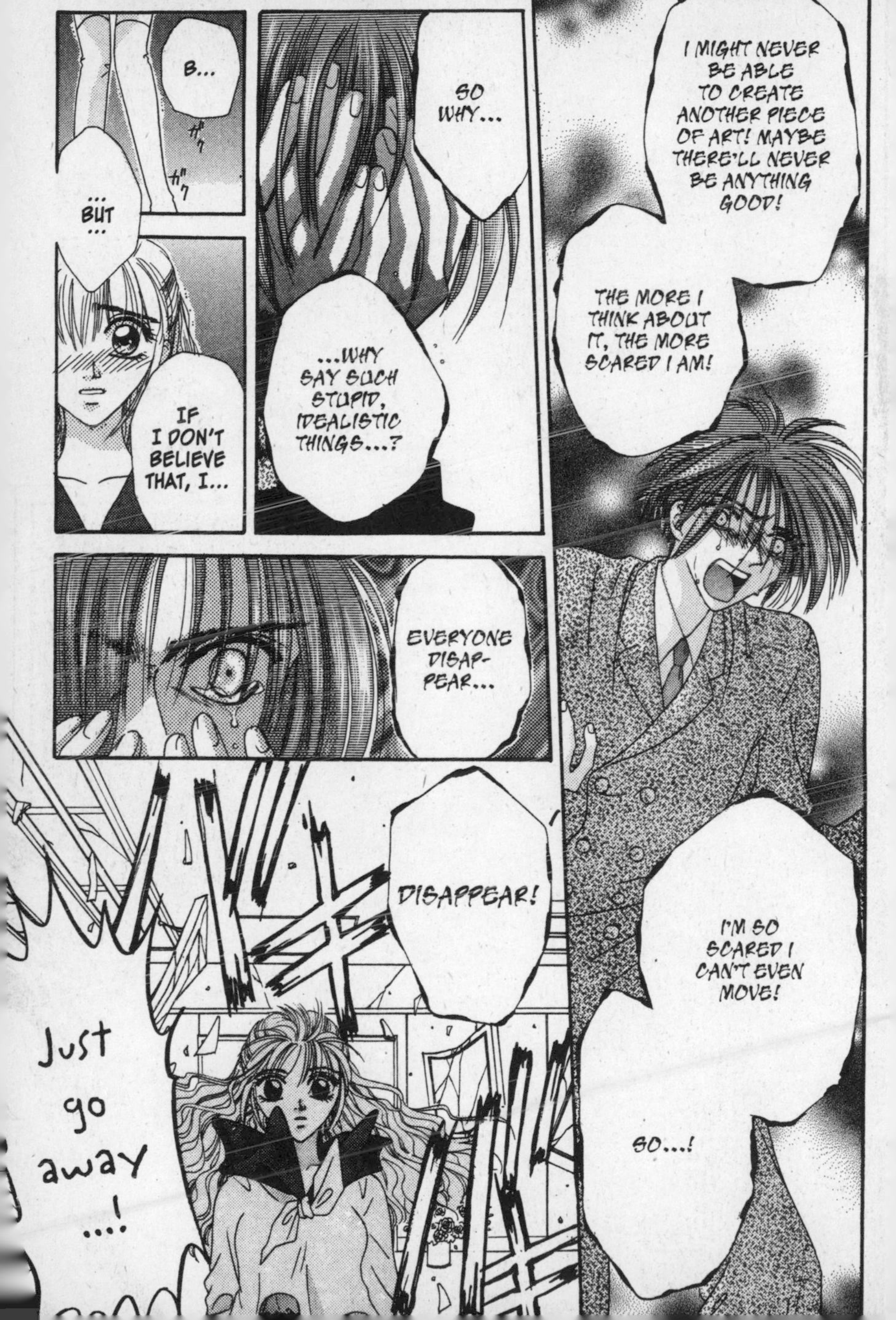
I MIGHT NEVER BE ABLE TO CREATE ANOTHER PIECE OF ART! MAYBE THERE'LL NEVER BE ANYTHING GOOD!
THE MORE I THINK ABOUT IT, THE MORE SCARED I AM!
I'M SO SCARED I CAN'T EVEN MOVE!
SO...!
SO WHY...
...WHY SAY SUCH STUPID, IDEALISTIC THINGS...?
B...
...BUT...
IF I DON'T BELIEVE THAT, I...
EVERYONE DISAP-PEAR...
DISAPPEAR!
Just go away ...!

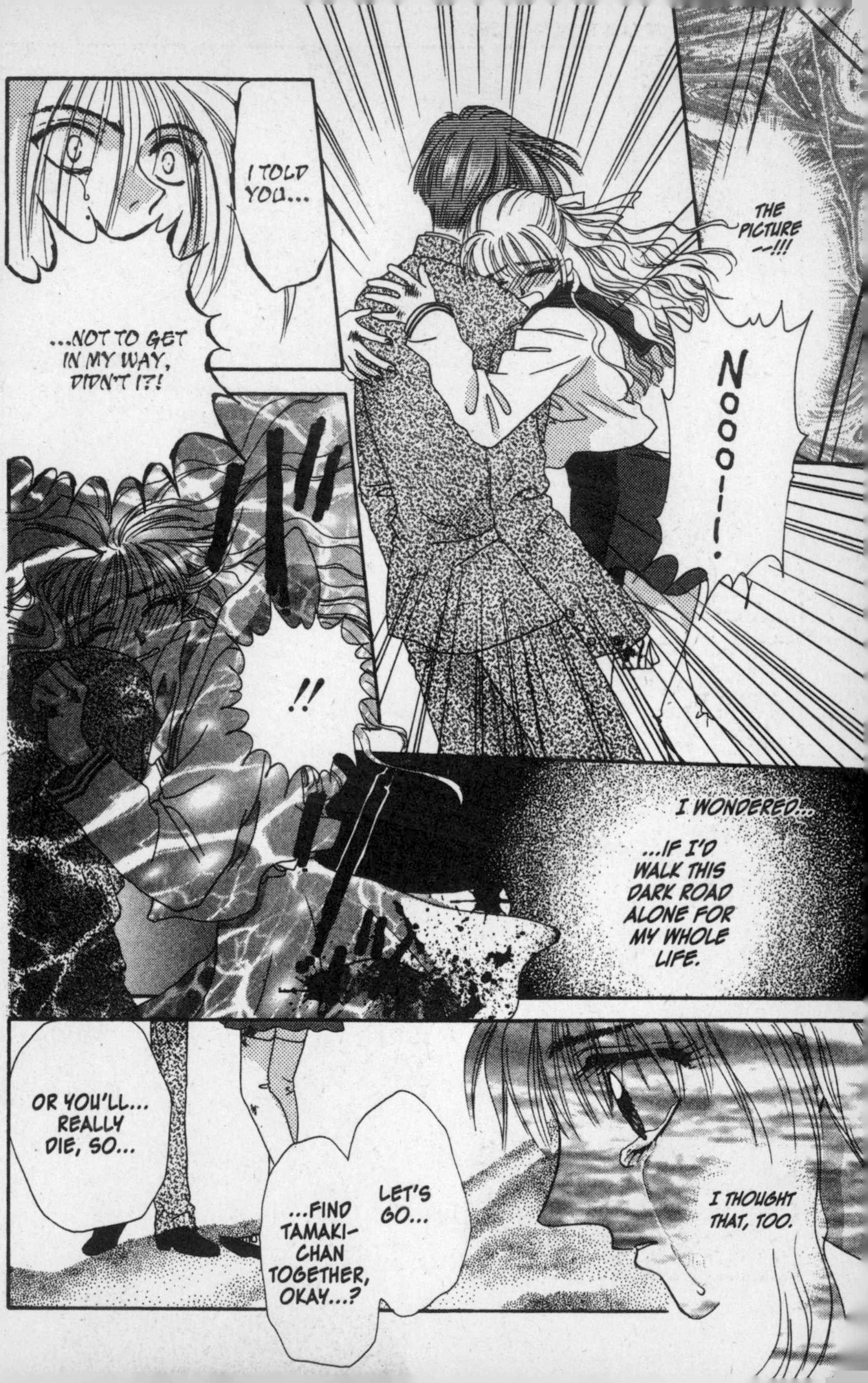
THE PICTURE --!!!
NOOOO!!!
I TOLD YOU...
...NOT TO GET IN MY WAY, DIDN'T I?!
!!
I WONDERED...
...IF I'D WALK THIS DARK ROAD ALONE FOR MY WHOLE LIFE.
I THOUGHT THAT, TOO.
LET'S GO...
...FIND TAMAKI-CHAN TOGETHER, OKAY...?
OR YOU'LL... REALLY DIE, SO...

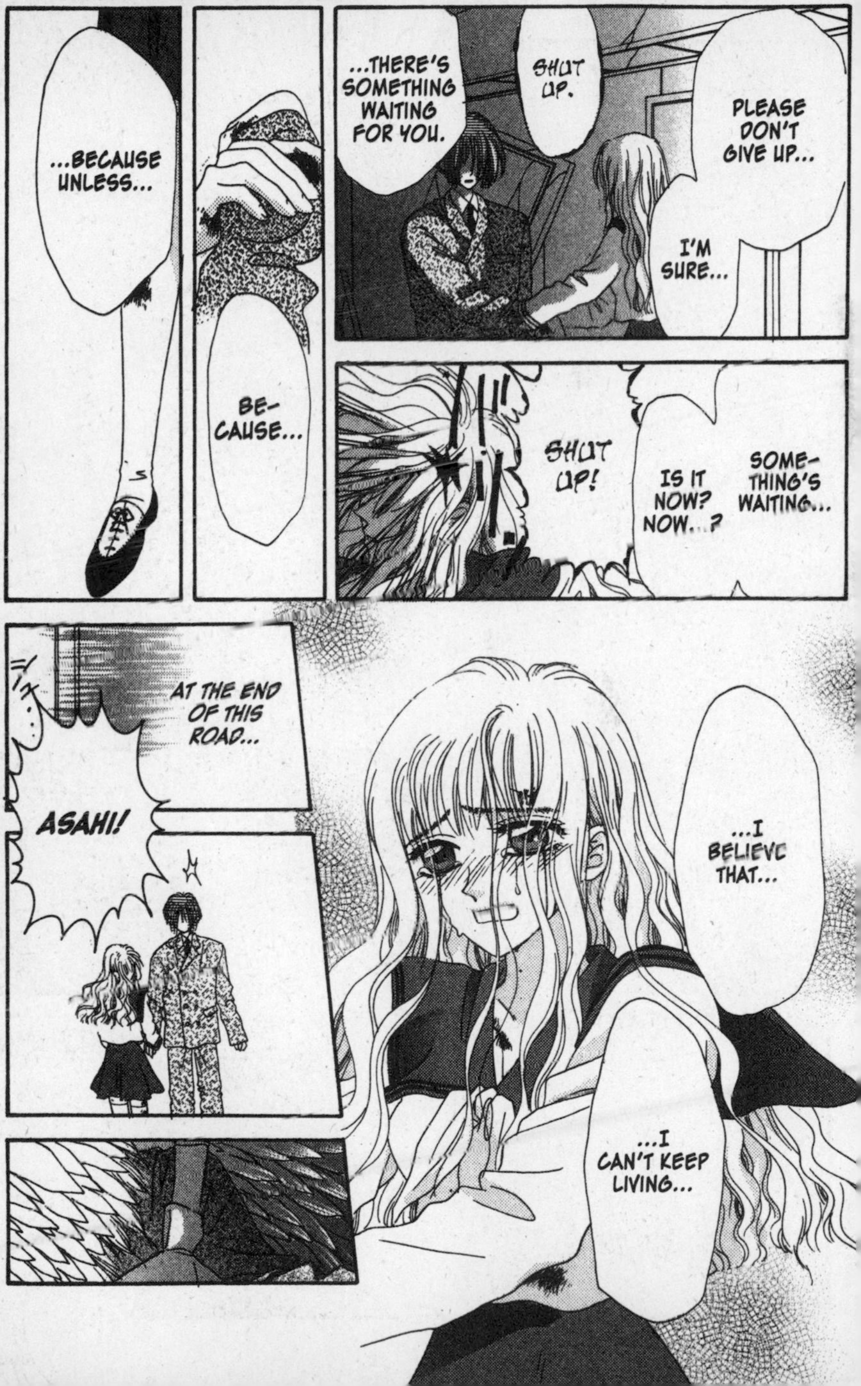
PLEASE DON'T GIVE UP...
I'M SURE...
SHUT UP.
...THERE'S SOMETHING WAITING FOR YOU.
SOME-THING'S WAITING...
IS IT NOW? NOW...?
SHUT UP!
BE-CAUSE...
...BECAUSE UNLESS...
...I BELIEVE THAT...
...I CAN'T KEEP LIVING...
AT THE END OF THIS ROAD...
ASAHI!

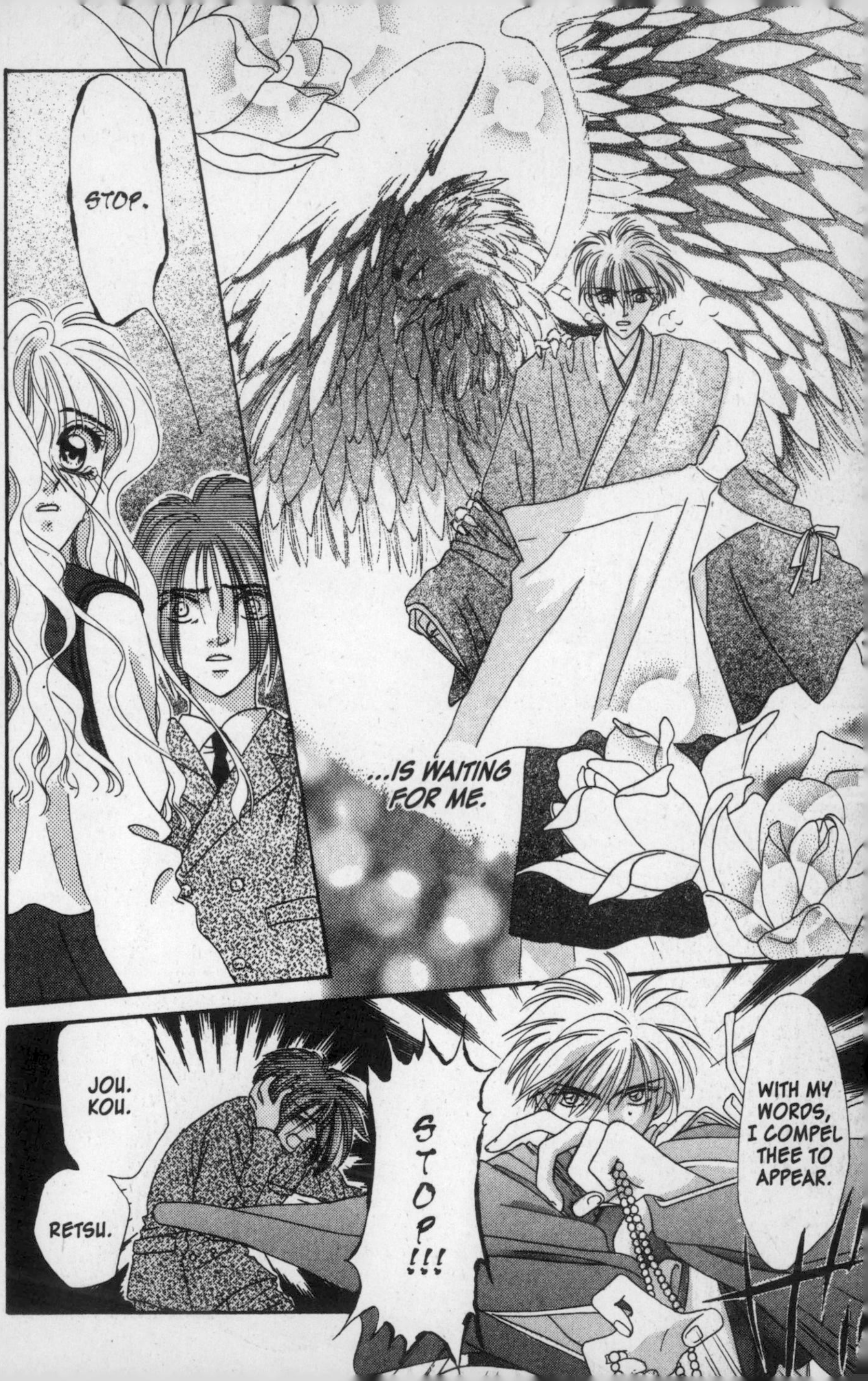
...IS WAITING FOR ME.
STOP.
WITH MY WORDS, I COMPEL THEE TO APPEAR.
STOP!!!
JOU. KOU.
RETSU.

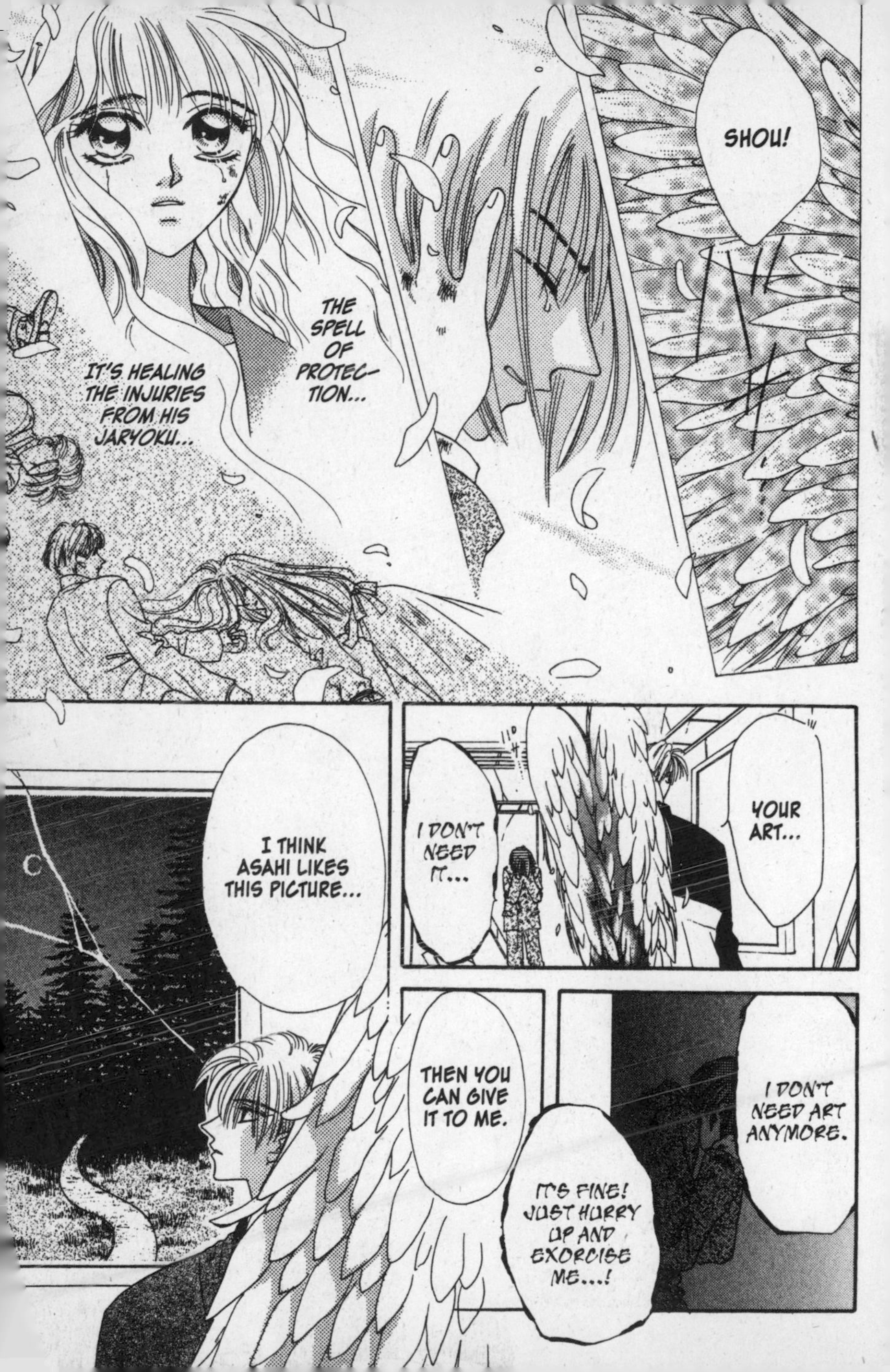
SHOU!
THE SPELL OF PROTECTION...
IT'S HEALING THE INJURIES FROM HIS JARYOKU...
YOUR ART...
I DON'T NEED IT...
I DON'T NEED ART ANYMORE.
IT'S FINE! JUST HURRY UP AND EXORCISE ME...!
THEN YOU CAN GIVE IT TO ME.
I THINK ASAHI LIKES THIS PICTURE...

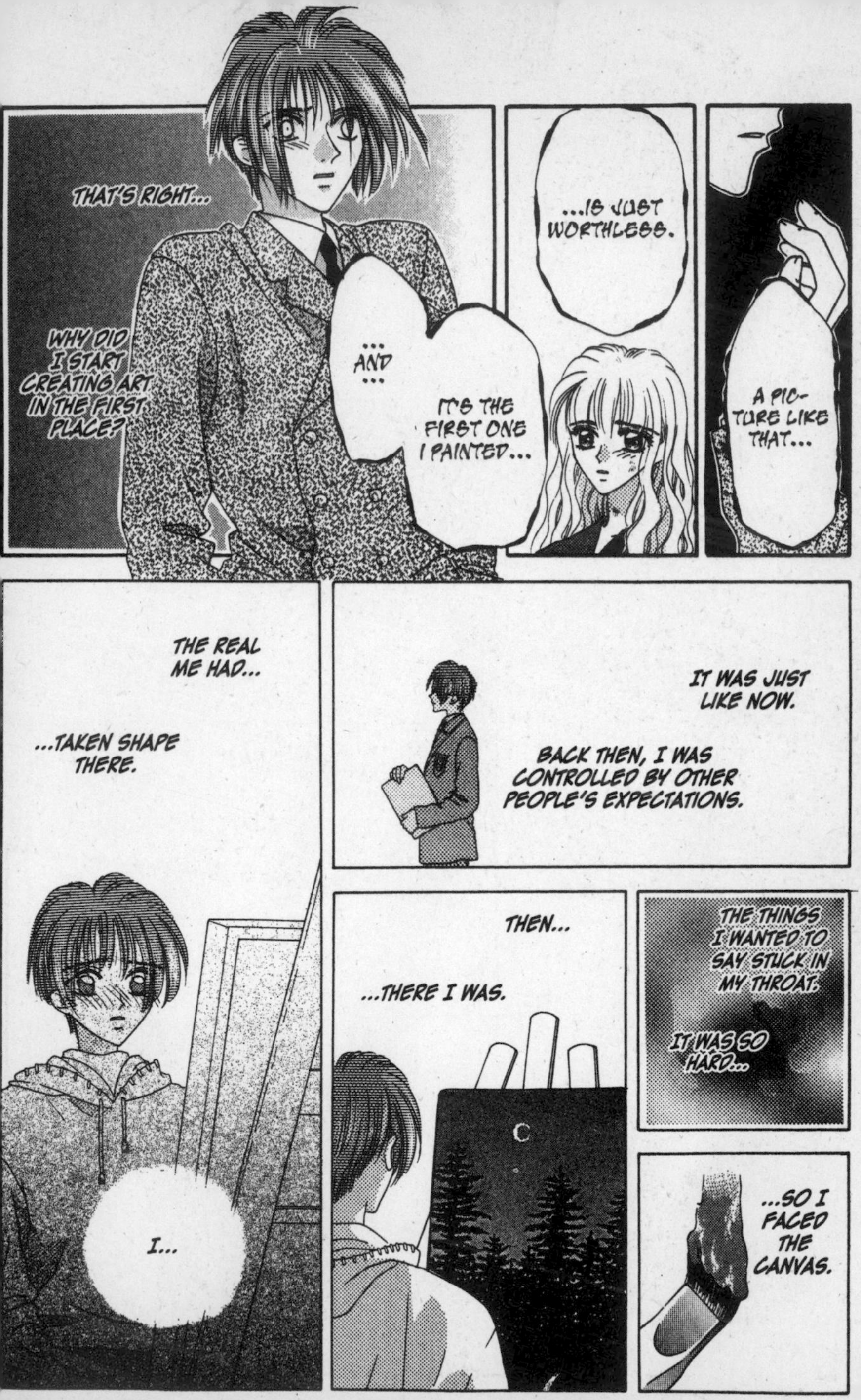

A PIC-TURE LIKE THAT...
...IS JUST WORTHLESS.
...AND... IT'S THE FIRST ONE I PAINTED...
THAT'S RIGHT...
WHY DID I START CREATING ART IN THE FIRST PLACE?
IT WAS JUST LIKE NOW.
BACK THEN, I WAS CONTROLLED BY OTHER PEOPLE'S EXPECTATIONS.
THE THINGS I WANTED TO SAY STUCK IN MY THROAT.
IT WAS SO HARD...
...SO I FACED THE CANVAS.
THEN...
...THERE I WAS.
THE REAL ME HAD...
...TAKEN SHAPE THERE.
I...

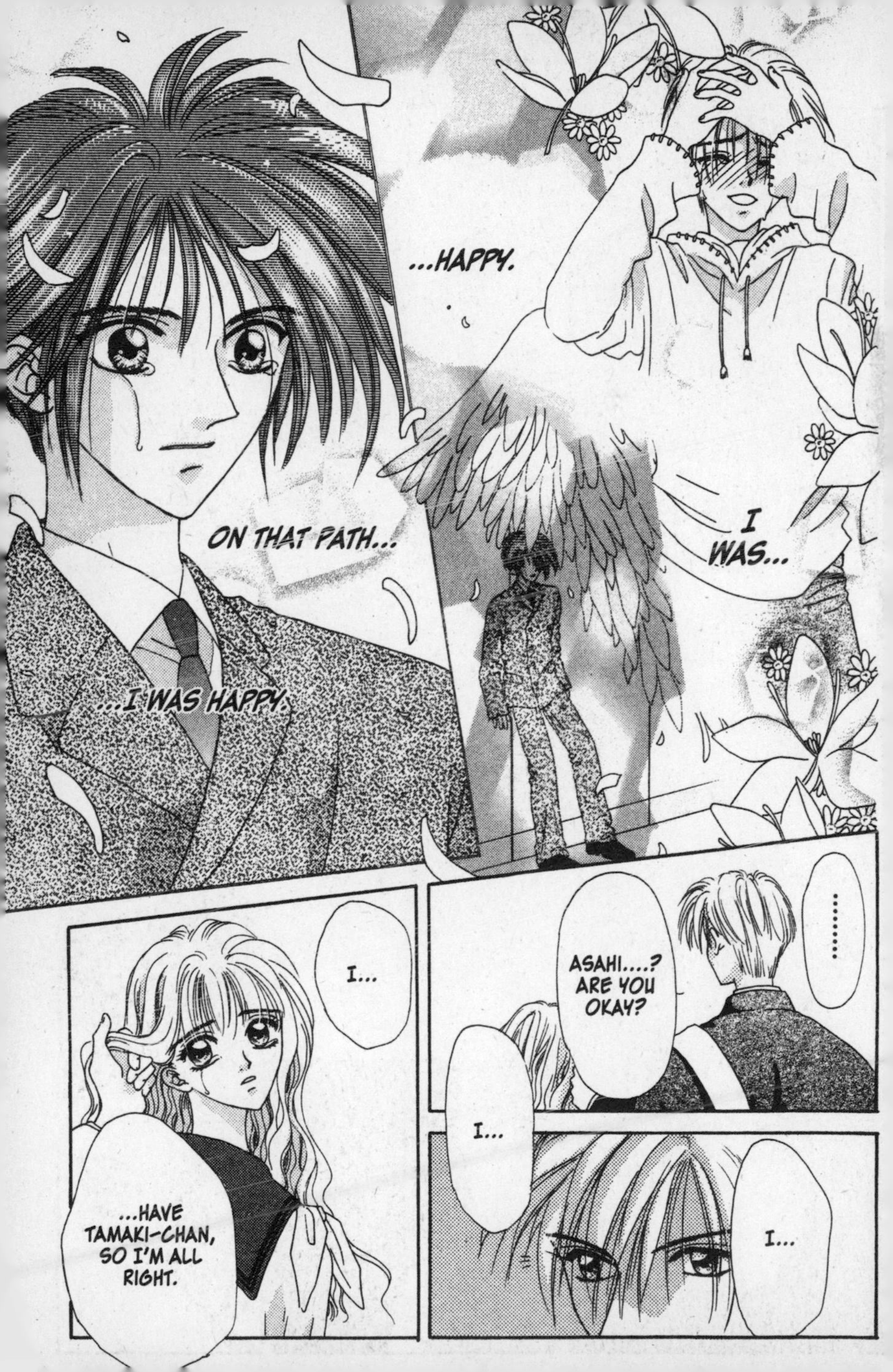
I WAS...
...HAPPY.
ON THAT PATH...
...I WAS HAPPY.
......
ASAHI....? ARE YOU OKAY?
I...
I...
I...
...HAVE TAMAKI-CHAN, SO I'M ALL RIGHT.

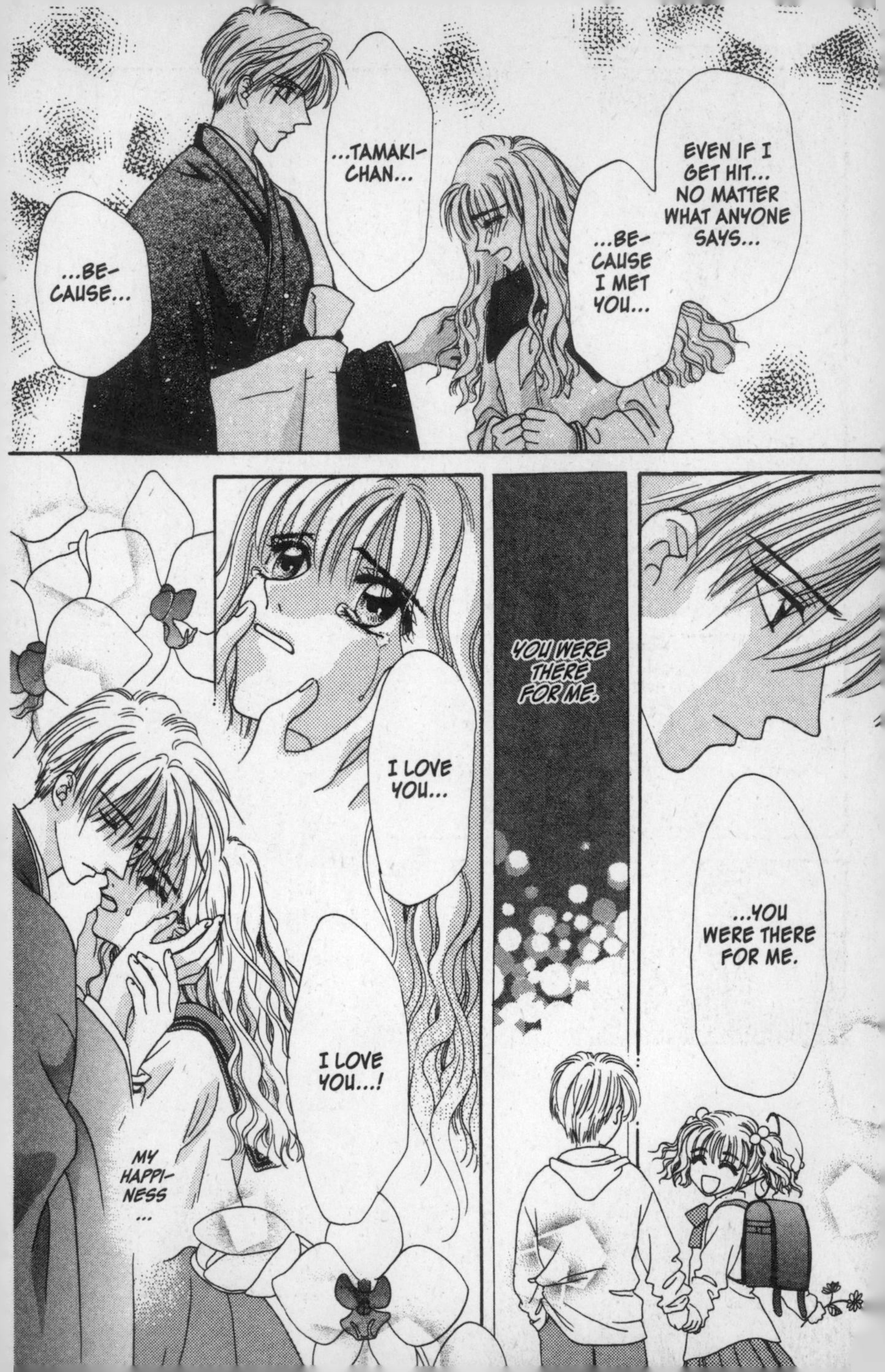
EVEN IF I GET HIT... NO MATTER WHAT ANYONE SAYS...
...TAMAKI-CHAN...
...BE-CAUSE I MET YOU...
...BE-CAUSE...
...YOU WERE THERE FOR ME.
YOU WERE THERE FOR ME.
I LOVE YOU...
I LOVE YOU...!
MY HAPPI-NESS ...

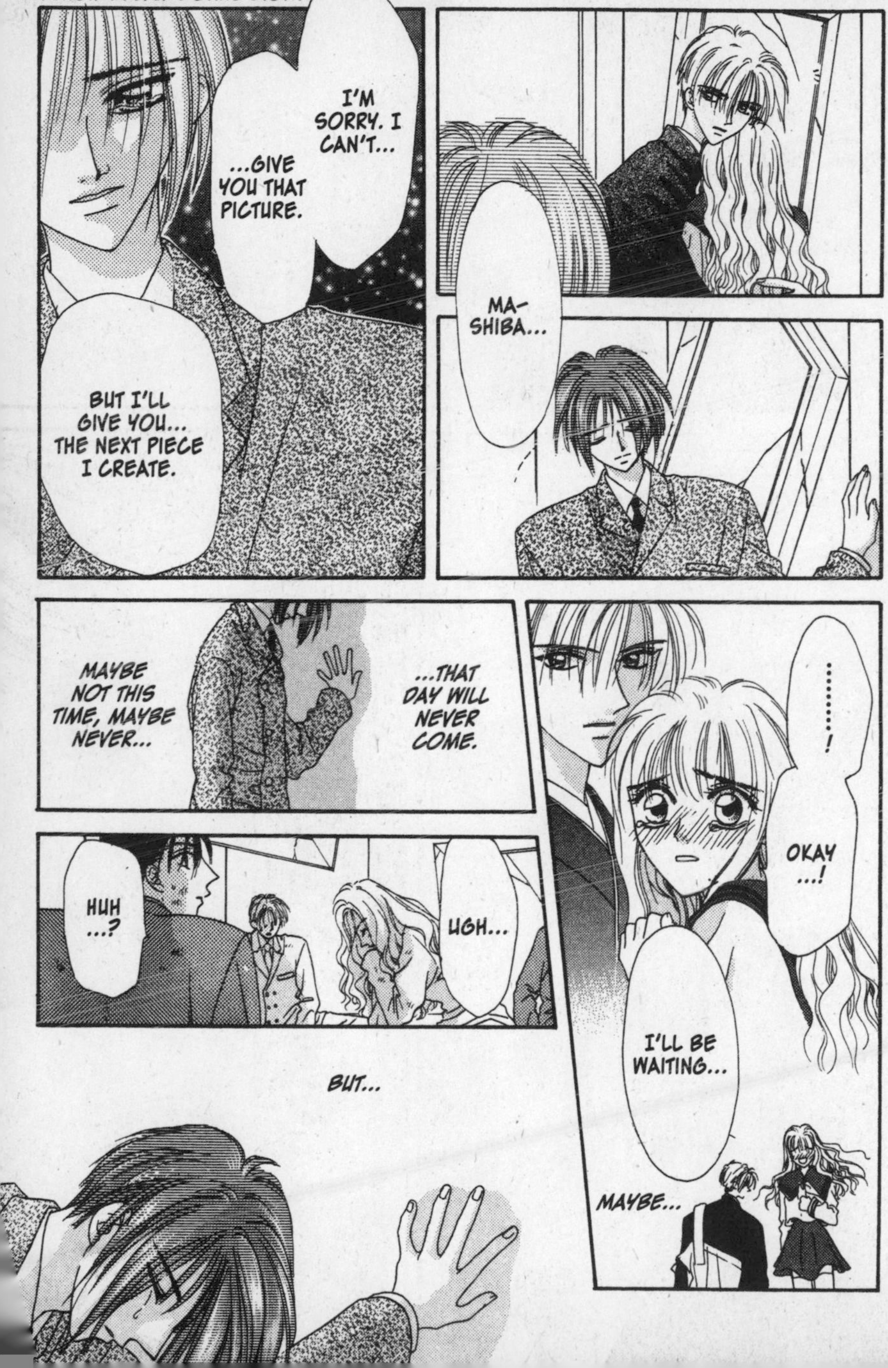
MA-SHIBA...
I'M SORRY. I CAN'T...
...GIVE YOU THAT PICTURE.
BUT I'LL GIVE YOU... THE NEXT PIECE I CREATE.
.......!
OKAY ...!
I'LL BE WAITING...
MAYBE...
...THAT DAY WILL NEVER COME.
MAYBE NOT THIS TIME, MAYBE NEVER...
UGH...
HUH ...?
BUT...

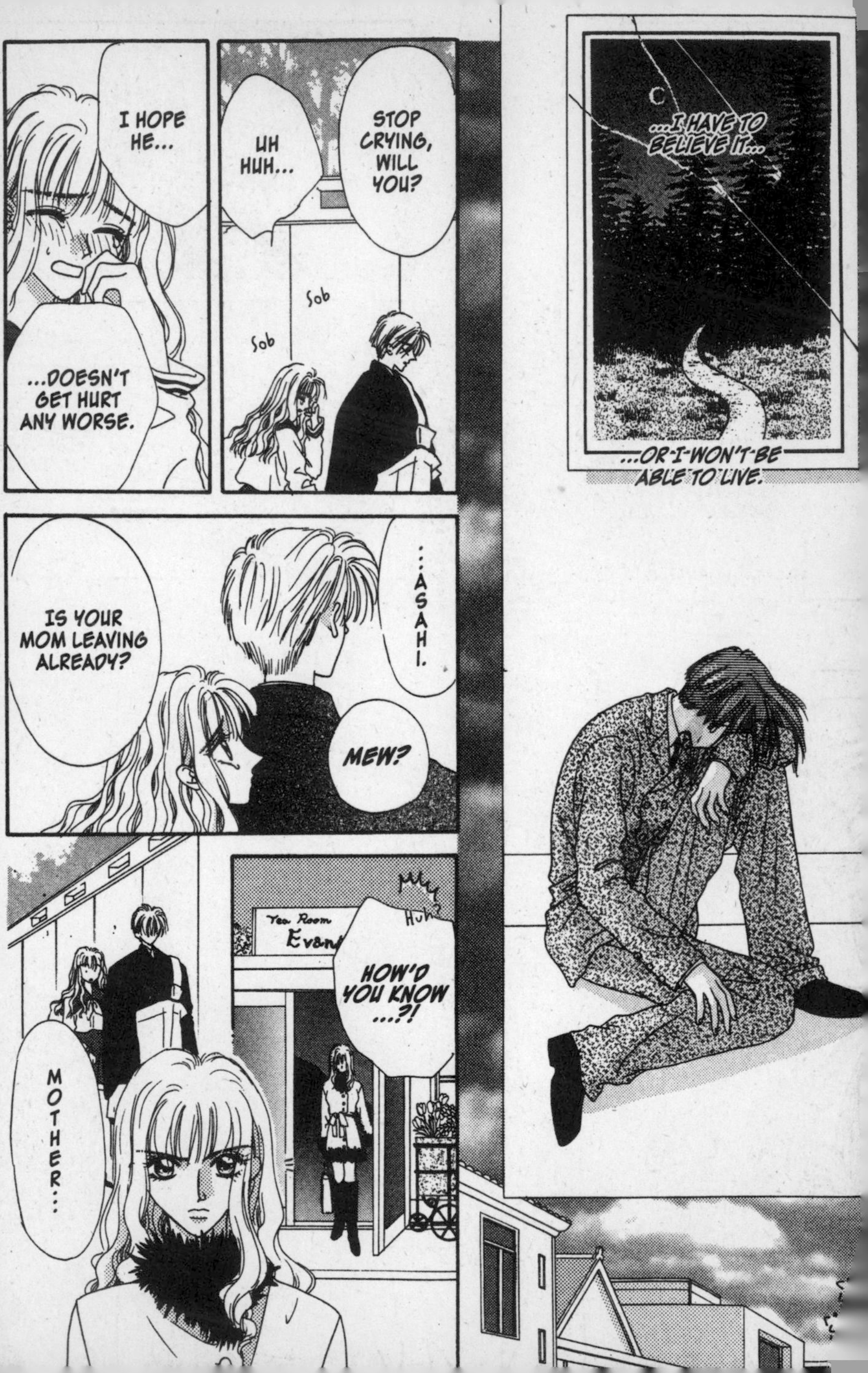
...I HAVE TO BELIEVE IT...
...OR I WON'T BE ABLE TO LIVE.
STOP CRYING, WILL YOU?
UH HUH...
Sob
Sob
I HOPE HE...
...DOESN'T GET HURT ANY WORSE.
...ASAHI.
MEW?
IS YOUR MOM LEAVING ALREADY?
Huh
HOW'D YOU KNOW ...?!
Tea Room
MOTHER...

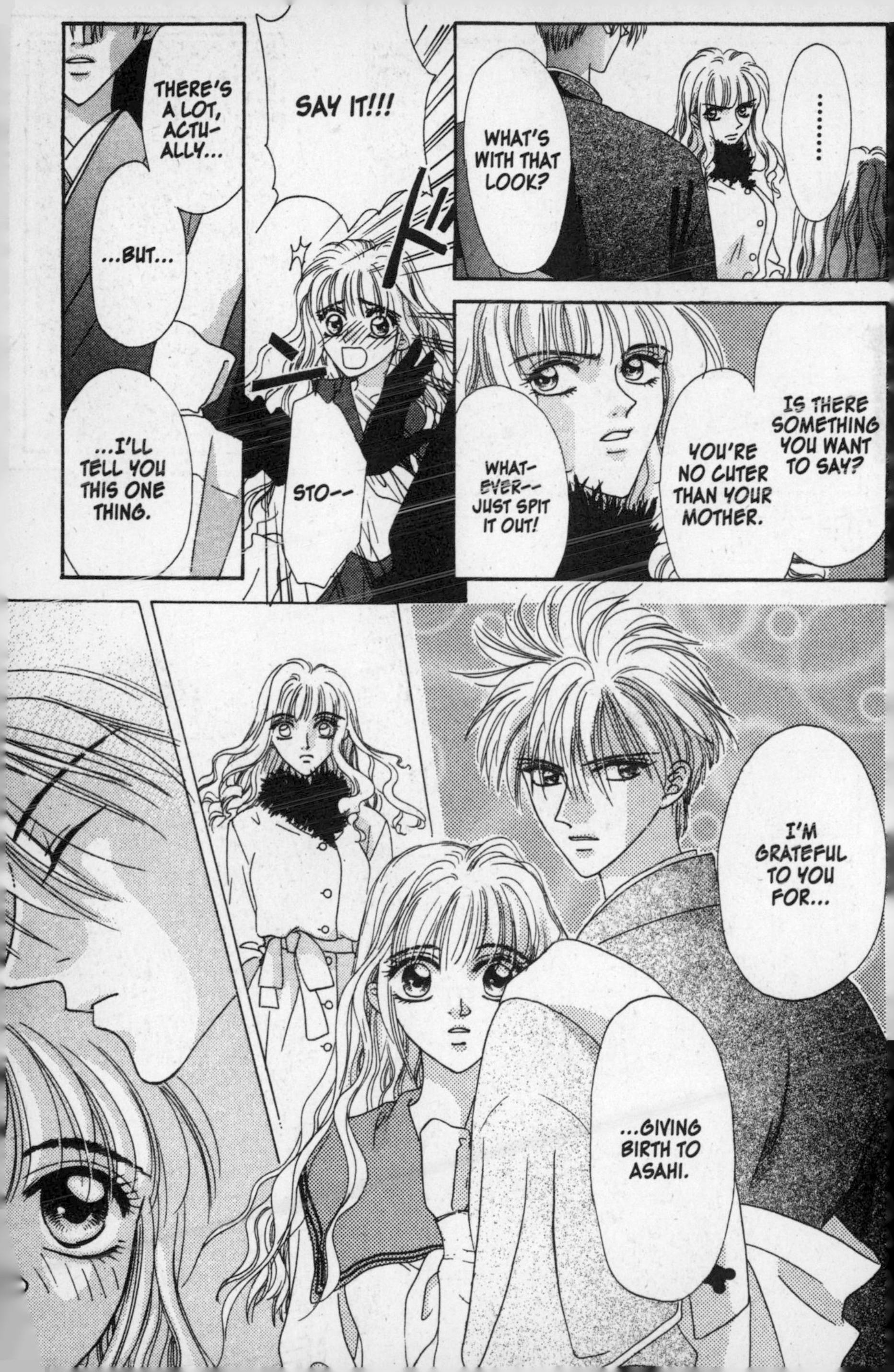
......
WHAT'S WITH THAT LOOK?
IS THERE SOMETHING YOU WANT TO SAY?
YOU'RE NO CUTER THAN YOUR MOTHER.
WHATEVER-- JUST SPIT IT OUT!
SAY IT!!!
STO--
THERE'S A LOT, ACTUALLY...
...BUT...
...I'LL TELL YOU THIS ONE THING.
I'M GRATEFUL TO YOU FOR...
...GIVING BIRTH TO ASAHI.

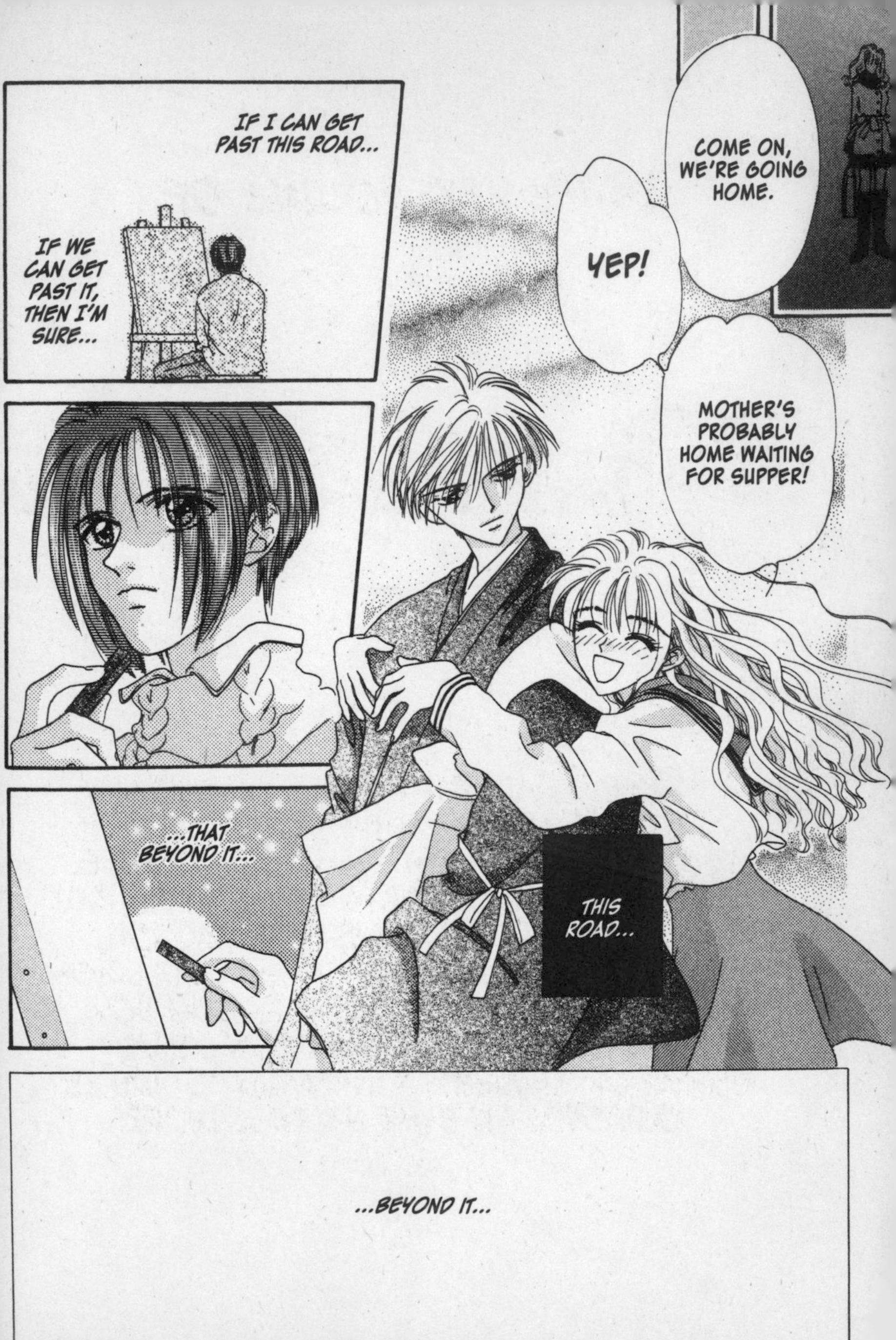
COME ON, WE'RE GOING HOME.
YEP!
MOTHER'S PROBABLY HOME WAITING FOR SUPPER!
THIS ROAD...
IF I CAN GET PAST THIS ROAD...
IF WE CAN GET PAST IT, THEN I'M SURE...
...THAT BEYOND IT...
...BEYOND IT...

PHANTOM DREAM BONUS STORY / THE END

IN THE NEXT VOLUME OF

Phantom Dream

THE FINAL BATTLE BETWEEN TAMAKI AND
HIRA APPROACHES, AND HIRA'S DARK PAST
IS REVEALED AT LAST. SAGA CONFESSES
HIS TRUE FEELINGS TOWARDS HIRA AND HIS
REASONS FOR BECOMING THE GOHOU,
AND KANAME REAPPEARS IN THE THRILLING
LAST VOLUME OF PHANTOM DREAM! HOW
WILL THE CONFLICT BETWEEN HIRA'S
HATRED OF HUMANITY AND TAMAKI'S DESIRE
TO PROTECT IT EVER BE RESOLVED?

STOP!

DEC 2009

This is the back of the book.
You wouldn't want to spoil a great ending!

This book is printed "manga-style," in the authentic Japanese right-to-left format. Since none of the artwork has been flipped or altered, readers get to experience the story just as the creator intended. You've been asking for it, so TOKYOPOP® delivered: authentic, hot-off-the-press, and far more fun!

DIRECTIONS

If this is your first time reading manga-style, here's a quick guide to help you understand how it works.

It's easy... just start in the top right panel and follow the numbers. Have fun, and look for more 100% authentic manga from TOKYOPOP®!

THE MANGA REVOLUTION · LEADING · LEADING · THE MANGA REVOLUTION · LEADING

漫画
革命